Understanding Bakhtin, Understanding Modernism

UNDERSTANDING PHILOSOPHY, UNDERSTANDING MODERNISM

The aim of each volume in **Understanding Philosophy, Understanding Modernism** is to understand a philosophical thinker more fully through literary and cultural modernism and consequently to understand literary modernism better through a key philosophical figure. In this way, the series also rethinks the limits of modernism, calling attention to lacunae in modernist studies and sometimes in the philosophical work under examination.

Series Editors:
Paul Ardoin, S. E. Gontarski, and Laci Mattison

Volumes in the Series:
Understanding Bergson, Understanding Modernism
Edited by Paul Ardoin, S. E. Gontarski, and Laci Mattison
Understanding Deleuze, Understanding Modernism
Edited by S. E. Gontarski, Paul Ardoin and Laci Mattison
Understanding Wittgenstein, Understanding Modernism
Edited by Anat Matar
Understanding Foucault, Understanding Modernism
Edited by David Scott
Understanding James, Understanding Modernism
Edited by David H. Evans
Understanding Rancière, Understanding Modernism
Edited by Patrick M. Bray
Understanding Blanchot, Understanding Modernism
Edited by Christopher Langlois

Understanding Merleau-Ponty, Understanding Modernism
Edited by Ariane Mildenberg
Understanding Nietzsche, Understanding Modernism
Edited by Douglas Burnham and Brian Pines
Understanding Derrida, Understanding Modernism
Edited by Jean-Michel Rabaté
Understanding Adorno, Understanding Modernism
Edited by Robin Truth Goodman
Understanding Flusser, Understanding Modernism
Edited by Aaron Jaffe, Rodrigo Martini, and Michael F. Miller
Understanding Marx, Understanding Modernism
Edited by Mark Steven
Understanding Barthes, Understanding Modernism
Edited by Jeffrey R. Di Leo and Zahi Zalloua
Understanding Kristeva, Understanding Modernism
Edited by Maria Margaroni
Understanding Žižek, Understanding Modernism
Edited by Jeffrey R. Di Leo and Zahi Zalloua
Understanding Nancy, Understanding Modernism
Edited by Cosmin Toma
Understanding Bakhtin, Understanding Modernism
Edited by Philippe Birgy
Understanding Cavell, Understanding Modernism (forthcoming)
Edited by Paola Marrati
Understanding Badiou, Understanding Modernism (forthcoming)
Edited by Arka Chattopadhyay and Arthur Rose

Understanding Bakhtin, Understanding Modernism

Edited by
Philippe Birgy

BLOOMSBURY ACADEMIC
NEW YORK • LONDON • OXFORD • NEW DELHI • SYDNEY

BLOOMSBURY ACADEMIC
Bloomsbury Publishing Inc, 1385 Broadway, New York, NY 10018, USA
Bloomsbury Publishing Plc, 50 Bedford Square, London, WC1B 3DP, UK
Bloomsbury Publishing Ireland, 29 Earlsfort Terrace, Dublin 2, D02 AY28, Ireland

BLOOMSBURY, BLOOMSBURY ACADEMIC and the Diana logo
are trademarks of Bloomsbury Publishing Plc

First published in the United States of America 2024
Paperback edition published 2025

Copyright © Philippe Birgy, 2024

Each chapter copyright © by the contributor, 2024

Cover design: Eleanor Rose
Cover image © Adobe Stock

All rights reserved. No part of this publication may be: i) reproduced or transmitted in any form, electronic or mechanical, including photocopying, recording or by means of any information storage or retrieval system without prior permission in writing from the publishers; or ii) used or reproduced in any way for the training, development or operation of artificial intelligence (AI) technologies, including generative AI technologies. The rights holders expressly reserve this publication from the text and data mining exception as per Article 4(3) of the Digital Single Market Directive (EU) 2019/790.

Bloomsbury Publishing Inc. does not have any control over, or responsibility for, any third-party websites referred to or in this book. All internet addresses given in this book were correct at the time of going to press. The author and publisher regret any inconvenience caused if addresses have changed or sites have ceased to exist, but can accept no responsibility for any such changes.

Library of Congress Cataloging-in-Publication Data

Names: Birgy, Philippe, editor.
Title: Understanding Bakhtin, understanding modernism / edited by Philippe Birgy.
Description: New York : Bloomsbury Academic, 2023. | Series: Understanding philosophy, understanding modernism | Includes bibliographical references and index. | Summary: "Explores and illuminates the impact of the Russian philosopher Mikhail Bakhtin on our understanding of literary modernism"– Provided by publisher.
Identifiers: LCCN 2023015240 (print) | LCCN 2023015241 (ebook) | ISBN 9781501381645 (hb) | ISBN 9781501381669 (epdf) | ISBN 9781501381652 (ebook)
Subjects: LCSH: Bakhtin, M. M. (Mikhail Mikhailovich), 1895–1975–Influence. | Modernism (Literature)
Classification: LCC PG2947.B3 U53 2023 (print) | LCC PG2947.B3 (ebook) | DDC 801/.95092–dc23/eng/20230817
LC record available at https://lccn.loc.gov/2023015240
LC ebook record available at https://lccn.loc.gov/2023015241

ISBN:	HB:	978-1-5013-8164-5
	PB:	978-1-5013-8168-3
	ePDF:	978-1-5013-8166-9
	eBook:	978-1-5013-8165-2

Series: Understanding Philosophy, Understanding Modernism

Typeset by Integra Software Services Pvt. Ltd.

For product safety related questions contact productsafety@bloomsbury.com.

To find out more about our authors and books visit www.bloomsbury.com and sign up for our newsletters.

CONTENTS

Series Preface xi
Notes on Contributors xiii
List of Abbreviations xvii

Introduction: Bakhtin at Interpretative Crossroads
Philippe Birgy 1

Part 1 Conceptualizing Bakhtin

1. From Heteroglossia to Contemporaneity: Bakhtin's Modernist History of the Novel 19
   Ken Hirschkop

2. Mikhail Bakhtin and the History of Literature: The Past in the Present and the Present in the Past 33
   Anker Gemzøe

3. On Death and Turn-Taking in Conversation: The Concept of Succession (*smena*) in Bakhtin's Late Philosophy 51
   Sergeiy Sandler

4. Bakhtin's Chronotope: Crisis Time and Great Time in Benjamin and Hölderlin 65
   Jeremy Tambling

5. Bakhtin's Scenarios of Selfhood: Modernism between Intersubjectivity and Transindividuality 81
   Ilya Kliger

6. Anticipation and Prevention: A Dialogical Approach to the Modern Unconscious 99
   Jonathan Hall

7   Bakhtin, Habermas, and the "Revenge of the Real" 115
    Michael E. Gardiner

8   Decolonizing Aesthetics: Bakhtin, Modernism, and
    Anti-Colonial Poetics 131
    Peter Hitchcock

Part 2 Bakhtin and Modernism

9   "New Philosophical Wonder": Bakhtin, Shklovsky, and
    the Re-enchantment of the World 149
    Daphna Erdinast-Vulcan

10 Gide, Bakhtin, and the Threshold of Modernism 163
    Tara Collington

11 Sensation and Abstraction: The Station as a Modernist
    Chronotope 179
    Anker Gemzøe

12 Bakhtin and the Protomodernist Dickens: From an
    Anthropological Perspective 199
    Michael Hollington

13 "An Irish Clown, a Great Joker at the Universe": Joyce
    and the Modern Carnival 213
    Yann Tholoniat

14 Mikhail Bakhtin, Modern Dance, and the Body's
    Unmediated Presence in the World 227
    Marsha D. Barsky and Robert F. Barsky

Part 3 Glossary

15 Introduction to the Glossary 245
    Sergeiy Sandler

16 Architectonics (*arkhitektonika*) 247
    Sergeiy Sandler

17 Author and Hero (*avtor i geroj*) 249
   Sergeiy Sandler

18 Becoming 251
   Jonathan Hall

19 Carnival 253
   Yann Tholoniat

20 Chronotope (*khronotop*) 255
   Sergeiy Sandler

21 Completion (*zavershenie*) 257
   Sergeiy Sandler

22 Contemporaneity (*sovremennost'*) 259
   Ken Hirschkop

23 Deed (*postupok*) 261
   Sergeiy Sandler

24 Dialogue/Dialogical/Dialogization 263
   Ken Hirschkop

25 Genre (*zhanr*) 265
   Sergeiy Sandler

26 Heteroglossia (*raznorechie*) 269
   Ken Hirschkop

27 I and other 271
   Philippe Birgy

28 Menippean Satire 273
   Yann Tholoniat

29 Outsidedness (*vnenakhodimost'*) 275
   Sergeiy Sandler

30 Present/Past/Future 277
   Philippe Birgy

31 Responsibility 281
    Philippe Birgy

32 Style 283
    Ken Hirschkop

33 Utterance (*vyskazyvanie*) 285
    Sergeiy Sandler

34 Word/Discourse (*slovo*) 287
    Sergeiy Sandler

Index 289

SERIES PREFACE

Sometime in the late twentieth century, Modernism, like philosophy itself, underwent something of an unmooring from (at least) linear literary history in favor of the multi-perspectival history implicit in "new historicism" or, say, varieties of "presentism." Amid current reassessments of Modernism and modernity, critics have posited various "new" or alternative Modernisms—postcolonial, cosmopolitan, transatlantic, transnational, geomodernism, or even "bad" modernisms. In doing so, they have not only reassessed Modernism as a category but also, more broadly, rethought epistemology and ontology, aesthetics, metaphysics, materialism, history, and being itself, opening possibilities of rethinking not only which texts we read as Modernist but also how we read those texts. Much of this new conversation constitutes something of a critique of the periodization of Modernism or Modernist studies in favor of Modernism as mode (or mode of production) or concept. *Understanding Philosophy, Understanding Modernism* situates itself amid the plurality of discourses, offering collections focused on key philosophical thinkers influential both to the moment of Modernism and to our current understanding of that moment's genealogy, archaeology, and becomings. Such critiques of Modernism(s) and modernity afford opportunities to rethink and reassess the overlaps, folds, interrelationships, interleavings, or cross-pollinations of Modernism and philosophy. Our goal in each volume of the series is to understand literary Modernism better through philosophy as we also better understand a philosopher through literary Modernism. The first two volumes of the series, those on Henri Bergson and Gilles Deleuze, have established a tripartite structure that serves to offer both accessibility to the philosopher's principle texts and to current new research. Each volume opens with a section focused on "conceptualizing" the philosopher through close readings of seminal texts in the thinker's oeuvre. A second section, on aesthetics, maps connections between Modernist works and the philosophical figure, often surveying key Modernist trends and shedding new light on authors and texts. The final section of each volume serves as an extended glossary of principal terms in the philosopher's work, each treated at length, allowing a fuller engagement with and examination of the many, sometimes contradictory ways terms are deployed. The series is thus designed both to introduce philosophers and to rethink their relationship to Modernist studies, revising our understandings of both Modernism and philosophy, and offering resources that will be of use across disciplines, from philosophy, theory, and literature, to religion, the visual and performing arts, and often to the sciences as well.

CONTRIBUTORS

Marsha Barsky is Chair of the Department of Dance at Kennesaw State University. She has served as Associate Professor and Director of Dance at Middle Tennessee State University (MTSU). Her research is on the overlap between the work of F. M. Alexander and M. M. Bakhtin, and its connection to modernity.

Robert F. Barsky is a Guggenheim Fellow and Professor of Humanities and of Law at Vanderbilt University. His most recent book, *Clamouring for Legal Protection: What the Great Books Teach Us About People Fleeing from Persecution*, has just appeared in paperback with Bloomsbury Press. His forthcoming book, tentatively called *Lyndon B. Johnson's White House and the Italian Villa in Bellagio: Negotiating Civil Rights and Refugee Law and in the Height of the Cold War*, will be completed in 2024.

Philippe Birgy is a Professor with the University of Toulouse Jean Jaurès, France, where he teaches critical methodology and literary theory as well as English and American philosophy. He has been editor-in-chief of the scholarly journal *Caliban* for 8 years. He is the author of *"Une terrible beauté": les modernistes anglais à l'épreuve de la critique girardienne* (Toulouse: PUM, 2005), and the editor of *Revoir 14: images après tout* (Rennes: Presses Universitaires de Rennes, 2017), *Crossroads* (*Anglophonia*, PUM, 2012), *Samuel Beckett: Drama as Philosophical Endgame* (Miranda, 2011).

Tara Collington is a Professor with the University of Waterloo (Canada) where she is Chair of the Department of French Studies. She is a specialist of twentieth- and twenty-first century French literature. She is the author of *Lectures chronotopiques: espace, temps et genres romanesques* (Montreal: XYZ, 2006), and co-editor, with François Paré, of *Diasporiques* (Ottawa: Éditions David, 2013) and, with Guy Poirier and Élise Lepage, of *Le défi de la fragilité: Autour des essais de François Paré* (Ottawa: Éditions David, 2020), winner of the Prix Gabrielle-Roy for Canadian literary criticism.

Daphna Erdinast-Vulcan is the author of *Graham Greene's Childless Fathers* (London and New York: Macmillan and St Martin's Press, 1989), *Joseph Conrad and the Modern Temper* (Oxford: Oxford University Press, 1991),

The Strange Short Fiction of Joseph Conrad: Writing, Culture, and Subectivity (Oxford: Oxford University Press, 1999), and *Between Philosophy and Literature: Bakhtin and the Question of the Subject* (Stanford: Stanford University Press, 2014).

Michael E. Gardiner is a sociologist who teaches and researches social theory. He focuses on theories of affect, the everyday, utopia, and dialogical social theory (in the work of Mikhail Bakhtin in particular). He is the co-editor of *Bakhtin in the Fullness of Time: Bakhtinian Theory and the Process of Social Education* (London: Routledge, 2020), *Boredom Studies Reader: Frameworks and Perspectives* (London: Routledge, 2017), and the author of *Weak Messianism: Essays on Utopia and Everyday Life* (Oxford: Peter Lang, 2013).

Anker Gemzøe is Professor Emeritus in Scandinavian Literature at the Department of Languages, Culture and Aesthetics, Aalborg University, Denmark, and at the Department of Scandinavian Languages and Literature, University of Bergen, Norway. He is the coordinator of the Center for Modernist Studies at Aalborg University. He is the editor of *Modernismens historie* [Modernismestudier 2] (København: Akademisk Forlag, 2003), the author of *Metamorfoser i Mellemtiden. Studier i Svend Åge Madsens forfatterskab 1962–86* [Metamorphoses in the Middle Time: Studies in the Works of Svend Åge Madsen] (Copenhagen: Medusa, 1997); "Nordic Modernisms," *The Oxford Handbook of Modernisms*, 2010), 851-72; "Modernism, Narrativity and Bakhtinian Theory," *Modernism* 1, ed. Astradur Eysteinsson and Vivian Liska (Amsterdam/Philadelphia: John Benjamins Publishing Company, 2007), and many other books and contributions to anthologies, on Modernism, grotesque realism, metafiction, intertextuality, Mikhail Bakhtin, Franz Kafka, James Joyce, T. S. Eliot, and a number of classical and modern Danish authors.

Jonathan Hall is a former Lecturer in Comparative Literature at the University of Hong Kong, and is currently an Honorary Research Fellow at the Bakhtin Centre, University of Sheffield. He is the author of several papers and articles on the Bakhtin Circle and related topics. He has recently published a book on the conflictual symbiosis of Bakhtin's and Voloshinov's monologism/dialogism dyad, *Reaction Formations: Dialogism, Ideology, and Capitalist Culture–the Creation of the Modern Unconscious* (Boston: Brill, 2019).

Ken Hirschkop is a Professor with the University of Waterloo (Canada). He is the author of *The Cambridge Introduction to Mikhail Bakhtin* (Cambridge: Cambridge University Press, 2021), *Linguistic Turns, 1890–1950: Writing on Language as Social Theory* (Oxford: Oxford University Press, 2019),

Mikhail Bakhtin: An Aesthetic for Democracy (Oxford: Oxford University Press, 1999) and has co-edited *Bakhtin and Cultural Theory* with David Shepherd (Manchester: Manchester University Press. First edition, 1989. Second, revised and expanded edition, 2001).

Peter Hitchcock's main research interests lie in literary theory, cultural theory, Marxism, Bakhtin, and working-class fiction, world literature and postcolonialism. He is the editor of *Biotheory: Life and Death under Capitalism*, with Jeffrey Di Leo (New York: Routledge, 2020); *The Debt Age*, with Jeffrey Di Leo and Sophia McClennen (New York: Routledge, 2018); *The New Public Intellectual*, with Jeffrey Di Leo (New York: Palgrave Macmillan, 2016); and the author of *Labor in Culture, or, Worker of the World(s)* (New York: Palgrave Macmillan, 2017); *The Long Space: Transnationalism and Postcolonial Form* (Palo Alto: Stanford University Press, 2010); *Imaginary States: Studies in Cultural Transnationalism* (Champaign/Urbana: University of Illinois Press, 2003); and *Dialogics of the Oppressed* (Minneapolis: University of Minnesota Press, 1993).

Michael Hollington is a retired Professor of English and Comparative Literature. He has held chairs in Australia and France, notably at the University of New South Wales and the University of Toulouse-Le Mirail, and taught on every continent. He has published widely on English literature from the Renaissance onwards, and also on literature in other European languages. He has written books on Charles Dickens, Katherine Mansfield, Walt Whitman, and Günter Grass, and edited anthologies of Dickens criticism. His recent projects include a book on Shakespeare's *Henry V* (Paris: Atlande, 2020), and *Dickens among the Modernists*, sections of which have appeared in a variety of academic journals.

Ilya Kliger is an Associate Professor in the Department of Russian and Slavic Studies, New York University. He specializes in the nineteenth-century Russian novel, the theory of the novel, literary theory, and the relationship between philosophy and literature. He is the author of *The Narrative Shape of Truth: Veridiction in Modern European Literature* (Pennsylvania: Pennsylvania State University Press, 2011), and co-editor, with Boris Maslov, of *Persistent Forms: Practicing Historical Poetics* (New York: Fordham University Press, 2016).

Sergeiy Sandler is a scholar and translator into English and Hebrew of Mikhail Bakhtin's works. He is the author of multiple articles on Bakhtin's philosophy, as well as of studies promulgating a Bakhtin-inspired approach to linguistics and the philosophy of language. He is the editor of *The Conversation Frame: Forms and Functions of Fictive Interaction* (Amsterdam: John Benjamins, 2016) with Esther Pascual, and has published an annotated translation of a collection of late essays and notes by Bakhtin in Hebrew (Tel Aviv: Resling, 2008). He is also a joint editor for the journal *Language under Discussion*.

Jeremy Tambling is a writer and critic who has been engaged with education and teaching at all levels and across the range, including holding the Chair of Comparative Literature in Hong Kong, and of Literature in Manchester. He is the author of many books, including *Histories of the Devil: From Marlowe to Mann and the Manichees* (London: Palgrave, 2017), *Hölderlin and the Subject of Tragedy: Readings in Sophocles, Shakespeare, Nietzsche and Benjamin* (Brighton: Sussex Academic Press, 2014), *Literature and Psychoanalysis* (Manchester: Manchester University Press, 2013), *On Reading the Will: Law and Desire in Literature and Music* (Brighton: Sussex Academic Press, 2012), *On Anachronism* (Manchester: Manchester University Press, 2010), *Allegory, The New Critical Idiom* (London: Routledge, 2009), *Wong Kar-wai's Happy Together* (Hong Kong: Hong Kong University Press, 2003), *Becoming Posthumous* (Edinburgh: Edinburgh University Press, 2001), *Lost in the American City: Dickens, James and Kafka* (New York: Palgrave, 2001), *Opera and the Culture of Fascism* (Oxford: Clarendon Press, 1996), and *Narrative and Ideology* (Milton Keynes: Open University Press, 1991).

Yann Tholoniat is Professor of British and Irish literature and arts at the University of Lorraine in Metz (France). He is the author of *"Tongue's Imperial Fiat": les polyphonies dans l'œuvre poétique de Robert Browning* (Presses Universitaires de Strasbourg, Strasbourg, 2009), co-editor with Christian Auer of *Culture savante, culture populaire en Écosse* (RANAM no. 40, 2007), and editor of *Culture savante, culture populaire dans les pays anglophones* (RANAM no. 39, 2006). His research interests fall within British and Irish novelists, Romantic and post-Romantic poetry, and Modernism in anglophone and Spanish-speaking countries. He is currently working in the field of animal studies related to nineteenth and twentieth-century English painting and sculpture.

ABBREVIATIONS

AA   *Art and Answerability: Early Philosophical Essays*, ed. Michael Holquist and Vadim Liapunov, trans. Vadim Liapunov (Austin: University of Texas Press, 1990).

BOS   "Bakhtin on Shakespeare: Excerpt from 'Additions and Changes to Rabelais,'" trans. Sergeiy Sandler, *PMLA* 129.3 (2014): 522–37.

CW1   *Sobranie sochinenij*, ed. Sergey Georgievich Bocharov and Nikolai Ivanovich Nikolaev, vol. 1 (Moscow: Russkie slovari, Jazyki slavianskoj kul'tury, 2003), 69–263.

CW2   *Sobranie sochinenij*, ed. Sergey Georgievich Bocharov and Leontina Sergeevna Melikhova, vol. 2 (Moscow: Russkie slovari, 2000).

CW3   *Sobranie sochinenij*, ed. Sergey Georgievich Bocharov and Vadim Valerianovich Kozhinov, vol. 3 (Moscow: Jazyki slavianskikh kul'tur, 2012).

CW4.1   *Sobranie sochinenij*, ed. Irina L'vovna Popova, vol. 4.1 (Moscow: Jazyki slavianskikh kul'tur, 2008).

CW4.2   *Sobranie sochinenij*, ed. Irina L'vovna Popova, vol. 4.2 (Moscow: Jazyki slavianskikh kul'tur, 2010).

CW5   *Sobranie sochinenij*, ed. Sergey Georgievich Bocharov and Liudmila Archirovna Gogotishvili, vol. 5 (Moscow: Russkie slovari, 1996).

CW6   *Sobranie sochinenij*, ed. Sergey Georgievich Bocharov and Liudmila Archirovna Gogotishvili, vol. 6 (Moscow: Russkie slovari, Jazyki slavianskoj kul'tury, 2002).

DI   *The Dialogic Imagination: Four Essays*, ed. Michael Holquist, trans. Caryl Emerson and Michael Holquist (Austin: University of Texas Press, 1981).

PDA *Problems of Dostoevsky's Art* (Leningrad: Priboi, 1929).

PDP *Problems of Dostoevsky's Poetics*, ed. and trans. Caryl Emerson (Minneapolis: University of Minnesota Press, 1984).

REL "Rhetoric, to the Extent That It Lies," trans. Irina Denischenko and Alexander Spektor, *Slavic and East European Journal* 61.2 (2017 [1943]): 203–15.

RHW *Rabelais and His World*, trans. Hélène Iswolsky (Cambridge, MA: The MIT Press, 1968).

SG *Speech Genres and Other Late Essays*, ed. Caryl Emerson and Michael Holquist, trans. Vern W. McGee (Austin: University of Texas Press, 1986).

TPA *Toward a Philosophy of the Act*, ed. Michael Holquist and Vadim Liapunov, trans. Vadim Liapunov (Austin: University of Texas Press, 1993).

Introduction

Bakhtin at Interpretative Crossroads

Philippe Birgy

Bakhtinian studies have been a site of constant debate throughout the major part of the twentieth century, as *The Annotated Bakhtin Bibliography* attests.[1] From the late seventies onward, it fueled a massive critical production. Many of these contributions minimized the context of Bakhtin's work so as to allow for a measure of flexibility in its interpretation, which opened up the range of possible applications, resulting in thought-provoking propositions.

> Bakhtin, it seems, offers something to everyone. He is invoked in the cause of liberal humanist criticism, idealist philosophy, Russian nationalism, Marxism, anti-Marxism, postcolonial theory and many more positions besides. Indeed, it often seems there are as many "Bakhtins" as there are interpreters.[2]

A rapid survey of the critical production on or around Bakhtin's concepts suffices to confirm that these have generated a very intense activity in Western Europe and America since his rehabilitation by scholars in the 1970s and increasingly so throughout the eighties and nineties when it developed into a field of study in its own right. At that same period, scholarly interest has shifted from the strictly literary studies to the philosophical—and particularly ethical—tenor of his texts, while also branching out into studies of diplomatic relations, applied linguistic and semiotics, the teaching of English as a second language (and more generally whatever involved dialogue and negotiation in two or more languages) as well as the philosophy of language.

In response to that expansion, the necessity of a more robust contextualization was felt, eventually leading, among other achievements, to the publication of the complete works of the philosopher in Russian, in an edition consciously aimed at exhaustiveness and concerned with the nuances of Bakhtin's original texts.[3] "Over the last quarter-century," Sergeiy Sandler observes in a paper delivered at the fifteenth International Bakhtin Conference in Stockholm in July 2014, "Bakhtin scholarship focused on unearthing the various influences on his thought, his sources."[4] Bakhtinian theory has thus also become a forum for dialogue on the political and intellectual background that had supplied him with food for thought or determined the limits of what he could safely write in insecure times, retracing (often contradictory) filiations in his personal history as well as in Russian history. Bakhtin's thought, *they* argue, was very much of its time. This situatedness, together with the fact that one of the main objects of his inquiry was the negotiation involved in the formation, progress, and mutation of the novel as an index of modernity, makes him particularly conducive to an examination of Modernism.

Diverse Interpretations

Among other things, Bakhtin's work seems to have anticipated the great themes of post-Modernism, as Eagleton remarks with a certain irritation in his review of Pechey's *The Word in the World*,[5] prompting diverse readings, not all of them antagonistic but offering debatable versions that played against each other and stimulated a conversation.

Concurrently, there has been apparently enough ground in his texts to accommodate a conservative Bakhtin, self-centered and careerist, in the eyes of those who resented his appropriation by a postmodern paradigm which they rejected—a postmodernism which, they felt, was not only inherently anti-Marxian but went against the grain of a long tradition of German idealism. The quarrels were partly ideological, and presumably also involved a reaction of spite in the face of the dismantling of a socialist worldview elaborated in the nineteenth century. And this could easily lead the defenders of the human values embodied in that tradition to stand up against all intellectuals who appeared to have resisted the communist revolution.

If we follow Anker Gemzøe, after the first scholarly boom and the return to the archive and to genetic criticism, came a third wave of critical interest, this time intent on reconsidering preceding critical interpretations of Bakhtin in the light of the historical data culled by the previous generation.

Yet the history of Bakhtin's reception and of what can safely be placed under his name remains at the heart of contemporary scholarly reflections, and Sergeiy Sandler proposes to go back to the thinker's first writings in order to restore the richness and variety of concepts that were later smoothed out, abridged, and refashioned, so as to recover lines of reasoning which might be used to support a critique of Modernism. Notably, the case for the notion of succession engages us in a reflection on tradition and other possible relationships to the past, a concern that determines Modernist thought since its historical consciousness preoccupies and motivates it. A reading of Modernism as the guilty conscience of modernity, a worried and hesitant position vis-à-vis modernity is especially congruent with such notions.

The Modernists' extreme self-consciousness, as they approached the project of finding a spontaneous expression and a purity of intention attuned to the historical conditions under which they operated, was bound to create such hesitations. For they were late-comers: they had only joined the fray after many weighty aesthetic and moral statements of intent had already been made, after Realism and Romanticism, after the announced triumph of rationality and the celebration of technological progress.

They followed train nonetheless, though remaining dubious of the unwarranted belief that, whatever came up, history was inexorably headed for the realization of the common good. They were equally circumspect when considering the democratic wager. Not that they dismissed the possibility of making literature with the voices of the multitude. But while embracing the variety of stylistic possibilities offered by idiolects, sociolects, and characterial styles, as Joyce did in *Ulysses* (see Yann Tholoniat, Chapter 13), they also weighted them against the dangers of dilution that affected the high style when it became exposed to the corrosive agents of a popular, untrained, and undisciplined language. All in all, Modernists were indeed very much concerned about their sources and what they could allow themselves to do with them. The simple proposal of a reinvention of literature as a program of restoration of a genuine drive toward the new entangles novelty and the old in a mind-boggling way that precludes any genuine celebration of absolute originality.

The present book looks both ways: the first part returns to the study of Bakhtin's texts while the second part goes in the extrapolative direction that Bakhtinian criticism has learned to contain. These two opposite orientations, centripetal or centrifugal according to Bakhtin's own terms, because they appear side by side, strive to achieve a balance between necessary elucidation and prospective applications.

The archive works and the consideration of the development of Bakhtin's theory in time have striven to stabilize the meaning and implication of the concepts he introduced. On the face of it, his concern with early modern literary forms and nineteenth-century realism have made him an obvious ally in the search for the historical continuity of a modernity that eventually culminates in the anticlimactic and contradictory achievement of the Modernists, their own historical situatedness inspiring them with a profound ambivalence. Eagleton remarks in his review of Pechey's book that the latter

> misses the true complexity of a European Modernism that was both ultramodern and anti-modern at the same time. Modernity is a matter of "abstract ideas and bloodless epistemology"; there is nothing to be said in favour of the Enlightenment (democracy? feminism? liberalism? universal rights?); and though Bakhtin suffered under the barbarous irrationalism of the Soviet regime, we are invited to admire "any group which has reason to suspect Reason."
>
> (Eagleton 2007)

But, surprisingly, Bakhtin's commentaries rarely dwell on the most outstanding literary movements that were contemporaneous to the period when he elaborated and set down the principles of his theory of textual comprehension. Notwithstanding, many features predispose his reasoning for an incursion into specific Modernist problematics. For it is also the site where a reflection on the opposition between theory and the individual act as a condition of existence is articulated—the latter being clearly linked, in the view of many observers, to American pragmatism, and to a questioning of universals and general principles which affect the world of the arts.

It also contains, perhaps most strikingly, since it was this aspect that caught the attention of commentators in the late sixties, a theory of generalized intertextuality. Bakhtin indeed demonstrated a keen awareness of what is circulating in a continuum of lessons learned and words received, of misunderstandings more or less assumed and constant accretion of meanings.

Concomitantly, he engages with a reflection on novelty and tradition, referring us to a complicated relationship to time, a perception of temporality that is manifested in the fabric of the Modernist novel. It also envisages tradition as transmission, concentrating on the modalities of influence and determination, on the way in which literary discourses respond to a multitude of preceding utterances, or projects themselves toward a conversation to come, by a revolutionary act that anticipates what will be said or can be said. Thus it stands self-consciously before posterity.

Understanding Modernism

Two dominant aspects stand out from the examination of Bakhtin's work in the context of Modernism that will be attempted in these pages. The first has to do with temporal perception. It highlights the part of historicity and periodization informing our apprehension of texts and cultural products. But this approach also takes into consideration the space–time configurations that Bakhtin designates as "chronotopes," for these allow one to overcome the limits of strictly historical perception and subsume distant experiences that are separated in time, thus opening up the subject to a modified consciousness of its temporal inscription. Such preoccupations are of course integrally native to Modernism in its reflexive movement, as it questions its position with regard to the vast panorama it seeks to encompass.

The contributions to this volume also reflect on the part of agentivity involved in change, becoming, and temporal displacement. Since the experience of modernity is one of swift change and rapid movement, it tends to perpetually leave one behind. The question of one's personal investment and active involvement in these cultural and social processes brought about by modernization comes to the fore in Bakhtin's investigation in such way that, when applied to the study of Modernism, it exposes or uncovers an ethical turn in Modernism.[6]

Anteriority: The Tradition of the Modern

Daphna Erdinast-Vulcan's article concentrates on the "loss of the relation to the Sacred" in turn of the century and early twentieth-century literature, and its presumed consequences on the development of subjectivity. Modernism, as a response to modernity, certainly involves a mulling over the possibility of some prelapsarian state of existence, some antiquity of the emotions and the perception of oneself, where the division and fragmentation of everyday life was less incapacitating than it later became at the dawn of the twentieth century—or so it seems to the contemporary critical observers of the period. Modernists never entirely shed that temptation to look back, however tentatively, to a moment when the separation of the subject from the world had not yet been effected by a triumphant rationality (Adorno and Horkheimer's formulation of this quandary being the most damning).[7]

Yeats' Modernism emerged from that nostalgic outlook and Lawrence's fiction favors a similar worldview. In spite of the progressive turn that necessarily marks feminism, some of its Modernist advocates elicit a similar ambivalence. Even Rebecca West's Evadne in "Indissoluble Matrimony"[8] loses herself in the primeval waters of a nearby lake, imaginatively becoming, in her husband's eyes, the embodiment of primordial instincts, while Mina Loy's "Feminist manifesto"[9] flatly discounts any political practice to reaffirm the original separateness of the male and female principles in a way that Lawrence could not have disapproved of.[10]

In contradistinction to this understanding of Modernism as the critical appraisal of a phase of historical development, some see it as a strictly bounded historical period while modernity would be the diffuse and undatable principle that presides over the changes affecting human life.[11] Whatever the case, the turn of the century is undoubtedly marked by a new primitivism and a new paganism in the arts which assiduously seek for an expression of the sacred that would be free from any theological overtone.

That same strange attraction to a lost past is detectable in the avant-gardes at a time when modern subjects seemed to alienate themselves from the natural world in order to control it, or at least to give themselves the impression of mastering it. And even as their embrace of mechanical progress is put forward in the futurists' manifestoes, they nonetheless mourn a form of presence in the world that would be more lively and attentive. Bakhtin could be aligned with this trend in intellectual life since, in Erdinast-Vulcan's words, he "sets out on a lifelong philosophical quest for an alternative 'first philosophy' which would proceed not by 'constructing universal concepts, propositions, and laws,' but by offering 'a description, a phenomenology of that world'" (Chapter 9).

Michael Hollington reminds us of an extant anthropological lineage leading to Bakhtin and Modernism which starts with Frazer and his voluminous study focused on sacrificial rituals. Anthropology is concerned with an infancy of the world, recalling its violence and cruelty as well as its forms of solidarity. And presumably because these still concern us, they are conjured up and brought back to us. At any rate one can recognize their operations in Joyce, as Tholoniat indicates, but also in Gide's *Les faux monnayeurs* (see Collington, Chapter 10) where Boris' suicide disturbingly refers us to the ancient order of primitive homeopathic magic and mysterious correspondences documented by Frazer. These ominous precedents also figure prominently in Eliot, both in his Catholic drama, where the reference to ancient tragedy is overshadowed by a Christ-like figure, and in the persona of the Fisher King in "The Waste Land."

Hollington emphasizes the carnivalesque aspect of Bakhtin's thought, which could be understood as being largely independent of his philosophical reflection proper—this, of course, would be a mistake, as it also elicits a kind of systematicity and closely ties up with Bakhtin's other conceptualizations. Besides the fact that the tradition of the comic novel is scrutinized and reinterpreted in terms of its relationship to time, the status of the subject, the hero and the author, etc., the seriousness of laughter and jest that Bakhtin foregrounds in his studies of literary genres also draws the outlines of a counter-philosophy or anti-philosophy.

Proposing Dickens as a precursor of the Modernist turn in literature, Hollington writes of a Modernist aspiration that led many turn-of-the-century artists to seek "strange gods." (The phrase comes from the title of a book that Eliot thought it safer not to re-publish, presumably, among other things, because of the anti-Semitic formulas it contained. The book also encapsulated Eliot's belief in some traditional way of life for common men, an agrarian model that has moved critics to talk of certain reactionary tendencies in his political outlook.)

Hollington highlights the attraction toward a popular and mostly oral and performative tradition linked to the small rural community, with its rites and stories, and opposed to a Modernism that many see as inseparable from urban and technological modernity. Yet neither Lawrence nor Eliot, let alone Yeats, can be said to strictly conform to this principle of division. And if Joyce figures among those who felt it necessary to relate to some ancestral precedent, he combines these earlier imaginative sources with new media, stressing the technological becoming of arts, rituals, and cultural formations when they are recast in the idiom of the press, of the music hall or the cinema.

If we follow Yann Tholoniat, it might be that the relation between Joycean prose and Bakhtin can perhaps be established in a literal way, through the former's recovery of a carnivalesque impulse. Since Joyce undertakes to ridicule all figures of authority so as to suggest the ambivalence of the sacrificial victim—the scapegoat embodied in King Carnival—, he easily falls into the categories established by the Russian philosopher. Just as Leopold Bloom and Stephen Dedalus suffer ridicule and persecutions, the inversions and subversions of hierarchies and binaries designate Joyce to public opprobrium and he accomplishes meta-literarily in his prose the staging of his condition as a modern author. Perhaps this reflexivity makes him a Modernist: not merely by the simple gesture of looking back on himself or of pondering on his own text, but by the self-recognition that results from this move and makes of him a critic of modernity, a commentator who follows the events and ideas of his time in order to underline their weaknesses and incongruities; someone who, being a modern, cannot write about anything other than the present time, but only does so by putting himself in a false or awkward position since he refuses to assume a pontificating tone. He thus manifests his artistic vocation as something that inevitably turns him into an outsider, out of step with progress or any steady historical unfolding, excluded from them by the drift of his art.

After Historicism: "In space things touch, in time things part"[12]

Most attempts at theorizing Modernism largely revolve around its historical situation, since it is assumed to be linked to the conditions of modernity (which are not necessarily explicit), or to its manifestations (but one must assume that there are deep-rooted problems causing such manifestations).

Modernism is, by its very name, precariously suspended from or butting against what it calls into question (notably, the faith in progress as the solution to human ailments and material destitution as well as the rational answer to moral crises). It depends upon the conditions of existence that it critically examines and tries to render in words. But its coordinates are unsteady. The French, Collington reminds us (Chapter 10), used the term "*modernité*" for what, in British-speaking countries, generally goes by the name of Modernism. Moreover, their construction of Modernism refers us to the nineteenth century. For Rancière, Modernism is coterminous with Flaubert's realism, and the sudden irruption of the mass of indiscriminate people and everyday objects into the field of literature which had been hitherto reserved for the evocation of the deeds and thoughts of superior people.

> The aesthetic regime of the arts dismantled this correlation between subject matter and mode of representation. This revolution first took place in literature: an epoch and a society were deciphered through the features, clothes, or gestures of an ordinary individual (Balzac); the sewer revealed a civilization (Hugo); the daughter of a farmer and the daughter of a banker were caught in the equal force of style as an 'absolute manner of seeing things' (Flaubert). All of these forms of cancellation or reversal of the opposition between high and low not only antedate the powers of mechanical reproduction, they made it possible for this reproduction to be more than mechanical reproduction. In order for a technological mode of action.[13]

The link between early French Modernism, Dostoevsky and Gide was signaled very early on by critics, Collington contends. Hall also argues that the fragmentation of consciousness and the suspension of time, which Bakhtin detects at key threshold moments in Dostoevsky's works, anticipate the more positive epiphanies or "breakthroughs" which are to be found in later, more clearly Modernist, literary works.

Ilya Kliger reconsiders two of the major historical assessments of Modernism (Chapter 5). The first is Berman's largely Marxist account of the movement in terms of social circumstances and relations between political forces, so that, in his view, Modernism is mostly determined by a phase of capitalism.

Anderson, on the contrary, situates it at the point of convergence between three factors: the institutionalization of academism in the arts, the new modes of communication, and the imaginative proximity of the revolution.[14]

Arguing that subjectivity plays out in Bakhtin's system according to three different models or scenarios, Kliger relates these to Anderson's typology. He associates the first trend to an "intersubjective" script whereby the subjective aesthetics of the individual is confronted to the normative evaluation of art. The second scenario hints at a mode of mediation and co-construction between (technological) objects and the human subject, and corresponds to what he describes as "transindividuality," while the last concerns the relationship between the individual and the collective forces (disjunctive manifestations).

The question of the perception of time is also at the heart of Tambling's reflection. For Bakhtin, the purpose of criticism is no longer to place the works in their historical context, but to trace the individual significance of time as it affects the subjects, the division it introduces within their constitution, splitting up their purported integrity. The notion of "crisis time," on whose explanatory power Bakhtin places such a high value, points at a temporal sensibility that places the subject at a crossroads or on the razor's edge. The figure of the split subject thus manifests an awareness of our being caught up in time. Bakhtin, as well as many of the contributor to this volume, fasten on this sense of "crisis time," the intensity and immediacy of felt life—a concern that closely parallels the sort of experience the Modernists were keen to explore and render in words at about the same period, as is evidenced in both Virginia Woolf and James Joyce's attempts at rendering the flow and circulation of ideas in the moment.

Along the same line, and with reference to Felski's arguments against neo-historicism, Gemzøe approaches Bakhtin as a literary critic who theorizes the history of literature. With historicism, according to Felski, "the literary work is entrapped within its period of origin" (see Gemzøe, Chapter 2). Such outlook forces us to ignore the position of the reader and, with it, to exclude any phenomenology of reading. Thus, Felski searches for an alternative view of texts other than their traditional assessment "as transcendentally timeless on the one hand, and imprisoned in their moment of origin on the other"[15] and endeavors to open up the boundaries of the literary field so as to consider its interrelation with and integration within the larger field of culture.

Gemzøe and Tambling echo each other in the rapprochement they propose between Shklovsky and Bakhtin, and especially in his formulation of the a-synchronous development of genres. The complex and conflicted relationship with the past that a-synchrony supposes, and the reflection on history are recognizable features of the Modernists' position vis-a-vis their literary sources and their stand in regard to preceding models is consequently ambivalent.

The questions of temporality and of the perception of time are thus indissociable from the experimental orientations of much of Modernism. If modernity affects the way we perceive and experience time, Modernism reflects on the most intimate consequences of this predicament and creates alternative perceptions to compensate for the obvious limitations of a strictly progressive outlook. The chronotope is Bakhtin's chosen figure to approach the question of the record and inscription of human time: "The chronotope concentrates, but it splits" as it invites us to figure the historical constitution of the subject in "the space of a moment." "Perhaps we could say that the chronotope is a concept aimed less at thinking about space than at visualizing historical time, and what that means," Tambling suggests (Chapter 4).

Bakhtin's analyzes are also consonant with Modernism as a reimagined and revolutionary perception of time that no longer separates temporal experience into segments, periods, formative moments, and logical and causal successions, but emphasizes the vivacious and vibrant immediacy of what presents itself, paying particular attention to the role of genres, which may or may not be inscribed or reinterpreted in time. And, in this instance, the chronotope of the threshold has a distinct status in Bakhtin's scheme because it stresses both interconnectedness and separation, thus problematizing what can possibly remain of a factual and chronological history when the relationship between past, present, and future is upset by the existence of "liminal spaces," which act as passageways but which also break apart as much as they join the totality of the experience, cutting the subject off from itself, even more so as its integrity is already largely a matter of rational reductions smoothing out the irregularities between successive states of consciousness.

The Ethical Turn

This change of direction is also manifested as an ethical turn, although its terms are rendered blurry because of the distinction between the aesthete and the moralist established in nineteenth-century critical discourse and pitting Shaw and Bennett against Wilde or Joyce. The simplistic distinction between a concern for the moral dimension of human action, on the one hand, and an exclusive attention given to the form, on the other, has never ceased to have repercussions on contemporary critical postures, and Bakhtin was bound to reject Gide as an aesthete, Collington argues, insofar as he appropriated the main criticism that realists and socially minded artists had to address to those who, on the face of it, seemed to put the quest of beauty above morality.

But as Daphne Erdinast-Vulcan has it, Bakhtin steers clear from this easy dichotomy and intimates that Dostoevsky lines up a model of writing or storytelling, and more generally of artistic production, with an ethical proposal unbound by the requisites of formal and aesthetic exigencies which recommends coherence and fully rounded characters, so that the craft of the writer and the ethical substance of the literary work are eventually made to coincide. What makes Dostoevsky's authorial abdication truly "Copernican" in its magnitude is that it grants literature the status of a "new paradigm of ethical subjectivity" (Erdinast-Vulcan, Chapter 9).

The ethical turn (or at least the mounting concern for an ethical appraisal of literature) appears to be contemporary with the success of new historicism in literary criticism at the dawn of the eighties. But as Gemzøe points out, in order to recover the moral significance of the novel it might be necessary for the critic to free himself from the antiquarian's reflex and from the exclusive attention given to the many deterministic forces that may seem to obliterate human agency. Yet wouldn't such a move be simply retrograde, a retreat toward that very old *new criticism* which was the first to construct an idiom fit for the study of Modernism—and which, in the process, eventually canonized the figures of the high Modernists? This diversion may seem dangerous, yet it cannot be avoided if we want to recapture a form of humane concern that is inseparable from phenomenology, and that has somehow been lost along the way. To be sure, Jameson himself was eager to warn his readers of the dangers of antiquarianism.

Tambling also reminds us that, as Bakhtin made amply clear, the most substantial achievements of literature unfold in "great time": "the future is essential to release the work from its own epoch; 'its fullness is revealed only in great time'. Thus, the Russian philosopher dismisses the idea that a text is to be understood in terms of a definable 'historical context'" (Chapter 4). Such an outlook breaks away from any historicism which considers the works and cultural productions of the past to be so thoroughly tied up to the circumstances of their production that they are dead and inert in the present unless these circumstances are artificially revived by the specialist. Whereas modernity represses the past, especially when it considers this past to be pre-modern, denying continuity and atomizing experience, art concentrates and combines different periods.

Bakhtin's view, Tambling observes, is parallel to Benjamin's since the latter also feared the consequences of a temporal perception in which the past would retreat before the straight line of progress and be gradually relegated to the background.

Benjamin highlights a paradoxical relationship of mutual production between past and present: "it can never be said that something was unambiguously lost in the past, for whatever is 'found' is both new and creates elements of the past." Thus, any specific time in the past can be seen as retaining its "now" time, an actuality that can be deployed in our present: "the present experience is the present and the past together," Tambling notes. Likewise, the chronotope allows a reversal of time.

Both Bakhtin and Benjamin make the case for a present that is saturated with words spoken elsewhere and before. Tambling consequently suggests that the chronotope can be envisaged as a dialectical image in Benjamin's sense, which brings two moments together and makes the transition from one to the other manifest. To take up Tambling's metaphor, just as light becomes visible when it changes or declines, thus ceasing to be transparent, the tangible existence of what is otherwise trivialized and rendered invisible by its immobility becomes perceptible when it is set in motion.

A "phenomenology of the historical present" (Kliger, Chapter 5), such as the one articulated by Bakhtin, suggests that the valences and attributions of the categories of self and other are mobile, and sheds a light on the phenomenon of non-synchronicity at work in Russian Modernism. But its consequences can also be felt internationally and they have been articulated in criticism in the form of the paradox of the new and the reactionary, the moderns being anti-moderns according to Antoine Companion.[16]

In Collington's view, Bakhtin thus acknowledges in Dostoevsky, even though none of the expected writers make any appearance in his text, the turn toward an "ethical modernism," according to Rabaté's phrase, a moment of hesitation before an entirely personal and responsible choice. And this preoccupation affects the craft of writing, resulting in a certain way of articulating the elements of the narrative which changes its expected flow (the conventional unfolding of dramatic incidents and of their moral consequences, the illustrative and pedagogical function of the exposition of exemplary lives) and forces it to depart from a linear succession of conventional sequences of events.

Arguably, such decisions are formative of the modern subject. In this (new) configuration, the protagonist/hero, poised on the liminal threshold, is confronted to the multiple solicitations of external "perturbations" or "noises" in relation to which he must take a stand. This moment of decision implies uncertainty but also the assumption of responsibility (see Glossary), without recourse to a deterministic alibi that would explain away his act.

That dispensation is not without it quirks, however. Building upon the conclusions of a preceding article which balanced Bakhtin with Habermas' enumeration of the prototypical situations of conversational exchanges, a painstakingly normative endeavor which, on the face of it, ignores the implications of pluralism, Gardiner delivers a tentative assessment of Bakhtin's political relevance. While Habermas' thinking does not take into account the individual singularity of each unique experience, Bakhtin flatly discounts abstractions in everything that concerns the interpersonal relationship since he puts forward a conception of language that is neither bounded nor policed. This acknowledgment of the open-endedness of social conversation led many critics to defend the view of a liberal Bakhtin celebrating difference.

Gardiner suggests reversing the order of priorities, for the exhilaration that the Bakhtinian perspective may procure, with its opening up of possibilities or "illimitation of the game," does not extinguish the need for the consensus Habermas insists on. Gardiner also suggests the inadequacy of Bakhtin's treatment of the exact sciences and the natural sciences as an unambiguous relationship between an inert object to be known and a knowing subject who performs all the thinking, as opposed to the objects of the human sciences which, being themselves subjects, would respond to and anticipate and contribute to the construction of knowledge. He thus proposes to extend the method associated by Bakhtin to the human sciences—involving a dialogue with a subject that is not passively exposed to the cognition of the observer but may respond unexpectedly to its expectations—so that it might also cover the whole field of scientific investigation.

I have saved Marsha and Robert Barsky's study of Modern\Discourse for the end because, although it exceeds Bakhtin's preoccupation with language, it highlights a set of recurrent notions problematized by the Modernists, relating them to the body as the locus of sense experience and empirical self-perception. Such notions include the forms of social life and the relation to tradition, the ethics of interactions and the changes affecting temporal perception, and these are equally mentioned by the other critical commentators brought together in this book.

Modern dancing, as a discipline, calls upon the mythology of some intuitive and spontaneous sense of what is apt and timely. This requirement is coextensive with its insatiable search for embeddedness in the present, for a situatedness which requires that no movement be isolated from those that have come before or from the actions of other dancers, although nothing in the dance must be too carefully premeditated or pondered.

All this marks out modern dancing as a training ground, a field of practice or action in the sense that Bakhtin gives to these words, that is neither entirely on the side of the rule and the regulated choreography—which would make it indifferent to the environment—nor unduly reliant on the fantasy of an outburst of private genius entirely unrelated to any external factor that might assist it or determine its performance.

Such a choreographic proposal could legitimately be taken as the paradigm of Modernism, notably because of its insistence on flows and continuous movements: it plays out the conflict between academicism and free form.[17]

All in all, the chapters of this book generally acknowledge the traces of a vibrant concern for the status of the modern subject in Bakhtin. As we interiorize the words of our antagonists and those of our collaborators, these words preserve all the intentions and nuances that they had in the foreign discourses against which we measure ourselves. Such an open constitution, Jonathan Hall suggests, inevitably fractures the individual's integrity. Yet this exposure also maintains the possibility of some sort of connectedness between speaking subjects.[18] The forms of commonalities that ensue nonetheless follow the modern trend which aims at the formation of the individual.

In this sense, there is nothing revolutionary in Bakhtin's claim, no desire of a radical refoundation of the socius or the private person on new theoretical grounds. It still addresses the question of moral responsibility along the lines of a German tradition partly fed by philosophical idealism. For Kliger, Bakhtin starts from the recognition of plurality as well as that of the unique place of the subject in order to develop an "inquiry into the conditions of the possibility of coherent experience, ethical action, and aesthetic activity." Phrases such as "sense of crisis" and "crisis of authorship" may suggest a watershed in the historical development of self-consciousness and self-concern. But this general instability, whether for the Modernist or for Bakhtin, is perhaps less a current landmark event in cultural history than the uncovering of a pre-existent condition. At any rate, it is not necessarily a problem that calls for a resolution, but perhaps rather an agent of defamiliarization and change that may indeed be called the "new," and that must be put to use in artistic composition since it cannot be ignored.

Notes

1 Carol Adlam and David Shepherd, eds., *The Annotated Bakhtin Bibliography* (London: Maney Publishing for the Modern Humanities Research Association, 2000).
2 Craig Brandist, *The Bakhtin Circle: Philosophy, Culture and Politics* (London: Pluto Press, 2002).
3 See Craig Brandist's review of the first volume of the edition, "The Oeuvre Finally Emerges," *Dialogism: An International Journal of Bakhtin Studies* 1 (1998): 107–14, and *Russian Studies in Literature* 50.4 (2014), which memorializes the launch of the complete works.
4 Sergeiy Sandler, "The Reinterpretation of Kant and the Neo-Kantians: On Bakhtin's Pattern of Appropriation," reprinted as "A Strange Kind of Kantian: Bakhtin's Reinterpretation of Kant and the Marburg School," *Studies in East European Thought* 67.3/4 (2015): 165–82.
5 Terry Eagleton, "I Contain Multitudes," review of *The Word in the World*, by Graham Pechey (Routledge, 2007), *London Review of Books*, December 29, 2007.
6 It might be that the Formalists' concern with spatiality and structure, as Ricoeur contends, has flattened and suppressed the "intelligence of the narrative," so much so that the mapping out of the text, a matter of landmarks and spatial positions, has taken precedence over the expression of a temporal sensibility in the examination and evaluation of Modernist works. But historicism, Anker Gemzøe reminds us, can equally result in the desiccation and naturalization of text.
7 Theodor W. Adorno and Max Horkheimer, *Dialectic of Enlightenment: Philosophical Fragments* (Stanford: Stanford University Press, 2002).
8 "Indissoluble Matrimony," *Blast* 1 (1914): 98–117.
9 Mina Loy, *The Lost Lunar Baedeker: Poems of Mina Loy* (New York: Farrar, Straus & Giroux, 1996 [1914]), 153–6.

10 In *Psychoanalysis and the Unconscious*, as well as in the characterization of his heroines (Mrs. Goddard in *Mr Noon* as well as Gudrun in *Women in Love*, for instance), D. H. Lawrence straddles a line between the acknowledgment of the urgent necessity to liberate female subjects from the moral and social determinations of gender, on the one hand, and an ardent defense of some primordial principle of sexual differentiation, on the other. His narrators frequently disavow the ultimate benefits of the assiduous campaigning pursued by the suffragists, insofar as the actual spiritual emancipation of women is concerned. They also mock the sort of bohemian and sentimentalized ecofeminism practiced by Gudrun. D. H. Lawrence, *Psychoanalysis and the Unconscious and Fantasia of the Unconscious* (Cambridge: Cambridge University Press, 2004), 66, 126–32; *Mr Noon*, (Harmondsworth: Penguin, 1996), 34–43; *Women in Love* (Harmondsworth, Penguin, 1986), 185–90.

11 For instance, after Lefebvre, Gardiner sees modernity as a presiding spirit (a matter of principle), whereas Modernism can easily be understood as a period (see Gardiner, Chapter 7).

12 E. M. Forster, *A Passage to India* (Harmondsworth: Penguin, 2000), 199.

13 Jacques Rancière, *The Distribution of the Sensible* (London: Continuum, 2004), 32.

14 For Anderson, these conditions vanish at the end of the Second World War.

15 Quoted by Gemzøe in Chapter 2; Rita Felski, "Context Stinks," *New Literary History* 42.4 (2011): 573–91 (575).

16 Antoine Companion, *Les Antimodernes, de Joseph de Maistre à Roland Barthes* [The Antimoderns, from Joseph de Maestra to Roland Barthes] (Paris: Gallimard, 2005).

17 Loïe Fuller's performances captured the interest of Yeats for this reason. See W. B. Yeats, "Nineteen Hundred and Nineteen," *The Collected Poems of W. B. Yeats* (New York: Scribner, 1996), 206. In a 1955 essay, Kermode quotes Loïe Fuller's statement that "motion and not language is truthful." "Poet and Dancer before Diaghilev," *Puzzles and Epiphanies: Essays and Reviews 1958–1961* (New York: Routledge, 1962), 1–28 (17).

18 Drawing from Bakhtin's early writings (and also in part, it must be said, from *Marxism and the Philosophy of Language* which he misattributes to Bakhtin), Todorov insists that the notion of an empathetic communication would not apply here, since Bakhtin stresses that the process of reception is, from the very start, one of dialogical confrontation with the language of the other, which excludes the possibility of a passive surrender to the intentions of the other's language. Tzvetan Todorov, *Mikhail Bakhtin: The Dialogical Principle* (Minneapolis: University of Minnesota Press, 1984), 22.

PART ONE

Conceptualizing Bakhtin

1

From Heteroglossia to Contemporaneity

Bakhtin's Modernist History of the Novel

Ken Hirschkop

On the face of it, Bakhtin did not like Modernist novels. His brief comments on Joyce and Proust, made in the long series of notes and musings, "On the *Bildungsroman*" (1937–39), echo the dominant Soviet critical line: Modernism is subjectivist, obsessed with the inner workings of the individual consciousness, distant from actual history. "Time," the "hero of [Proust's] multivolume novel," Bakhtin remarks, "has become purely subjective extension, in which a historical event and the most intimate microscopic domestic experiences are given the same weight."[1] Joyce is condemned for being "an almost borderline case of withdrawal from real time and all its real historical dimensions" (ibid.). From the writings, as well as the interviews, we sense Bakhtin's preference was for canonical European realism, exemplified by the traditional English, French, and Russian masters: Dickens, Balzac, Flaubert, Turgenev, Dostoevsky, and so on.

At the same time, Bakhtin was crazy for *modernity* and argued, with noticeable enthusiasm, that the novel was its representative and embodiment in the sphere of literature. Admittedly, it took him some time to come around to this view. In *Problems of Dostoevsky's Art* (1929), he characterized monologism as not only bad form for novels but also as an ideology, a philosophy, the principles of which stand "behind the entire ideological culture of modernity."[2] Monologism was identified with the positivism—the belief that natural science was the sole acceptable form of knowledge—ascendant in the early part of the twentieth century. A few years later, however, the roles were reversed, and monologism found itself lumped together with the ancient power of myth and a number of antique and authoritarian figures (priests, political leaders, etc.). In "Discourse in the Novel" (1930–36), the blossoming of the novel is dated to the Renaissance and its emergence is a literary complement to the rise of modern science. The long, historical, and rarely discussed fifth chapter of that essay opens with the claim that the novel is "the expression of a Galilean linguistic consciousness,"[3] that it is the beneficiary of a "radical revolution in the fate of human discourse" (*CW3*: 122; *DI*: 367) and it closes with an encomium to the "epoch of great astronomical, mathematical, and geographical discoveries," the "epoch of the Renaissance and Protestantism, which destroyed the verbal and ideological centralization of the Middle Ages" (*CW3*: 170; *DI*: 415).

So: Modernism bad, modernity good. Given the meanings of the two terms, that isn't a self-contradictory position. But Bakhtin's account of the latter is actually inflected by the former: the modernity that characterizes the novel is *Modernist* in shape and flavor. The novels he likes to write about may be modern but not, in the usual sense, Modernist. But his account of how they work and what they do transforms them into Modernist masterpieces. Their Modernism lies in their conception of historical time.

What's a Modernist version of historical time? The unmodernist version is what we know as "progress," famously condemned by Walter Benjamin in the notes on "On the Concept of History." Progress, in the mind of the corrupted German Social Democrats, he argued, was "something boundless" and "inevitable—something that automatically pursued a straight or spiral course."[4] It was an immense, all-powerful force that compelled humanity as a whole to improve its lot steadily and incrementally: in science, in morality, in its political institutions, in its technological prowess, and its economic prosperity. In this version of modernity, human reason carried the peoples of the world forward with an irresistible momentum (though it was understood that some peoples moved forward faster than others). In Anglophone circles, it is allied to the "Whig version" of history, the Victorian faith in the forward movement of humankind (led, as it happened, by the British Empire).

The idea that history itself might have a direction, that there was forward movement built into it, came into its own in eighteenth-century Europe, and its emergence has been carefully documented by the intellectual historian Reinhart Koselleck. In roughly the middle of that century the term *Histoire* finds itself replaced by "the collective singular form of *Geschichte*, which since about 1780 can be conceived as history in and for itself in the absence of an associated subject or object."⁵ As a consequence of this change, "[t]ime becomes a dynamic and historical force in its own right," (Koselleck 2004: 236), pushing the denizens of the world onwards and upwards toward ever greater achievements. Bakhtin seems to mimic Koselleck's account when he dates the dominance of the novel to the second half of the eighteenth century⁶ and insists that this dominance reflects a "new era of world history" (*CW3*: 609; *DI*: 4), an era characterized by a new conception of historical time. But the forward movement of history could be conceived of in different ways, depending on how one thought about the relation of the future to the present. And it's here that the conception of historical time embodied in the novel, which Bakhtin calls "historical becoming" in the 1930s and "contemporaneity" in the 1940s has a Modernist twist lacking in Koselleck's conception.

That twist concerns the future and its relation to the present. In the conception of modernity we know as progress, the future is a mere continuation of the present, not differing in scale or ambition. But Bakhtin believed in a future that was radically unlike the present, a messianic promise of dramatic transformation and redemption that in a sense always threatened to upend present circumstances and worldviews. This was not a literal or embodied future, an achieved or even achievable state of perfection, but a virtual point through which ideals of justice, love, and human perfectibility applied pressure on the present. Bakhtin set out this vision most sharply in his writings of the early 1940s, perhaps because at that point it seemed like the past was threatening to overwhelm the present. The novel is founded not, he wrote in 1943, on "the ordinary course of life, but faith in miracles, in the possibility of its radical violation."⁷ Describing the vision of Flaubert at about the same time, Bakhtin claimed that novelistic images presupposed "[a] sharp feeling (a distinct and sharp consciousness) of the possibility of a completely different life and a completely different worldview than the life and worldview available in the present."⁸ Echoing Walter Benjamin's invocation of the Angel of History, who sees the past as "one single catastrophe, which keeps piling wreckage upon wreckage," (Benjamin, 2003: 392), Bakhtin argued that "The present day (when it commits violence) always seems to be a servant of the future. But this future is a future continuation, a succession of oppressions, not an exit into freedom, a transfiguration" (Bakhtin 2017 [1943]: 206, 207).

The moment of sudden freedom, the release from the burden of history, is Bakhtin's version of the Modernist "shock of the new," the radical difference that the art and writing of the early twentieth century insisted was a sudden, unpredictable intervention in the "ordinary course of life."⁹ In Bakhtin's case, the shock of the new is the shadow that a messianic future casts on the present, as an ever-present possibility of a life transformed. And what stands in the way of this necessary shock is that old foe of avant-garde art, the stolid and risk-averse bourgeoisie. Like so many other Modernists, Bakhtin will *épater les bourgeois* in the name of something scandalously different: the promise of transformation is blocked by the repetition of the "current comfortable truths," a "bourgeois-philistine optimism (an optimism not of the better but of the secure)," which relies on the solidity "of one's own domestic everyday life" (*CW5* [1940s]: 131). It's the bourgeois obsession with security and stability that blinds us to the possibilities that a messianic future holds open.

It is, arguably, the same bourgeois obsession with security and stability that causes literary historians and critics to overlook this historical time, this contemporaneity, in the novels of the past. For Bakhtin's Modernist history of the novel does not identify the Modernist sense of time, that messianic pressure on the present, with early twentieth-century Europe. Instead, he claims to find the seeds of this conception in classical Antiquity, in Saturnalia, ancient comedy, Roman satire, and so forth, and then again, in bolder form, in the popular-festive culture ("carnival") of the Middle Ages and Renaissance. It then blossoms in the "modern" novel, beginning in the eighteenth century, and finds its most striking expression in the nineteenth-century novels on which Bakhtin focuses his analyses. Does one find Modernist time in actual Modernist novels? It's hard to say what Bakhtin thinks about this, above all because by the mid to late 1930s, when Bakhtin began to concentrate on this question, it was impossible to openly discuss the Modernism of twentieth-century Western Europe or what could be called Modernism in Russia (for example, the prose of Zamiatin, Olesha, Bulgakov, and Pilniak; the poetry of Akhmatova, Pasternak, and Maiakovskii).[10] Instead, Bakhtin endorsed Modernism through his interpretative, critical work: he found Modernist time in prose that had been understood differently, as bourgeois and incremental; he—to borrow a Modernist phrase—fanned the messianic sparks of the past so that a bright line of pre-Modernist Modernism became visible.

And although one finds the most explicit and striking articulations of this conception of historical time in the writing of the 1940s, it in fact pervades Bakhtin's work on the novel from the beginning and, I want to argue, constitutes the backbone of the novelistic project in all of Bakhtin's critical work. We tend to think of Bakhtin's theory of the novel as lurching from stylistics to narratology, from dialogism to the chronotope and eventually to carnival—but these are in fact different sides of a single, evolving but cohesive novelistic project, elaborated in the years from 1930 to 1946.

To say that historical time is central to Bakhtin's studies of "discourse in the novel" may be surprising. The essay of that name is typically understood as a celebration, a call for recognition of the diversity of linguistic forms, the multiplicity of styles that novels depend and focus on. It's an attack on the dominance of monolingualism, the cultural force of standard languages, and the "code model" of language that underpins them, in the name of heteroglossia and linguistic diversity. "The style of the novel,"

Bakhtin famously intones, "lies in its combination of styles; the language of a novel is a 'system' of languages."[11] But the undoubted emphasis on what we might call the synchronic heterogeneity of linguistic forms can draw our attention away from what Bakhtin claims novels actually do, what makes them a form of art. For, as he makes clear throughout the essay, the novel does not merely reproduce the variation, the stylistic diversity, that constitutes so-called heteroglossia: it "artistically organizes" it, creating and reshaping that basic linguistic diversity so that it embodies "the forces of historical becoming that stratify a language" (*CW3*[1930–36]: 76; *DI*: 325). To this end novels are expected to deviate "from the empirical actuality of the represented language" (*CW3* [1930–36]: 90; *DI*: 336) and may even engage in the "free creation of elements which are completely alien to the actuality of a language but are in the spirit of the given language" (*CW3* [1930–36]: 91; *DI*: 336-7). When Bakhtin asks, rhetorically, what it is that distinguishes the extra-artistic transmission of an alien language from the artistic representation of such a language, he notes that the extra-artistic forms "do not strive to see and strengthen behind utterances the image of a social language realizing itself in them, but not exhausted by them—an *image*, and not a positive empirical given of the language" (*CW3* [1930–36]: 110; *DI*: 356).

The distinction between the image of a language and its dialectological givenness, the form it takes in everyday practical life, is bound to what Bakhtin alternately calls intentionality and ideology. While discourse in the novel is bound to speakers and contexts—is, in the modern sociolinguistic sense, heavily indexical—the fates of those individuals only matter insofar as they represent an ideological project that transcends them. A novel, Bakhtin insists, is "a dialogized representation of an ideologically freighted discourse" (*CW3* [1930–36]: 87; *DI*: 333), which it is the plot's job to test, frame, and expose. Intentionality and ideology are, one could say, the forces that drive us toward the future, realized in but never exhausted by linguistic material. When a novelist represents a style in distant, ironic terms, the point is not to limit its reach, but to reveal the intentionality that is at once embodied in it and beyond it. That is why, speaking of Rabelais, Bakhtin can say that the truth is never expressed directly in its own words, but "sounds only in the parodic-unmasking accentuation of lies" (*CW3* [1930–36]: 63; *DI*: 309). As Bakhtin stresses, in the novel it's language that's relativized, not the intentions that animate it. The novel makes language the visible vehicle of historical becoming. At least Bakhtin thinks it does.

When Bakhtin's attention turns, after he completed "Discourse in the Novel," first to the *Bildungsroman* and Goethe, and then, to the chronotope and to Rabelais, he is examining a different dimension of this novelistic modernity, the extent to which it is cashed out in distinctive narrative forms and patterns. As is usually the case with Bakhtin, it's difficult to say why he changed direction at this point in time (although we know with some certainty *when* he changed direction: in the fall of 1937, when he withdrew from the publisher *Sovetskiĭ pisatel'* the manuscript for "Discourse in the Novel" and proposed in its place a manuscript on Goethe and the *Bildungsroman*).[12] A good guess would be that he thought he could latch on to ongoing debate in the Soviet Union about the nature of literary realism and the role of the hero within the novel, and that he believed he could recast his project as a contribution to that debate. In the event, the book on Goethe and the *Bildungsroman* was never completed, and instead of a book we have that very long sequence (over 700 pages in manuscript) of notes I mentioned at the beginning, "On the *Bildungsroman*," in which Bakhtin begins serious work on the *Bildungsroman*, only to change direction once more in the middle of his notes, switching out Goethe for Rabelais and the *Bildungsroman* for the chronotope.

But we can see how Bakhtin thought it might work. The history of realism, as it is recounted in the *Bildungsroman* notes, is remarkably straightforward and progressive. In the beginning, we have prose narratives in which nothing changes: neither the hero (who is often a traveler, an adventurer, or a lover separated from his beloved) nor the world in which the narrative takes place. There follows the earliest version of the *Bildungsroman*, with roots in classical Greece but maturity only in the Renaissance and Enlightenment, in which "[t]he human being became, but not the world itself" (*CW 3* [1937–39]: 331; *SG*: 23). In this grab-bag of texts from different periods, the heroes strive and change, but this change "took place against the immobile background of a world that is finished and at its foundation completely solid" (ibid.). With Goethe's appearance, the summit of the form is reached, perhaps a little too soon. Now, as Bakhtin puts it, the hero "becomes *together with the world*, the historical becoming of the world is reflected in him" (ibid.). In other words, the Modernist conception of historical time that animated the stylistic profile of the modern novel was now embodied in a definite kind of plot; it achieves distinct narrative expression. But historical becoming, as it appears in these notes, acquires a somewhat muted hue: it is exemplified in the transition from one historical era to another (the hero is posed "on the border between two epochs, at the point of transition from one to the other" (ibid.), as if Bakhtin had incorporated Stalinism's notorious "stagist" view of historical change into his conception. There is transformation, but it seems to lack the abruptness and unpredictability we find later.

If this was some kind of compromise, it didn't last long. By the middle of the text, Bakhtin has a new concept, the chronotope, and a new literary exemplar, Rabelais. The text known as "Forms of Time and of the Chronotope in the Novel"—which is effectively the second half of the long sequence of *Bildungsroman* notes, later edited for publication—at first traces the evolution of narrative chronotopes up from Antiquity to the Renaissance. At that point "the future" makes its first explicit appearance as a category in Bakhtin's work, in a discussion of its deformation in what Bakhtin calls "historical inversion." The passage is worth quoting in full:

> The essence of such inversion is that mythological and artistic thinking locates in the past such categories as the goal, the ideal, justice, perfection, a harmonious condition of human and society, etc. Myths about paradise, about a Golden or heroic age, about ancient truths, and later representations of a state of nature, of natural rights, and so on, are expressions of this historical inversion. Putting the matter in somewhat simplified terms, one could say that something is represented as already having existed in the past which could or should be realized only in the future, which, in essence, has the form of a goal or obligation, and in no way the reality of a past.
> (CW3 [1937–39/1973]: 400–1; DI: 147)

Such inversions "empty and thin out the future, they bleed it white" (CW3: 401; DI: 148). But the future they empty out is not a state of paradise located at the end of time rather than the beginning, but a messianic promise with the "form of a goal or obligation," a sense of justice and harmony that enforces a moral obligation on everyone in the present. Historical becoming is thus the change and movement that comes from human striving toward a goal, even if that goal is a virtual point.

This means, as well, that whatever dramatic transformations occur, they take place within history, not as the result of some divine intervention into it. Historical inversions, Bakhtin notes, are "readier to erect something above actuality (above the present) along the vertical of high and low than to go forward along the horizontal axis of time" (CW3: 401; DI: 148). By contrast, a properly Modernist conception of historical time assumes that moments of transfiguration are a consequence of human historical effort, not sudden raids on history from above. In notes on Rabelais written at the same time, Bakhtin will emphasize "Perfection along the *horizontal* of time. Not the raising of the spirit, but historical progress through children and grandchildren."[13]

We will never know for sure what prompted this sharper formulation of the idea of historical becoming, what led him to talk about the status of the future and the horizontals and verticals of the cosmos; but we can make a good guess. We know that in the 1930s Bakhtin made a detailed résumé of Ernst Cassirer's *The Individual and the Cosmos in Renaissance Philosophy*, in which the latter discussed how Nicholas of Cusa destroyed the verticality of the medieval cosmos. We know he also made a résumé of the second volume of Cassirer's *Philosophy of Symbolic Forms* (having mentioned the first volume in "Discourse in the Novel"), making special note of the passages where Cassirer argued that monotheism had introduced a new *"feeling for the future"* that made possible the distinctive "time of human *history.*" And we know that in the summer of 1937, just as he was embarking on this long rumination on the nature of novelistic narrative, he spent many hours talking with his friend Matvei Kagan, who had studied with Cassirer and with Cassirer's mentor Hermann Cohen (who had made the Messianism of the Hebrew Prophets the keystone to human, moral history) and who himself created a philosophy of historical becoming.

The chronotope essay seems to have led Bakhtin to Rabelais and to popular-festive culture and its topsy-turvy transformations. But it also led him to a long and sustained exploration of the conception of time embodied in the novel, to which he now gave a new name: contemporaneity (*sovremennost'*). The exploration takes place in extensive, ruminative form in a very long manuscript which Bakhtin's editors have titled "On Issues in the Theory of the Novel" (*CW3* [1940–41]) and in concise form in the two lectures he gave on the novel in Moscow: "From the Prehistory of Novelistic Discourse" in 1940, and "The Novel as a Literary Genre" (better known as "Epic and Novel") in 1941. In these works, Bakhtin sets out his case for the relation between the novel and contemporaneity:

> The discovery of the novel, more precisely, the discovery that creates this genre, is the discovery of contemporaneity, of passing actuality, having neither beginning nor end. This "present" is not an abstract-temporal determination, but a value and formal-artistic category. It defines the orientation of the author, the orientation of his discourse, the tone, the formal structure, etc.[14]

What was distinctive about this present, the present understood as contemporaneity, is that it "is essentially and in principle unfinished: according to its very essence it demands continuation, it moves into the future, and the more actively and consciously it moves forward into this future, the more tangible and essential is its unfinishedness."[15] Note the verb: it *demands* continuation. The present does not move into the future as an abstract physical fact—because one damn thing always follows another—but because the future pulls it forward, like an ethical magnetic pole. Bakhtin's account of this "transitory present" is sometimes interpreted as if he were pointing out that as life goes on, shit happens, and we should draw some ethical conclusions from that. But the account insists on the exact opposite: there aren't ethical consequences of the "bare fact" that time passes—time passes as a consequence of the ethical pressure the future places on the present.

As mentioned above, the contemporaneity of novelistic writing has consequences for the formal structure and discourse of novels. In "The Novel as a Literary Genre" Bakhtin will focus on two formal features in particular: the position of the author in relation to the world it narrates, and the representation of the hero (at the time, a hot topic in Soviet literary debate). "Towards a Prehistory of Novelistic Discourse" will focus on how contemporaneity structures discourse in the novel.

Contemporaneity applies most literally to the position of the author in the novel: "The author of a novel himself composes, himself sees and experiences (brings in from his own life) the world he depicts. The heroes are his friends and are acquainted with his readers, who should recognize them (as types and characters whom they meet in reality). 'Onegin, my dear friend ... '" (*CW3*: 568). "A novelist," Bakhtin observes, "can appear in the field of representation itself in any authorial pose, can represent real moments of their own life or make allusions to them, can get mixed up in their heroes' conversations, can openly polemicize with their literary enemies, etc." (*CW3*: 631; *DI*: 27). This is familiar ground for the theory of the novel: the genre takes the disenchanted, secular everyday life of contemporaries as its subject, is grounded in empirical description of the social world, and is—as a consequence—devoted to a kind of empirical, sensory realism. But the novelist (Bakhtin's successful, ideal novelist, at any rate) isn't merely observing and recording: because these are its contemporaries, and because the world is its contemporary world, it is already part of the conversation, so to speak ("The hero is located in a zone of possible contact with the author, in a zone of dialogical contact" (*CW3* [1940a]: 517n; *DI*: 45m). The novelist, the argument implies, is forced to become historical, because they cannot avoid being entangled, caught up in the disputes and the forward movement of the world they represent. Of course, matters are not quite as simple as Bakhtin makes out: the novelist is not just caught up in the onward rush of the modern—their job is to craft, to create the very contemporaneity the novel embodies. They do so in a number of ways. First, by means of an ironic stance that pervades the novel in its plot and its tone. Like Georg Lukács—to whose work Bakhtin refers throughout the late 1930s and 1940s—Bakhtin sees irony as constitutive of the structure of the novel ("There cannot be an authentic and mature culture—artistic, social, everyday—without some element of irony and self-mockery" (*CW3* [1940–41]: 573)). But he draws a different conclusion from it: whereas Lukács sees irony in the novel's failure to reach epic wholeness in the age of fragmented capitalism, for Bakhtin it is a sign of the limited, but self-transcending quality of every significant human utterance or action. The possible future, you could say, ironizes every present action and event.

But contemporaneity also finds expression in the forward pressure, the tension of the plot. Epic works—Bakhtin's continual point of comparison in "The Novel as a Literary Genre"—furnish no suspense or surprise, because the story must end a particular way and we know it is so. Novels, by contrast, are marked by a "specific 'interest in continuation'" (what will happen next?) and an "interest in the ending" (how will it end?) (*CW3* [1941]: 635; *DI*: 32).[41] In his "Introduction to the Structural Analysis of Narratives," Roland

Barthes had claimed of the kernels of narrative movement, which he called cardinal narrative functions that "what constitutes them is not spectacle (the importance, volume, rarity, or power of the action articulated), it is, so to speak, risk: the cardinal functions are the moments of risk of the narrative; between these points of alternative [actions]."[16] Bakhtin's argument makes a historical, generic distinction: epic works are precisely about the spectacle of rare, unfolding events; novels are characterized by the riskiness of the events within them, and their narrative drive depends on maintaining the "spontaneity of an unfinishable present" (*CW3* [1941]: 631n; *DI*: 27) by means of plotting.

It is hardly a surprise that at this point in time Bakhtin casts Dostoevsky as the standard bearer of Modernism. In a text written a year or two after the lectures, he will imply that in the ordinary novel, and perhaps in ordinary life, "The human being is surrounded by the world, his room, his apartment, by nature, by landscape—he lives inside the world and acts in it; dense, warm masses of the world are around him; he is within the external world, not at its boundaries."[17] But Dostoevsky puts his characters in "the narrow space of a threshold, a boundary, where it is not possible to settle in, find comfort, obtain a foothold, where one can only step over, transgress" (Bakhtin, 2017 [1943–46]: 223/223). In *Crime and Punishment* Raskolnikov seems to be constantly skulking in doorways, but the more general point is that there's a variety of plot devices whereby novelists can discomfit and disorientate their heroes, throwing them off their guard and compelling them to contemplate the possibility that everything could be very different. For Bakhtin this discomfort is an essential element of a contemporaneity, and it's what distinguishes Modernist time from the narrative arcs we usually associate with the *Bildungsroman* and its novelistic kin.

A character—a "hero"—caught up in contemporaneity is therefore fundamentally unsettled. Bakhtin will point out that "in the novel the inadequacy of the hero to its fate and position is a leading theme" although this itself is a reflection of the larger "inadequacy of the entire world order" (*CW3* [1940–41]: 578). Such inadequacy "is bound to the ideological initiative of the hero and the author itself" (*CW3* [1940–41]: 578): both the hero and the author are continually pulled into the future. As a consequence, the hero's representation "is a pictorially incoherent image, not collected and not closed up, going beyond itself, radiating patches and emanations around itself" (*CW3* [1940–41]: 571). But one can put this more simply: novels attempt to represent subjectivity, understood not as consciousness, but as a continual, essentially unending movement forward. "A human being never coincides with itself"—that's what Bakhtin means by subjectivity—"insofar as it is always participating in the future" (*CW3* [1940–41]: 573).

The unsettled quality of the hero extends to its language, which, in a way, returns us to our starting point—discourse in the novel. "From the Prehistory of Novelistic Discourse" was delivered as a lecture in 1940 at the Gorky Institute in Moscow; Bakhtin clearly wanted to use the occasion to make public the ideas that had been sitting unread in "Discourse in the Novel." Accordingly, the lecture opens with an analysis of various passages from Pushkin's poem "Eugene Onegin" (interestingly, the paradigm of novelistic writing!). Bakhtin points out for us the various ways in which Pushkin has stylized various speech forms in the poem, endowing them with a distinctive linguistic profile and ideological drift. The language of each of the main characters—Lensky, Onegin, Tatiana—is rendered an object of representation and what the poem delivers is not direct speech but "images of languages" that are at the same time "images of world views and their living bearers—people, thinking, speaking and acting in historically and socially concrete circumstances."[18]

Having made the general point about the novel and about style, Bakhtin spent the remainder of the lecture describing the novel's ancient satirical and parodic precursors, in which the project of representing a language is developed and refined.

What's less clear in the lecture, but more explicit in some of the writings contemporary with it, is how satire and parody—and thus the stylizing, ironizing features of the novel—derive from the condition of contemporaneity. Contemporaneity, although it only flowers in the modern age, can be found even in the texts of classical Antiquity. In what Bakhtin calls the low, parodic-travestying, or serio-comical genres, contemporary actuality "serves as their object and, more importantly as the starting point of understanding, evaluation and formation" (*CW3*: 626; *DI*: 22). Parody depends on the destruction of authoritative tradition, on familiarity and equalization of subject and object. You could almost say that the simultaneity necessary to contemporaneity is a metaphor for equality of status—to be a contemporary is to be equal, or at least familiar.[19]

Is it an irony to point out that Pushkin himself founded a literary journal called *The Contemporary*? In any case, Bakhtin argues it is Pushkin's familiarity with the languages that appear in "Eugene Onegin" that makes their dialogization inevitable. A language present to you, in the sense that it approaches you, makes inquiries, demands a response, can't be treated as neutral strings of words. In Bakhtin's words, "the author actually *converses* with Onegin" (*CW3* [1940a]: 518; *DI*, 46): because it is impossible to relate to his language, once made contemporary, in any other way. Which means that the novelist and the languages they novelize can't help but be pulled ahead by the future.

One final text, and one final quotation. When Bakhtin wrote his article on "Satire" for the *Great Soviet Encyclopedia* (written in 1940, not published until 1996), he made a point of stressing that satire was never a purely negative exercise, bent on unmasking, bringing down to earth, and cutting down to size. Satire, no matter what its form, always contained "ambassadors of the future ('ideals')" as he called them.[20]

He followed this remark with a comment about Marxism–Leninism and the growth of the future in contemporary actuality. The comment on his political present may or may not have been in earnest. But the remark about satire was: contemporaneity was never an endless present in his theory, but always something animated by what lay, far in the distance, before it.

Notes

1. "On the *Bildungsroman*" [1937–39], in *CW3*, 218–335 (324). English translation in "The *Bildungsroman* and its Significance in the History of Realism," in *SG*, 218–335.
2. *PDA*, 76. English translation in *PDP*, 80. Where there is an English translation of the relevant text by Bakhtin, the first reference refers to the Russian original and the one following the available translation (I have often, however, altered the English translation). Where there is a single reference the translation is mine from a Russian original.
3. "Discourse in the Novel" [1930–36], in *CW3*, 9–179 (121). English translation in *DI*, 259–422 (366).
4. Walter Benjamin, "On the Concept of History," in *Selected Writings*, vol. 4: *1938–1940* (Cambridge, MA: Harvard University Press, 2003), 389–400 (394).
5. Reinhart Koselleck, *Futures Past: On the Semantics of Historical Time* (New York: Columbia University Press, 2004), 236.
6. M. M. Bakhtin, "The Novel as a Literary Genre" [1941], in *CW3*, 60843 (611). English translation as "Epic and Novel," in *DI*, 440 (5).
7. M. M. Bakhtin, "Rhetoric, to the Extent that it Lies," *Slavonic and East European Journal* 61.2 (2017 [1943]): 202–15 (202, 203).
8. "On Flaubert" [1940s], in *CW5*, 130–7 (132).
9. The reference is to the 1980 BBC TV series *The Shock of the New*, put together by the art historian Robert Hughes, and the book that followed in its wake.
10. An additional problem was that the term Modernism was rarely used in the Soviet Union and when it was, it often referred to Russian Symbolist writers.
11. "Discourse in the Novel" [1930–36], in *CW3*, 9–179 (15). English translation in *DI*, 259–422 (262).
12. The new proposal and a letter from the publisher acknowledging the switch appear in transcription in the editorial notes to the *Bildungsroman* book, in *CW3*, 757–9.
13. "Notebooks on Rabelais" [1938–39], in *CW4*, 605–75 (668).
14. M. M. Bakhtin, "On Issues in the Theory of the Novel" [1940-41], in *CW3*, 557–607 (568).

15 "The Novel as a Literary Genre" [1941], in *CW3*, 608–43 (633). English translation as "Epic and Novel," in *DI*, 4–40 (30).

16 Roland Barthes, "Introduction to the Structural Analysis of Narratives," in *The Semiotic Challenge* (Oxford: Basil Blackwell, 1988 [1966]), 95–135 (109).

17 M. M. Bakhtin, "On Questions of Self-Consciousness and Self-Evaluation," *Slavonic and East European Journal* 61.2 (2017 [1943–46]): 218–32 (220/221).

18 M. M. Bakhtin, "From the Prehistory of Novelistic Discourse" [1940a]), in *CW3*, 513–51 (523). English translation in *DI*, 41–83 (49).

19 Bakhtin, it's worth pointing out, was not the only scholar at the time who thought ancient Greek and Roman writing contributed something vital to the modern novel; this was also the part of the argument made by Erich Auerbach in his *Mimesis* (written in Istanbul, also during the war), where some of the same texts Bakhtin singles out contribute the seeds of novelistic realism that will flourish eventually in Balzac. Erich Auerbach, *Mimesis: The Representation of Reality in Western Literature* (Princeton: Princeton University Press, 1953 [1946]).

20 M. M. Bakhtin, "Satire," in *CW5* (2012 [1940b]), 11–38 (34). English translation in Ilya Kliger and Boris Maslov, *Persistent Forms: Explorations in Historical Poetics* (New York: Fordham University Press, 2016), 369–91 (390).

2

Mikhail Bakhtin and the History of Literature

The Past in the Present and the Present in the Past

Anker Gemzøe

Bakhtin neither developed a unified and definitive literary-historical theory nor a unified theory of the word, dialogue, polyphony, the chronotope, and the carnival. He does, however, present a wide range of inspiring suggestions for literary history writing, each with an original understanding of particular literary and cultural-historical contexts. In connection with these approaches, though sometimes independently of them, he has formulated a number of methodological reflections on the history of literature. Combined, they constitute a highly topical approach, worth considering on equal terms with some of the most interesting current positions in this field. In the present article I attempt to tie together some of Bakhtin's significant statements about, and contributions to, the history of literature, with an intent to give an impression of their rich variety as well as trace their main lines of cohesion. Together with other elements of placing Bakhtin in the history of modern criticism, I will profile Bakhtin in the context of a comparison and contrast to the influential stand on literary history taken by Rita Felski.

In Bakhtin's "Response to a Question from the *Novyj Mir* Editorial Staff"[1] we find a late, extremely important reflection on the history of literature.

The primary question of the journal concerned the current state of Soviet literary research. Bakhtin develops his view of literary history in response to the secondary question: what he considers the most urgent tasks of literary studies. This answer is imaginative, suggestive, immensely condensed. It concerns "the literature of past epochs"—not *modern* literature and literary criticism, "although it is precisely here that we find most of the important and immediate tasks" (*SG*: 2).

"First of all, literary scholarship should establish closer links with the history of culture. Literature is an inseparable part of culture and it cannot be understood outside the total context of the entire culture of a given epoch" (*SG*: 2). With this primary delineation, Bakhtin positions himself in opposition to "narrow specification" characteristic of Russian Formalism, new criticism, and similarly many variants of contemporary structuralism. Schools of theory such as these, he claims, have ignored questions of interrelation and interdependence between various areas of culture. They have often forgotten not only that the boundaries between these areas are not absolute, but that, historically, they have been drawn in different ways. Often, they fail to recognize that the most intensive and productive life of culture takes place at and across the boundaries between these separate areas and not where or when these areas "have become enclosed in their own specificity" (*SG*: 2). Literature has been narrowly confined inside epochs, generally historically defined. Writing aptly about the effects of period-defined literary history, he claims that if the literature of an epoch is studied without attention to the powerful, popular currents of culture at large, it is usually trivialized and reduced to the fashionable quarrels in newspapers and literary reviews.

He then unfolds his critical alternative:

> If it is impossible to study literature separately from an epoch's entire culture, it is even more fatal to encapsulate a literary phenomenon in the single epoch of its creation, in its own contemporaneity, so to speak. We usually strive to explain a writer and his work precisely through his own time and the most recent past (usually within the epoch, as we understand it). We are afraid to remove ourselves in time from the phenomenon under investigation. Yet the artwork extends its roots into the distant past. Great literary works are prepared for by centuries, and in the epoch of their creation it is merely a matter of picking the fruit that is ripe after a lengthy and complex process of maturation. Trying to understand and explain a work solely in terms of the conditions of its epoch alone, solely in terms of the conditions of the most immediate time, will never enable us to penetrate into its semantic depths. Enclosure within the epoch also makes it impossible to understand the work's future life in subsequent centuries; this life appears as a kind of paradox. Works break through the boundaries of their own time, they

live in centuries, that is, in *great time,* and frequently (with great works, always) their lives there are more intense and fuller than they are within their own time.

(*SG:* 3f)

Here we come across the leitmotif of the great time of literature and culture. Semantic phenomena can exist latently, he continues, and become visible only in the new contexts of subsequent epochs. Shakespeare is a prime example. Genres are especially important:

> Genres (of literature and speech) throughout the centuries of their life accumulate forms of seeing and interpreting particular aspects of the world. For the writer-craftsman the genre serves as an external template, but the great artist awakens the semantic possibilities that lie within it [...] The author is a captive of his epoch, of his own present. Subsequent times liberate him from this captivity, and literary scholarship is called upon to assist in this liberation.
>
> (*SG:* 5)

Thus, Bakhtin confronts Spengler's influential theories of eras as closed cultures. Instead, he argues, each cultural unity is an open unity and part of the non-linear development of human culture. In every culture "lie immense semantic possibilities that have remained undisclosed, unrecognized, and unutilized" (*SG:* 6).

For a creative understanding, it is crucial

> for the person who understands to be *located outside* the object of his or her creative understanding—in time, in space, in culture. For one cannot even really see one's own exterior and comprehend it as a whole, and no mirrors or photographs can help; our real exterior can be seen and understood only by other people, because they are located outside us in space and because they are *others.*
>
> (*SG:* 7)

This is a remarkable text in which more of Bakhtin's essential approaches and concepts are gathered than in perhaps any other text. Here we not only find the idea of culture's most intensive life existing at the boundaries between different fields, of the crossing lines, the great dialogue of the epoch, as well as the long life of genres, chronotopes, images, and plot types of the dialogue between distant times—indeed, we witness a return to nothing less than the fundamental phenomenological "architecture" of his early works, with its correlation of bodies and gaze directions in space and time, and the herein implied outsideness and excess of seeing.

In addition, we must note Bakhtin's significant distancing from theoretical trends that are certainly not yet things of the past. Not least, Bakhtin gives an apt, critical characterization of a conception of literary history predominant in educational systems all over the world to this day, including university scholarship: the unilinear writing of (literary) history, conceived as a series of epochal boxes, each of which is claimed to be permeated by one and the same *problematic/idéologème*. In its current forms, it represents the combined, heavy legacy of traditional historicism as well as the structural thinking of the 1960s and onwards, including the all-governing paradigm (Thomas Kuhn) or *l'épistémè* (early Michel Foucault) of epochs abruptly replacing one another.

All of these "problematic" concepts have great heuristic value, however, and are parts of complicated intellectual developments. The concept of *ideologeme*, to take one example, was used by Pavel Medvedev[2] in *The Formal Method in Literary Scholarship* (1978), whose first statement is this: "Literary scholarship is one branch of the study of ideologies."[3] It is used as a concept for established, fixed ideological systems: "Every ideological product (ideologeme) is part of the material social reality surrounding man, an aspect of the materialized ideological horizon" (Bakhtin, and Medvedev 1978: 8). But to Medvedev it is a main point, that literature does not ordinarily take its content from such closed systems:

> This is the reason that literature so often anticipates developments in philosophy and ethics (ideologemes), admittedly in an undeveloped, unsupported, intuitive form. Literature is capable of penetrating into the social laboratory where these ideologemes are shaped and formed.
> (Bakhtin, and Medvedev 1978: 17)

Julia Kristeva reintroduced the concept with explicit reference to Medvedev in the essay "Le texte clos" ("The Closed Text," dated 1966–67).[4] It is also important in "Le sens et la mode" ("Meaning and Fashion," 60–89), her reflections on Roland Barthes' *Système de la mode* (1967). In both cases she paradoxically combines vast, "box-like" descriptions of closed systems with a fundamental challenge to such systems as well as corresponding modes of description, in favor of forms of negation inherent in "productivity," "text," "écriture," "paragramme," etc.

The *Tel quel* group, of which Kristeva was a prominent representative at the end of the 1960s, marked on the one hand a peak of "box-thinking" in colossal, generalizing analogy systems (e.g., the *numismatics* of Jean-Joseph Goux), on the other a breaking up from structuralism in favor of a "post-structuralist" interest in intertextuality, processes, contradictions, heterogeneous manifolds, "rhizomes," and the like. A similar development can be observed in main structuralist figures such as Roland Barthes and Michel Foucault.

Rita Felski on Living Literature and Stinking Context

In the following, I will seek to profile Bakhtin in relation to the well-argued and influential position represented by Rita Felski, using key words from her book *The Uses of Literature*[5] and her article "Context Stinks,"[6] which offers a polemical summary of her view of the current state of literary history. Already in *The Uses of Literature*, a useful and rather undogmatic "manifesto" pinpointing some of the essential functions of literature, she takes as her starting point a confrontation with a number of dominant "schools": *ideology critique, symptomatic reading, deconstruction*, and a number of subsequent forms of "critical reading," including "the hermeneutics of suspicion." These approaches, imbued with a normative negativity, replace dialogue with diagnosis: "More and more critics are venturing to ask what is lost when a dialogue with literature gives way to a permanent diagnosis, when the remedial reading of texts loses all sight of why we are drawn to such texts in the first place" (Felski 2008: 1).

Though more positive toward different forms of neo-historical readings, she draws attention to the danger of a simplified historical approach: "the work is anchored at its point of origin, defined in relation to a past interplay of interests and forces, discourses and audiences" (Felski 2008: 10). Thus, the literary work is entrapped within its period of origin. At the end of the book, she elaborates on this point: "Historical criticism enriches our understanding of the work of art, but it can also inspire a stunted view of texts as governed entirely by the conditions of their origin, leaving us hard-pressed to explain the continuing timelessness of texts, their potential ability to speak across centuries" (Felski 2008: 120).

An important consequence of this is that the critic is impelled to disregard her or his own (historical) position as a reader. The interaction between texts and individual readers is, however, crucial to all kinds of literary studies—both within and even more so outside of literature as an academic discipline. In a confrontation with an avant-garde attitude that she claims to be influential in much literary theory, she formulates the following key points for a committed use of literature—recognition, enchantment, knowledge, and shock—as an approximate parallel to the classic aesthetic terms anagnorisis, beauty, mimesis, and the sublime. The ultimate goal of her approach is to contribute to a "neo-phenomenology that blends historical and phenomenological perspectives, that respects the intricacy and complexity of consciousness without shelving sociopolitical reflection" (Felski 2008: 18).

Bakhtin is absent in this positioning. In the chapter about "Recognition"—when Felski discusses ambivalent reactions to *The Well of Loneliness*, probably the most read novel on lesbianism, while simultaneously the most hated by lesbian readers—any reader acquainted with *Problems of Dostoevsky's Poetics* will miss the wide perspectives in Bakhtin's analysis of Devushkin's aggressive reaction (in Dostoevsky's *Poor Folk*) when he recognizes every trait of himself as an "objectified" portrait in Gogol's short stories about poor clerks.

In the chapter on "Knowledge," Bakhtin is in fact referred to, together with Paul Ricoeur and Dorrit Cohn among others, but merely in the form of an adjective, and in a rather tired way:

> Such observations bring to mind heavily canvassed Bakhtinian themes of polyphony and heteroglossia, yet in the current critical scene such themes are often eviscerated of any determinate content and watered down into reassuring bromides about the dialogic or subversive qualities of novelistic form. Heteroglossia, however, describes the moment when linguistic distinctions match up with socio-ideological ones, when historical divisions are actualized and verbalized in unique configurations of lexis, grammar, and style.[7] Such utterances can highlight patterns of social stratifications, forcing us to see how linguistic distinctions match up with political ones, how words partake of asymmetrical and unequal worlds.
> (Felski 2008: 94)

The imagery—"heavily canvassed," "eviscerated of any determinate content," and "watered down into reassuring bromides"—significantly testifies to the selective superficiality and consequential wearing down to clichés of references to Bakhtin's oeuvre "in the current critical scene." Despite the sympathetic attempt,[8] by reference to a secondary source, to revive the half-dead Bakhtinian body on the scene, neither Bakhtin nor Hirschkop figure in the book's "Index."

In the article "Context Stinks," aptly published in *New Literary History*, Felski gives another pointed programmatic formulation of her conception of literary history. In her continued confrontation with "the hermeneutics of suspicion," here focused on the concept of "context," she involves the sociologist Bruno Latour. These are the main theses of the article:

> 1) that history is not a box—that conventional models of historicizing and contextualizing prove deficient in accounting for the transtemporal movement and affective resonance of particular texts—and 2) that in doing better justice to this transtemporal impact, we might usefully think of texts as "nonhuman actors.
> (Felski 2011: 574)

In her conclusion, she considers the possibility of redefining the text/context distinction, "rather than abandon[ing] it," but rejects it: "the remorseless pressure of context's prior usage, I wager, is likely to coax us back into the familiar mindset of container versus contained" (Felski 2011: 589). "The context concept is itself an actor," she claims, and recommends that we put it "temporarily in abeyance" (Felski 2011: 590).

Hardly a good idea. Felski's polemical statement has some good points and defends a reasonable critical position. But while the introduction of Latour is interesting, why resort to a (new) sociological terminology, considering that a main polemical target is the crudeness of influential schools of sociology in literary studies? More importantly, why should precisely *context* be singled out as the main villain of the unilinear, self-contained thinking she rightly dismisses? Felski's critical stand should be commended, but in stating her alternative, she disregards so many formulated theories of literary history that one may legitimately accuse her of kicking in open doors.

Context and Code, According to Bakhtin

The most widely open door is certainly that of Mikhail Bakhtin. When, in her programmatic article, Felski seeks alternatives to seeing texts "as transcendentally timeless on the one hand and imprisoned in their moment of origin on the other" (Felski 2011: 575), one could argue that she formulates one of Bakhtin's central intentions. I have already demonstrated above that Bakhtin, in his "Response to a Question … " presents a scathing critique of the very same conception of literature as she does. And although effectively separating himself from depersonalization through his personalist philosophy, he too operates with "nonhuman actors." In the late notes of "The Problem of the Text" he often shifts between a personalized and a nonhuman optic, e.g., when writing about "The text as a unique monad that in itself reflects all texts (within the bounds) of a given sphere. The interconnection of all ideas (since they are all realized in utterances)."[9] Furthermore, he very often treats genres (like the Menippean satire and the polyphonic novel), chronotopes, cultural traditions and even influential individual works as nonhuman actors.

Instead of merely rejecting the concept of context, however, he has subjected it to a critical revision, has redefined and expanded it. For literature, context encompasses the entire literary tradition. Bakhtin's use of context reminds us of T. S. Eliot's conception of literary history in its entirety as a constantly modified "ideal order."[10] Context includes traded styles, discourse forms and, not least, genres.

Furthermore, literature is, as stated above, embedded in the wider context of culture. Bakhtin once again affirms this in "From Notes Made in 1970–71," at the same time clearly demarcating his position from crude sociologism: "Literature is an integral part of the totality of culture and cannot be studied outside the total cultural context. It cannot be severed from the rest of culture and related directly (bypassing culture) to socioeconomic or other factors" ([1970–71] *SG*: 140). Context obviously involves both past, present, and future relations. And yet again in the concise style characteristic of his late notes, in "Toward a Methodology for the Human Sciences" Bakhtin restates this point:

> Contexts of understanding. The problem of *remote contexts*. The eternal renewal of meanings in all new contexts. *Small time* (the present day, the recent past, and the foreseeable [desired] future) and great time—infinite and unfinalized dialogue in which no meaning dies.
> ([1970–71] *SG*: 169)

Context also includes the author's own previous utterances (the authorship). Finally, it includes the reader's context, an essential precondition for the constant renewal of the text. For Bakhtin, understanding implies a correlation with other texts and reinterpretation in ever new contexts, those of each new reader. From a point of departure in the text, we move backward to past and forward to future contexts.

The location, function, and significance of the concept of context in Bakhtin differ from that of many of his contemporaries, e.g., from its meaning and function in Roman Jakobson's famous communication model.[11] Jakobson's approach was influenced by his collaboration with communication engineers. The terminology of the model is mainly mechanical: as in telegraphy, a ready-made message, a manifestation of a pre-established code, is transferred from an addresser to addressee. For Bakhtin, communication, including reading, is an event:

> Semiotics deals primarily with the transmission of ready-made communication, using a ready-made code. But in live speech, strictly speaking, communication is first created in the process of transmission, and there is, in essence, no code.
> ([1970–71] *SG*: 147)

Bakhtin opened a diverse literary landscape between the abysses formed by a timeless transcendental view of texts on the one hand and the confinement of them to their moment of origin on the other. Especially important is his approach to the concept of context: "Context and code. A context is potentially unfinished; a code must be completed. A code is only a technical means of transmitting information; it has no cognitive, creative significance. A code is an intentionally killed context" (ibid.).

Concerning context, it may be claimed that Felski reproduces the misleading conception nurtured by the targets of her just criticism: she confuses context and code.

A Multi-Linear and Multi-Directional Literary History

Throughout his life, Bakhtin was critical of Russian Formalism. "Art is rich—it is not arid, not specialized. The artist is a specialist only as a master-craftsman, that is, only in relation to the given material," Bakhtin exclaims in "The Problem of Content, Material, and Form in Verbal Art" (1924), his passionate and incisive scholarly demarcation from the Formalists (*AA*: 278). Similarly, he also approved of the main critical points in Pavel Medvedev's before mentioned—very differently formulated[12]—*The Formal Method in Literary Scholarship* (1928). No doubt he must have been sympathetic to Medvedev's criticism, not of the Formalists but of "three fatal methodological errors" of traditional Russian literary history, the third of which he formulated as follows:

> It finalized and dogmatized basic ideological points reflected by the artist in his work, thus turning active and generating problems into ready theses, statements, and philosophical, ethical, political, religious, etc. conclusions. It did not understand or consider the vital fact that the essential content of literature only reflects generating ideologies, only reflects the living process of the generation of the ideological horizon.
> (Bakhtin, and Medvedev 1978: 19)

This reformulation of Medvedev's before quoted main point of literature's capacity to penetrate into "the social laboratory where these ideologemes are shaped and formed" (17) has an obvious kinship to Bakhtin's ideas of the double-voiced word, dialogue, and polyphony.

In spite of several important differences, Bakhtin is clearly influenced by many fundamental assumptions of Russian Formalism, not least its multi-linear conception of literary history and its ideas about the importance of a dialogical-polemical "push factor" in the dynamics of literary development. These conceptions had been anticipated by others,[13] but were brilliantly and poignantly reformulated by Viktor Shklovsky in the powerful, inventive style of his pioneering essays, collected in *Theory of Prose* (1925):

> The history of literature progresses along a broken path. If we were to arrange all of the literary saints canonized since the seventeenth century along one line, we would still fail to produce a single line of descent that might allow us to trace the history of literary form ... In each literary epoch there exists not one but several literary schools. They exist in literature in a state of simultaneity. However, one of them represents a canonized crest in its evolution, while the other schools coexist without such canonization in a state of obscurity ... At this very time, however,

new literary forms are emerging out of the lower stratum of society to replace the old ones. The old forms, no more consciously felt than grammatical forms are in speech, have lost their artistic character to assume an official status that precludes sensation.[14]

The main features of this dynamic conception of the history of literature (and art) as a dialectic between canon and deviation were inspired by the German aesthetician Broder Christiansen's work *Philosophie der Kunst* (1909), as it is demonstrative in this passage:

> The deviations from the convention of the day and from the fashion style ... could be included as elements in a work ... But these qualities of divergence [Differenzqualitäten] disappear with time; as soon as the canon is no longer valid, the basis of the deviation is missing. Such works themselves join in creating a new convention, displacing the old one, and in doing so they saw off the branch that bears it. For their performance needs the background of the old.[15]

Based on Christiansen's key concept of "Differenzqualitäten," Shklovsky[16] remarks in his usual poignant and whimsical style:

> I would like to add the following as a general rule: a work of art is perceived against the background of and by association with other works of art. The form of a work of art is determined by its relationship with other pre-existing forms ... All works of art, and not only parodies, are created either as a parallel or an antithesis to some model.
> (Shklovsky 1990: 20)

The quoted passage can be seen as an early anticipation of all later theories of intertextuality. In its crude form, it can very well be characterized as a simplified model of the history of literature "driven by an endless spiral of surprise-habituation-surprise" that "oversimplifies and underestimates the impact of literary works by yoking them emphatically to a single moment" (Felski 2008: 115). Shklovsky's multifaceted use of literature's built-in *push* factor, e.g., involving children's phenomenology of perception, is, however, less abstract and formalistic than it is often assumed. In Bakhtin's case, the existential, phenomenological, and historical horizon is evidently even wider.

One of the works in which Bakhtin most clearly elaborates on the literary-historical conceptions of Russian Formalism is *Discourse in the Novel* (1934–35). This is paradoxical, since the motivating polemic of this treatise is directed against one of the favorite concepts of Formalism (with exceptions, notably Shklovsky), namely the poetic language, "poetic discourse." However, in the polemically simplified reversal of the usual relation of dominance between poetry and prose, and in following the tendency toward abstract generalizing, this book, for better or worse, shows some kinship with Formalism. Especially relevant is the multi-linear perspective on literary history in the summarizing chapter "The Two Stylistic Lines of Development in the European Novel," in which Bakhtin illustrates some important philosophical and historical consequences of his previous stylistic and genre-related studies of artistic prose fiction:

> The novel is the expression of a Galilean perception of language, one that denies the absolutism of a single and unitary language ... The novel begins by presuming a verbal and semantic decentering of the ideological world, a certain linguistic homelessness of literary consciousness, which no longer possesses a sacrosanct and unitary linguistic medium for containing ideological thought.
>
> (*DI*: 366f)

In his own way, he expands the multi-linear literary-historical thought of Formalism. Similarly, the central concepts in his concluding "methodological observations" are clearly dialogical developments of Formalism's approach to the dynamics of literary evolution. Both of the essential concepts in Bakhtin's perspectives on literary evolution—"the process of *canonization* and the process of *re-accentuation*"—are very much his own, yet they bear an unmistakable trace of Shklovsky's pioneering essays.

Historical Poetics

The essays collected in "Forms of Time and of the Chronotope in the Novel. Notes toward a Historical Poetics" were written mainly around 1937–38, probably as parts of a larger project on the *Bildungsroman*. Most of the surviving essays, however, were later published in Russian, approved and with a postscript from Bakhtin. These "Concluding Remarks" are dated 1973 and thus constitute some of his last utterances. Three small fragments on the *Bildungsroman* and Goethe were published separately (and will be addressed in the next section).

These essays return to one of Bakhtin's earliest commitments, most obviously expressed in the manuscript published under the title "Author and Hero in Aesthetic Activity" (*AA*). But while a phenomenological approach to space and time is important here, it is nonetheless subordinated to an interest in the author–hero-relation. Topical configurations of time and space, typical chronotopes, are now read as keys to a historical typology of prose fiction, especially its earliest forms and cultural preforms preceding the Renaissance.[17] This historical poetics of the chronotope focuses foremost on genres, and, more or less derived from them, on the chronotopes that are typical of a given genre. Still taking into account his old point of departure in human characters (heroes, types, "masks"), Bakhtin touches upon a number of literary, chronotopic, motifs. Here he deals with plot types in more depth than anywhere else and is increasingly interested in forms of popular culture. In his conception of the novel and, finally, in his basic assumptions, it is a decisive divergence that literary masters of time and gradual formation, like Rabelais and Goethe, figure as valid alternatives to Dostoevsky's spatial and synchronous optics.

As already indicated, Bakhtin only occasionally—most consistently in his "Concluding Remarks"—focuses on the title concept of the chronotope, instead moving freely between levels and topics such as hero, plot, motif, genre, mode (laughter, for example) and cultural form. As a fragile framework of thought for these preludes to a historical poetics, we sometimes see a schematic outline of a history of thought, implying a certain logic of progress, that is, a normative and teleological depiction of literature's historically conditioned development of such forms of representation which are most adequately suited to show human development and historical change.[18]

This figure of thought corresponds in its main outlines to a Hegelian and Marxist way of thinking, which was also common—in more or less caricatured, "vulgar" simplifications—in the official Soviet philosophy during Bakhtin's lifetime. Bearing in mind, however, that Ernst Cassirer's significance for Bakhtin has been increasingly emphasized,[19] it is clear that the Hegelian elements in the chronotope dissertation have their background and kinship in Cassirer, rather than in Soviet philosophy. Ken Hirschkop, who approves of the figure of intellectual progress in the essays on the chronotope, puts it this way: "Bakhtin's own narrative, the narrative of the development of the chronotope, is therefore not merely descriptive, but normative, tracing the achievement of a historical existence deemed valuable in itself" (Hirschkop 1999: 179). Hirschkop is right; this figure of thought can be found here and, as mentioned, elsewhere in Bakhtin's writings.

In my perception, however, the contradicting voices prevail. Bakhtin's conception of literary history differs not only sharply and on many levels from the unilinear, teleological adoration of progress and glorification of the perfect present time that was the official Soviet norm, but also from the tendency toward schematism in Cassirer's *geistesgeschichtliche* Hegelian approach. Bakhtin focuses a provocative and eye-opening light on all the "advanced" storytelling devices that were in fact already developed in Antiquity. It was commonplace in literary scholarship to see the novel exclusively as a product of the Renaissance—a view generally held by Lukács, regardless of the important changes in his position (and his discreet reservations about Stalinism's worst simplifications).

Bakhtin's approach to genre and chronotope harbors an idea of a motley coexistence of time and space forms, incompatible with a figure of progress that valorizes fixed points in an ascending historical line. In keeping with this, he demonstrates many surprising connections, e.g., between the archaic romance of chivalry and Modernism which cannot be arranged on a single line of development at all. Strikingly, he is more interested in the figure of metamorphosis, with its mixture of archaism and modernity, than in more "developed" forms for the rendering of human and historical change. And if, after all, we take the development logic at face value, it represents at the very least a quite broad, impertinent swipe at the official norm since it is not Soviet art and literature which eventually creates the conditions for an adequate mode of representation of human and historical change, but Rabelais, Grimmelshausen, and Goethe.

The literary history writing in the Rabelais book is somewhat less theoretical in its orientation, but nevertheless offers an unsurpassed practical demonstration, which is especially inventive in the last chapters. Some of Bakhtin's most subtle and meticulous textual analyses are found in the large chapter six on "The Images of the Material-Bodily Lower Stratum" in Rabelais' novel. In themselves, these readings—of the infant experiments with swabs in *Gargantua*, of Epistemon's resurrection in *Pantagruel*, and of Gargantua's famous letter to his son in the same book—are testimonies of an unsurpassed textual sensibility. Moreover, and even more importantly, they serve as a springboard for a magnificent outline of the historical transition of the Renaissance as an upheaval of the chronotope, that is, a revolution in the time and space coordinates, and in the image of human nature.

Then, in seemingly capricious order, follow accounts of very heterogeneous but strangely interconnected phenomena. Among them we find forms of negation: grotesque chronotopic negations turning the world upside down and inside out; the more abstract and intellectual game of negation (as in "The Story of Nemo"); the ambivalent fusion of praise and abuse in *blazons*; the dynamic nonsense of the *Coq-à-l'âne*. In the last chapter, on "Rabelais' Images and His Time," Bakhtin once again settles accounts with a faulty "biographism" that privatizes and trivializes great historical movements, reducing them to mere biographical details. He nonetheless offers a more traditional and concrete placement of Rabelais' novel, partly in the region of Rabelais' adolescence, partly in the contemporary political history of conflicts and wars in one of Europe's most turbulent periods. But from here Bakhtin moves from Rabelais' encyclopedic knowledge to his historically specific and unique consciousness of language. Bakhtin's description of the active multilingualism of the Renaissance is fascinating–confronting languages, dialects, and sociolects, weakening the boundaries between appellants and proper names, between proper names and nicknames, and containing a grotesque handling even of numbers. Together with the previously mentioned approaches, this invigorated language history and literary-historical symptom reading constitutes a deeply original new conception of literary history.

Bakhtin's "Evolving Emerging Method"

In one of the fragments on the *Bildungsroman*,[20] Bakhtin characterizes Goethe by his exceptional ability to "*see time*, to *read time*, in the spatial whole of the world and, on the other hand, to perceive the filling of space not as an immobile background, a given that is completed once and for all, but as an emergent whole, an event" (*SG*: 25). Goethe called his approach "die entwickelnde entfaltende Methode," with an intent to read the traces of passing time through a combination of the seeing eye and complex thought processes. In a city like Rome, he sees, as frequently demonstrated in his *Italienische Reise* (1816), a spatial densification of historical time, a great chronotope of history, a unique expression of the fullness of time:

> The main features of this visualization are the merging of times (past with present), the fullness and clarity of the visibility of the time in space, the inseparability of the time of an event from the specific place of its occurrence (*Localität und Geschichte*), the visible *essential* connection of time (present and past), the creative and active nature of time (of the past in the present and of the present itself), the necessity that pervades localized time, the inclusion of the future crowning the fullness of time in Goethe's images.
>
> (*SG*: 41f)

Goethe's vision of everything as visible, concrete, and material, but under constant change, also implied an aesthetics—not least an idea of the novel. The novel was to reproduce the complex whole of the world. The novel's particular potential as a genre lies in its capacity to provide a historical and encyclopedic picture of an entire epoch. This idea of the novel was later continued and further developed by the young Friedrich Schlegel.

With his characterization of Goethe's vision, Bakhtin characterizes—almost better than anywhere else—his own view of the significant world. This applies to both the visible world (the spatial and temporal phenomenology of bodies and gazes, which he took as his point of departure, and which is latently ubiquitous in his work) and to the world of the word. This parallel is obvious when, in his notes from 1970–71, he affirms: "There can be no such thing as an isolated utterance. It always presupposes utterances that precede and follow it. No utterance can be either the first or the last. Each is just a link in the chain, and no one can be studied outside this chain" (*SG*: 136).

In "Rabelais and Gogol: The Art of Discourse and the Popular Culture of Laughter,"[21] however, there is a formulation of Bakhtin's "evolving emerging method," on the level of the history of literature, which includes the chronotope, dialogue, genre, and style—a methodological reflection on the perspectives of regarding Gogol in the context of living popular speech:

> We reject the primitive notion, usually formed in normative circles, of a certain linear progression. Actually, it turns out that each essential step forward is accompanied by a return to the beginning ("primordial state") or, more precisely, to the renewal of the beginning. Only memory and not oblivion can move forward [...] Of course, seen in this way, the terms "backward" and "forward" themselves lose their closed absoluteness. Instead, their interaction opens up the living and paradoxical nature of movement, studied and interpreted differently by philosophy from the Eleatic school to Bergson.
>
> (Bakhtin 1983: 45)

With this important demarcation, we find ourselves again in the broad literary-historical perspectives of "Response to a Question from the *Novyj Mir* Editorial Staff." Bakhtin reaches and reads far back in history. At the same time, he is future-proof. His view of literary history—of Antiquity, the Renaissance, the nineteenth century—does not disregard his own time. It is distinctly modern. According to Bakhtin, literary prose has emerged as an exploration of the unfinished present moment, the new, the future-oriented in it. The novel, the first form of literature based entirely on written texts, is anti-canonical, indeed, anti-generic by nature. The journalistic preoccupation of fictional prose with the latest news, the emerging present, is expressed in the genre designations of "novella" and "novel," both signifying novelty, newness.

In fact, Bakhtin has been internationally inspiring for the study of such contemporary currents and movements as magic realism, Modernism, and postmodernism, not only in prose but in poetry as well. A Bakhtinian approach has even been used and recommended for the analysis of new electronic texts. Bakhtin's position on literary history is complex but coherent. His "evolving emerging method" constitutes a distinctive historical and rhetorical Formalism which, through a sensitive consciousness of form, takes equal aim at the content, the existential, and the social. It is a position that creates dialogue between literary and cultural history and connections between rhetoric, media studies, and linguistics.

Rooted as it is in Bakhtin's conception of literary history, times past become more interesting. Simultaneously, it is possible to calmly draw correlations to current text fields in which new forms and connections are constantly being developed. Thus, addressing the microscopic particulars of current texts prompts us to embark on formative historical journeys, leading around the world and far back in time. The attempt to capture and vitalize the present, the brand new, is a literary endeavor that is of course far from new. Fact and fiction, forms of communication in life and in literature are intertwined. Every communication takes place in genres, even when the setting is anti-canonical and genre critical. All genres, especially the literary ones, contain something archaic and primitive, a transpersonal, creative memory of the long lines in the development process of literature. Literature lives in the present but stretches its roots far back into the great time of culture. Even when a literary text seems most topical and original, it usually draws on ancient forms–genres, scenarios, chronotopes, images, and forms of rhetoric. In his approach to the history of literature, Mikhail Bakhtin, has opened original ways of seeing time in space as well as reading the past in the present and the present in the past.

Notes

1. First published in *Novyj Mir*, 11 (1970), in *SG*, 1–9.
2. A participant to the so-called "Bakhtin school" which also included Valentin Voloshinov.
3. M. M. Bakhtin and P. N. Medvedev, *The Formal Method in Literary Scholarship: A Critical Introduction to Sociological Poetics* (Baltimore and London: Johns Hopkins University Press, 1978), 3.
4. J. Kristeva, *Semeiotike. Recherches pour une sémanalyse* (Paris: Éditions du Seuil, 1969), 113–42.
5. R. Felski, *The Uses of Literature* (Oxford: Blackwell Publishing, 2008).
6. R. Felski, "Context Stinks," *New Literary History* 42.4 (2011): 573–91.
7. Here Felski has a general note reference to K. Hirschkop, *Mikhail Bakhtin: An Aesthetic for Democracy* (Oxford: Oxford University Press, 1999).
8. In this context, there is no room to take up the discussion about the adequacy of the "free" translation of "heteroglossia."
9. M. M. Bakhtin, "The Problem of the Text in Linguistics, Philology, and the Human Sciences: An Experiment in Philosophical Analysis," in *SG*, 103–31 (105).
10. T. S. Eliot, "Tradition and the Individual Talent," *The Sacred Wood: Essays on Poetry and Criticism* (London: Faber & Faber), 50.
11. R. Jakobson, "Closing Statement: Linguistics and Poetics," in *Style in Language*, ed. T. A. Sebeok (Cambridge, MA: The MIT Press, 1966). Tzvetan Todorov has presented a "Bakhtinian" alternative to Jakobson's communication model. T. Todorov, *Mikhaïl Bakhtine. Le principe dialogique* suivi de *Ecrits du cercle de Bakhtine* [Mikhail Bakhtin: The Dialogical Principle followed by Writings of the Bakhtin Circle] (Paris: Éditions du Seuil, 1981). In my doctoral thesis, I have taken up his good idea, correcting and further developing an illustrative "Bakhtinian communication

model," followed by extensive commentaries. A. Gemzøe, *Metamorfoser i Mellemtiden. Studier i Svend Åge Madsens forfatterskab 1962–1986* [Metamorphoses in the Middle Time: Studies in the Work of Svend Åge Madsen from 1962 to 1986]) (København: Forlaget Medusa, 1997), 40–6.

12 But attributed by many–in my opinion wrongly–to Bakhtin, hence the reference with double authorship. The problem of the "disputed texts" will not be discussed here. In any case, the harsh tone in parts of Medvedev's criticism of the Formalists indicates a "necessary" fellow traveler attitude, revealing the terrifying growing reach of Stalinist control over intellectual life in the Soviet Union at the time.

13 For example, Ferdinand Brunetière and Broder Christiansen.

14 V. Shklovsky, *Theory of Prose* (Funks Grove, IL: Dalkey Archive Press, 1990), 189f.

15 B. Christiansen, *Philosophie der Kunst* [Philosophy of Art] (Hanau: Clauss und Feddersen, 1909), 122f., my translation.

16 Broder Christiansen's book was published in Russian in 1911. This German philosopher, important to the Formalists (not only Shklovsky but also other leading Formalists such as Boris Eichenbaum, Yury Tynyanov, and Roman Jakobson), is unidentified in Benjamin Sher's translation into English. His name is simply rendered in its Russian transcription (Khristiansen), as absurd as if an English translation of a Russian book on the Second World War were to constantly refer to "Gitler."

17 See more about the chronotope in my article "Sensation and Abstraction: The Station as a Modernist Chronotope" in Chapter 11, this volume.

18 An especially interesting variant of a similar pattern of development can be found in Bakhtin's lecture "Epic and Novel" (1941).

19 For example, by Brian Poole and Graig Brandist. Significant verbal and intellectual similarities can be found especially in Cassirer's *Philosophy of Symbolic Forms* (1923–29). G. Brandist, "Bakhtin, Cassirer and Symbolic Forms," *Radical Philosophy* 85 (1997): 20–27; B. Poole, "Bakhtin and Cassirer: The Philosophical Origins of Bakhtin's Carnival Messianism," *The South Atlantic Quarterly* 97.3/4 (1998): 537–78.

20 "The *Bildungsroman* and Its Significance in the History of Realism" (Toward a Historical Typology of the Novel), in *SG*, 10–59.

21 M. M. Bakhtin, "Rabelais and Gogol: The Art of Discourse and the Popular Culture of Laughter," *Mississippi Review* 17.3 (1983): 34–50. Incidentally, the first text by Bakhtin translated into Danish, in L. S. Andersen, ed., *Marxistisk litteraturanalyse* [Marxist Analysis of Literature] (København: Rhodos, 1970). The inclusion in a *Marxist* analysis of literature evidently implies a rather broad, undogmatic understanding of the term.

3

On Death and Turn-Taking in Conversation

The Concept of Succession (*Smena*) in Bakhtin's Late Philosophy

Sergeiy Sandler

> *There's nothing serious in mortality.*
> (SHAKESPEARE, *MACBETH*, ACT II, SCENE 3)

Introduction: Personalism and Holism in Bakhtin's Thought

An apparent tension often noted in Bakhtin's work is that between personalism and holism. On the one hand, Bakhtin resists any attempt to bring the human person to completion, or to subsume the individual under some kind of collective subject, as a form of violence.[1] On the other hand, he speaks of the carnival crowd and of the body of an entire people[2] and of an ultimate whole containing "all ends and meanings,"[3] larger than the individual. This tension has been an important concern for Bakhtin scholarship over the years.[4]

A closer reading, though, shows the tension here is merely apparent.

In his early works, Bakhtin embraces a radical reversal of traditional philosophical priorities.[5] Traditionally, that which is the same for everybody in all contexts is taken to *underlie* that which differs from one context and perspective to the next. Thus, one could think of space as an abstract geometric entity, and represent it, say, on a map. The content of the map is objective; everybody would agree on it. But the way *I* experience space is not map-like. I don't observe it in its entirety from some external vantage point; I am situated *here*, and am looking in a particular direction. Moreover, different locations in space mean different things to me, they have values and emotions attached to them, and I view the space around me and the things in it differently depending on my intentions and actions.

So, my space is subjective, not objective. And yet, Bakhtin insists, it is *my*, and other people's, space, not the space of a map, that is ultimately real.[6] No amount of objective knowledge about a point in space and its surroundings can tell how a person experiences this space, or indeed whether there is any person there to experience it at all. On the other hand, one can create a map by studying many people's recollections of their experiences and abstracting the relevant information from them (*CW1*: 29).[7]

Bakhtin also claims that I, as a subject, am not self-sufficient—the world as it exists for me does not contain myself in it (*CW1*: 66–8; *TPA*: 72–5). To fully become a subject, I need to obtain a coherent image of myself as a whole, and this I can only receive as a gift from *others*.[8] I am constituted by others as a subject. The same claim has been made by several other philosophers, most notably by Hegel.[9] But whereas Hegel then goes on to subsume both *I* and *other* under the higher unity of a *we* (and later the highest unity of Absolute Spirit), and whereas some other thinkers who similarly claimed I am constituted by the other[10] tried to subsume both *I* and *other* under the unity of objective reality, Bakhtin is notable for resisting such temptations. He insists on maintaining the plurality of *I* and *other* as irreducible.[11]

Up to this point, it would appear that Bakhtin, in his early works at least, would resist any notion of a whole that spans multiple individuals (and possibly even a whole that spans only one). But this is not quite the case. Take, for example, this quote from *Toward a Philosophy of the Act*:

> Aesthetic seeing is a justified seeing, if it does not go beyond its limits, but insofar as it claims to be a philosophical seeing of the united and unique being, in its eventness, it is inevitably doomed to pass an abstractly demarcated part for the actual whole.
>
> (*CW1*: 20; *TPA*: 17)

In this quote, if we oversimplify a bit, "aesthetic seeing" refers to a view contained within the bounds of a single consciousness.[12] The phrase "the united and unique being, in its eventness" is probably best understood as referring to being as a whole, but not just to the physical world or to objective reality, but rather to a greater totality, which also includes all conscious beings, with their subjectively constituted worlds.[13] An attempt to claim that "aesthetic seeing" is "a philosophical seeing of the united and unique being" would thus be an attempt to unite the totality of being within the purview of one consciousness, an attempt identified with philosophical idealism, perhaps most notably with Hegel (1977). The critique Bakhtin levels against such an attempt is not that the whole it pretends to grasp does not exist, but rather that it tries to pass a part for the whole. Pay attention to this turning of the tables, as we will encounter it again.

For Bakhtin, it *does* make sense to speak of the entirety of being—with all the individual subjective perspectives and deeds that it contains—as a *whole*. What is wrong is the attempt to reduce this whole to a single consciousness, or to a theoretical abstraction. The whole of being would somehow have to contain an irreducible plurality of consciousnesses, while nevertheless remaining an organic whole.

That said, Bakhtin does not offer us a full positive description of how to conceive of this organic supra-individual whole. The whole—be it the whole of an individual subject, the whole that unites life and culture, or the whole of being writ-large—is *posited* (*zadan*), not given. In his earliest surviving text, attempting to explain himself to a lay audience, Bakhtin puts it thus "Art and life are not one, but they *ought to become one* in me, in the unity of my responsibility."[14]

Later on in his writings, Bakhtin focused on more concrete forms and traditions of depicting the supra-individual whole in the proper way. Bakhtin heralded Dostoevsky's polyphonic novel precisely as a whole that is able to contain multiple consciousnesses of equal rights to the author—a major breakthrough in the quest for representing both the individual and the supra-individual whole in literature.[15] Bakhtin marks the connection to his earlier project explicitly and conspicuously early on in the introduction to the book on Dostoevsky:

> It is not the multiplicity of destinies and lives in a unitary objective world, in the light of a unitary authorial consciousness, that unfolds in [Dostoevsky's] works; rather, it is precisely the *multiplicity of consciousnesses of equal rights, with their worlds*, that are combined here, while maintaining their distinctness, into *the unity of a certain event*.
> (*CW2*: 12; *CW6*: 10; *PDP*, 6; italics added in the last phrase)

Bakhtin later studied the history of literature, and especially of the novel, to trace the traditions which laid the ground for thus depicting both the individual and the supra-individual whole.[16] He studied spatio-temporal forms for expressing an individual's position and perspective, and the interaction of several individuals, in his work on chronotopes.[17] And, of course, he discussed carnival as a traditional form of human relation to the supra-individual whole in his book on Rabelais and other related works.

The Contexts and Scales of Succession

The term "succession" (*smena*) begins appearing in Bakhtin's writings in the mid-1930s[18] and remains significant at least until the mid-1960s. "Succession" has not been studied much, if at all, as a Bakhtinian term, partly because it has been inconsistently and incorrectly translated. It was most frequently rendered as "change," which makes it look inconspicuous (and is also very misleading in many contexts).[19] I will try to argue that it is in fact a pivotal, and surprisingly constant, term in Bakhtin's writings.

The term "succession" appears in several different contexts in Bakhtin's works. Already in the 1930s, Bakhtin refers to succession as an element in how time is being perceived and aesthetically expressed. He speaks of the succession of seasons and other natural cycles (*CW3*: 247, 369; *DI*: 113), but also of the succession of historical times (*CW3*: 213, 369; *DI*: 113). In some contexts, we find also references to a succession of languages, truths, political powers, and regimes[20] or to a succession of forms assumed by a person, a metamorphosis (*CW3*: 374–5; *DI*: 118–19).

All these senses of succession appear repeatedly throughout Bakhtin's book on Rabelais. Especially frequent is the phrase "succession and renewal" (*smena i obnovlenie*),[21] referring above all to *the succession of human generations*. It is used in an optimistic tone: the old will be succeeded by the new and thus renewed; it will become bigger and better (see, for example, *CW4.1*: 73–5; *CW4.2*: 17–19, 93, 95–6, 294–5; *RHW*: 9–11, 81, 83, 294–5).[22] But the succession of generations is also presented in a darker context in the notes from the mid-1940, titled "Additions and changes to *Rabelais*." Here Bakhtin speaks of an individual's hostility to succession, that is, hostility to being replaced by a successor. The starkest example Bakhtin offers is that of Shakespeare's tragic hero Macbeth:

> Macbeth begins with the murder of his father (Duncan is a stand-in for a father: he is a relative, he is gray-haired, etc.)—here he is the heir, here he accepts succession; he ends up slaying babes (standing in for sons)—here he is a father, rejecting succession and renewal (decrowning). This is the suprajuridical crime of any self-asserting life (implicitly containing, as

its constitutive moment, the murder of one's father and the murder of one's son), the suprajuridical crime of a link in the chain of generations, hostilely separating itself, tearing itself apart from what precedes and what follows.

(*CW5*: 85–6; *BOS*: 527)

Whether it is discussed in an optimistic or in a dark tone, succession clearly implies *death*. Macbeth has to die, violently and prematurely, to be succeeded on the throne. Rabelais' Gargantua, in his letter to his son Pantagruel (discussed at length in *CW4.1*: 420–7; *CW4.2*: 433–9; *RHW*: 404–10), is filled with hope for the future, but that future also involves his own death, to be succeeded by his bigger and better son, and by his son's future children.

Finally, we find the term "succession" featured prominently in what might at first appear to be a surprising context in the draft linguistic article, "The problem of speech genres," written in the 1950s. In "The problem of speech genres," Bakhtin defines an utterance (*vyskazyvanie*) as a segment of speech delimited by the *succession of speaking subjects* (*smena rechevykh sub`ektov*), that is, by the transition from one speaker to another in a dialogue.[23]

So, is Bakhtin saying that turn-taking in conversation is like death? Perhaps. But I think he would rather want to put it the other way around: death is like turn-taking in conversation. Bakhtin is inclined not to take death too seriously. At one point (*CW5*: 83; *BOS*: 525), he likens death to a stage magic trick (called in Russian "*korobka vorovka*"—"the thieving box"): the illusionist places an object or person inside a box, and then that object or person disappears, only to soon reappear elsewhere in the hall.

And if death is like speaker transition in a conversation, then life is like an utterance. Indeed, the utterance is clearly connected to Bakhtin's early term "deed" (*postupok*), it is one type of deed, and "[My] life as a whole can be considered as a kind of composite deed" (*CW1*: 8; *TPA*: 3). Bakhtin leans into this analogy, to the point that you might claim it is not an analogy at all, that he literally views a whole life as one kind of utterance. Especially in his latest writings, Bakhtin attributes *meaning* not only to the individual utterance but also to a person's ultimate position vis-à-vis the world, and, by implication, to the human life as a whole (see, for example, *CW5*: 345; *PDP*: 286; *CW6*: 50–1; *PDP*: 39–40).[24] Bakhtin seeks that meaning in the *responses* both the utterance and the human life receive: "What I call 'meanings' are *answers* to questions. That which answers no question is devoid of meaning for us" (*CW6*: 409; *SG*: 145). Bakhtin also speaks of times, epochs, and cultures as, in a sense, engaged in dialogue with one another.[25]

Consider the truly vast range of phenomena that the term "succession" applies to. Bakhtin speaks of the succession of major historical epochs, of natural cycles, of generations, of individual lives, but also of individual utterances, of turns in a conversation, and indeed of ever smaller elements within an utterance:

> But in any utterance, if we study it to a greater depth in the concrete circumstances of social interaction through speech, we shall discover a whole series of concealed and half-concealed alien words, with different degrees of alienness. The utterance is therefore all furrowed, as it were, by the distant and barely audible resonances of speaking subject successions and dialogic overtones, boundaries between utterances that have been weakened to their limit.
>
> (*CW5*: 198; *SG*: 93)

Succession and the Construction of the Whole

Succession thus marks a *liminal* zone in time. It is a boundary between persons, between I and the other. Such boundaries were central to Bakhtin's philosophy from the very outset, but the notion of "succession," especially from the 1950s on, gives this interest in boundary lines an almost structuralist twist. Succession is a transition from one perspective to another—from self to other—*viewed as an element in the construction of a larger whole*. One might think of succession as one of those neat formulas from a Claude Lévi-Strauss anthropological analysis.

An even closer analogy would be with the role of negation in Hegelian dialectics. In Hegel's philosophical system, everything, up to and including the Absolute Spirit—the consciousness that encompasses being as a whole—is constructed by the recursive application of dialectical negation (Hegel 1977: 10). Bakhtin similarly views the ultimate whole of being (at least as it exists for us, conscious beings) as constructed out of repeated, unending, successions, at any point.

Already in the 1920s, Bakhtin spoke of culture as being entirely located on boundaries: "A domain of culture has no inner territory: it is entirely located on boundaries, the boundaries pass everywhere, through each of its aspects, the systematic unity of culture goes down to the atoms of cultural life, reflected in each of its drops like the sun,"[26] and again in the early 1960s: "The human being has no inner sovereign territory, he is all and always on the boundary" (*CW5*: 344; *PDP*: 287).[27]

Continuing the comparison with Hegel, succession is indeed a form of negation, of self-negation, too, as it involves death or some other form of ceding the floor, giving up my place in others' favor. In *Toward a Philosophy of the Act*, Bakhtin spoke in a related context of "absolute self-exclusion"

(*CW1*: 68; *TPA*: 75). However, as is usually the case with Bakhtin, the analogy with Hegel breaks down where it matters (to Hegel) the most. And recall the contrast Bakhtin famously draws in his late notebooks between dialogue and dialectics (*CW6*: 430; *SG*: 147). Negation is a *logical* operation in that it eventually describes the thought process of a single mind. Structuralist formulas are also conceived of as logical. Succession is the exact opposite: It marks precisely what one consciousness cannot possibly contain. A whole constructed through successions is organic, but irreducibly plural; any single-perspective view of this whole is merely a part pretending to be the whole.

The parts, delimited by succession, are not subsumed under the whole, nor explained by the unitary principle of the whole. Instead, they *interact to form the whole*, and ideally do so freely and responsibly.

Attitude to Succession as a Litmus Test

But aren't we getting ahead of ourselves? Who said "succession" is even the same term across all its contexts of use? After all, Bakhtin often uses the same word with a different meaning, depending on the context.[28] However, I would argue, assuming that "succession" means the same thing in all these contexts allows making very intuitive connections between different aspects and periods in Bakhtin's work. Think of succession as a coherent term—and things start falling into place.

An important way in which the notion of succession helps connect different aspects of Bakhtin's philosophy has to do with how Bakhtin uses one's attitude toward succession as a sort of litmus test. If the whole (of some phenomenon in question) is accessed the right way, succession is embraced merrily and fearlessly, celebrated; otherwise, it is ignored or met with hostility.

Macbeth, as you recall, is hostile to succession. He is therefore fundamentally criminal, committing "the suprajuridical crime of any self-asserting life" (*CW5*: 85; *BOS*: 527). Macbeth is a *tragic* hero. Tragedy, as Bakhtin explains (*CW5*: 80; *BOS*: 524), is not supposed to be self-sufficient; it presents its object in its serious aspect, and has to be supplemented by the satyr play (as it was in ancient Athens) to restore the object's wholeness. Considered on its own, it would be *a part passing itself for the whole*. Macbeth seeks to be such a part, to remain on the throne forever. On a larger scale, the agelasts and other comical villains of Rabelais' novel are hostile to the succession of historical epochs and of truths and beliefs (as expressed most clearly in *CW4.1*: 265–6: *CW4.2*: 287–8: *RHW*: 267–8). They claim to represent the *only* truth, the *only* legitimate order of things, and thus, again, are trying to pass a part—one truth and order—for the whole.

Moving now to the context of a dialogue or a conversation, what would be the equivalent of Macbethian hostility to succession? How would one refer to an utterance that seeks to be the *only* utterance, proclaiming the *only* truth, that is oblivious to its predecessors and rejects the possibility of a response? The answer easily suggests itself: I have just described *monologism*, and criticized it in the exact terms Bakhtin does (e.g., in *CW5*: 350–1: *PDP*: 292–3).

Finally, Bakhtin's critique of various linguistic theories focuses on their refusal to take succession into account—be it the succession of speaking subjects that delimits the utterance, or the successions found within the utterance, its various dialogic relations with past and future utterances and its internal dialogic structure. By ignoring succession and attempting to reduce linguistic meaning to abstract objective signification, the linguistic theories Bakhtin criticizes fail to properly grasp their object of study (see, e.g., *CW5*: 174–7, 183–91; *SG*: 73–5, 80–7: *CW6*: 203–7: *PDP*: 181–5).

Dialogue and the Ultimate Whole

What does this imply regarding what Bakhtin has to say positively about the supra-individual whole? In his book on Rabelais and other works from the early 1940s, Bakhtin speaks of this whole as one that inspires an emotional tone of merry fearlessness (while itself being "indifferent"—*CW5*: 10). But whereas carnival offers a relatively nebulous sense of how such a whole is possible, Bakhtin's linguistic explorations in the 1950s allow a considerably more concrete picture to be drawn.

An utterance contains multiple successions of speaking subjects within it, while remaining a coherent whole (with an author). Any conversation is a whole containing the utterances (the turns) making it up, with speaker succession happening repeatedly. In the process, the individual speakers and their utterances do not lose their individuality. *No simple static meaning can be assigned* to the conversation as a whole, nor to each individual utterance. An utterance only becomes meaningful when it meets a responding utterance, and then gains new meaning with each new response:

> There can be no "meaning in itself"—it exists only for another meaning, i.e., exists only together with it. There can be no unitary (one) meaning. Consequently, there can be neither a first nor a last meaning, it is always between meanings, a link in a chain of meaning, which alone, as a whole, can be real. In the course of historic life this chain grows infinitely, and therefore each of its separate links is renewed again and again, born again, as it were.
>
> (*CW6*: 410; *SG*: 146)

And as goes the meaning of an utterance, so goes the meaning of a human life. the moment of succession is the moment of death, but the meaning is *reborn, bigger and better* with every new response it receives (and note how well the carnival theme I just alluded to fits into this vision now).

Note that the concept of dialogue as developed in Bakhtin's late writings is not quite the same as his uses of the term in his earlier works (mostly in the first edition of the book on Dostoevsky). Bakhtin now conceives of the ultimate whole of being, at least as it exists for us, as a big dialogue. It spans the individual perspectives that succeed each other in it the way a conversation spans the utterances that succeed each other in it. It is a unity that contains a true plurality of irreducible individual perspectives within it.

In his latest writings, Bakhtin puts a lot of effort into arguing that the ultimate whole of dialogue cannot be brought to completion, i.e., cannot be assigned a definite final meaning (e.g., *CW6*: 434–5: *SG*: 170). Otherwise, the whole of dialogue could be made to fit into the purview of a single consciousness, making it no different from Hegel's Absolute Spirit. Moreover, no final meaning for the ultimate whole means no final meaning for the individual life, for the single utterance, nor for any of the voices making that utterance up. Thus, all individual perspectives, and all meanings, also transgress the limits of any one consciousness. Indeed, my own perspective, even though it is constituted by my consciousness, always transgresses the limits of this consciousness. I received myself as a gift from others—tells us early Bakhtin—and I will go on receiving this gift after I die—late Bakhtin adds.

The ever-incomplete nature of the ultimate whole, now conceived of as an infinite dialogue, is the subject of some of the most oft-quoted passages in Bakhtin's latest notes, perhaps most famously, in the paragraph that was (how symbolic!) once *erroneously* considered to be his last, and that now, I hope, can be read in a somewhat new light:

> There is neither a first nor a last word and there are no bounds to the dialogic context (it stretches both into the boundless past and into the boundless future). Even *past* meanings, i.e., ones born in the dialogue of past centuries, can never be stable (brought to completion once and for all, finished)—they will always be altered (while being renewed) in the process of dialogue's subsequent, future development. At any moment in the development of dialogue there exist immense, boundless masses of forgotten meanings, but in certain moments in the subsequent development of dialogue, in its course, they shall be remembered again and come back to life in a renewed (in a new context) shape. Nothing is absolutely dead: every meaning shall have its own feast of rebirth. The problem of *major time*.
>
> (*CW6*: 434–5; *SG*, 170).

Conclusion

This description, evocative as it sounds, still tells us much more about what dialogue as a whole is *not* than about what it *is*. This is no accident. A true image of the whole forever remains posited as a task, not given. Most of what Bakhtin has to say about it amounts to a sort of negative theology.[29]

Nevertheless, Bakhtin did make a truly novel attempt to reimagine the very idea of what a whole is, with the notion of succession at its center. This, in turn, led him to offer a fresh and unusual take on various cultural phenomena, which often opened the door to truly original applications. His approach to literary works, famously, spawned a whole academic industry. But there is still a lot of potential to unlock in other fields as well. For instance, linguists and communication scholars have only relatively recently begun to uncover the potential of looking at language in a thoroughly Bakhtinian way, with a focus on the succession of speaking subjects not only between but also within utterances.[30] In that respect, Bakhtin (with his friend Valentin Nikolaevich Voloshinov, though it is Bakhtin's works that contain the more advanced development of the main Bakhtin-circle linguistic themes) was many decades ahead of his time. The way Bakhtin applies the notion of succession to language, where it allows breaking up linguistic material into dialogically defined units, holds a particularly large productive potential for linguistics in the future, at least in my humble opinion.

In this paper, I painted a picture of Bakhtin not as the hardline anti-systematic thinker some claimed he was,[31] but also not as a passive follower of the philosophical systematizers he looked up to in his youth.[32] Instead, he sought to be systematic on his own novel terms, and his concept of succession illustrates what such a systematic approach looks like, and why it is not quite like any other philosophical system we know.

Bakhtin's drive to radically rethink first philosophy (a term he repeatedly invokes in *TPA*), to reject the established solutions to the major problems of modern Western thought, without, however, succumbing to cynicism about the very possibility or desirability of seeking such solutions, reflects what might be called a Modernist ethos. In this sense, Bakhtin was indeed a man of his time. At the same time, Bakhtin always strongly resisted the temptation, so prevalent in Modernist art and philosophy, of grounding his thought in seemingly basic and elementary principles: in logic, in simple geometric forms, or in isolated individual subjective experience. Instead, from the outset, Bakhtin questioned the very supposition that these principles are elementary, that high-level abstractions reveal something fundamental about reality. His preference was always for taking the bull of complexity by the horns. In that sense, despite his relatively traditional style of writing and lack of rebel mannerisms, Bakhtin offered a deeper, and potentially more fertile, rebellion against tradition than did most of his contemporaries.

Notes

1. M. M. Bakhtin, "Toward a Reworking of the Dostoevsky Book," in *PDP*, 283–302 (292); M. M. Bakhtin, "1961 god. Zametki," [1961, Notes]), in *CW5*, 329–60 (349); M. M. Bakhtin, "Ritorika v meru svoej lzhivosti …" [Rhetoric, Insofar as it is False …], in *CW5*, 63–70; *REL*, 205–15. All quotes from Bakhtin's work are in my translation. References to Bakhtin's writings are given to the Russian *Collected Writings* edition, and, when available, to the relevant place in a published English translation.

2. *RHW*, 19, 322–5, 358, 367; M. M. Bakhtin, "Fransua Rable v istorii realizma (1940)" [François Rabelais in the History of Realism (1940)], in *CW4.1*, 11–505 (26, 82, 319–22, 362–3, 373); M. M. Bakhtin, "Tvorchestvo Fransua Rable i narodnaja kul'tura srednevekov'ja i Renessansa" (1965) [The work of François Rabelais' and the Folk Culture of the Middle Ages and the Renaissance (1965)], in *CW4.2*, 7–510 (29, 346–9, 385, 394).

3. M. M. Bakhtin, "K filosofskim osnovam gumanitarnykh nauk" [On the Philosophical Foundations of the Human Sciences], in *SW5*, 7–10 (10).

4. See, for example, Gary Saul Morson and Caryl Emerson, *Mikhail Bakhtin: Creation of a Prosaics* (Stanford, CA: Stanford University Press, 1990); Sergeiy Sandler, "Tema karnavala v kontekste filosofii M. M. Bakhtina" [The Place of Carnival in the Context of Mikhail Bakhtin's Philosophy], *Studia Litterarum* 1.3–4 (2016): 10–28; Sergeiy Sandler, "The Pros and Cons of Deconstructing Bakhtin: A Reflection on Boris Groys," *Dialogic Pedagogy: An International Online Journal* 5 (2017): 23–38; Anthony Wall, "A Broken Thinker," *The South Atlantic Quarterly* 97.3/4 (1998): 669–98.

5. I discuss these aspects of Bakhtin's early philosophy in greater detail elsewhere. See especially Sergeiy Sandler, "Bakhtin and the Kierkegaardian Revolution," *SSRN Electronic Journal* (2012), doi: 10.2139/ssrn.2558247; Sergeiy Sandler, "Language and Philosophical Anthropology in the Work of Mikhail Bakhtin and the Bakhtin Circle," *Rivista Italiana Di Filosofia Del Linguaggio* 7.2 (2013): 152–65; Sergeiy Sandler, "A Strange Kind of Kantian: Bakhtin's Reinterpretation of Kant and the Marburg School," *Studies in East European Thought* 67.3–4 (2015): 165–82.

6. This prioritization of the subjective over the objective is a central theme of Modernism, especially as it comes as part of a broad rejection of the philosophical traditions of modernity—cf. M. M. Bakhtin, "K filosofii postupka" [On the Philosophy of the Deed], in *CW1*, 7–68 (29). But, I hasten to add, Bakhtin cannot be uncontroversially labeled as a Modernist. For example, unlike many of his Modernist contemporaries, Bakhtin makes no reference in any of his extant writings to industrialization or other forms of technological progress as a theme. And, as for the stress on subjective

experience in Modernist literature, Bakhtin highly values the work of such stream-of-consciousness writers as Proust and Joyce. M. M. Bakhtin, "O Flobere" [On Flaubert], in *CW5*, 130–7 (134). But he also views it as representing "the monologization [...] of dialogue." M. M. Bakhtin, "Dialog" [Dialogue], in *CW5*, 207–9 (208).

7   See also *TPA*, 28–9.

8   M. M. Bakhtin, "Author and Hero in Aesthetic Activity," in *AA*, 4–256 (100, 143); M. M. Bakhtin, "Avtor i geroj v esteticheskoj deiatel'nosti" [Author and Hero in Aesthetic Activity], in *CW1*, 69–263 (165ff., 175, 210).

9   Georg Wilhelm Friedrich Hegel, *Phenomenology of Spirit*, trans. Arnold Vincent Miller (Oxford: Oxford University Press, 1977), 109–11.

10 For example, Paul Natorp, *Sozial-Idealismus* (Berlin and Heidelberg: Springer Berlin Heidelberg, 1922), 232–3.

11 As I explain in greater detail in "Bakhtin and the Kierkegaardian Revolution" and "A Strange Kind of Kantian."

12 The word "aesthetic" comes from the Greek *aisthesthai*, "to perceive." This original sense of the word is reflected in Bakhtin's use of such terms as "aesthetic seeing" and "aesthetization" in his early writings in reference to how the world is perceived by an individual consciousness, while the now more customary association of "aesthetics" with the arts is secondary. In this, Bakhtin follows Kant (cf. the "Transcendental Aesthetic" part of Immanuel Kant's, *Critique of Pure Reason*, trans. Norman Kemp Smith (New York: Macmillan, 1929) and others.

13 An event (*sobytie*—this Russian word can also be read as *so-bytie*, literally, "co-being") for Bakhtin always indicates some kind of interaction between multiple subjects, and, in particular, between me and others.

14 M. M. Bakhtin, "Art and Answerability," in *AA*, 1–3 (2), italics added; Bakhtin, "Iskusstvo i otvetstvennost'" [Art and Responsibility], in *CW1*, 5–6 (6).

15 *PDP*, *PDA* (republished as M. M. Bakhtin, "Problemy tvorchestva Dostoevskogo" [Problems of Dostoevsky's Oeuvre], in *CW2*, 5–175); M. M. Bakhtin, M. M., "Problemy poetiki Dostoevskogo" [Problems of Dostoevsky's Poetics], in *CW6*, 6–300.

16 M. M. Bakhtin, "Discourse in the Novel," in *DI*, 259–422; M. M. Bakhtin, "Slovo v romane: K voprosam stilistiki romana" [The Word in the Novel: On Questions of the Stylistics of the Novel], in *CW3*, 9–179.

17 M. M. Bakhtin, "Forms of Time and of the Chronotope in the Novel: Notes toward a Historical Poetics," in *DI*, 84–258; M. M. Bakhtin, "Formy vremeni i khronotopa v romane" [Forms of Time and of the Chronotope in the Novel], in *CW3*, 340–503.

18 There is already one instance of the word appearing in a potentially relevant context in "Author and Hero," back in the 1920s (*CW1*, 222; *AA*, 158), and a couple of instances in "Discourse in the Novel" (*CW3*, 40, 65; *DI*, 287, 312) and in the surviving materials for Bakhtin's lost book on Goethe and the

Bildungsroman and the essay on the chronotope, which developed from them (*CW3*, 369, 374, 383; *DI*, 113, 118–19, 210). See also: M. M. Bakhtin, "K 'Romanu vospitanija'" [For *the Bildungsroman*], in *CW3*, 218–335 (247, 321); M. M. Bakhtin, "Roman vospitanija i ego znachenie v istorii realizma" [The *Bildungsroman* and its Significance in the History of Realism], in *CW3*, 180–217 (213).

The term becomes all but ubiquitous in the 1940 manuscript of the book on Rabelais (Bakhtin 2008a) and in the drafts toward the book. M. M. Bakhtin, "Tetradi k 'Rable'" [The Rabelais Notebooks], in *CW4*, 605–75.

19 In addition to "change," the term has been rendered as "shift" or "replacement," and, on rare occasions as "diversity," "displacement," "progression," or "alternation." The word "succession" has first been used as a rare variant for rendering *smena* by Hélène Iswolsky in her translation of Bakhtin's book on Rabelais (*RHW*, 41, 81, 142), alongside her usual choice of "change." As we shall see presently, Bakhtin uses this term in several distinct contexts, and while "succession," obviously, is not a perfect match for what Bakhtin is trying to say in Russian, it does have the advantage of working at least reasonably well in all these contexts, which is why I am consistently using "succession" as the English translation of *smena* in this chapter.

20 M. M. Bakhtin, "From the Prehistory of Novelistic Discourse," in *DI*, 41–83 (66–7); M. M. Bakhtin, "Iz predistorii romannogo slova" [From the Prehistory of the Novelistic Word], in *CW3*, 513–51 (536–8); M. M. Bakhtin, "K voprosam teorii romana" [On Questions of the Theory of the Novel], in *CW3*, 557–607 (561).

21 We find this collocation already in drafts from the 1930s (*CW4.1*: 616, 634, 657), but it appears Bakhtin started using "succession" and "renewal" in conjunction with one another more frequently later on. About half of the instances of "succession and renewal" in the book on Rabelais, as published in 1965, are not yet there in the 1940 manuscript.

22 The discussion of crowning/decrowning rituals in the fourth chapter that Bakhtin added to the second edition of his book on Dostoevsky (*CW6*, 140–3) also offers a condensed exposition of the different contexts in which Bakhtin uses the term "succession" throughout his carnival writings. This is very clear in the Russian original, though more difficult to notice in the English translation without knowing what to pay attention to. Caryl Emerson was consistent in using "shift" to translate *smena* in this passage (*PDP*, 124–7), and reading it with this fact in mind can help get a hang of the significance of succession (or "shift") for Bakhtin's understanding of carnival.

23 M. M. Bakhtin, "The Problem of Speech Genres," in *SG*, 60–102 (71ff.); Bakhtin, M. M., "Problema rechevykh zhanrov" [The Problem of Speech Genres], in *CW5*, 159–206 (172ff.).

24 Also: M. M. Bakhtin, "Toward a Methodology for the Human Sciences," in *SG*, 159–72 (170); M. M. Bakhtin, "Rabochie zapisi 60-kh—nachala 70-kh godow" [Working Notes from the 1960s to Early 1970s], in *CW6*, 371–439 (434–5). And, indeed, meaning also applies to being as a whole (see, e.g.,

CW5, 8; CW6, 395–7, 1986a). Also: M. M. Bakhtin, "From Notes Made in 1970-71," in SG, 132–58 (137–8).

25 For example, in M. M. Bakhtin, "Response to a Question from the *Novy Mir* Editorial Staff," in SG, 1–9 (3–7); M. M. Bakhtin, "Otvet na vopros redaktsii 'Novogo mira'" [Answer to a Question from the Editors of *Novyj Mir*], in CW6, 451–7 (453–7).

26 M. M. Bakhtin, "The Problem of Content, Material, and Form in Verbal Art," AA, 257–325 (274); M. M. Bakhtin, "K voprosam metodologii estetiki slovesnogo tvorchestva" [On Questions of the Methodology of the Aesthetics of Verbal Creation], in CW1, 265–325 (282).

27 Notice not only the fact that Bakhtin used almost the exact same wording in two texts written thirty-seven years apart, but also that he is talking about a cultural domain, and culture as a whole, in one text, and about a human being in the other. This is very telling, and recurs throughout Bakhtin's writings: he clearly thinks there is some kind of isomorphism between the totality of being, the individual human being seen as a whole, and any number of organic wholes in between. Often, especially in his early writings, it is not always easy to tell which of these wholes Bakhtin is talking about. This is perhaps most strikingly illustrated in the passage from Bakhtin's late notes on "The witness and the judge" (CW6, 396–7; SG, 137–8), where he speaks of the relation of consciousness to the material world as parallel to the relation of the other to the I-for-myself.

28 Sergeiy Sandler, "Whose Words Are These Anyway?" in *Dialogues with Bakhtinian Theory*, ed. Mykola Polyuha, Clive Thomson, and Anthony Wall (London, Ontario: Mestengo Press, 2012), 227–42.

29 I am using the word "theology" advisedly. The theological allusions in many of the Bakhtinian ideas discussed here are quite obvious—for example, to the unity of plural individuals in the person of the Christian God, or to the resurrection of the dead at the end of times in the passage just quoted.

30 François Cooren and Sergeiy Sandler, "Polyphony, Ventriloquism, and Constitution: In Dialogue with Bakhtin," *Communication Theory* (2014); John W. Du Bois, "Towards a Dialogic Syntax," *Cognitive Linguistics* 25.3 (2014): 359–410; Oswald Ducrot, *Le Dire et le dit* [What is Said and the Act of Saying] (Paris: Les Éditions de Minuit, 1984); Boris Gasparov, *Speech, Memory, and Meaning: Intertextuality in Everyday Language* (Berlin: De Gruyter, 2010); Per Linell, *Approaching Dialogue* (Amsterdam: John Benjamins Publishing Company, 1998); Esther Pascual, *Fictive Interaction* (Amsterdam: John Benjamins Publishing Company, 2014); Arie Verhagen, *Constructions of Intersubjectivity* (Oxford: Oxford University Press, 2005).

31 Susan Stewart, "Shouts on the Street: Bakhtin's Anti-Linguistics," *Critical Inquiry* 10.2 (1983): 265–81.

32 As claimed, insofar as Bakhtin's philosophy is concerned, by Craig Brandist, *The Bakhtin Circle: Philosophy, Culture and Politics* (London: Pluto Press, 2002) and others.

4

Bakhtin's Chronotope

Crisis Time and Great Time in Benjamin and Hölderlin

Jeremy Tambling

Thinking in Dostoevsky is often wildly allusive, appearing as flashes of insight, rather than as connected rationalism. When Raskolnikov is on his way through St. Petersburg to commit murder, Dostoevsky shows how much goes on in his head:

> Passing the Yusupov Gardens, he began to consider the construction of tall fountains in all the squares, and how they would freshen the air. Following this train of thought he came to the conclusion that if the Summer Gardens could be extended right across the Champs de Mars and joined to those of the Mikhalylovsky Palace, it would add greatly to the beauties and amenities of the city. Then he suddenly began to wonder why, in all big towns, people chose of their own free will to live where there were neither parks nor gardens, but only filth and squalor and evil smells. This reminded him of his own walks in the neighbourhood of the Haymarket, and brought him back to himself. 'What rubbish!' he thought. 'It would be better not to think at all'.[1]

Thought is generated by passing through places, particularly parks and squares, and market-squares, places which could, by the addition of fountains, be made peaceful, paradisal; and places impose thinking which is transitional, creating thought about that which is in process, able to move. Thus, in fantasy, the physical transportation of part of the architecture of the observed scene to join it to somewhere else becomes possible. Simultaneously, the imaginative non-rational nature of this thought questions irrationality itself—why people choose not squares but squalor to live in; that then makes Raskolnikov realize that he lives in the area of the Haymarket, which is both squalid and a square, and makes him consider his enlargement of thought as pointless. Therefore, it is better not to think—as indeed someone about to commit murder must shut off thought and its dialogism, and its creativity, a sign of which appears in his wish to freshen the air in a contradictory care for others. Raskolnikov in mentally planning St. Petersburg is thinking in a Napoleonic way—as both Napoleon I and Napoleon III. The latter is remembered inside *Crime and Punishment* as the author of a history of Julius Caesar, but both uncle and nephew planned Paris, the latter more definitively through Baron Haussmann's demolitions in the 1850s, creating boulevards which cleared out working-class areas and marketplaces—akin to St. Petersburg's Haymarket. Raskolnikov's fantasies are of being a Napoleon, having commanding authority over the shape of cities. That shows in how he thinks; and that Paris is present in this thinking is evident from his reference to the Champs de Mars. One city-space, a public square, is inside another in another city; to think of one city is to think of another, because cities have plural identities.

This record of contradictory thinking generated while walking in city-spaces, which suggests such "modernist" texts as *Ulysses* or *Mrs Dalloway*, seems to be halfway toward giving an insight as to what is meant by the "chronotope" as Bakhtin conceptualizes this in "Forms of Time and of the Chronotope in the Novel" (1957–58). We can move toward a definition of the chronotope via those spaces of Raskolnikov, for Bakhtin writes that "the autobiographical and biographical self-consciousness of an individual and his life" were "first laid bare and shaped in the public square" (*DI*: 131). This is the square of the common people, such as the Haymarket, an example of "the square of bazaars, puppet theatres, taverns" (132) The square, the most privileged site of heteroglossia because of its promiscuous assemblage of people, was

> a remarkable chronotope, in which all the elevated categories, from that of the state to that of revealed truth, were realised concretely and fully incarnated, made visible and given a face.
>
> (132)

The square here–the site of pageant plays, and so of tragedy, as Bakhtin notes Pushkin saying–may remind us of Rabelais, or of the marketplaces of Pieter Breugel (1525–69), showing "The battle of Carnival and Lent" (1559), where different seasons come together in a moment which is a crisis of victory or defeat for each, or in "Children's Games" (1560), which is also conflictual, full of movement, bringing people together and dividing them at the same time. The individual appears, as does the square, "open on all sides" (*DI*: 132). Bakhtin is fascinated by spaces which layer different times together, along with different stories, different experiences, like those of the *picaro*, which move together in time. In the realist novel there is a tendency for single spaces, single rooms to be presented, as in Stendhal or Balzac, but then comes Dostoevsky, where one form of chronotope among many is prominent: "the chronotope of *threshold*; it can be combined with the motif of encounter, but its most fundamental insistence is as the chronotope of *crisis* and *break* in a life … the breaking point of a life, the moment of crisis" (*DI*: 248).

This particular chronotope, whose metaphorical use is also obvious in ordinary speech and in talk of the "liminal" has reference to *Crime and Punishment*, where stepping over the threshold, a subject of the last moments of Part 3, and of transgressing (*prestuplenie*), crossing over becomes vivid. It makes the threshold the space of a moment, so that crossing it reveals the subject. It brings the "actual historical person" (84) into visibility, as Svidrigailov appears in Raskolnikov's attic-room, but in a way which reveals him, as a split subject, just as the name Raskolnikov implies psychic splitting, from the verb *raskolot*, meaning to split. The chronotope concentrates, but it splits; the threshold divides the person who crosses over in the instant. Raskolnikov in the squares shows his divided thought, and it also shows that people are divided: as he reflects, give them cleanliness and they will still prefer squalor. Different people are momentarily in either space which the threshold divides and connects. Duchamp's oil painting "Nude Descending a Staircase" (1912) conveys a splitting of the subject; a staircase being, for Bakhtin, an example of a threshold, for he supplements the threshold with other spaces: "the staircase, the front hall, and corridor, as well as the chronotopes of the street and square that extend those spaces into the open air" (*DI*: 248). In this chronotope, time is essentially instantaneous; it is as if it had no duration and fell out of the normal course of biographical time. In discussing Dostoevsky's use of such spaces, "the only time possible is *crisis time*, in which a moment is equal to years" (*PDP*: 196).

If the threshold is "the chronotope of *crisis, of break* in a life" (*DI*: 248), this contrasts with Tolstoy who according to this argument of Bakhtin, "did not value the moment, he did not strive to fill it with something fundamental and decisive: one rarely encounters the word 'suddenly' in his works" (249). Perhaps Tolstoy is less of a city-writer than Dostoevsky; with Bakhtin's word "suddenly" we may compare Walter Benjamin finding shock as definitional for city life, as when thinking of Baudelaire's "A une passante," where the woman passing by and seen for a moment, makes for "un éclat et puis la nuit" (a flash, and then night).[2] In this way Baudelaire—the writer of Paris— and Dostovesky—the writer of St. Petersburg—come together as writers of that which is distinctively modern.

The essay from which we have been quoting, "Forms of Time and of the Chronotope in the Novel," whose title gives a double emphasis to time, opens by calling the chronotope that which gives "the intrinsic connectedness of temporal and spatial relationships" (*DI*: 84), their "connectedness" being only in the specific sense that to think about spatiality means to think about time. The chronotope is a provocation to thought in a way which exceeds the specific examples given by Bakhtin: their literality points to something else. Perhaps we could say that the chronotope is a concept aimed less at thinking about space than at visualizing historical time, and what that means. To explain that statement is the object of this chapter which in order to do so will try to expand Bakhtin's wonderfully affirmatory provocations to thought, extracted in a time not favorable to such utopian thinking, by drawing on Walter Benjamin's theses in "On the Concept of History," and on a poem by Hölderlin, "Friedensfeier." Poetry contrasts with the novel-form, for Bakhtin, but Hölderlin's poem has nothing of monologism within it. Consideration of these texts will not move us away from Bakhtin.

Bakhtin writes that "time, as it were, thickens, takes on flesh, becomes artistically visible" (*DI*: 84). In the chronotope, one sees time, which is perhaps exactly what Heidegger means by "temporality."[3] Temporality seems to be a sudden perception that one is in time, and in the moment; for Kierkegaard, whom Heidegger partially follows, anxiety is the experience of the moment.[4] It is not that we are in time and look out from that vantage-point; rather temporality is the sense of being in "crisis time" as something in which we are caught. Awareness of time in this way is the opposite of what Wagner writes when he has Gurnemanz sing to Parsifal in Act 1 of the opera *Parsifal* that time becomes space ("*Du siehst, mein Sohn, zum Raum wird hier die Zeit*"). There, time lengthens itself out. It becomes non-striated, smooth, unambiguous, and homogeneous, to use a word which Walter Benjamin employs, and, above all, it becomes static, a word which Bakhtin uses to contrast with the idea of "becoming" (128). In the chronotope, by contrast to Wagner, there is a "materialising of time in space" (250), not dissolving it or rendering it immaterial in comparison to the sacred and hierarchical space of the Grail. In *Parsifal*, the idea that "time thickens" is as strange as it is in Shakespeare, when Macbeth says "light thickens" (*Macbeth* 3.2. 50), which could mean that it becomes less mobile (as light is always a play of light and shadow moving), or that it darkens, which means that it enters into visibility; at the time of fading, light can be seen *as* light, less as a transparent medium which is seen through. Bakhtin further says that the chronotope exhibits "time's fullness" (*DI*: 147), but this fullness is not completion, it reverts to the idea of splitting—to "the uncovering of social contradictions," a statement which declares Bakhtin's Marxism. The single rooms of the realist novel obscure such social contradictions, and they imply an orderly progress from one to another. The city, the marketplace, the liminal space, bring them together; they show that different historical times are at work for different people; differences which cannot be swaled away by talking about "progress." In film, the analogue for thinking about time in the instant is montage, the demonstration of splits and of contradictions in individual shots, and the space between them.

Bakhtin then says that there can be seen in such a chronotope an "historical inversion," wherein what must belong to the future, that is, thinking about "purpose, ideal, justice, perfection, the harmonious condition of man and society," i.e., those things which speak to Bakhtin's Marxism, are actually placed in the past, in the myth of a Golden Age. That would suggest that the chronotope allows for another inversion, in which what is said of the past becomes a possibility for the future. Thus, all the historical examples of narrative Bakhtin marshals–the Greek Romance with its "adventure time" (*DI*: 89), a time which is unpredictable–the novel of Apuleius and of Petronius, stressing metamorphosis; the folkloric and chivalric narrative; the Rabelaisian, and the time of the realist novel–are all imminent and possible in the present. Nothing remains behind. What Bakhtin gives here is the reverse of an historicist sense's sense of time, where what is of the past must be left in the past. The chronotope allows another sense of time as always containing a redemptive possibility in itself. And such a thought would relate to Bakhtin's other stress, on polyphony, which assumes a plural in what may seem to be an individual's single state, or single utterance.

In a final series of notes in *Speech Genres and Other Late Essays*, "Methodology for the Human Sciences" (1974), Bakhtin concludes with what is effectively a critique of historicism:

> There is neither a first nor a last word and there are no limits to the dialogic context ... Even *past* meanings, that is, those born in the dialogue of past centuries, can never be stable (finalised, ended once and for all) —they will always change (be renewed) in the process of subsequent, future development of the dialogue. At any moment in the development of the dialogue there are immense, boundless masses of forgotten contextual meanings, but at certain moments of the dialogue's subsequent development along the way they are recalled and invigorated in renewed form (in a new context). Nothing is absolutely dead: every meaning will have its homecoming festival. The problem of *great time*.
> (*SG*: 170)

"Great time" is opposed to "small time," which implies a concern only with the present and with the foreseeable future (167, 169), and it was annotated by Bakhtin earlier on, when, in "Responses to a Question from *Novy Mir*" (1970) he observed that "works break through the boundaries of their own time, they live in centuries, that is, in *great time*" (*SG*: 4). That idea is then enlarged upon when saying that a work may gain in significance, but only if it has absorbed past centuries; that is, it cannot belong entirely to "today" (4). He adds that the future is essential to release the work from its own epoch; "its fullness is revealed only in *great time*" (5). In that way, Bakhtin dismisses the idea that a text is to be understood in terms of a definable "historical context" which is knowable, and he pulls the text away from a positivism which makes history the master-discipline in reading literature, so much so that the reading of texts seems at present to have been subsumed into "cultural history." That positivism is partly reinforced by "new historicism" in the way that this has been allowed to reinforce a historicist reading of texts, even if new historicism insists that history exists in textual forms which themselves need to be read, and whose meaning is not determinate. New historicism still assumes that it is speaking with the dead when it addresses a text of the past.[5] In contrast, Bakhtin refuses to believe that anything of the past is dead.

We must pair, and at the same time, differentiate, Bakhtin's interest in the chronotope and that of "great time." The chronotope is the non-place—threshold, corridor, staircase, and, to take another space which is crucial in *Crime and Punishment*, the bridge. These are richly charged, urban features which enable a passage from one to another crisis-point, but which in doing so split identity as surely as happens to Raskolnikov in the market place. It shows identity was never one thing, and that in such a moment which it reveals, an absolute reversibility is also possible. It questions the separation of past and future; thus a way of thinking of "great time" would make the chronotope a concentration and combination of different epochs. That is part of what Bakhtin means in saying, as seen before, that "time thickens." If it is a character of modernity, whose root meaning comes from the Latin for "today" (*hodie*), that it atomizes time, as in the industrial practices of Taylorism, denying continuity, and that it contains a movement to repress the past, especially that which it deems to be pre-modern, dismissing past texts, past experiences as irrelevant to the present, then, in contrast, Bakhtin's argument will seem Modernist, in that it fights against that new and hegemonic culture.[6] "Great time" has something in common with what Bakhtin speaks of relative to Rabelais' world of the marketplace; it is the place of grotesque realism, showing bodies which are unfinished—for the body "outgrows itself, transgresses its own limits" (*RHW*: 26). The unfinished body which makes for an unfinished character, matches "great time," also unfinished, so that what constitutes it remains unknown. In that way, "great time" matches the time of the novel, as opposed to "the world of the epic 'absolute past', [which is] walled off by an unapproachable boundary from the continuing and unfinished present."[7] Bakhtin refers to this as "the problem of great time."[8] It is a problem to consider, not only because it contests historicism, but because it combines the chronotope with something extended, with a literary history in which the past reappears in the present, and so makes the present filled with something other to it. Perhaps carnival is the image of the "homecoming festival" of which Bakhtin speaks.

If "great time" assumes that time may focus within it all moments, and all splits, it will benefit from being compared with Walter Benjamin, who was also fascinated by carnival as an exceptional state, as he shows in a short story, "Conversation above the Corso: Recollections of Carnival time in Nice" (1935),[9] Benjamin makes equal attempts to refute historicism, a concept he makes real and oppressive in the well-known aphorisms which mark "On the Concept of History," which were his last writings, and were published posthumously.[10] He considers revolutionary time as the opposite of historicism when he argues: "The concept of mankind's historical progress cannot be sundered from the concept of its progression through a homogeneous, empty time" (XIII).[11]

This concept, which he attacks, is part of a rejection of the concept of "progress," which depends first on a belief that how things were can be narrated by the historian—here Benjamin cites Leopold von Ranke (1795–1886) of the University of Berlin—and, further, that history reveals itself in steady, orderly growth, where the past recedes as development takes place. Such a writing of history must ignore what has been dumped in the movement of progress; what Benjamin elsewhere calls "everything untimely, sorrowful, and miscarried."[12] To do justice to that, he implies, requires a different writing: allegory. In "On the Concept of History," Benjamin specifically takes aim at Germany's Social Democrats whom, an editorial footnote says (399), had been formed in 1863 originally as a Marxist organization, but had become social-reformist, and had been the largest political party in the Weimar republic. They represented belief in progress.

The alternative to historicism appears in the following aphorism, which opens with a citation from the journalist and satirist Karl Kraus (1874–1936), "Origin is the goal," an aphorism earlier expanded upon in an essay on Kraus' writings (1931). Here, the world is, as Kraus says, "a wrong, deviating, circuitous way back to Paradise." The "origin" Benjamin there calls "a seal of authenticity," and "the subject of a discovery that has a curious element of recognition."[13] That means that we do not start with the origin; rather, it must be discovered, found, and what is found can only be known from the standpoint of knowing the future, and so establishing the richness and diversity of what has been. The psychoanalytic implications of a finding being a re-finding will be noted; for the "lost object" of Freudian and Lacanian analysis—a Modernist conception which might be paralleled from Proust—is only "found" in a process of recognition which confuses chronology: it can never be said that something was unambiguously lost in the past, for whatever is "found" is both new and creates elements of the past which are preserved in the images of language whose provenance is never known. What is found revivifies the past, or recreates it: "The object is by nature a refound object. That it was lost is a consequence of that—but after the fact. It is thus refound without our knowing, except through the refinding, that it was ever lost."[14]

The language of recognition, the sense that cognition contains re-cognition, but of what belongs to no assignable past time or place, defeats the idea that its terms can be assigned to one time, one place. Aphorism XIV follows:

> History is the subject of a construction whose site is not homogenous, empty time, but time filled by now-time [*Jetztzeit*]. Thus, to Robespierre, ancient Rome was a past charged with now-time, a past which he blasted out of the continuum of history.
>
> (XIV)

A hint as to how to read a text of the past is there: to read it is to find—unless we are fixed on knowing its "historical context" —which we presume we *can* know—that it retains its "here-and-now time," and that this is equally available in the time of the now. Hence, "revolutionary classes," at their moment of action, are aware "that they are about to make the continuum of history explode," because the past is not irrecoverable, in the sense that its energies are still there, and usable.

> The Great Revolution [i.e. the Russian Revolution] introduced a new calendar. The initial day of a calendar presents history in time-lapse mode. And basically it is this same day that keeps recurring in the guise of holidays, which are days of remembrance.
>
> (XV)

Revolution resets the clock, but Benjamin's interest is more in the calendar, a word which designates the first day of each month, and thus stresses events in red-letter mode, red letters being especially marked for holy days. The first day of each month presents things in "time lapse" photographic mode which is defined by *OED*, giving a first citation of 1926, as "designating the technique of taking a sequence of photographs at set time intervals to record events that occur imperceptibly slowly, so that when the resulting film is played at normal speed the action is speeded up and perceptible." A time-lapse film thus does not give "empty homogeneous time"; there are no gaps; it makes time in which everything happens, consequentially, indeed explosively, like showing a flower burst into openness. Time is explosive, and it has an apocalyptic—i.e, a revelatory—tendency. This has a similar stress to the one implied in the formula "The origin is the goal." Each moment has its predecessors contained within it. This leads into another argument: Benjamin says that the "historical materialist," by which term he means the non-Hegelian Marxist (for a Hegelian Marxist would be committed to progress, and even to the inevitability of revolution):

cannot do without the notion of a present which is not a transition, but in which time takes a stand [*einsteht*] and has come to a standstill [*Stillstellung*]. For this notion defines the very present in which he himself is writing history. Historicism offers the "eternal" image of the past; historical materialism supplies a unique experience with the past.

(XVI)

The past means something; the present experience is the present and the past together. Again, this aphorism takes issue with "historicism" when this is defined as a conviction that the past can be known chronologically, as cause and effect, one event bringing on another event. Benjamin speaks of it as "mustering a mass of data to fill the homogeneous, empty time" (XVII). For the person writing as an historical materialist:

thinking involves not only the movement of thoughts, but their arrest as well. Where thinking suddenly comes to a stop in a constellation saturated with tensions, it gives that constellation a shock, by which thinking is crystallised as a monad.

(XVII)

The monad contains all potentialities, but nothing can be said about it in terms of objective description; in *Origin of the German Trauerspiel* (1928), Benjamin writes that "the idea is a monad," which makes ideas discontinuous from each other; and makes each unpredictable, unknown; but "each idea contains the image of the world" (Benjamin 2019: 27).

"Now-time" is the moment, the *Augenblick*, which is Nietzsche's subject in *Thus Spake Zarathustra*, a text certainly known to Bakhtin (and to Benjamin: Nietzsche is cited in "On the Concept of History"). The *Augenblick* is the gateway which is alluded to in thinking of eternal return, where Zarathustra makes it that which breaks with the desolating thought that everything must be repeated, that we are condemned to eternal repetition, which might be another way of formulating what is meant by "empty homogeneous time." Zarathustra asks: "are not all things knotted together so tightly that this moment draws after it *all* things that are to come?"[15] The thought of a chronology which repeats itself, as one thing after another, is undone by considering the moment—the twinkling of an eye—as changing everything, as St Paul thinks of it as the moment of resurrection, when "we shall all be changed" (I Corinthians 15:51–2). Everything within past and future is contained therein, with the possibility of reversing direction within it. Benjamin glosses it as "now-time"—i.e., *Jetztzeit*–in XVIII as being "the entire history of mankind in a tremendous abbreviation" (396), and as such a concentration, it resembles the chronotope as the antithesis of homogeneous empty time (and empty includes a reference to what is spatial, the opposite of, say, the market-square: awareness of a full space and a full time come together). Homogeneous time has no difference, nothing "other" within it. It is the time of monologism, or the dream of an administered state in which everything of otherness is repressed, or the time of pseudo-events, manufactured by the media, in which what is new is always a repeat of what has happened before: eternal repetition. Benjamin identifies it with what historicism yields, because this is in the service of a thinking of time which discards the past as it happens. Great time similarly opposes such historicism.

In fragments which were drafts for "The Concept of History," Benjamin draws in another concept, "the dialectical image":

> History deals with connections and with arbitrarily elaborated causal claims. But since history affords an idea of the fundamental citability of its object, this object must present itself, in its ultimate form, as a moment of humanity. In this moment, time must be brought to a standstill.

The dialectical image is an occurrence of ball lightning that runs across the whole horizon of the past.

> Articulating the past historically means recognising those elements of the past which come together in the constellation of a single moment .... In drawing itself together in the moment–in the dialectical image—the past becomes part of humanity's involuntary memory. The dialectical image can be defined as the involuntary memory of redeemed humanity.[16]

Benjamin speaks of "citability," and this idea should be compared with Bakhtin's dialogism, where every utterance is saturated with the language of the other, and where speech turns out to be quoting utterances whose provenance is not certain to the speaker. Indeed, it exists as "involuntary memory," a concept Benjamin takes, of course, from Proust. Full citability is akin to the idea, which Benjamin knew, coming from the theologian Origen, of *apokatastasis*: the time of the restitution of all things (Acts 3:21), a belief for which Origen was counted a heretic, that there would be a universal salvation, the very fires of hell being extinguished, "that God may be all in all" (I Corinthians 15:28), but without the monologism or triumphalism that is implied in that statement.

The "dialectical image," which assumes that every moment contains a contradiction within it which shows up in a flash of diverse images, Benjamin calls, in his *magnum opus, Das Passagen-Werk*, translated as *The Arcades Project,* "a caesura in the movement of thought."[17] The caesura, as a break, an interruption, the *Stillstellung* which has been translated as a "standstill," borrows from the theoretical writings of the poet Friedrich Hölderlin (1770–843). So Benjamin acknowledges in his essay on Goethe's

Elective Affinities, where he brings it—as part of Hölderlin's discussion of tragedy—into association with "the expressionless" [*das Ausdrucklose*], which shatters the appearance of continuity, of the ability of art (or indeed of history) to proceed fluently on its course of "semblance," confident in being able to give a positivist-inspired narrative representing events. In the caesural break, Benjamin writes in the *Elective Affinities* essay, "every expression simultaneously comes to a standstill."[18] The "standstill," and the dialectical image are conjured up in the electrical phenomenon of ball lightning, in which an electrical phenomenon shows up for a second as a ball in the sky: an alternative world (like the monad). Whereas Benjamin stresses a breakage, an aporia, a halting, Bakhtin's chronotope seems to privilege a passage through, but the difference between these two is less real than apparent. Above all, "only dialectical images are genuine ... and the place where one encounters them is language" (*Arcades*: N2a, E, 462). The sense of language as containing the plurality of a double sense, even a dialectical sense, in an utterance, is akin to Bakhtin saying that "language, as a treasure-house of images, is fundamentally chronotopic" (251). For language assimilates time, and an utterance is old and new at the same time.

The word "passage" just used (Bakhtin speaks of the corridor) may recall the Parisian arcades themselves, which may be called Benjamin's chronotope. In the series of aphorisms "Paris, the Capital of the Ninetenth Century," which fronts *The Arcades Project*, Benjamin quotes from a nineteenth-century guide-book to Paris:

> These arcades, a recent invention of industrial luxury, are glass-roofed, marble panelled corridors extending through whole blocks of buildings, whose owners have joined together for such enterprises. Lining both side of these corridors, which get their light from above, are the most elegant shops, so that the *passage* is a city, a world in miniature.
>
> (3)

Perhaps Bakhtin might have wanted to add the arcade to the list of chronotopes, however many differences might have been stressed; there is no emphasis in Bakhtin on the "arcades as temples of commodity capital" (Benjamin: A2, 2, 37). Such ideas belong to a Western Marxism different from Bakhtin's and more responsive to commodity capitalism. But in the arcades things come to a "standstill" (A3a, 7, 42), and they combine times and places–oriental bazaars, the appearance of winter-gardens, or hot-houses, the sense that, as for Dickens, shops in them were a "door to romance" (A11, 3, 57)—i.e., they exist as thresholds. In what the Arcades produce, the department-store, "the customers perceive themselves as a mass" (A12, 5, 60) which means that they see themselves; the "religious intoxication of great cities" which Baudelaire speaks of shows in them, as "temples consecrated to this intoxication" (A13): producing a "dérèglement des tous les sens." And perhaps all that is implied in the chronotope. Benjamin quotes Balzac on "the great poem of display" (A1, 4), meaning Paris; and that of course affects Dostoevsky, remembering the fashionable Nevsky Prospect in St. Petersburg, and Gogol's fantastic realism in describing it. Balzac's sense of Paris enters Dostoevsky's sense of St. Petersburg. One city enters into the way another city is thought, which is a point that was noted with Raskolnikov's mental city-planning. It comes near to illustrating what is meant by the dialectical image.

But we have seen that "great time" has a festal sense for Bakhtin, which is the reverse of the artificial paradise that is created in the Parisian arcades, and, for that reason, we may conclude by considering Hölderlin's poem, "Friedensfeier" (Celebration of Peace), in order to think about the potentialities of great time. "Friedensfeier" itself points toward "great time," for though it was written at the time of the Treaty of Lunéville (signed February 9, 1801, that which momentarily sealed peace between France and the Holy Roman Empire), it was not discovered as a holograph manuscript until 1954, in the Biblioteca Bodmeriana in Geneva, and it was first published that year. It is a posthumous document, therefore, which takes its place inside the twentieth century, as a text that is Modernist in its difficulty, but which dates from a hundred and fifty years earlier. Benjamin, one of Hölderlin's best commentators, along with Adorno, could not have known it; and probably not Bakhtin either. And though the hymn, and its drafts, was written 1801–02, it is "late style," since Hölderlin virtually ceased writing, because of his madness after 1806: it is the late style of a young poet.

The poem is in twelve stanzas (triads of 12, 12, and 15 lines) whose mode derives from Pindar, the poet who celebrates the festal, and it begins by imagining the setting out of a feast after a storm, with loving guests assembled, and with them, perhaps, "den Fürsten des Fests"—the prince of the feast-day (15).[19] Readers of Hölderlin preoccupy themselves with the positivist question, who is this? But there is no single answer, for "great time" disallows periodizing and making single identifications. In a recognition, which cannot be a literal memory, but which is more like a re-finding of the "lost object," the second verse seems to say that he may see this prince in person ("ihn selbst zu sehn," 15). But it is not clear that he is present; the mode of this poem is that "Heavenly ones" are "not manifest in wonders, nor unseen in storms" (103–4: "nicht/Im Wunder offenbar, noch ungesehn im Wetter"). The "Fürsten" could be the sun, or Napoleon, or Peace, or the "Vater" (75—though he is not specific to any religion), or Christ, who in Christian interpretation of Isaiah 9:6 is "the Everlasting *Father*, the Prince of Peace":

Nichts vor dir,
Nur Eines weiss ich, Sterbliches bist du nicht.
Ein Weiser mag mir manches erhellen, wo aber

Ein Gott noch auch erscheint,
Da is doch andere Klarheit.

(20–4)

("Nothing of you but one thing I know: mortal you are not. A wise man might illuminate much for me but when a god also appears there is another clarity.")

We are within a chronotope which seems to be ancient Greece, where Christ and Napoleon would both be oddly placed catachrestic figures. Peace here is more than the Napoleonic "peace"; it is said, in a later stanza, that mother and child can look on it ("Und schauet den Frieden," 125). But despite this seeing, the poem hovers between desiring a manifestation, or realization, in the present, which is that of no realizable time, of what has been fragmented, and lost, and knowing that there can be no full presence, a point from Derrida, but also derivable from Bahktin, whom Hölderlin seems to anticipate, not in showing the subject as split, as in the novel, but in showing that no state is complete in itself, nor susceptible to either positivist or historicist definition. The combination of peoples and events make this also an image of "great time," when different moments converge upon a now (*jetzt*—27, 39) which the poem celebrates.

This "Fürsten" is associated with "des Donnerers Echo" (32), with Zeus, and Dionysus, and with a past thousand years of warfare, which have rolled from East to West, and are still heard in the storm which is there and not there (121). Neither identity nor time is single, the "Fürsten" is new but not new: "von heute aber nicht, nicht unverkünder ist er" ("but not of today nor undeclared is he," 25). The time and people, at the end of stanza 3, are called to be renewed, and the fourth stanza invites especially one who is well disposed to men, who was "dort unter syrischer Palme" ("there, under the Syrian palm," 42), which might seem to be Christ (alluding to John, Chapter 4), save that the Syrian in Hölderlin's elegy "Brod und Wein" is also Dionysus, the Asian god. This one is called "youth" ("Jüngling," 48), and the fourth stanza closes with a sense that even heavenly values are in transition, changing, not caught in a metaphysics which would give them a permanent identity; because, as for Bakhtin, thought is never finished, never fixed:

So ist schnell
Vergänglich alles Himmlische, aber unsonst nicht. (50, 51)

("Thus speedily fleeting is everything heavenly, but not for nothing.")

The poem is fascinated with time as marked by the divine, and the sixth stanza evokes one who is a son, a "Ruhigmächtiger" (73, "quietly powerful") one, a "Herrn der Zeit" (—"Lord of Time," 79—which might suggest Saturn and so the return of the golden age).

Schiksaalgesez ist diss, dass Alle sich erfahren,
Dass, wenn die Stille kehrt, auch eine Sprache sei.

(83, 84)

("It is a law of destiny that each shall experience the other, that, when the silence turns, there shall be a language too.")

The poem looks for a turn ("kehr"), when silence, that of the feast-day, that of the pause associated with the "standstill," as a crisis time, alters, giving way to conversation, whose dialogism intimates "great time." Hence the affirmation of stanza 7:

Viel hat von Morgen an,
Seit ein Gespräch wir sind, und hören voneinander,
Erfahren der Mensch; bald sind wir aber Gesang.

(91–3)

("From morning on humans have learned from each other since we have been a conversation, and listened to each other, but soon we are song.")

It is now the day's end–after its progress through morning to the evening ("Abenstunde," 11). There has been song before (72), for time has never been empty, even before this desired moment of the turn, but the promise now is of carnival; of speech giving way to song, where separate identities disappear, and humans are taken up in the song which ends separate utterance. Jochem Schmidt, one of Hölderlin's commentators, refers to Heraclitus B40: "Much learning does not teach sense—otherwise it would have taught Hesiod and Pythagoras, and again Xenophanes and Hecataeus."[20] Here, however, dialogism means that there has been learning, and teaching, but nonetheless there will be its replacement by festal song, and this gives a reminder of what carnival means for Bakhtin: freedom from "the profound tragedy of the *individual* life itself, condemned to birth and death."[21]

That promise of song, of celebration of peace which is nonetheless aware of the "other" to peace, and which continues to have an intuition ("Ahnen," 127), which means that there is no finality here, not quite the attainment of Kraus' paradise—occurs on the basis of one who is "not absent" ("nicht fehlt," 109)—but the negative is important—who appears at the "Abend der Zeit" ("evening of time," 111), He is still the "Jüngling" (112) who was called to the "Fürsten des Festes." The grammar is ambiguous whether Christ, if it is he, is the "Fürsten," or not. There is no absolute. As the chronotope disallows single utterance, "great time" means that historical roles are not complete expressions, and they cannot be where identities, ages, and times, are not singly specifiable. Hölderlin's poem confronts, by writing about it, the problem of an apocalyptic "great time"; this continues as it speaks differently in a present it could not foresee; letting the older still roll forward into the present, and not be lost.

The "homecoming festival" of which Bakhtin speaks in conceptualizing "great time" is strikingly imaged in Hölderlin's poem, and renewed as a thought in the 1950s. And Benjamin, and Bakhtin, are equally writers whose work appeared most fully after their deaths, showing that the "here-and-now" quality of *Jetztzeit* makes the chronotope a distinctively utopian conception, always potentially realizable, however emphatically negative the conditions within which the possibility is framed. It has needed Modernism and the legacies of Modernism, to attempt to parallel these concepts of "great time" and the "chronotope" in literary forms, but as concepts, they burst out of any periodization, which indeed they question.

Notes

1 Fyodor Dostoevsky, *Crime and Punishment*, trans. Jessie Coulson, ed. George Gibian (New York: Norton, 1989), 62.
2 Walter Benjamin, "On Some Motifs in Baudelaire," *Selected Writings*, vol. 4: *1938–1939*, ed. Howard Eiland and Michael W. Jennings (Cambridge, MA: Harvard University Press, 2003), 329, and discussion of Baudelaire, 323–4.
3 Martin Heidegger, *Being and Time*, trans. John Macquarrie and Edward Robinson (Oxford: Blackwell, 1962), 376–7.
4 Søren Kierkegaard, *The Concept of Anxiety*, ed. and trans. Reidar Thomte and Albert B. Anderson (Princeton: Princeton University Press, 1980), 81.
5 Jeremy Tambling, *Becoming Posthumous: Life and Death and Literary and Cultural Studies* (Edinburgh: Edinburgh University Press, 2002), ix.
6 Stephen Kern, *The Culture of Time and Space 1880–1918* (London: Weidenfeld & Nicolson, 1983).
7 M. M. Bakhtin, "Epic and Novel," in *DI*, 3–40 (30).
8 David Shepherd, "A Feeling for History? Bakhtin and 'The Problem of Great Time'," *The Slavonic and East European Review*, 84 (2006): 32–51. See also William D. Lindsey, "'The Problem of Great Time': A Bakhtinian Ethics of Discourse," *The Journal of Religion* 73 (1993): 311–28; Barry Sandywell, "Memories of Nature in Bakhtin and Benjamin," in *Materialising Bakhtin: The Bakhtin Circle and Social Theory*, ed. Craig Brandist and Galin Tihanov (London: Macmillan, 2000), 94–118.
9 Walter Benjamin, *Selected Writings*, vol. 3, ed. Michael W. Jennings, Howard Eiland and Gary Smith (Cambridge, MA: Harvard University Press, 1999), 25–31. I discuss this in my *Histories of the Devil: From Marlowe to Mann, and the Manichees* (London: Palgrave, 2016), 97–100.

10 See H. D. Kittsteiner, "Walter Benjamin's Historicism," trans. Jonathan Monroe and Irving Wohlfarth, *New German Critique* 39 (1986): 179–215.
11 Walter Benjamin, "On the Concept of History," *Selected Writings*, vol. 4, 394–5.
12 Walter Benjamin, *Origin of the German Trauerspiel*, trans. Howard Eiland (Cambridge, MA: Harvard University Press, 2019), 174.
13 Walter Benjamin, "Karl Kraus," *Selected Writings*, vol. 2, 451.
14 Jacques Lacan, *The Ethics of Psychoanalysis: The Seminar of Jacques Lacan VII*, trans. Dennis Porter (London: Routledge, 1992), 118.
15 Friedrich Nietzsche, *Thus Spoke Zarathustra*, trans. Graham Parkes (Oxford: Oxford University Press, 2005), 136.
16 "Paralipomena to 'On the Concept of History'," *Selected Writings*, vol. 4, 403.
17 Walter Benjamin, *The Arcades Project*, trans. Howard Eiland and Kevin McLaughlin (Cambridge, MA: Harvard University Press, 1999), N10a, 3, 475.
18 Walter Benjamin, "Goethe's *Elective Affinities*," *Selected Writings*, vol. 1, ed. Marcus Bullock and Michael W. Jennings (Cambridge, MA: Harvard University Press, 1996), 340–1.
19 Friedrich Hölderlin, *Sämtliche Werke und Briefe* [Complete Works and Letters], ed. Michael Knaupp (Munich: Carl Hanser, 1992), vol. 1, 361–6. Translations mine but see *Friedrich Hölderlin: Poems and Fragments*, trans. Michael Hamburger (London: Anvil Press, 2004), 522–33.
20 Jochem Schmidt, ed., *Hölderlin: Sämtliche Gedichte: Text und Kommentar* (Frankfurt: Deutscher Klassiker, 2005), 923: see *Early Greek Philosophy*, ed. Jonathan Barnes (Harmondsworth: Penguin, 1987), 105.
21 Quoted in Ken Hirschkop, *Mikhail Bakhtin: An Aesthetic for Democracy* (Oxford: Oxford University Press, 1999), 182 and 287.

5

Bakhtin's Scenarios of Selfhood

Modernism between Intersubjectivity and Transindividuality

Ilya Kliger

In his review of Marshall Berman's classic work on European Modernism, *All That is Solid Melts into Air*, Perry Anderson advances an alternative and, by his lights, more precise historical delineation of the period. To Berman's linear-dialectical account, Anderson opposes a "conjunctural" alternative, refusing to conceive Modernism in culture as coterminous with modernity itself, and instead placing it at the point of convergence among three socio-historical developments: "the codification of a highly formalized academism in the visual and other arts [...] institutionalized within official regimes of state and society still massively pervaded [...] by aristocratic or landowning classes"; "the emergence within these societies of the key technologies or inventions of the second industrial revolution: telephone, radio, automobile, aircraft and so on"; and "the imaginative proximity of social revolution."[1] According to Anderson, Modernist responses to these conditions were, as a general matter, structured by a basic ambivalence. The drive to be free from the constraints of status-laden academism in the arts coincided with opposition to the middle-brow and the valorization of high culture that could itself be assimilated to "an aristocracy of the spirit." Anderson's second historical coordinate invited reflections on the dialectic of mastery and servitude in human metabolism with nature (Marx, *Economic and Philosophical Manuscripts*), with a stream of technological breakthroughs and inventions signaling rapid and potentially unlimited expansion of human capacities alongside nightmares of denaturing and enslavement. Finally, the expectation (or reality) of social revolution signified both possibility and collapse, provoking utopian hopes and millenarian fears, which passionately played out in the cultural domain. Anderson summarizes his brief account as follows: "European modernism in the first years of [the twentieth] century thus flowered in the space between a still usable classical past, a still indeterminate technical present, and a still unpredictable political future. Or, put another way, it arose at the intersection between a semi-aristocratic ruling order, a semi-industrialized capitalist economy, and a semi-emergent, or -insurgent, labor movement."[2] Anderson dates Modernism's end quite precisely with the Second World War. Only after 1945 did the openings afforded by the tripartite conjuncture shut down: in the West, bourgeois democracy was firmly established, stemming the threat of social revolution and aristocratic *revanche*; at the same time, full-scale industrialization along the Fordist model took hold. "There could no longer be the smallest doubt as to what kind of society this technology would consolidate: an oppressively stable, monolithically industrial, capitalist civilization was now in place."[3] As the conjuncture dissolved, Modernism dwindled in the West. Despite individual achievements, the extraordinary cultural richness of the first half of the century could be neither sustained nor replicated.

Few motifs were as deeply rooted in all aspects of Modernist culture as the motif of crisis besetting the figure of the human. This crisis of humanism—of individualism, or of the subject—became the focus of intense, anxiety-ridden exploration: both explicit and mediated through a variety of cultural forms. With Anderson's model in mind, the problematic of "the crisis of humanism," too, can be understood in relation to three axes of the Modernist conjuncture. In relation to the sclerotic persistence of old-regime categories (both aesthetic and social), the subject appears as the destroyer of forms and the subverter of conventions, while also claiming privileged status as unconstrained creator, acting both within an autonomous domain and for the benefit of society as a whole. In light of the problematics of the anticipated (or accomplished) social revolution, the question of the subject takes the form of the relationship between members of the cultural elite and the popular masses. Finally, the experience of technological amplification is also that of subjective dispersal and dissolution, while expanded mastery over nature can come at the price of servitude to the machine.

In what follows, I would like to introduce still further specificity into the conjunctural account of Modernism by paying special attention to the scenarios of subjectivity—and, correspondingly, of sociality—broadly operative in the work of Mikhail Bakhtin. Three such scenarios in particular will be central here: the scenario of intersubjectivity, effecting a complex mediation between social/aesthetic authority and subjective/aesthetic emancipation; the scenario of (disjunctive) manifestation, staging the enmeshment of the individual and the masses within the horizon of social revolution; and finally the scenario of transindividuality, operating broadly in Bakhtin's texts but coming especially to the fore during a (previously untranslated) discussion of a technological metaphor in a poem by Vladimir Mayakovsky. In speaking of "scenarios" rather than "theories" or "conceptions" of subjectivity, I mean to emphasize their elastic and mobile character. I will treat them less as products of explicit deliberation and systematic exposition than as *ad hoc* imaginaries articulated in orthogonal contexts (for example, in the course of inquiry into the phenomenology of narrative, history of genre, philosophy of language, aesthetic theory, etc.), coexisting and even comingling with the evocative imprecision characteristic of Bakhtin's work as a whole.[4]

Authority and Immanence: Scenarios of Intersubjectivity[5]

It is possible to describe the foundational gesture of Bakhtin's phenomenology as that of rendering transcendence immanent. At stake among other things is an attack—by no means unique within "modernist" thought—against idealist notions of the transcendental self, whose capacity for grasping the world from a thoroughly disembedded, worldless position functions as the guarantee of true knowledge. In *Problems of Dostoevsky's Art* (*Problemy tvorchestva Dostoevskogo*, 1929), Bakhtin characterizes the presupposition as follows: "This faith in the self-sufficiency of a single consciousness in all spheres of ideological life is not a theory created by some specific thinker; no, it is a profound structural characteristic of the creative ideological activity of modern times, determining all its external and internal forms" (*CW2*: 61; *PDP*: 82). The transcendental, cognitive, or contemplative stance is, in this account, symptomatic of modernity's paradoxical tendency both to de-personalize and to subjectivize knowledge, to refer it to that "within" each of us which is not unique to us, which we share with others.

The problem for Bakhtin is not universality itself, but how it is conceived within the parameters of transcendental idealism (and phenomenology), namely, the tendency to align universality (and therefore authority) with the individual. Bakhtin "begins" by rejecting this alliance, which, in the book on Dostoevsky, appears as narrative monologism, a kind of revealing caricature of the idealist subject. His position echoes that of the founders of historical materialism, who state in *The German Ideology* that "the first premise of all human history is [...] the existence of living human individuals."⁶ Key and irreversible, for Marx–Engels and for Bakhtin alike, is both existence and plurality. When it comes to existence, Bakhtin insists:

> I occupy a place in once-occurrent Being that is unique and never-repeatable, a place that cannot be taken by anyone else and is impenetrable for anyone else. In the given once-occurrent point where I am now located, no one else has ever been located in the once-occurrent time and once-occurrent space of once-occurrent Being [...] That which can be done by me can never be done by anyone else [...] This fact of *my non-alibi in Being*, which underlies the concrete and once-occurrent ought of the answerably performed act, is not something I come to know of and to cognize but something I acknowledge and affirm in a unique or once-occurrent manner.
>
> (*CW1*: 38–9; *TPA*: 40)

Existence amounts to the absence of alibi, the impossibility of absenting oneself from the concrete "event of Being," except in bad faith. As for plurality, Bakhtin conceives it too, in concrete—which is to say non-numerical—terms, as a plurality of materially embedded, non-coinciding subjects standing in irremediably asymmetrical relationships to each other: "From my own unique place only *I-for-myself* constitute an *I*, whereas all others are others for me" (*CW1*: 43; *TPA*: 46). The notion that I am just like others, that we are all human, share the same essence, die, etc.—all of these facts are supplied by abstract cognition. But when it comes to the concrete experience of plurality, non-coincidence and asymmetry is all we have. It is from these assumptions of radical immanence and asymmetrical plurality that Bakhtin sets out to develop his own quasi-transcendental analysis, an inquiry into the conditions of the possibility of coherent experience, ethical action, and aesthetic activity.

One consequence of our unique and unrepeatable position in the world is that the categories of self and other are non-interchangeable. From within the categories of I-for-myself I experience myself as an open-ended, forward-striving impulse. I cannot experience my own birth or death, nor perceive the whole of my body, nor be rid of the sense that meaning, knowledge, and satisfaction are tasks, ever still to be achieved. Others-for-me, meanwhile, can appear complete in time and space, I can both experience and envision their birth or death (if I attempt to imagine my own, I start treating myself as "another"); I conceive of them as in some sense "whole," in possession of a certain "character" or "temperament," as well as a coherent life-trajectory, or fate. Bakhtin speaks of a "surplus of vision" which I possess vis-à-vis all others, and others possess vis-à-vis me (*CW1*: 104; *AA*: 22–3). What further complicates matters—and what finally gets us to intersubjectivity proper—is that we are all, according to Bakhtin, constituted as a ratio of the two phenomenological axes. This is because I inevitably internalize elements of another's surplus of vision in relation to myself and thereby come to experience myself in part within the categories of otherness, as an other. This operation can be understood as one of communicative and, more broadly, socio-historical stabilization, whereby an otherwise wide-open, unbounded self acquires relative object-like determinateness, which is in turn assimilated, appropriated, rejected, re-evaluated, and so on, within the categories of the I-for-myself.[7]

Bakhtin's immanent analysis of intersubjectivity, then, takes as its starting point not a division within the self between the ideal space of the transcendental and the real space of the empirical but rather the basic fact of differential localization in—and the ineluctable sociality of—"the event of Being." In his early manuscript on aesthetics, *Author and Hero in Aesthetic Activity (Avtor i geroi v esteticheskoi deiatel'nosti*, mid-1920s), this analysis proves fruitful for a reconstruction of the history of aesthetic forms (predominantly of narrative representation) as an account of changing self–other, or author–hero, configurations.[8] Of particular relevance for our discussion are passages treating the distinction between "Classical" and "Romantic" constructions of literary character. The Classical character, for Bakhtin, is dominated by the category of otherness: the character is firmly embedded in (external, but deeply internalized) structures of communal authority. Dominant here is

> *the value of one's kin*, conceived as a category of validating otherness, which involves me as well in the axiological sphere of its accomplishment. *I do not initiate life* [...] I only *continue* the sequence (the acts of thinking as well as the acts of feeling and the acts that constitute deeds). I am bound by an indissoluble *relation of sonship* to the fatherhood and motherhood of my kin or kind.
>
> (*CW1*: 238; *AA*: 178)

By contrast, the uprooted I-for-myself dominates in the Romantic character construction, while the collective, authorial otherness confronts a crisis of legitimacy. Here, all external determinations are undermined, everything that does not arise from within the self-consciousness of the self is questioned; all customary ways of life lose authority and turn into empty conventions. The center of temporal gravity shifts from the solid past of tradition to the open-ended future of the project. We find ourselves in the midst of a historical predicament that Bakhtin designates as "the crisis of authorship" (*CW1*: 259–60; *AA*: 202–3).

It is at this point that the historical dimension traversing Bakhtin's scenario of intersubjectivity appears most clearly on the surface. Indeed, "crisis of authorship" is Bakhtin's diagnosis of the present (though not unprecedented) moment, in the field of aesthetic activity and in social life alike. This crisis expresses itself on the one hand in the loss of distance, evident both in Russian Symbolism and in the avant-garde, between art and life: "the very place of art in the whole of culture, in the event of being, is reevaluated; any traditional place of art appears to be unjustified; [...] it is impossible to be an artist, it is impossible to become totally part of this limited sphere; the point is not to surpass others in art, but to surpass art itself" (*CW1*: 258; *AA*: 202). At the same time, in life itself, we witness the disappearance of tradition, the devaluation of "outward appearance, the exterior, manners of comportment, etc.; the communal way of everyday life, etiquette, etc." (*CW1*: 259; *AA*: 204).

That Modernism in the strict sense is indeed here at stake, evident from Bakhtin's invocation of Fyodor Dostoevsky (an iconic figure not only for Russian but also for European Modernism) and Andrei Belyi (a leading Symbolist poet, novelist, and theorist): the two register in their work the historically specific intersubjective structure that bespeaks the crisis of authority. Bakhtin's work on Dostoevsky goes on to develop the consequences of such crisis in great detail. A character in Dostoevsky is said to relate to others not as a "landlord to peasant, property-owner to proletarian, well-to-do bourgeois to déclassé tramp," not as "someone dressed in the concrete and impenetrable garb of his class or social station," but directly as a self-consciousness to another self-consciousness (*CW2*: 75; *PDP*: 104). With this devaluation of external markers of hierarchy and order, the category of the self/hero comes to predominate, while the other/author is recast from a benevolently embedding community to an authoritarian monologist, incapable of hearing, or unwilling to listen to the voices of other selves. Thus, on the one hand, traditional order is reduced to the figure of the solitary individual, the monologic author who, in standing radically above his characters, presumes to possess an "alibi in Being," and exempts himself from intersubjective dynamics; on the other hand, we have the order-less, other-less self-for-itself of the Dostoevskian hero, hostile to boundaries, conventions, and definitions, unseemly and unformed.

Aligned with the history of narrative form, of representation, and ultimately, of culture, Bakhtin's phenomenological scenario of intersubjectivity assimilates and displays a genuinely Modernist preoccupation with the tension between traditional social and aesthetic forms (are they living, or are they dead?) on the one hand, and forces of social and aesthetic insurgency (are they renewing or destructive?) on the other. Where Bakhtin's own ultimate sympathies lie is less important here than the fact that his scenario of intersubjectivity encodes–we might even say, consists of–elements of a social phenomenology of the historical present. Endowed with a historical dimension, such a phenomenology registers the sliding of the category of the *author/other*, for example, from the modality of the archaic-communal (chorus) to that of the modern-individual (monologist) as well as the corresponding rearticulation of *the hero/self* from socially bounded to radically self-conscious. It is not simply the case, in other words, that the categories of the *other/author* are associated with tradition and those of the *self/hero* with modernity. Rather, the intersubjective situation itself is to be read as simultaneously both. In this way, Bakhtin's scenario of intersubjectivity encapsulates the experience of non-synchronicity so starkly in evidence in the Russian inflection of European Modernism.[9]

The Chorus and the People: Scenarios of Manifestation

The second scenario of selfhood (and hence, once again, of sociality), to which I would like to turn now, is tacitly presupposed in what is perhaps Bakhtin's most far-reaching contribution to the study of literature and culture: the concept of heteroglossia (*raznorechie*). Developed primarily in the essay *Discourse in the Novel* (*Slovo v romane*, 1930–34), his account of heteroglossia draws attention to the workings of language as a shifting field of always pre-existing and ever-changing discursive articulations: individual as well as collective. These articulations, as Bakhtin understands them, are highly diverse in nature. One of his lists includes "the Ukrainian language, the language of the epic poem, of early Symbolism, of the student, of a particular generation of children, of the run-off-the-mill intellectual, of the Nietzschean and so on" (*CW3*: 44; *DI*: 291). What gives us the right to characterize all of these discursive formations as "languages" and to treat them as in some sense the same? The following passage develops Bakhtin's response:

> In actual fact, however, there does exist a common plane that methodologically justifies our juxtaposing [these phenomena]: all languages of heteroglossia, whatever the principle underlying them and making each unique, are specific points of view on the world, forms for conceptualizing the world in words, specific world views [...] By stressing the intentional dimension of stratification in literary language we are able, as has been said, to locate in a single series such methodologically heterogeneous phenomena as professional and social dialects, world views, and individual artistic works, for in their intentional dimension one finds that common plane on which they can be juxtaposed, and juxtaposed dialogically. The whole matter consists in the fact that there may be, between "languages," highly specific dialogic relations; no matter how these languages are conceived, they may all be taken as particular points of view on the world.
>
> (*CW3*,: 44–6; *DI*: 291–3)

The implicit scenario here is that of manifestation, according to which the subject is conceived as speaking the language of a group, a social rather than individual language, which he or she embodies, actualizes, brings into the world. It is instructive to juxtapose this "mature" passage with an earlier one, from *Author and Hero*, on the lyric:

> Lyrical self-objectification, too, is full of deep trust that has been rendered immanent to its powerful, authoritative, and lovingly affirming form, i.e. immanent to the author—the bearer of the consummating unity of form. In order to make my lived experience sound lyrically, I need to feel [...] the other in myself, my own passiveness in the possible chorus of others [...] In a lyrical work, I have not yet stepped forward out of the chorus in the capacity of its hero-protagonist, that is, as a hero who still retains the chorally determined axiological bodiedness of his soul or otherness, but who already feels his own solitariness—in the capacity of the tragic hero (the solitary other). In a lyrical work, I am still wholly within a chorus and I speak from within a chorus.
>
> (*CW1*: 232; *AA*: 170)

The logic of the passage may appear paradoxical: in the lyric, I speak of myself, assert myself, "sing" myself—in the presumed (or, most strongly perhaps, presupposed; not invented) voice of the collective other. I am most myself when I speak with, or "from within" the authority of the chorus, with the assurance of what Bakhtin calls "choral support." A curious, but by now not unfamiliar, slippage occurs when modern (solitary) lyric turns out to imply archaic chorus as its condition of possibility. It is not difficult to recognize a Nietzschean subtext here; and Bakhtin leaves no doubt of it by invoking, several sentences earlier, "the spirit of music" (*CW1*: 231).[10] At stake in Nietzsche, as in prior Romantic and post-Romantic interpretations of the Greek tragic (and lyric) chorus, is a certain vision of the relationship between individual and community. This community is conceived as both archaic and eschatological within a tripartite historical schema of original unity within the collective; current state of individuation and fragmentation, and hoped-for reunification at hand. The precise outlines and timing of this reunification—this modern antiquity—differ from account to account. The most prominent Russian Modernist popularizer of Nietzsche's work (especially of his work on tragedy) was the Russian Symbolist poet and theorist Vyacheslav Ivanov, for whom the resurrection of public choral performance and the new communalist sociality that such performance would enact became associated with social revolution. Ivanov greeted the events of February 1917 with great enthusiasm and entered the competition for a new national anthem with his "Choral Song of New Russia," a Populist-Symbolist text, celebrating political liberty, national brotherhood, and the universalization of the peasant commune (*mir*).[11] For a brief time, he played a prominent role in the Bolshevik cultural administration, promoting the spread of mass festivals. In one of his articles from the time, he argued: "It is necessary to facilitate however possible the inculcation, distribution and development of the chorus; to keep large choruses at the expense of the municipality and to patronize the activity of choral societies; [...] in a word, to create out of the chorus a vital and artistically effective organ for the enthusiastic expression of popular thought and popular will."[12]

Ivanov's Populist Dionysianism reappears in Bakhtin, transformed and complicated within the context of a two-pronged inquiry into structures of subjectivity and history of form. The thematics of the chorus will reappear regularly in his work, in various ways construing configurations of collectivity and selfhood. Bakhtin's passage on "choral support" suggests a model of harmonious co-thriving of community and individuality, on the grounds of stable and benevolent authority: in manifesting the community, the speaking/singing self expresses its own innermost feelings and thoughts. Individualism and communalism meet at the highest point of each: "Individualism can determine itself positively and feel no shame about its own determinateness only in an atmosphere of trust, love, and possible choral support. The individual does not exist outside otherness [*vne drugosti*]" (*CW1*: 232–3).[13] We are here as it were "prior" to (but also perhaps "past") the opposition between the individual and the group.

Several years later, the image of the chorus will reappear in *Problems of Dostoevsky's Art*, this time as a chorus of "battling and internally divided voices" (*CW2*: 153; *PDA*: 250). In the terms developed in *Author and Hero*, such a polyphonic chorus arises in the midst of a "crisis of authorship," a loss of legitimate authority and belonging. In *Problems of Dostoevsky's Art*, Bakhtin historicizes this innovation in a more materialist spirit as a function of a catastrophic intrusion of capitalism into "an untouched multitude of diverse worlds and social groups" unprepared for the change (*CW2*: 27; *PDA*: 20). Capitalism disembeds individuals from the isolation of traditional social groups, both hierarchical and geographical, and brings them together in their very separateness. What results in Dostoevsky is a disjunctive chorus, in which speakers are linked by relations of mutual suspicion and dependence, of paranoia and clinging, insistent on protecting their own boundaries and yet unable to disentangle their speech from the intrusive voices of others. Here, then, the scenario of manifestation acquires an extra twist. Speakers no longer express socially determined points of view on the world; they no longer ventriloquize distinctive languages. Instead, their fragmented and internally conflicted discourse expresses the fragmented and internally conflicted structure of the social chorus, an anti-chorus, so to speak, an ultimate unity that (provisionally) appears as its opposite.

The final scenario of manifestation that is important to consider here can be found in Bakhtin's discussions of the deep history of genre. What accounts for the links of Dostoevsky's poetics to the tradition of carnival folklore is not the author's "subjective memory," Bakhtin writes, "but the objective memory of the very genre in which he worked" (*CW6*: 137; *PDA*: 121). At issue is the process whereby deep layers of unofficial, collective, and anonymous folk culture make their way into the works of individual authors, regardless of—and sometimes even despite—their intentions. On this view, intention, and intentionality more broadly, is no longer understood as the condition of the possibility of experience proper, but rather as the condition of the possibility of a certain, limited kind of experience: it locks the subject within the confines of what Bakhtin calls "the small," the confines of everyday, private, practical considerations, rendering us blind to the vast areas of human experience, especially in its collective forms. The foregrounding of subjectivity, Kantian and phenomenological alike, correlates here with the condition of social isolation, the predicament of being cut off not only from the masses but from the "great experience of humanity" as a whole. "In small experience," Bakhtin writes in his notebooks from the 1940s, "there is one cognizer (everything else is an object of cognition), one free subject (everything else is dead things), one who speaks (everything else is unresponsively silent). In great experience everything is alive, everything speaks [...] I am object-like in a subject-like world" (*CW5*: 78).[14] "Genre memory," "great time," "great memory" are all figures that connote a choral substrate, inflected in distinctly Populist terms and called upon to free the otherwise-all-too-individual subject from its isolation and to root it in a form of deep historical and democratic sociality. What from the point of view of a certain ("bourgeois") individualism might appear terrifying—the experience of being overwhelmed by the masses and by the archaic past, the writer's surrendering of control—is here staged as liberating and conducive to creativity and innovation.[15]

The Self and Technics: Scenarios of Transindividuality

The scenario of the intersubjective encounter relies, as we have seen, on a vision of two symmetrically organized consciousnesses confronting each other within an asymmetrical "event of Being." Bakhtin superimposes upon this model a certain history of (especially narrative) form, in terms of which the phenomenological scenario acquires a distinctly Modernist valence as an attempt to grapple with the evanescence and spectral persistence of tradition, both aesthetic and political. Thus, not only is the intersubjective situation conceived as a field of tension between the decorousness of authorial stability and the scandal of heroic transcendence, but it also evinces a symptomatic ambiguity when it comes to the figure of the author himself. The author can be collective (the chorus), but also individual (the monologist)—in the first case, its bestowments of bounded solidity to the hero are welcome; in the second case, they are mere impostership and violence, and deserve to be debunked.

Visions of historical non-synchrony play an important role in the scenario manifestation as well. So does the image of a collective author (the communal flourishing of individuals), which here reappears in three distinct but interrelated guises: as "choral support," "polyphonic discord," and "archaic de-individuation." Here we encounter a set of variations on the Populist theme of social unification as the condition of individual fulfillment. Thus, even the internally fragmented and socially alienated participants in capitalist polyphony must be grasped in their inexorable (though disavowed) togetherness, while the memory and anticipation of the emancipating chorus enacts, once again at the level of the history of culture and forms, the vision of a classless, genuinely democratic world.

The third scenario of selfhood prominent in Bakhtin's work comes through most clearly in a fragment from the early 1940s—a uniquely substantive confrontation with a major figure within Russian Modernism. The fragment at issue likely represents notes toward a projected article on the poetics of Vladimir Mayakovsky. One particular passage stands out for its use of a technological metaphor in Mayakovsky's poem "To Our Youth" (1927) as a springboard for a broad-ranging discussion of subjectivity. It is worth citing at length:

> "*We roar* with [the roar of] the steam-engine *to the point of hoarseness*" and "*I fly* through canyons with whistles subdued."[16] The boundary between the human being and the thing is drawn in a new way here. The poet of the older generation separates himself from the thing very sharply: the train roars, not I. I am concentrated inside myself, while the roaring train is part of my surroundings [...]. I am alienated from the thing, I do not feel myself as a responsible co-participant in its task. In reality the passenger, of course, roars with the steam train. For if we fly along in a train (with the train), then we also roar with the train; it is not our surroundings, but we ourselves, expanded and elongated by technology; the boundary of the human being extends beyond the train [...] Such images that shift boundaries and expand the human being–expanding in the dimensions of *material growth*–can be artistically convincing only under the condition that the human being ceases to be an enclosed and finalized egocentric *inner* little world which only experiences and contemplates; that he becomes enfleshed, not separate from the collective, sharply activated, involved in the movement and work of people and things [...] One joins things not from the inside, but rather intertwines with them in the zone of external material contact.
>
> (CW5: 60–1)[17]

The opening image of the passengers roaring with the roar of the steam-engine (*revem parovozom do khripoty*) relies on a vision of conduit or exchange, whereby the train and the riders prove permeable to each other's affects. The steam-engine transmits its capacity to roar to "us"; "we" transmit to it the intense, personal, (perhaps triumphant, perhaps strained) tone of the sound. Both the steam-engine and "we" become hoarse in the process; together, we—the engine and the collective speaker—meet at the point of hoarseness. At stake, for Bakhtin, is a new vision of the subject which no longer stands over and against the objective world and other people, a kind of "kingdom within a kingdom," but is rather placed entirely within the "zone of material contact"—and through and through active—with(in) the world. Such material contact enables free exchange of properties and affects among people and things, an exchange that constantly defines and redefines boundaries.

The fragment mixes the motif of technological extension of human capacities with two other familiar Modernist motifs: those of radical innovation and social revolution. To begin with, we have a discussion of Mayakovsky's resistance to the demands of aesthetic decorum:

> "Falsified by beauty"—unmasked by aesthetics. Beauty and finalizedness. Can becoming be beautiful. Beauty, finalizedness, and belonging to the past. *The struggle of the old with the new*. New wholes are being created within new boundaries: the decomposing old and the unready [*negotovyi*] new. But from this, two-bodied and bitonal chaos toward a new monumentalism. This struggle of the new with the old in the history of world literature and in folklore created a whole system of images.
>
> (*CW5*: 61)

Mayakovsky appears here as the poet of unfinalizable becoming, which breaks through the canons of beauty just as it flees the historical past. The motif of the "crisis of authorship" reappears here no longer embedded within the scenario of intersubjectivity; it is no longer linked, in other words, with the hypertrophy of self-consciousness at the expense of stable social categories and naturalized boundaries. "The old and the new" no longer represent different hypostases of the subject (respectively, the stability of the conservative other and the open-endedness of the innovating self). Rather, "the old and the new" marks the distinction between the version of subjectivity as a self-enclosed, bounded, transcendental-empirical ego and the kind of self that is, in Bakhtin's own words once again, "enfleshed, not separate from the collective, sharply activated, involved in the movement and work of people and things." This latter, in turn, is the (post-)revolutionary subject par excellence, possible only "in our country" (*CW5*: 51). Regardless of the sincerity of this final claim, regardless, in other words, of whether Bakhtin thought such a society has actually been established (chances are, he didn't), the scenario captures the pathos of Mayakovsky's poem and coheres more broadly with a prominent Modernist take on the social revolution as such.

The scenario of selfhood presupposed, and partially elaborated, in the fragment on Mayakovsky places Bakhtin within the tradition of thought that has recently been referred to as "transindividualist." Accounts of the tradition tend to highlight two major sources of intellectual inspiration: Gilbert Simondon's recent work on technology in light of a broader inquiry into the ontology of persons, collectivities, and things; and the twentieth-century revival of interest in the philosophy of Baruch (Benedict) Spinoza. Vittorio Morfino encapsulates Simondon's critique of the philosophical tradition, both dualist and substantivist, as resting on two basic presuppositions: "1) the thesis of the primacy of individuation over the individual; and 2) the thesis of the primacy of the relation over the terms [of the relation]."[18] The two principles manifest themselves most clearly in the interaction between human beings and technics, insofar as such interactions call "into question the putative stability of the individual."[19]

While scholars have pursued fruitful links between Bakhtin's "dialogism" and Simondon's transindividualist ontology,[20] Bakhtin's relationship to Spinoza has remained largely unexplored. Yet we can glean suggestive hints at affinity from the few brief remarks that Bakhtin dedicates to the Dutch philosopher, mentioned almost exclusively in connection with Goethe. To begin with, we know that he planned to include a section on Spinoza and Goethe in the ill-fated book on the *Bildungsroman* (CW3: 206). In the extant notes, Spinoza and Goethe are briefly compared with regard to their respective conceptions of time. According to Bakhtin, Goethe refuses to follow "his teacher" in seeing the world *sub specie aeternitatis* and understands it instead as a process of "productive-creative" becoming (CW3: 311). Yet, in fact, this understanding of nature corresponds closely to Spinoza's conception of substance as a whole and infinite chain of causal modifications.[21] Indeed, in the book on François Rabelais (*Tvorchestvo Fransua Rable i narodnaia kul'tura srednevekov'ia i renessansa*, 1965), Spinoza makes another appearance as an inspiration behind Goethe's carnivalesque conception of nature as both complete and forever self-modifying (CW4.2: 272; RHW: 254). Finally and most substantively, in a letter responding to Ivan Kanaev's book on Goethe as a poet-naturalist, Bakhtin points with evident approval to a major convergence between Goethe and Spinoza; on the question of the relationship between essence and appearance, and between subject and object.

According to Bakhtin, both understand essence as something that necessarily appears, actualizes itself in the phenomenal world, rather than stay hidden behind (or within) phenomena. Both also place the subject of knowledge inside what it strives to know, conceiving of it as a connatural part of nature (CW3: 710). This rejection of both essence-substance and subject-object dualisms is nowhere as evident in Bakhtin's own work as in his scenarios of transindividuation. To quote once again from the passage on Mayakovsky: "One joins things not from the inside, but rather intertwines with them in the zone of external material contact." Or, from the approximately contemporaneous dissertation on Rabelais:

> The grotesque body is not separated from the rest of the world. It is not a closed, completed unit; it is unfinished, outgrows itself, transgresses its own limits. The stress is laid on those parts of the body that are open to the outside world, that is, the parts through which the world enters the body or emerges from it, or through which the body itself goes out to meet the world [...] The unfinished and open body (dying, bringing forth and being born) is not separated from the world by clearly defined boundaries; it is blended with the world, with animals, with objects.
> (*CW4.1*: 33)[22]

Prominent here once again is the image of transindividual exchange, of the passing of matter and properties across permeable, provisional boundaries, thresholds of individuation that serve as possibility conditions of individuality itself.

Corresponding to the image of the grotesque body in the realm of language, we find a certain kind of double-voiced speech, which Bakhtin defines in *Problems of Dostoevsky's Art* as "discourse with an orientation toward someone else's discourse" (*CW2*: 96; *PDP*: 199). Here we have once again the phenomenological notion of orientation, a logic within which of the two voices contained in the utterance we know which is representing which, which stands for the subject and which for the object. But then Bakhtin turns to the third, in some ways most representative, version of double-voiced discourse in Dostoevsky: the version he calls "active." Bakhtin writes: "Another's discourse in this case is not reproduced with a new intention, but it acts upon, influences, and in one way or another determines the author's discourse, while itself remaining outside it" (*CW2*: 92; *PDP*: 195). And a little later: "One word acutely senses alongside it someone else's word speaking about the same object, and this awareness determines its structure" (*CW2*: 93; *PDP*: 196). Here the intentional structure of discourse—the structure within which we take words from other people and endow them with the accents that express our own stance in the world—encounters a basic limit. The other's word and one's own end up side by side, each inflecting each, and we don't quite know who is speaking. The subject-object opposition is replaced by the relational structure of side-by-sidedness, an interplay of mutual individuation.

The images of the roaring techno-human in Mayakovsky, of the grotesque body in Rabelais, of speech warped within the forcefield of other speech in Dostoevsky—all play out the scenario of transindividuality. Together with the other two scenarios we have considered, it traces a specifically Modernist alternative to what appears to Bakhtin and many others as the culturally dominant notion of a bounded, transcendentally centered, independent, and masterful self. I have resisted assigning these scenarios to specific stages of Bakhtin's thought, since all three are perhaps best seen as traversing much of his work, overlapping and weaving into each other, at times easily distinguishable, at times not. Hints of the transindividual scenario can be detected in Bakhtin's discussion of the wholly immanent "event of Being," while the intersubjective author–hero paradigm haunts his entire oeuvre. The wager of this essay has been that it may nevertheless be useful to disentangle them rather than assume a unified vision of subjectivity operative throughout.

Such disentangling has the additional benefit of anchoring Bakhtin's work more firmly within the Modernist moment. We have seen that, as specific instantiations of the Modernist critique of modern subjectivity, Bakhtin's scenarios resonate strongly with elements of Anderson's conjuncture. Intersubjectivity ambivalently encodes—and elaborates the consequences of—the tension between formal-social order cathected on the past and the tendencies of its future-directed overcoming. The script of manifestation stages various configurations of the self's relationship to the collective, in various ways internalizing the entrance of mass movements onto the stage of history, crystalized in the (hoped for, feared, or actual) event of a social revolution. Lastly, the discourse of transindividuality proves responsive—even if it is by no means reducible—to the promise of technological amplification.

Anderson does not dwell on Russian and Soviet Modernism specifically. The situation there was in some ways uncharacteristic. The moment was powerfully traversed by a successful revolution and some decade and a half later largely died an "unnatural death" with the consolidation of Stalin's cultural politics. Yet, on the whole, the circumstances that provoked the set of responses we can identify as "modernist" were in place. As everywhere, such responses were of course plural, each articulating the conjuncture in a distinctive way. Bakhtin's scenarios of selfhood highlight both general trends and local peculiarities, or accentuations. One of the latter emerges to the foreground in the context of his form-historical take on intersubjectivity. What we find here is a vision of the self–other dynamics that are closely tied to the non-synchronous condition of early twentieth-century Russia, pre- and post-revolutionary alike. This condition has been diagnosed by Lev Trotsky as one of "uneven and combined development," in which very old (feudal) economic, social, and cultural forms coexisted and interacted with radically new (capitalist) ones.[23] Another local emphasis, linked more closely to the script of manifestation, involves the native tradition of progressive intelligentsia populism (Narodnichestvo), bemoaning the intellectuals' alienation from the common people and envisioning how it can be overcome. Finally, the concept of transindividualism was taken up in the wake of Simondon's coinage and Louis Althusser's rereading of

Marx through Spinoza in part as a way of thinking beyond the alternative between (bourgeois) individualism and (Stalinist) collectivism. One peculiar characteristic of Russian Modernism, as it is articulated in Bakhtin's work, consists in the fact that the urgency of finding just such an alternative is detectable already there.

Notes

1 Perry Anderson, *A Zone of Engagement* (London and New York Verso, 1992), 34.
2 Ibid., 36.
3 Ibid., 37.
4 Galin Tihanov has suggestively characterized the Bakhtinian stance as that of "decentered humanism without subjectivity." The following discussion is in part an attempt to specify the nature of this decenteredness. See Galin Tihanov, *The Birth and Death of Literary Theory: Regimes of Relevance in Russia and Beyond* (Stanford: Stanford University Press, 2019), 108.
5 For a detailed and wide-ranging discussion on intersubjectivity in Bakhtin, see Daphna Erdinast-Vulcan, *Between Philosophy and Literature: Bakhtin and the Question of the Subject* (Stanford: Stanford University Press, 2013).
6 Karl Marx and Friedrich Engels, *The German Ideology, Including Theses on Feuerbach and the Introduction to the Critique of Political Economy* (Amherst: Prometheus Books, 1998), 37.
7 For a lucid discussion of this intersubjective structure, see Michael Holquist, *Dialogism: Bakhtin and His World* (New York: Routledge, 1990), 25–9.
8 Ken Hirschkop vividly invokes the entanglement of history and phenomenology in *Author and Hero* when he writes that "the aesthetic work wants to tell us something about the style and substance of existing intersubjectivity." See Ken Hirschkop, *Mikhail Bakhtin: An Aesthetic for Democracy* (Oxford: Oxford University Press, 1999), 62.
9 See Harsha Ram, "Russia," in *The Cambridge Companion of European Modernism*, ed. Pericles Lewis (Cambridge: Cambridge University Press, 2011), 113–35.
10 Ibid. For a detailed account of Bakhtin's "Nietzscheanism," especially in relation to the Polish born–scholar Tadeusz Zieliński, see James M. Curtis, "Mikhail Bakhtin, Nietzsche and Russian Pre-Revolutionary Thought," in *Mikhail Bakhtin*, ed. Michael E. Gardiner, vol. 1 (London: Sage Publications, 2003), 228–48.
11 Vyacheslav Ivanov, *Sobranie sochinenii*, vol. 4, ed. D. V. Ivanov, O. Deshart and A. B. Shishkin (Brussels: Foyer Oriental Chrétien, 1987), 60.
12 *Vestnik teatra*, no. 26 (May 16, 1919): 4. Cited in Robert Bird, *The Russian Prospero: The Creative Universe of Viacheslav Ivanov* (Madison: University of

Wisconsin Press, 2006), 32–3. See also Ilya Kliger, "Dostoevsky and the Novel Tragedy: Genre and Modernity in Ivanov, Pumpyansky and Bakhtin," *PMLA* 126.1 (2011): 73–87.

13 *AA*, 171–2; translation slightly emended.

14 The passage is translated in David Shepherd, "A Feeling for History? Bakhtin and 'The Problem of Great Time'," *Slavonic and Eastern European Review* 84.1 (2006): 41–2. See also Ilya Kliger, "Genre Memory in Bakhtin," *Persistent Forms: Explorations in Historical Poetics*, ed. Ilya Kliger, and Boris Maslov (New York: Fordham University Press, 2016), 227–51.

15 For an account of Bakhtin's links to the Russian Populist tradition, see Craig Brandist, "Bakhtin: Marxism and Russian Populism," in *Materializing Bakhtin*, ed. Craig Brandist and Galin Tihanov (London: Macmillan, 2000), 70–93.

16 V. Mayakovsky, "To Our Young Generation," in *Selected Works in Three Volumes*, vol. 1: *1985*, 201–5; V. Mayakovsky, *Polnoe sobranie sochinenii*, vol. 8: *1958*, 14–18. Translation modified. As becomes evident soon, Bakhtin is particularly intrigued here by the poet's use of the instrumental case to highlight a kind of mixing between the human and the technological, an exchange of properties between them. Thus: "revem parovozom do khripoty" and "lechu usshcheliami svisty priglushiv."

17 All translations from this fragment are mine; "On Questions of the Theory of The Novel: On Laughter. Mayakovsky," in *Beyond the Canon: Bakhtin* (Boston, MA: Academic Studies Press, 2021).

18 Vittorio Morfino, "On Étienne Balibar's 'Philosophies of the Transindividual'," trans. Dave Mesing, *Australasian Philosophical Review* 2.1 (2018): 88.

19 Jason Read, *The Politics of Transindividuality* (Leiden and Boston: Brill, 2016), 107.

20 See, for example, Olga Goriunova, "The Force of Digital Aesthetics: On Memes, Hacking, and Individuation," *The Nordic Journal of Aesthetics* 47 (2015): 54–75; and Ondřej Procházka, "A Chronotopic Representations as an Effect of Individuation: The Case of the European Migrant Crisis," *Language in Society* 49.5 (2020): 717–43.

21 Étienne Balibar glosses Spinoza's notion of causality as follows: "'To cause' is an operation by which something modifies or modulates the way something else operates (or produces its effects). Such an operation is of course itself modified or modulated *ad infinitum*. But the infinite connection does not take the form of independent linear series, or genealogies of causes and effects […] it typically takes the form of an infinite network of singular *modi*, or existences, a dynamic unity of modulating/modulated activities." See E. Balibar, "Spinoza: From Individuality to Transindividuality," *Mededelingen vanwege het Spinozahuis*, vol. 71 (Delft: Eburon, 1997), 12.

22 Ibid., 26–7. Ann Jefferson speaks of the carnival body as "transindividual" without linking the term to the philosophical tradition. See Ann Jefferson, "Bodymatters: Self and Other in Bakhtin, Sartre and Barthes," in *Bakhtin and*

Cultural Theory, ed. Ken Hirschkop and David D. Shepherd (Manchester and New York: Manchester University Press, 2001), 201–28.

23 For an early elaboration of the concept of non-synchronicity (*Ungleichzeitigkeit*) see Ernst Bloch, *Heritage of Our Times*, trans. N. Neville and Stephen Plaice (Berkeley: University of California Press, 1990), 37–184. Lev Trotskii, *Istoriia russkoi revoliutsii*, 3 vols. (1931–33; reprint edn. Moscow: Respublika, 1997), vol. 1: 35.

6

Anticipation and Prevention

A Dialogical Approach to the Modern Unconscious

Jonathan Hall

Dialogism and "Becoming"

I start from the well-known point about Bakhtin's philosophy of language: namely that he and his Marxist co-thinker Voloshinov rejected the proto-structuralism of Saussure's view of the centrality of the underlying atemporal system (*la langue*). Consequently, they also rejected Saussure's version of the *linguistique de la parole* as merely secondary. For Bakhtin and his co-thinkers, the Saussurean order is reversed. It is the linguistics of the "utterance" (*vyskazyvanie*), i.e., language in use, that is primary. This means that exchanges, collaborations, and dialogues of various kinds are actually the creative source of the structures that come into being in the history of whatever society, or fraction of society, is being analyzed. Dialogical exchanges, which should definitely include practical collaboration, create new possibilities of meaning, so the "utterance" (or the thinking behind it) does not merely conform to the limits supposedly imposed by a pre-existing linguistic system. Structures certainly exist and they can be analyzed for different purposes, but such analyses necessarily abstract them from the social processes of exchange, collaboration, and occasional conflicts from which they have arisen, and in which they continue to exist. In their historical existence they are constantly liable to modification (and sometimes occlusion), under the pressure of the dialogical relations which have brought them into being.

As he turned toward linguistic dialogism as the basis of consciousness, Bakhtin consistently emphasized the creativity of the "utterance" and the human capacity for change or "becoming" (*stanovlenie*). This turn toward the dialogical relationship with others retained his earlier concern with the ethical choices which every individual has to make. But the dialogical turn also brought with it the linked temporal concepts of creativity and "becoming." These were borrowed from Ernst Cassirer's *Philosophy of Symbolic Forms*, but Bakhtin's and Voloshinov's originality consisted in making social dialogism itself the condition of possibility for "becoming" (Cassirer's *werden*), i.e., openness to a different future, which Cassirer himself had taken from Humboldt. The capacity for change, which is for Bakhtin and Voloshinov the necessary corollary of the dialogical process, is a constant potential even when it does not lead to major changes in consciousness and may actually be resisted. I will return to this resistance, because it is the source of the occlusion mentioned above.

Caryl Emerson, the translator of Bakhtin's *Problems of Dostoevsky's Poetics*, points out the closeness of Bakhtin's arguments on dialogical "becoming" to the theories on childhood development of his compatriot and contemporary, L. S. Vygotsky.[1] Bakhtin, Voloshinov, and Vygotsky share the view that external dialogues are the basis for internal development. For all three thinkers, individuality is not a quasi-natural autonomy subsequently subjected to socialization through the language system. On the contrary, individuality is itself the outcome of prolonged social developments of increasing differentiation and complexity. But, although Bakhtin and Voloshinov refer briefly to the dynamics of childhood speech development, they consider dialogical interaction in a broader perspective because it is the source of every human being's capacity to reflect on their previously internalized forms of understanding from a position of distanced "outsideness" (*vnenakhodimost'*). Those internalized structures are the social-historical outcome of past utterances and responses to them, but their basis in the dialogical process means that they are always provisional and open to a different future. However, given the inseparable relationship between dialogism and "becoming," especially in Bakhtin's arguments from the 1930s onwards, there is a paradox in the fact that he points to Dostoevsky as providing the most striking examples of dialogism. He is right to do so, but it is paradoxical because, as Bakhtin himself emphasizes, Dostoevsky's works are marked by an almost complete absence of "becoming." There is no significant development in terms of either characterization or plot.

I would argue (as I have in my *Reaction Formations*)[2] that this is not a mere absence of "becoming" but its negation, or in psychological terms its repression. However, the negated/repressed possibilities are nonetheless registered as a potential for change in the internal dialogism explored by Dostoevsky.

Bakhtin advances two approaches for dealing with this Dostoevskian paradox. One is formal and the other historical, but in his overall argument they supplement each other. On the formal side, Bakhtin argues that the plots in Dostoevsky's novels fulfill a purely pragmatic function. They are artfully structured so as to bring about the maximum collision and confrontation between the different viewpoints and evaluative "voices" borne by the characters, both in their inwardly dialogized self-consciousness and in their relationship to other characters. In short, emplotment in Dostoevsky's major works is not a controlling apparatus manipulated by an omniscient author to give himself the definitive "last word." On the historical side, Bakhtin makes an argument for Dostoevsky's realism, namely that the collision of "voices," both between and within Dostoevsky's heroes, accurately reflected the social reality in the Russia of his time when capitalism was developing late and with catastrophic speed. Unlike the slower development of capitalism in the West, in Russia the previously distinct and merely coexisting worldviews were brought into collision by the rapid development of capitalism. Bakhtin quotes Otto Kaus and the leading Russian Marxist Anatoly Lunacharsky (and his expressed agreement with Bakhtin) in support of this argument. Where other critics had attempted to trace developmental patterns, and even a dialectic, in Dostoevsky's works, Bakhtin argues that such developmental patterns are indeed to be found in Western novels (the *Bildungsroman*, for example) where they reflected the slower development of capitalism in the West. But Russia provided Dostoevsky with the cultural preconditions for the explosive confrontations in his novels, which Lunacharsky called the fragmentation or splintering (*rasshcheplenie*) of consciousness. Lunacharsky maintained that this fragmentation also characterized the catastrophic effects of early capitalism in Shakespeare's England, where it was the precondition for Shakespeare's immense creativity, just as it was later for Dostoevsky. (*PDP*: 35) So, despite Dostoevsky's well documented opposition to the socialism of his day, he was a creative artist who perceived the explosive contradictions concealed within the appearances of normality in his society, and in his writing he responded to them. Like the heroes of the royalist Balzac, whom he admired, Dostoevsky's principal characters embody the energy and the emergent individualist consciousness which was threatening the author's own conservative loyalty to "all that was sacred" (to borrow Marx and Engels' expression). This is what made Dostoevsky's writing truly dialogical.

Anticipation and Internal Struggle

In Bakhtin's thinking on the relationship between dialogism and "becoming," anticipation is a key term. He argues that every utterance is shaped by the anticipated responses of its addressee(s), and this makes anticipation central to his dialogical concept of consciousness itself:

> [But] from the very beginning, the utterance is constructed while taking into account *possible responsive reactions*, for whose sake, in essence, it is actually created. As we know, the role of *others* for whom the utterance is constructed is extremely great. We have already said that the role of these others, *for whom my thought becomes actual thought for the first time (and thus for my own self as well)* is not that of passive listeners, but of active participants in speech communication. From the very beginning, the speaker expects a response from them, an active responsive understanding. The entire utterance is constructed, as it were, in anticipation of encountering this response.
>
> (*SG*: 94, emphases added)

Bakhtin writes that through the anticipated response of his addressees "my thought becomes actual thought for the first time." But, since anticipation is defined by him as an orientation toward the "*possible responsive reactions*" of others, dialogism provides a space for desire and anxiety because, unlike the traditions of rhetoric as a means for controlling the addressee, it acknowledges a real difference between an anticipated response or range of "possible responses," and an actual response which may or may not occur.

In the case of external dialogues, the speaker's or writer's expectations are obviously provisional, since they are constantly open to the possibility of new unexpected rejoinders and points of departure. In short, external dialogism allows a certain temporality to come into play as an orientation toward a not yet disclosed future. But Bakhtin's argument on "inward dialogism" is more complex. It shows that since anticipation shapes not only the verbal act but also the thought even prior to its external articulation, it seeks to bridge inwardly the gap between the utterance and any possible response. That is how it constitutes a desire to elicit a response on the part of an addressee. But it may also be an anxious desire to prevent or forestall the responses which it anticipates. This inescapably uncertain nature of anticipation is not fully assessed by Bakhtin because he generally treats the dialogical relationship as though it were fully constituted by an actual two-way interaction (as do most commentators), without giving adequate consideration to the specific temporality of anticipation as a disturbing factor. Nonetheless, even in his earlier essay, "Discourse in the Novel," Bakhtin evokes the internal pressure of anticipation:

> [But] this does not exhaust the internal dialogism of the word. It encounters an alien word not only in the object itself: every word is directed towards an *answer* and cannot escape the profound influence of the answering word that it anticipates ....
>
> Forming itself in an atmosphere of the already spoken, the word is at the same time determined (*opredelyaetsya*) by that which has not yet been said but which is needed and in fact anticipated by the answering word.[3]

Bakhtin's insistence that the utterance is always an address to some other, or plural others, is the basis for his theory of the way in which those others' *possible* responses are already anticipated by the speaker (or writer) who includes them in the very formation of his thought. So the anticipated responses are his imaginary constructs, even though they are formed on the basis of his past personal encounters and/or the collective social experience which he has internalized (through the "speech genres"). This inner attitude toward a response that has not yet occurred can vary in kind and intensity. Sometimes it is relatively trivial. A speaker's or a writer's expectations may be fulfilled or not, without dire consequences. He/she may be relaxed about the response to come, or even genuinely interested in the new or unexpected response which the dialogical encounter might disclose. In the latter case, the dialogical utterance is exploratory, and even experimental. This is the openness of dialogism celebrated by many commentators. But quite frequently the speaker's or writer's desire for a particular response, or his/her anxious desire to control it, can be very intense.

In his late essay, "The Problem of Speech Genres," Bakhtin cites his own experience as writer and speaker to discuss the role of anticipation:

> When constructing my utterance, I try actively to determine [*aktivno opredelit'*] this response; on the other hand, I try to anticipate it, so this anticipated response, in turn, exerts an active influence on my utterance (I parry objections that I foresee, I make all kinds of provisos, and so forth).[4]

His "I" here is a generalized "I," because this is not primarily a confessional utterance but a theoretical citing of the personal to make the general point. Despite the fact that dialogical relations are frequently taken by commentators, and by Bakhtin himself, as the basis for his social ethics of responsibility (*otvetstvennost'*), this discussion of anticipation makes it clear why the relationship of a speaker's utterance to the anticipated responses of others is not necessarily collaborative and benign. The dialogical engagement can sometimes take the form of a struggle in which the others being addressed are not just necessary partners enabling the utterance to exist, but may be at the same time internalized antagonists to be overcome. This argument is spelled out in very striking terms in his earlier essay of the 1930s, "Discourse in the Novel." In that essay, the capacity to formulate one's own thoughts involves a struggle against others' prior possession of the "word":

> The word in language is half someone else's. It becomes "one's own" only when the speaker populates it with his own intention, his own accent, when he appropriates the word, adapting it to his own semantic and expressive intention. Prior to this moment of appropriation, the word does not exist in a neutral and impersonal language (it is not, after all, out of dictionaries that the speaker gets his words!), but rather it exists in other people's mouths in other people's contexts, serving other people's intentions: it is from there that one must take the word, and make it one's own. And not all words for just anyone submit equally easily to this appropriation, to this seizure and transformation into private property.
>
> (*DI*: 293)

The speaker's or writer's engagement in a struggle against all others' intentions in order to make the utterance his own "private property" is surprising and perhaps rather ironic. Private property, like "the word in language," is still a social form. But Bakhtin goes on to make the point that many responsive utterances produced by others remain implacably alien to the individual speaker's intentions, refusing expropriation:

> Language is not a neutral medium that passes freely and easily into the private property of the speaker's intentions; it is populated–overpopulated– with the intentions of others. Expropriating it, forcing it to submit to one's own intentions and accents, is a difficult and complicated process.
>
> (*DI*: 293)

This argument by no means confirms the mutual cooperation required by Bakhtin's ethical values. Property and expropriation are metaphors for the internalized power struggle which he is describing here. Language remains "overpopulated ... with the intentions of others" (i.e., it is multi-voiced or, in Bakhtin's terms, "polyphonic"). The speaker (or writer) is indeed indebted to the prior utterances of others, but to speak or even to think in his "own" voice he is engaged in a competitive struggle to subordinate them to his own intentions. The internalization of this social struggle is a key point, since it makes individual subjectivity an arena of historical struggle. It is remarkable that Bakhtin locates his own embattled anticipation as a writer and thinker in the context of the struggle for uniqueness and dominance which he criticizes and generalizes as specific to "capitalist" culture.

The Threshold

In his "Notes towards a Reworking of the Dostoevsky book" (1961),[5] Bakhtin returns to the question of Dostoevsky's relationship to the catastrophic emergence of capitalism in Russia, which he had discussed in the earlier work. He now links it to his concept of the "threshold" but he begins by reaffirming his view that Dostoevsky's dialogism testifies to "the impossibility of the existence of a single consciousness." That is because consciousness is a process which "takes place on the *boundary* between one's own and someone else's consciousness, on the *threshold*" [original emphases]. Bakhtin continues:

> Thus does Dostoevsky confront all decadent and idealistic (individualistic) culture, the culture of essential and inescapable solitude. He asserts the impossibility of solitude. The very being of man (both external and internal) is the *deepest communion. To be* means *to communicate* .... To be means to be for another, and through the other, for oneself. A person has no internal sovereign territory, he is wholly and always on the boundary; looking inside himself, he looks *into the eyes of another* or *with the eyes of another.*
>
> (*PDP*: 287)

Although Bakhtin writes that a "single consciousness" is an "impossibility," he also argues that it is in effect a really existing impossibility, produced by "the culture of essential and inescapable solitude" which he identifies specifically as the culture of capitalism: "Capitalism created the conditions for a special type of inescapably solitary consciousness. Dostoevsky exposes all the falsity (*lozhnost'*) of this consciousness as it moves in its vicious circle" (*PDP*: 288). Bakhtin refers to the "impossibility of solitude," but I have called it above a "really existing impossibility." By this paradox I mean that the solipsist aspiration is real, in the sense of having an effective social and historical existence, but its goal is unachievable. The deceptive lure of complete mastery is a lie (Bakhtin's *lozhnost'*) which leads ineluctably to the failure to achieve it. Dostoevsky's confrontation with this lying culture, which fosters the solipsist desire for autonomous mastery as though it were an achievable goal, consists in his exploration of its baleful effects. This is not a matter of a merely utopian exposition of the ethical superiority of the dialogical mutuality which capitalist culture negates (in Dostoevsky's case, that would mean a Christian apologia for such an alternative), but of uncovering the fundamental connection between its external competitive aggression and its inward self-destructive drives. The compulsion to dominate all others who appear as potential competitors on the external scene, is matched by the drive to silence their claims for dominant superiority on the internal one. This is where the dialogical novelist surpasses the polemical journalist.

Voloshinov's Non-Freudian Version of Repression

Like Bakhtin, Voloshinov understands the dominant "official ideology" as a would-be monological discourse struggling for control within the field of dialogical signs which are the actual basis of all consciousness. He identifies the ideological struggle in question as one between opposing "social value judgements." But the dialogical nature of this struggle means that its monological goal is never a fully achieved state, even when it may appear to be. Although it seeks a final state of assured dominance, no ideology can actually eliminate the underlying dialogism out of which it has arisen, and which continues to be its historical condition of possibility. This dialogical understanding of linguistic dominance, which is close to Gramsci's dialectical "hegemony," raises key issues.[6] Voloshinov defines the "ideological sign" as the scene of a struggle for unity, for class dominance, and for ahistorical universal validity. He theorizes this "striving" for dominance in terms of the specifically Marxist dialectic of the class struggle. Under the conditions of historical struggle, the "vital and mutable" dialogical sign reveals its other aspect as a "refracting and distorting medium":

> The very same thing that makes the ideological sign vital and mutable is also, however, that which makes it a refracting and distorting medium. The ruling class strives to impart a supraclass, eternal character to the ideological sign, to extinguish [*pogasit'*] or drive inwards [*zagnat' vnutr*] the struggle between social value judgements which occurs within it, to make the sign uniaccentual.[7]

This inwardness of the oppositional discourses, whose extinction Voloshinov theorizes here as the discursive aim of ruling class ideology in pursuit of its own "uniaccentuality" (monologism), is not the same as his and Bakhtin's usual concept of the inwardness of the sign. In general, their concept of this silent "inwardness" means that it is continuous with the sign's external existence. As Voloshinov observes: "Every sign *as* sign is social, and this is no less true for the inner sign than for the outer sign" (Voloshinov 1973: 34). This continuity across the difference between inner and outer speech is grounded in the dialogical nature of the sign, and it provides the link between individual consciousness and social communication. In short, it is simply the given nature of the sign as such in Bakhtin's and Voloshinov's dialogical theory of consciousness. But that is precisely why "to extinguish" [*pogasit'*] an oppositional discourse, or "to drive it inwards" [*zagnat' vnutr*] in the sense of imposing a silence, would not be a simple denial of external expression. It would amount to driving it completely from consciousness. And, since such a monological state of consciousness is impossible (consciousness being, for Bakhtin and Voloshinov, dependent on dialogical engagements), it is identified as a desired goal, not as an achieved result. One does not have to be an orthodox Freudian to observe that any discourse which is driven inwards in this second sense, is "repressed" or prevented from direct expression, but is not actually obliterated.[8] It continues to exist within the imposed redirection, which Voloshinov identifies as refraction and distortion. Consequently, at moments of personal or social crisis, it can return within and against the very consciousness that seeks to negate it.

For Freud, the "return of the repressed" always takes place in the form of "displacement" (or its alternative: "condensation"), since otherwise it would not be able to elude the repressive vigilance of the internal censorship. He discusses these strategies as the means whereby the repressed contents of the unconscious achieve a limited and distorted measure of expression. They assume the guise of metaphors and/or metonymic substitutions in order to evade the ever-vigilant internal censor (the *superego*). In Freud's theory, the active initiative is entirely on the side of the repressed contents. They achieve their limited measure of expression by recourse to a whole series of metaphorical or metonymic disguises, which it is the task of the analyst to decipher in order to reconstruct the patient's repressed unconscious desire. But if Freudian thinking on "displacement" and "condensation" is reconsidered as the outcome of an inward dialogical encounter in which a discourse struggles to impose its dominance or to maintain it, these rhetorical strategies actually assume a double guise. The corollary to Freud's thesis, which would be necessary from the point of view of dialogical analysis, is that "displacement" and "condensation" are really effects produced by the dominant discourse itself in its struggle for unchallengeable control.

Here Voloshinov's view of ideology as ongoing embattled *addressivity*, seeking (but never fully achieving) absolute dominance, comes into its own. It means that the rhetorical strategies outlined by Freud should be considered as negotiations between the monological drive toward dominance on the one hand, and the aspirations constrained by it into postures of concealed resistance on the other. The repressive discourse can only remain dominant on condition that it negotiates ("dialogically" one has to say) with the challenge "from below," that is to say, from those opposing others which it struggles to designate as "lower" since they cannot be entirely erased. This is significant because Voloshinov's conception of the ideological sign as a "refracting and distorting medium," whose "vital mutability" permits expression to opposing discourses but only through the deviations which he identifies as refraction and distortion, is not as far as it might appear from the Freudian or Lacanian concept of "displacement" through metaphor or metonymic substitution. But in Voloshinov's formulation, as the dominant discourse struggles to become truly monological it actively produces the unconscious, because the unconscious is that range of opposing aspirations or desires which cannot be completely erased, and are therefore subjected to the refractions of preventive repression. The *Oxford English Dictionary* definition of "prevention" is helpful here. Its primary meaning is "anticipation," but its more familiar secondary meaning introduces the key paradox: prevention is that form of anticipation which tries to ensure that the anticipated event does not occur, as in "preventive medicine," or indeed any other preventive measures. These anticipatory measures include the law, which exists in order to prevent an event by forbidding it. Of course, when these discursive acts of preventive anticipation are (or at least, seem to be) purely external, they are easily understood because they operate openly in an acknowledged intersubjective social space. But internalized (intra-subjective) prevention is inescapably paradoxical. In that internal space, the anticipated "event" (Bakhtin's dialogical *sobytie*[9]) is prevented from emerging into full consciousness. That does not mean that the inner dialogical event is totally erased. It persists, but only as a potential which is anticipated and therefore anxiously prevented (or "foreclosed"), at least insofar as the subject remains subordinate to the dominant discourse.

So, despite his aversion to the Freudian connotations of the term, Voloshinov outlines a theory of the unconscious. In his argument it emerges as the outcome of an internalized social struggle. But, even more significantly, his theorization of refraction and distortion is directly linked to the struggle against the threat of change by the dominant, or "hegemonic," discourse. Freud himself famously stated that the unconscious "knows no time" but, seen from a dialogical standpoint, the unconscious is actually brought into being by the drive to negate the very possibility of change. Unsurprisingly, therefore, it does not know what it refuses to know. And yet, there is a real internal struggle because, although the possibility of change may be feared, it can also be desired with almost equal intensity by the inwardly fissured modern subject. To use Bakhtin's terminology, this is a struggle which always takes place on a "threshold."

The Threshold of Consciousness: Dostoevsky as Early Modernist?

Caryl Emerson notes that Bakhtin specifically rules out a Hegelian schema of progression, calling it a monological mode of understanding (*PDP*: xxxii). This observation is undeniably correct. For example, Bakhtin writes that "the unified, dialectically evolving spirit, understood in Hegelian terms, can give rise to nothing but a philosophical monologue" (*PDP*: 26). But Bakhtin also notes that there is blindness as well as insight in "Dostoevsky's visualizing power," because it remained "locked in place at the moment that diversity revealed itself":

> Dostoevsky's extraordinary capacity for seeing everything in coexistence and interaction is his greatest strength, *but his greatest weakness as well* [my emphasis—JH]. It made him deaf and dumb to a great many essential things; many aspects of reality could not enter his artistic field of vision. But on the other hand this capacity sharpened, and to an extreme degree, his perception in the cross-section of a given moment, and permitted him to see many and varied things where others saw one and the same thing. Where others saw a single thought, he was able to find and feel out two thoughts, a bifurcation; where others saw a single quality, he discovered in it the presence of a second and contradictory quality. Everything that seemed simple became, in his world, complex and multistructured. In every voice he could hear two contending voices, in every expression a crack, and the readiness to go over immediately to another contradictory expression; in every gesture he detected confidence and lack of confidence simultaneously; he perceived the profound ambiguity, even multiple ambiguity, of every phenomenon. But none of these contradictions and bifurcations ever became dialectical, they were never set in motion along a temporal path or in an evolving sequence.
>
> (*PDP*: 30)

When Bakhtin praises Dostoevsky's ability to see the "complex and multistructured" reality concealed within apparent unity, and to detect the "profound ambiguity, even multiple ambiguity, of every phenomenon," his insight into Dostoevsky's novelistic discourse is truly illuminating. But what is excluded from this acute "field of vision" is precisely the temporality of "becoming." Bakhtin notes that this absent process finds expression only as a fissure or "crack," with no temporal outcome or resolution. There is only the possibility of sudden reversal ("the readiness to go over immediately to another contradictory expression") or the coexistence of contradictory attitudes within his heroes' split subjectivity, whose every gesture displays "confidence and lack of confidence simultaneously." This is a frozen temporality of unresolved crisis, in which the narrative time of movement toward resolution, whether dialectical or evolutionary, is precluded.

In his late essay "Forms of Time and Chronotope in the Novel" (1937–38), Bakhtin discusses "the chronotope of the threshold" in similar terms: "it can be combined with the motif of the encounter, but its most fundamental instance is as the chronotope of *crisis* and *break* in life." A crisis is the moment of "the decision that changes a life (or the indecisiveness that fails to change a life, the fear to step over the threshold)" (*DI*: 248). In Dostoevsky's novels, this threshold in time, when the dialogical "encounter" engenders either change or the recoil from change, corresponds to a threshold in physical space. But Bakhtin's key point is the compression of time into a single moment:

> In Dostoevsky, for example, the threshold and related chronotopes—those of the staircase, the front hall and corridor, as well as the chronotopes of the street and the square ... are the main places of action in his works, places where crisis events occur, the falls, resurrections, renewals, epiphanies, decisions, that determine the whole life of a man. In this chronotope, *time is essentially instantaneous* [emphasis added]; it is as if it has no duration and falls out of the normal course of biographical time.
> (*DI*: 248)

Bakhtin does not discuss the most complex example of the Dostoevskian "chronotope of crisis time," which is to be found in *The Idiot*. This occupies several pages before the nearly fatal encounter between Prince Myshkin and Rogozhin in the darkened stairwell, which precipitates the momentary epileptic annihilation of the prince's consciousness (the "little death" forestalls a real one). In Dostoevsky's narration, this obliteration is itself anticipated by the prince's inner sense of the approaching crisis. During the interim he recalls his earlier meditations on the prior insight provided by the epileptic "aura" immediately before such moments. The subsequent obliteration is a moment of unspeakable horror but, even so, the prior moment of timeless insight outweighs it:

> What indeed was he to make of this reality? For that very thing had happened. He *had* had time to say to himself at that particular second that, for the infinite happiness he had felt in it, it might well be worth the whole of his life. "At that moment," he once told Rogozhin in Moscow during their meetings there, "at that moment the extraordinary saying that *there shall be time no longer* becomes, somehow, comprehensible to me. I suppose," he added, smiling, "this is the very second in which there was not time enough for the water from the pitcher of the epileptic Mahomet to spill, while he had plenty of time in that very second to behold all the dwellings of Allah."[10]

In his reflections on these moments, Prince Myshkin debates inwardly whether they might be mere symptoms of his disease, but he counters this inner voice by affirming that even if they are morbid symptoms, they yield precious insights. So, he clings to his symptoms, despite his horror. This undoubtedly draws on Dostoevsky's reflections on his own experiences, which many critics have noted. In *The Idiot*, the epileptic moment is also apocalyptic, as the hero's quotation from the Book of Revelations above makes explicit. The moment itself is unbearably destructive but it is inseparable from the joyful glimpse of the universal harmony beyond time.

This is not just a personal reflection, or the persistence of an outmoded metaphysics of timeless truth beneath the transient illusions of worldly experience, but a literary precedent of a major preoccupation in Modernist literature. It anticipates the "epiphanies" celebrated and explored in a great number of Modernist works, when the "doors of perception" (Aldous Huxley) open and allow the subject to escape mentally from the limitations of historical time, or at least from that triumphant monological linear narrative which defines the present as a continuation of the past (and which therefore determines the future too). In many Modernist works, the moments of highest insight are not disastrous breakdowns but positive breaks from the disaster of modern normality. They are not so much breakdowns as breakthroughs. They produce insights into the interconnections between phenomena concealed within the routinized experiences of everyday normality. Like Baudelaire's "Correspondances," or Rimbaud's "*dérèglement de tous les sens*," they make the writer a seer (Rimbaud's *voyant*) into a reality normally concealed by the clichés of daily existence and its repressive succession of non-signifying events. But in Modernist works such liberating insights are not reserved for the Romantic "seer" or religious/mystical prophet alone. These moments of "epiphany" (Joyce et al.) are discoverable within the prosaic mundanity of everyday discourse, which normally conceals them. They may be disruptive (or even traumatic as in Dostoevsky's case), but they are moments when empty meaningless time is suspended in favor of heightened awareness. For Virginia Woolf, for example, they are moments of "shock" (and perhaps of remembered trauma too) which make it possible for her to penetrate the deadening and repressive "cotton wool" of daily existence. In many other writers too, they are the source of artistic creativity because creation is not an invention *ex nihilo* but a discovery or revelation of alternative suppressed/repressed possibilities. These alternatives have to be uncovered (dialogically) through reworking the inherited "language of the tribe," but not necessarily to "purify" it (T. S. Eliot), because that might well mean repressing its potential for a different future. Perhaps this uncovering could even be described as a glimpse of the normally unreachable "totality" theorized by Lukács. If so, when Henry Ford famously dismissed history as just "one damn thing after another," his empty succession should be understood by us as an ideological effect of late capitalism. Not only does the ideology of modern capitalism dismiss the revolutionary creativity of its own bourgeois past (and perhaps also the potential guilt over its continuing brutality), but above all it denies the possibility that the social and intellectual order which has emerged from that past could have been different; or, to put this in the more radical terms which Walter Benjamin might recognize, the past, which appears to have seamlessly become the present, actually still preserves the buried potential for surpassing and overturning what *is*. Although many Modernist writers are politically reactionary, Modernist "epiphanies" bring out the inherited potential for a different future, which the everyday ideology of fully developed (globally established) capitalism struggles to make unthinkable, mostly with remarkable success. That successful self-perpetuation is the catastrophe of modern capitalism. Its repressed potential for "becoming" is explored by literary Modernism, but in general it only becomes available to conscious thought at moments of impending ideological breakdown.

Notes

1. Caryl Emerson, "The Outer Word and Inner Speech: Bakhtin, Vygotsky, and the Interpretation of Language," *Critical Inquiry* 10.2 (1983): 245–63.
2. Jonathan Hall, *Reaction Formations: Dialogism, Ideology, and Capitalist Culture–The Creation of the Modern Unconscious* (Boston: Brill, 2019 / Haymarket, 2020).
3. M. M. Bakhtin, "Discourse in the Novel," in *DI*, 259–422 (280). The English "determined" is perhaps too strong. *Opredelit'* means "to determine" or "to define," but in the reflexive form, the emphasis on causality is less pronounced. The *Oxford Russian–English Dictionary* gives its range of meanings: "To be formed; to take shape; to be determined."
4. *SG*, 95. I have departed from McGee's translation of the original *ya starayus' ego predvoskhitit'* ("I try to anticipate it," i.e., the other's response) which he renders as: "I try to act in accordance with the response I anticipate."
5. Appendix II in *PDP*, 283–302.
6. See Peter Ives, *Gramsci's Politics of Language* (Toronto: University of Toronto Press, 2004); Michael E. Gardiner, *The Dialogics of Critique* (London: Routledge, 1992). Both provide illuminating discussions of the political dimensions of Bakhtin's and Voloshinov's thought on language and consciousness. But the potential in Bakhtinian thought for a reconsideration of the unconscious as historically produced is not addressed.
7. V. Voloshinov, *Marxism and the Philosophy of Language* (New York: Seminar Press, 1973), 23.

8   Freud's metaphor of the unconscious as a conquered city comes close to this perspective. The city of repressed or pacified discourses causes disturbances and can even rebel.
9   In a translator's footnote to Bakhtin's *Problems of Dostoevsky's Poetics*, Caryl Emerson notes: "*Sobytie* (event) and its adjective *sobytiinyi* (full of event potential) are crucial terms in Bakhtin. At their root lies the Russian word for 'existence' or 'being' (*bytie*), and ... *so-bytie* can be read in both its ordinary meaning of 'event', and in a more literal meaning as 'co-existing, co-being, shared existence or being *with* another'," *PDP*, 281, footnote 6.
10 Fyodor Dostoevsky, *The Idiot* (Harmondsworth: Penguin, 1963), 259.

7

Bakhtin, Habermas, and the "Revenge of the Real"

Michael E. Gardiner

An important component of Bakhtin studies over the last forty-odd years has been the scholarly engagement of the Russian thinker's ideas with a variety of interlocutors. This includes contemporaries that directly influenced his thinking (Scheler, the Russian Formalists), or, despite having ideas that paralleled his own in many respects, seemingly did not (Buber, Vygotsky). But this approach has also involved a wide swath of more recent figures from, well, Adorno to Žižek. As regards the latter development, however, the oeuvre most often compared with Bakhtin is likely that of the German critical theorist Jürgen Habermas. There are good reasons for this. For instance, both individuals believe that ethical commitment is intrinsic to scholarly inquiry; that the dialogical qualities of language-use are central to the formation of societies and cultures, and indeed of human selfhood; and, relatedly, that ideologically and materially ingrained asymmetries of power have to be understood and confronted with respect to the intersubjective constitution of communities themselves. Such thematic and normative dovetailings have, at the same time, been subject to widely diverse interpretations. Some commentators have claimed stark differences between these two figures. As an example, Habermas' preference for a singular public sphere,[1] in which debate is governed by transparent, universalistic principles ideally leading to the affirmation of validity claims and rational consensus,[2] is opposed to Bakhtin's preference for underscoring the heterodox nature of diverse social domains and proliferating "speech genres." Because dialogue in the multifaceted societies of modern times skews toward the agonistic and dissensual, which cannot be "suspended" in the disembodied and essentially cognitivist moment of Habermasian "ideal speech," it is held that Bakhtin's carnal and carnivalesque subversions of officialdom provide a sociocultural imaginarium more compelling than Habermas' decorporealized and presumptively staider, more sober reflections.[3] Others, notably Ken Hirschkop[4] argue that Bakhtin's stress on the "expressivity" of discourse as shaped historically by the novelistic genre itself can usefully supplement Habermas' approach by foregrounding style (or formal complexity) as well as ethical substance vis-à-vis interactions in the public sphere. Conversely, Greg Nielsen[5] forges a different path, suggesting that if there is too much abstract "system" and overly rigid conceptual boundary maintenance in Habermas, Bakhtin's thought is too "loose," anarchic, and protean to grasp the liniments of modern societies in more recognizably sociological terms, requiring us to situate normative critical theory in a conceptual space somewhere "between" Bakhtin and Habermas.

Many of the contrasts drawn between Bakhtin and Habermas turn on their respective positions in terms of the promises and pitfalls of modernity itself. Here, it is worth following French sociologist and philosopher Henri Lefebvre's[6] stricture that, whereas "modernism" can be understood as a somewhat general historical periodization separating past from present, as manifested in various ideas and cultural forms, "modernity" represents a more reflexively critical (and self-critical) stance aiming to construct a viable knowledge of our own times. Habermas, as is well-known, positions himself as the lonely proponent of a "redeemed" modernity, although this must always be interpreted as an "incomplete project" because its emancipatory promise as to the full instantiation of reason, at both the individual and societal levels, is always threatened by untrammeled market forces or the technocratic misuse of legal-bureaucratic power. Regardless, for Habermas[7] science and technology have a significant role to play in developing and sustaining a highly developed civilization. Although he is critical of "scientism," broadly understood, scientific and technological imperatives are not intrinsically oriented toward the domination of society and nature, as the original generation of critical theorists generally assumed. For his part, Bakhtin regards modernity as a complex and contradictory era, combining an awareness of its deleterious effects, such as reification and alienation, with an appreciation of its nascent potential to further the cause of human freedom. For instance, he continually underscores the liberatory and egalitarian character of modern vernacular speech and social relations; celebrates the demise of monolithic mythological and religious systems and the emergence of an authentic social heteroglossia; and praises the modern subject's ability to grasp "real historical time," and, resultantly, the efflorescence of "human discernment[,] mature objectivity and the critical faculty" (*DI*: 40). In Bakhtin's view, however, modernity's antimonies are more pervasive and deeply rooted than Habermas might allow, and cannot be easily pacified or contained. This is reflected in Bakhtin's tendency to see rationalism, in its modern European guise, as a "purified" form of specular perception and abstract thought effectively purged of affective or embodied qualities, which must be countered, not by a hyper-aestheticized Romanticism premised exclusively on intuition or feeling, the route more straightforward anti-Modernists have often taken, but a practical and ethical attunement with respect to the time-space situatedness of Being itself (understood as embodied, architectonic "event") in relation to similarly located, flesh-and-blood others. This helps to explain why numerous interpreters of Bakhtin have regarded him as a "postmodern" thinker, or perhaps as straddling some hypothetical line between modernity and postmodernity.[8]

By any standard, the engagement of Bakhtin with Habermas (or vice-versa) has generated many rich and fruitful discussions, serving to clarify the unique contours of each thinker's worldview, as well as indicate further lines of possible investigation or even potential rapprochements or syntheses. And yet, for whatever reason, this particular mode of inquiry seems to have run its course, as the number of publications comparing the two reached its high-water mark around the mid-2000s. An invitation to participate in the present volume provides us with an opportunity to reflect once more upon Bakhtin and Habermas' respective thoughts as to the wisdom or value of "redeeming" modernity, and the manifold implications that flow from this, but from the luxury (if that's the right word) of our contemporaneous vantage point. To state the obvious, much has happened since the bulk of the literature referred to above emerged—the financial collapse of 2007–8 and subsequent consolidation of "austerity regimes" worldwide; accelerating climate breakdown due to an ever more ruthless "extractivist" mode of capital accumulation; political polarization and the ascendance of the far right, in lockstep with what Pierre Dardot and Christian Laval[9] refer to as the "hyper-authoritarian" phase of neoliberalism; and a global pandemic (directly connected, it must be said, to the climate issue and the attendant loss of wilderness and biodiversity) that, at the time of writing, has only been fitfully curtailed, with the world's poor and marginalized populations (sadly but predictably) bearing the brunt of catastrophic health and economic effects. This is not to imply that Habermas' vision of modernity is now largely redundant, or that reading Bakhtin ceases to provide valuable insights into, for example, the nature of embodiment, ethics, or dialogue. But it might mean that what Benjamin Bratton[10] calls the "revenge of the real"—colossal, essentially material forces such as Covid-19, global warming, or the uses and abuses of our planetary-level technosocial infrastructure—are irreducible to questions of ideological conviction or ethical perspective and must be confronted effectively and managed rationally by our species as a whole. As such, the goal here is to reconsider the relevance of Bakhtin and Habermas, and their nexus, in our brave new post-Anthropocentric world. Hindsight, as the old saw goes, is twenty–twenty; nevertheless, seeing what remains of value in such positions, and what should be questioned and possibly discarded, might prove of use as we continually revise our assessment of major thinkers and how they can continue to inform thought and action in the present moment and beyond.

To being our investigation, in an influential essay Nancy Fraser[11] reminds us that all critical inquiry is effectively "bifocal," responding "simultaneously to political conditions and to intellectual developments" which, in turn, cultivates a "sense of engagement with one's opponents." Yet, it is equally self-evident that such circumstances change, and former adversaries do not appear as error-prone today as they might have appeared at earlier times (although some certainly do!). Complicating this picture is that heterodox thinkers like Bakhtin can be subject to very different interpretations across many disciplines and subfields. To focus briefly on one of these tendencies, over the course of the 1990s and 2000s a loose constellation of Left-leaning readers of Bakhtin, which might include this chapter's author, sought to challenge liberal readings downplaying the more radical implications of his thought, oddly colored by anachronistic Cold War baggage as they appeared to be. Despite many differences, there seemed to be an overarching desire among participants of this former grouping to promote a secular, materialist Bakhtin, one not wholly averse to the language of "class struggle," albeit by reference to an "open," anti-dogmatic Marxism. In retrospect, this image of Bakhtin was often tinged with a horizontalist and somewhat populist or anarchistic spontaneism, befitting an era of alter-globalization, postcolonial, and broadly anti-capitalist struggles as pursued by diverse and largely self-organized "new social movements." Bakhtin's "dialogical" brand of humanism, with its emphasis on "otherness" and carnivalesque inversions, seemed starkly at odds with the lofty and imperious masculinism of classical bourgeois liberalism, but also a discredited Marxism–Leninism, and hence more compatible with the recognition of sociocultural difference and "decentered," marginalized subjectivities.

Such a Left appraisal of Bakhtin was by no means lacking internal tensions and contradictions, and never, perhaps correctly, added up to something like ideological coherence. Although it would be foolish to deny there was, and indeed remains, considerable value in this scholarship, as suggested above our present conjuncture is a very different one. This prompts a reconsideration of Bakhtin as a boundlessly subversive, radical-populist, anti-statist figure. More specifically, Bakhtin's privileging of the immediate, the sensual, and the particular, an integral part of his belief in the axiological and ethical centrality of everyday life, does not seem entirely well suited to the profound challenges of today's "wicked problems," including pandemics, massive structural inequalities, or global warming. These phenomena would seem to make demands on our capacity not only for theoretical abstraction and cognitive distancing (*à la* Habermas) with the goal of conceptualizing universalities, and concomitantly of more sweepingly inclusive notions of social obligation and justice, but also the mass mobilization of entire populations and effective deployment of vast technical infrastructures of mitigation (or "deep adaptation") through institutionalized forms of power (that can be, it is hoped, much more democratically—and equitably—managed than has hitherto been the case). Put differently, Habermas' penchant for rational politics and a moral realism infused with universalistic and consensual aspirations acquires more allure in such circumstances.

By no means does Bakhtin wholly eschew the need for theoretical abstraction or concept-building (or the lighter touch of what he calls a "sense of theory"). Yet, for him, the ethical and epistemological dangers of theoreticism are ever present, because they are "hard-wired" into modernity itself, and must always be interpreted through the "eventness" of situated daily interactions. The purely cognitive relation to our world epitomized by modernity is reflected in the unabashedly utilitarian character of science and technology, in which any activity is justified by reference to the overriding goal of technical efficacy and control. Bakhtin's valorization of "direct experience" has, in recent decades, been echoed in a variety of disciplines and approaches, largely because it appears to constitute an antidote to the pitfalls of abstract theorizing for its own sake. There is a danger here, however, of fetishizing the putative "immediacy" of the mundane social world as some sort of guarantor of the centrality of embodied perception and experience over and against other ways of knowing and doing. For example, the appeal to immediacy tends to overlook things like the organization of sociocultural life by what Habermas[12] calls the "steering media" of money, information, and power, or myriad structural determinations of one kind or another. Arguably, beyond small-scale tribal groupings some degree of "abstraction" necessarily emerges in social life, and is best understood as a form of mediation allowing us to transcend the "physical and cognitive limits of human anatomy."[13] The belief there is some "primordial," non-abstract social reality we can somehow "return" to is, arguably, neo-Aristotelian fantasy. Abstraction is therefore not a spectral divorce from the real, but something generated by material processes themselves, insofar as the "concrete" is always shot through with the "abstract."

This brief discussion of abstraction might sensitize us to certain limitations of Bakhtin's ethics of personalism, particularly given the nature and scale of the issues that confront our species in the twenty-first century. The most well-known of these is probably the existential threat of global warming. (Perhaps surprisingly, this was not entirely unknown to Bakhtin's generation, as the now popular, if flawed term "Anthropocene"—a geological era defined by human activity, especially the effects of carbon emissions on climate—was originally coined by a Soviet climatologist in the early 1970s.) One influential attempt to think through the philosophical and ethico-political implications of this phenomenon is the work of humanities scholar Timothy Morton, especially via his notion of the "hyperobject."[14] Hyperobjects include such disparate entities as evolution, black holes, or nuclear radiation; they lack clearly delineated properties or compartments, and exist in a nebulous (but utterly "real" and irreducibly material) realm that cannot be easily fathomed directly by human observation, intelligence, or imagination. This opacity occurs because of a "transcendental gap" existing between the thing itself and any data we can accrue about it, and so the latter can only proffer tiny slivers of insight into any hyperobject's workings. Their very spatio-temporal inchoateness (for instance, the deep half-lives of uranium or plutonium) defy received ideas of what "things" themselves are, which of course has been the preoccupation of metaphysics, natural philosophy, and science for millennia. Focusing specifically on the climate issue, Morton argues that because there is no longer any "base" horizon on which human thoughts, perceptions, and actions can be reliably premised, the world we have come to know and inhabit over the course of the Holocene has become radically dematerialized, and is effectively "dead."

This has myriad implications for a Bakhtinian worldview. For one thing, hyperobjects certainly make their effects palpable at the level of the everyday (new invasive species appear virtually every year to devastate local flora and fauna; formerly rare occurrences like atmospheric haze from impossibly distant forest fires are now commonplace), but direct perceptual experience can no longer give us any fundamental purchase on the nature and tendencies of the hyperobject *qua* hyperobject. The latter simply cannot be comprehended by our usual analogies, perceptions, and metrics, and seems to transcend the very sphere of tangible everydayness altogether. "Climate" here can only be grasped, partially and indirectly, as a "real abstraction" inferred statistically through vast amounts of data collated from globally dispersed remote sensing devices or Antarctic ice core samples, pieced together and subject to interpretation by thousands of climate scientists. If we can no longer talk about the banalities of "weather" in a trivial, everyday sense, it is because weather itself has been wholly absorbed into largely ineffable climate systems that are becoming increasingly unstuck by the day, and hence such talk acquires a portentous, uncanny quality. It is also far from clear what ethical "answerability," for Bakhtin manifested necessarily in the everyday lifeworld and restricted largely to self/Other encounters, now means in a world where seemingly trifling activities (the daily commute, heating our home) contributes directly, if in incalculably small, imperceptible, and complexly mediated ways, to the accumulation of higher levels of atmospheric carbon dioxide that will substantively affect the planet's climate 100,000 years from now.

To take this line of inquiry further, it has become conventional, following the likes of Caryl Emerson, Wlad Godzich, or Tzvetan Todorov, to describe Bakhtin's ontology as an exclusively "subject-subject" one.[15] "The Other," Godzich declares, "cannot possibly be an object" (10, 11). To suppose otherwise would be to subscribe to a "narrative of violence" forcibly imposing sameness on difference, which is modernity's original sin.

This ontological dualism further implies a sharp contrast between the natural and "human" sciences. Whereas the former study the world of mute "givenness," material causations and brute determinations of one kind or another, Bakhtin's exclusive concern is with speaking subjects and texts that construct and convey meaning intersubjectively, in constitutively unpredetermined or "unfinalized" ways. However, there are myriad possible objections to Bakhtin's stance here. As Thomas Nail[16] shows in *Theory of the Earth*, even outwardly mundane physical processes are not governed by rote mechanical causality, but are dynamic, non-linear, and open-ended in nature, as well as inextricably intertwined with all possible biological forms and wider cosmological forces in infinitely complex ways. Morton similarly argues we cannot draw arbitrary lines between the human and ecological/material worlds. This means we are inescapably "objects" too, biological and physical entities existing in and through (and indeed ultimately constituted by) a "pluriverse" of innumerable other objects, technical apparatuses, elemental material forces, and nonhuman entities and lifeforms. This realization prompts him to coin the term "interobjectivity" in order to supplant the blinkered and essentially idealist connotations of "intersubjectivity." Needless to say, such insights complicate our received notions of ethics, politics, causality, responsibility, what exactly it means to be "human," and much else besides.[17]

Perhaps a brief consideration of the Covid-19 pandemic might help clarify what is at stake. Bratton, author of *The Revenge of the Real: Politics for a Post-Pandemic World*, shares much of Morton's intellectual heritage, and it is not too far a stretch to characterize the former's understanding of pandemics as conforming largely to the latter's idea of the hyperobject. Covid-19 is a hyperobject because of the coronavirus' terrifyingly exponential spread and planetary reach, boundless capacity for rapid mutation, synergetic relationship with the human genome (and capitalist globalization, including the acceleration of global warming), or biochemical interaction with vaccines. This implies multiple levels of interactive complexity that the usual human sociocultural formulations, or individual perceptions and affects, cannot fathom, much less respond to effectively. The real is revengeful in this case because minute bundles of genetic material (that by some scientific definitions are not even alive) manage to "exploit" deep system failures in our existing types of social organization, modes of governance (technosocial or otherwise), economic arrangements, and so on. Since a full-blown social constructivism arrives dead on arrival here, Bratton plumps instead for an "epidemiological model of society" (hereafter *EMOS*). This allows us to move decisively away from libertarian individualism (the default form that subjecthood takes under neoliberal capitalism), bolstered as it is by a notion of untrammeled personal sovereignty or autonomy, toward an acknowledgment of the irreducibly symbiotic relationships among people, systems, nonhuman entities, and things, all sutured together into extensive and intensive networks operating in multiscalar fashion, from the quantum level to that of the farthest reaches of the cosmos itself. Here, mediation trumps immediacy, everyday particularity is only a localized, and potentially deceptive instantiation of much wider dynamic flows and processes, and ethics must be based more on a logic of cause and effect, or consequentialism, rather than relying exclusively on autonomous, subjective judgment, because the latter simply cannot navigate effectively or responsibly these murky and dangerous waters. This explains why Bratton advocates for a "positive biopolitical politics," premised on a high level of techno-scientific refinement and infrastructural robustness. In the context of the current pandemic, this allows for complex models to be constructed and applied, linking the full gamut of epidemiological, ecological, and socio-behavioral phenomena together in comprehensible and manageable form. Collective self-composition in this fashion is not about Orwellian-type thought control or punitive surveillance, but rather the effective marshaling of heuristics, statistical inference, and so forth, in the service of meeting essential human needs in an empathetic and solidaristic fashion.

Does such a Brattonian project of collective self-composition fall prey to the sort of grandiose, abstract "metanarrative" characteristic of modernity that, as has been so often suggested, Bakhtin consistently rejected? To give but one example, Peter V. Zima[18] reads Bakhtin along Lyotardian lines, suggesting the Russian philosopher espoused a "chaotic polyphony" anathema to the grand, unifying metaphysics of Hegelianism or orthodox Marxist–Leninism. Nevertheless, Bratton's "revenge of the real" implies that the irruption of material forces ultimately creates a common existential fate for not only our species but also bears on the very ecosystemic integrity of the planet itself, including the overarching thermodynamic equilibria that have allowed the Holocene to exist, and with it human civilizations themselves. Without seeking to dissolve culture into nature or vice-versa, Anthropocene (or Capitalocene, or Eurocene, or post-Holocene, or whatever we wish to call it) times demand a heightened awareness of the manifold imbrications co-constitutively linking them, which at least gesture toward a species-level set of commonalities and overlapping interests. For Canadian philosopher Todd Dufresne,[19] one of the many ironies of the present conjuncture is that it implies a time of "anthropocenity," a sort of post-post-humanism. It is by no means the case that all humans are "in it together" identically, in terms of the likely catastrophic future we face. But, in another, overarching sense we do share a common fate, as the mountain redoubts and fortified islands of Silicon Valley billionaires will not save even them in the end. Strangely, this might be said to represent the realization of Hegel's "universal history," albeit in the form of what Dufresne calls the "democracy of suffering." This is arguably about as "metanarrative" as it gets. Whether this suffering binds us together in a kind of "negative community" or not, there is a chance we can go beyond our current necropolitics so as to embrace a politics of life, of shared joy and vitality, and mutual aid, metanarratives be damned.

To return to the question of Bratton's *EMOS*, how in more detail might the relationship between the respective ideas of Bakhtin and Habermas figure here? In terms of Bakhtin, recall Emerson's position that although the Russian thinker respected scientific and technical inquiry (but allegedly "had no feeling" for nature (Emerson 2003: 298)), he maintained consistently that "object-object" relations were irrelevant to the humanities. As Bakhtin starkly put it, "we do not address inquiries to nature and she does not answer us"; hence, the human cannot be considered as facticity, as part of nature (*SG*: 114). Yet *EMOS*, or for that matter the concept of hyperobjects, show us how problematic, even anachronistic this position is. If nothing else, our time-space of unfolding climate catastrophe shows us that nature does not represent "the unchangeable conditions of physical existence,"[20] as Bakhtin maintains, simply because we are now acutely aware that cumulative human activity has altered, probably irreversibly, such conditions at the planetary level. Furthermore, the "object-oriented ontology" that inspires Morton or Bratton blurs the boundaries that, for Emerson (2003: 304), Bakhtin maintained by sharply delineating "conscious subjects" from "inanimate, inert objects"—not least because "inanimate" does not necessarily, or even typically, mean "inert," as Nail (2021) convincingly demonstrates. Again, we are objects as much as subjects, inextricably enmeshed in a wider world of dynamic materialities, scalar flows, biophysical entities: the interobjective. To see oneself as an object among other objects might seem as "reifying" or "dehumanizing" to some, and indeed Bakhtin's corpus is dedicated largely to resisting this "modern" tendency to quantify or objectify subjects. But events like the pandemic force upon us the realization that, whether we like it or not, our material body is caught up in innumerable causal relations that saturate the world, in often "granular" and undetectable ways without the techno-scientific means to sense them, collect data, identify pertinent regularities, and act on them effectively. To take a timely and relevant example, the biomedical treatment of the sick body requires a relationship of distanciation and abstraction, not one of affective intimacy. The body here cannot be conceptualized as a singularly unique entity, but rather as a "generic" one with qualities that are "readable" through clinical assessment and the ongoing refinement of "pattern recognition." This is particularly true in something like pandemic conditions, where institutions, resources, and medical staff alike are strained to the absolute limit (see Bratton 2021: 105–6). If this is what Bakhtin referred to pejoratively as an "alibi for Being," but saves lives and prevents unnecessary suffering, especially in circumstances of deep systemic crisis, so be it.

Governing successfully the positive biopolitics Bratton envisages necessitates the continual enhancement of our collective intelligence, and that of a shared "commons," which in turn requires at least minimal consensus on what is needed, what is valuable, what has to be altered, and that which can be sustained (although these can certainly change over time, given the accumulation of new evidence, constantly fluctuating conditions, and so forth). In the present situation, this means we need some measure of rational consensus around, say, accepting the efficacy and safety of vaccines and assuming the collective risk of their universal application, or for that matter the pursuit of regulatory and planning measures designed to curtail market forces and the uncontrolled carbon emissions resulting from this. Here, the ethical universalism of a Habermasian communicative action model, by explicitly connecting practical action to reason, arguably holds more promise than a Bakhtinian heteroglossia, however "dialogical" the latter might be. For whereas Habermas believes a democratically organized polis can reign in (or at least temper) the real and potential abuses of technocratic scientism, or theoreticism, Bakhtin simply lacks such a theory of politics altogether. For Ken Hirschkop (381), the means by which we can transcend particularity and discharge our broader social responsibilities should occur through the mass participation of citizens with respect to modern political institutions. In abandoning political activity as such for the terrain of philosophy, however, Bakhtin cannot conceive of any real counterweight to modernity's darker side, apart from the centrifugal spontaneism of carnivalesque energies or the cultivation of an ethical sensibility oriented toward "Otherness."

Hirschkop is correct to argue that Bakhtin himself had no coherent account of the political, but that has not prevented many from deriving a kind of proto-politics of radical, antinominal populism from his literary treatment of carnival. However, such a conception of "history from below," held to undermine a "purified," hidebound reason functioning at the behest of centralized, hierarchical power, does not resonate today in quite the same manner. As is well-known, Bakhtin traces carnival's ancient wellsprings to Greek philosophy (especially Socrates and the Cynics), as well as Menippean satire, running through the Roman Saturnalia and Medieval festivals. This prompts him to valorize "folk-festive" humor and sardonic laughter as inherently healthy and subversive, and to uphold the notion that comic inversion is not dissimulation or trickery for its own sake, but rather integral to carnival's plebeian counter-power. Yet a seemingly offhand comment from German philosopher Peter Sloterdijk's *Critique of Cynical Reason* might complicate this idea of "popular cynicism."[21] Under certain conditions, Sloterdijk suggests, the cynical cheekiness of Diogenes of Sinope and his spiritual heirs down through the ages can be appropriated by the powerful and caught up in a "dialectic of disinhibition." When this happens, formerly staid and buttoned-down elites, and their propagandists and apologists, "let go affectively," tapping into an explosive vein of faux outrage and sarcastic abuse so as to consolidate influence and power. Sloterdijk penned these observations during the ascendance of the original

"New Right" in the late 1970s and early 1980s, but it is hard not to see this moment as a harbinger of a much more widespread phenomenon today: the Right-populist mobilization of mass affective sentiments so as to systematically mock, denigrate, and generally de-legitimate the aspirations and perspectives of certain groups (the "liberal" folk-devil, immigrants and refugees, sexual minorities, racialized domestic populations, those who slavishly "submit" to such pandemic protocols as lockdowns or vaccine mandates). This culminates in the feverish socio-political divisiveness and polarization we are all too familiar with today. Key here is that what Italian thinker Franco Berardi[22] calls the "lumpen-bourgeoisie" now dominates political life in many countries. The likes of Bolsonaro, Trump, Modi, and many others expertly marshal transgressive "profanation," the blasphemic mortification of the official worldview, and the usual norms and rules that govern social life, amplified dramatically by the ubiquity of profiteering social media, so as to galvanize supporters and cement their rule. In other words, the carnivalesque can inform both bottom-up *and* top-down hegemonic power, and whether a genuinely oppositional cynicism (or "kynicism," in Sloterdijk's terms) can be rescued from the current morass is very much an open, and indeed urgent, question.

In this anxious and divisive context, a dose of Habermasian sobriety and reasoned discourse might not go completely amiss. This might help to explain Bratton's argument that effective, democratic governance necessarily involves the deployment of an "abstractive reason," a "focused, secular, technical reason beyond the horizon of any location, moment, or lifetime" (Bratton 2021: 152). Obviously, consolidating this culture of abstractive, critical rationalism would involve clashes of opinion as regards the nature and level of data collection and interpretation, how social modeling is constructed, or the specific uses to which infrastructural apparatuses are put. But it does seem that Bakhtin's preference for value dissensus and heteroglossia "all the way down," and for opacity over transparency in the exercise of communicative exchange, militates against such society-wide— or indeed planetary-level arrangements. The corollary is that spontaneous forms of localized resistance to perceived forms of social control and repression, without regard for the wider interconnections at play, do not seem entirely appropriate in the present conjuncture. Something like Hakim Bey's "Temporary Autonomous Zones,"[23] effervescent bubbles of anarchic freedom, cannot conjure up vaccines or ventilators, or for that matter networked solar panels and windfarms, on anything like the quality and scale required. Here again, Habermas' firmer commitment to connecting public with private reason, to science and technological innovation, and the pursuit of reasoned consensus through dialogue, might well stand us in better stead.

Bratton connects the ethos of sovereign libertarianism, one that has been (as mentioned) stoked by neoliberalism and social media platforms in recent decades, to what he calls "hyperinteriorized individuation." To be fair to Bakhtin, this in no way describes his position. The bourgeois idea of autonomous selfhood is that we somehow arrive fully formed in the social world as preconstituted monads, and then subsequently enter into contractual or quasi-contractual arrangements with others, with the maximization of market efficacy operative as *de facto* determining variable. Bakhtin, by contrast, is adamant that we cannot think of human thought or agency without the realization that we are always already connected to others, and indeed constituted through these relations, a process without ultimate closure or finality. This "primordial" interrelatedness, what Bakhtin refers to as the realm of "supra-existence," is prior to, and forms the basis of, any further individuation. It follows that he does not valorize subjectivism or narcissistic interiority; in fact, Bakhtin's project can be interpreted as a sustained attack on the epistemological and moral precepts of bourgeois individualism, which he roundly condemns as a "culture of essential and inescapable solitude" (*PDP*: 287). Furthermore, if language is the primary basis of human consciousness and identity, it can only be understood as a collective resource "owned" by no one, and, moreover, is not a private but an expressly *public* phenomenon. As such, our collective participation in linguistic exchanges and the joint production of meaning is undoubtedly a powerful antidote to the egocentricity and social pathologies of "hyperinteriorized individuation."

At times, Bakhtin does seem to inch toward Bratton's notion of "collective intelligence" or the Autonomists' "general intellect."[24] It is also possible to find traces of a "proto-ecological" perspective in certain of Bakhtin's writings, especially in the Rabelais book; alternatively, one could extrapolate something like a distributed ecological sensibility from his account of alterity (and several authors have done each of these things). Michael Holquist even claims that Bakhtin borrowed freely from the biological sciences in terms of thinking about societies as consisting of living subjects situated and interacting in specific time-space locales.[25] It is certainly true that Bakhtin, especially in his writings on carnival, views the human body as something inextricably enmeshed with the collective (interesting from the epidemiological point of view). There are, additionally, occasional intimations of a line of thinking in Bakhtin's corpus that parallels Morton's hyperobjects or Bratton's interobjectivity. This might also include Bakhtin's notion of "great time," which evokes the anonymous sweep of collective human endeavor with respect to the continuous creation of language and culture persisting across vast stretches of time and space, or his fragmentary musings on Goethe, especially the latter's ability to "see" geohistorical changes in landscapes over eons, thereby conceptualizing humanity and nature as dynamically interrelated. However, these are relatively isolated insights and limited in scope—for one thing, the biology or population models Bakhtin draws upon do not really go beyond purely metaphorical usage, and the idea of extending this intuition to the world of physical matter per se is never fully pursued. Bakhtin's putative "materialism" is ultimately undercut by his commitment to neo-Kantian idealism and the *Geisteswissenschaft* philosophies of Husserl or Dilthey, cleaving as he does to a subject-subject ontology and a phenomenological emphasis on everyday particularism. As such, Bakhtin's image of the "human" remains anchored in a philosophical anthropology that, however resolutely intersubjective, is, again, detached from the world of biophysical forces, imbrications, and causations, which, by maintaining the separation of nature and culture, reinscribes Cartesian dualism at another level. For Bratton (39), our participation in the biopolitical collective is necessarily "public, communicable, and intersubjective," but this crucially turns on the centrality of material bodies and "biochemical assemblages" caught up in much wider ontologies and dynamic processes. Put differently, we must go beyond a purely phenomenological account of interconnectedness, whether socially mediated or not, and grasp the essential point that the "solidarities that bind us cannot be reduced to direct experience" (Bratton 2021: 71). Bakhtin's perspective is certainly pre-eminently concerned with an ethos of "care" and solicitousness vis-à-vis the other, but by focusing on immediate and unique particularities to the exclusion of other, often more relevant considerations, is at odds with Bratton's call for "abstractive reason."

By way of a concluding remark, for his part Habermas[26] realizes that scientific abstraction has its place (in the form of techno-scientific inquiry into the natural world to meet biological human needs), and that moral reasoning requires both affective distanciation and a commitment to what Bakhtin himself, in *Towards a Philosophy of the Act*, disavows as the "universality of the ought" (*TPA*: 25). "Purposive rationality" certainly has its place here, as one cannot really envisage the functioning of a modern, complex society without it—so long as hegemonic scientism is avoided by confining utilitarian logic and practices to appropriate domains of strategic action and knowledge-constitutive interests.[27] Moreover, this doesn't necessarily imply an anthropocentric Prometheanism at odds with a more ecocentric perspective. As Robert J. Brulle argues convincingly, the pursuit of Habermasian ideal speech understood as a "regulative ideal" does not simply hold the promise of, for instance, enhancing social solidarity, imbuing deliberative exchanges with ethico-political legitimacy, or upholding valid knowledges over scientifically spurious or conspiratorial forms. Since it concerns process over normative content, Habermasian communicative action can be extended to considerations of human/nature relations, particularly since it is simply rational to claim that, for human communities to prosper, a vibrantly functioning and diverse planetary ecosystem also has to exist. "Enactment of a communicative ethics," writes Brulle, "is thus a necessary prerequisite to the creation of an ecologically sustainable society."[28] One might end here with the observation that Bakhtin's thought has, in various Leftist formulations, lent itself very well over the last several decades to what we might call a "locally" resistant anti-capitalism. But it is perhaps less well suited to the epochal task of transitioning to a viable mode of post-capitalist governance on a planetary scale. Every meaning will have its "homecoming festival," but only if we have a home to return to.

Notes

1 Jürgen Habermas, *The Structural Transformation of the Public Sphere* (Cambridge, MA: The MIT Press, 1989).
2 Jürgen Habermas, *Communication and the Evolution of Society* (London: Heinemann, 1979).
3 See Michael E. Gardiner, "Wild Publics and Grotesque Symposiums: Habermas and Bakhtin on Dialogue, Everyday Life and the Public Sphere," in *After Habermas: New Perspectives on the Public Sphere*, ed. Nick Crossley and John Michael Roberts (Oxford: Blackwell, 2004), 28–48; Gregory T. Garvey, "The Value of Opacity: A Bakhtinian Analysis of Habermas's Discourse Ethics," *Philosophy and Rhetoric* 33.4 (2000): 370–90.
4 Ken Hirschkop, "Justice and Drama: On Bakhtin as a Complement to Habermas," in *After Habermas: New Perspectives on the Public Sphere*, ed. Nick Crossley and John Michael Roberts (Oxford: Blackwell, 2004), 49–66.
5 Greg Marc Nielsen, *The Norms of Answerability: Social Theory between Bakhtin and Habermas* (Albany: State University of New York Press, 2002).
6 Henri Lefebvre, *Introduction to Modernity* (London: Verso, 1995), 1–2.
7 Jürgen Habermas, *Toward a Rational Society: Student Protest, Science, and Politics* (London: Heinemann, 1971).
8 Clemens Friedrich, "Philosophical Modernity and Postmodernity in Russia? M. M. Bakhtin's Polyphony of Voices in the Dialogue," *The European Legacy* 22 (1997): 356–62.
9 Pierre Dardot and Christian Laval, *Never-Ending Nightmare: The Neoliberal Assault on Democracy* (London: Verso, 2019).
10 Benjamin Bratton, *The Revenge of the Real: Politics for a Post-Pandemic World* (London and New York: Verso, 2021).
11 Nancy Fraser, *Unruly Practices: Power, Discourse and Gender in Contemporary Social Theory* (Minneapolis: University of Minnesota Press, 1989), 2, 3.
12 Jürgen Habermas, *The Theory of Communicative Action*, vol. 2: *A Critique of Functionalist Reason* (Boston: Beacon Press, 1987).
13 Alex Williams, "The Politics of Abstraction," in *Speculative Aesthetics*, ed. Robin Mackay et al. (Falmouth: Urbanomic, 2014), 62–71 (68).

14 Timothy Morton, *Hyperobjects: Philosophy and Ecology after the End of the World* (Minneapolis: University of Minnesota Press, 2013).
15 Caryl Emerson, "Bakhtin at 100: Art, Ethics, and the Architectonic Self," in *Mikhail Bakhtin*, vol. 2, ed. Michael E. Gardiner (London: Sage, 2003), 296–314; Wlad Godzich, "Correcting Kant: Bakhtin and Intercultural Interactions," in *Mikhail Bakhtin*, vol. 2, ed. Michael E. Gardiner (London: Sage, 2003), 3–13; Tvetzan Todorov, "Epistemology of the Human Sciences," in *Mikhail Bakhtin*, vol. 2, ed. Michael E. Gardiner (London: Sage, 2003), 279–95.
16 Thomas Nail, *Theory of the Earth* (Stanford: Stanford University Press, 2021).
17 See Bruno Latour, *Reassembling the Social: An Introduction to Actor-Network-Theory* (Oxford: Oxford University Press, 2005), 25.
18 Peter V. Zima, "Bakhtin's Young Hegelian Aesthetics," in *Mikhail Bakhtin*, vol. 2, ed. Michael E. Gardiner (London: Sage, 2003), 14–28 (17).
19 Todd Dufresne, *The Democracy of Suffering: Life on the Edge of Catastrophe, Philosophy in the Anthropocene* (Montreal: McGill-Queen's University Press, 2019).
20 Barry Sandywell, "Memories of Nature in Bakhtin and Benjamin," in *Mikhail Bakhtin*, vol. 4, ed. Michael E. Gardiner (London: Sage, 2003), 3–24 (21).
21 Peter Sloterdijk, *Critique of Cynical Reason* (London: Verso, 1988), 103.
22 Franco Berardi, *Félix Guattari: Thought, Friendship, and Visionary Cartography* (London: Palgrave Macmillan, 2008), 26.
23 Hakim Bey, *TAZ: The Temporary Autonomous Zone, Ontological Anarchy, Poetic Terrorism* (New York: Autonomedia, 1991).
24 Michael E. Gardiner, "Bakhtin and the 'General Intellect'," *Educational Philosophy and Theory* 49.9 (2017): 893–908.
25 Michael Holquist, "Dialogism and Aesthetics," in *Mikhail Bakhtin*, vol. 1, ed. Michael E. Gardiner (London: Sage, 2003), 367–85 (381).
26 Jürgen Habermas, *Moral Consciousness and Communicative Action* (Cambridge, MA: The MIT Press, 1990), 180.
27 Jürgen Habermas, J., *Knowledge and Human Interests*, 2nd edn. (London: Heinemann, 1978).
28 Robert J. Brulle, *Agency, Democracy, and Nature: The U.S. Environmental Movement from a Critical Theory Perspective* (Cambridge, MA: The MIT Press, 2000), 47.

8

Decolonizing Aesthetics

Bakhtin, Modernism, and Anti-Colonial Poetics

Peter Hitchcock

It is about the other that all the stories have been written.[1]

One central aim of postcolonial and decolonial critique has been to demystify and deconstruct the colonial logic of modernity. While this is primarily a socio-political project, within this genealogy much attention has been focused on aesthetics and the ways in which modernity is expressed; unsurprisingly, such analysis has offered an encounter with Modernism in that regard. The sometimes less than ambivalent contours of the engagement in part reflects the difficulty of adjudicating the disjunctions between modernity and Modernism (which modernity, which Modernism or are they ever only singular in themselves and in conjunction?), even though in conventional cultural history the normative logics of the former appear decisively challenged by the aesthetic exceptions and experimentations of the latter. Indeed, the depth of Modernism's own counter-critique, particularly beyond its European representation, at once necessitates sensitivity to the claims of decolonial defamiliarization concerning modernity. The resistance of Modernism, however acute, is not necessarily a break with modernity's project; thus, any decolonial delinking must account for extensions of modernity even within the energetic aesthetics of postcolonial Modernism, seen for instance in the peripheral surrealism of the Caribbean and Africa and also in elements of the realist poetics of anti-colonialism. Concepts of antinomy and contradiction (especially around race, gender, and class) throw significant light on the discourses in play and the radical gainsay in addressing them. Here, rather than describe what is a burgeoning field of inquiry (already long beyond "Au bout du petit matin," to borrow from Césaire),[2] I wish to address briefly how Bakhtin's own peripheral poetics, both to Modernism and modernity, might aid in a more agonistic understanding of decolonial aesthetics. If Bakhtin's relationship to Modernism often depends on what is not said (a silence overdetermined by the specific norms of his political context) Modernism's place for decoloniality is insistently symptomatic. By placing Bakhtin at the intersection of Modernism and postcolonialism we might critically figure the theoretical provocations of all three. Perhaps in the dialectic of their concrete hesitancy one could yet propose an aesthetic logic for how decolonial discourse proceeds? And in that articulation, with a Janus-faced nature in Bakhtinian conceptualization (here between Modernism and postcolonialism) we could also extend and deepen resonant approaches to modernity as such.

The contours of postcolonial studies have changed dramatically in recent years. At the beginning of the twentieth century, for example, Neil Lazarus[3] underlined that, when it came to the postcolonial literary, aesthetics still seemed confined to a canon of one, Salman Rushdie, and such theory, when it addressed postcolonial literature at all, tended to fit a heavily vetted list of possibilities to a pre-formed and oft-repeated set of prescriptions around themes of anti-nationalism, anti-Eurocentrism, suspect History, and a studied or conventional "cosmopolitanism" that Timothy Brennan had identified and skewered in the late 1990s.[4] Furthermore, such interventions often suspended engagement with the material conditions of postcolonial writing and reduced literary expression itself to a practice of detached discursivity. For his part, Lazarus rightly bemoans that too much postcolonial critique of the time remained wedded to a limited collocation of questions overlooking a vibrant variegation of literature across the globe (especially non-Anglophone) and texts tending to be more overtly political and collective in their understanding of processes of decolonization. The reason I mention Lazarus' assessment here is not only for contrast with the present, but because he frames postcolonialism using the story of Modernism. Specifically, Lazarus refers to Raymond Williams' *The Politics of Modernism* as a lesson for postcolonial critique.[5] Williams takes the position that Modernism intervenes on the terrain of modernity by challenging aesthetic assumptions and by forgoing nostalgia through turning to bold experimentation in language and form. This is commonplace in the field but Williams' point, however, is that Modernism also became a space of selectivity subject to narrow definitions of what was properly Modernism while excluding other types of cultural expressivity as anachronistic, or, worse, derivative. He calls for a critical discrimination of Modernisms the better to understand the material components of its social formation and to head off the false universalization of what is otherwise a contested and much broader cultural genealogy. What Lazarus picks up on is the critique of canonization and institutionalization that Williams presents, which Lazarus suggests is a pertinent analogy for the limits of postcolonialism he reviewed. I will return to Williams' work on Modernism below but here would ask whether Lazarus' diagnosis of postcolonialism still obtains and, concomitantly, whether situating Bakhtin between Modernism and postcolonialism contributes to a vibrant rearticulation of all three? If, as Robert Seguin[6] suggests, Bakhtin's ideas "are always already a way of at least implicitly staging the modernist/postmodernist debate," how might one more forcefully register the disjunctions and continuities of what constitutes Modernist/postcolonialist dialogicity?

To some extent, the narrow criteria that restricts postcolonialism, according to Lazarus (taking up the spirit of Williams' approach), are bound by a will to universalism that flattens specific claims of decolonizing discourse in the cause of field consolidation (an institutional unconscious often unaddressed in the otherwise bold pronouncements of innovation and intervention). Despite the acuity and complexity of Homi Bhabha's sentencing in Lazarus' key example, it is actually easy to assume a cultural dominant rather than, let us say, the entangled, problematic combined and uneven development of anti-colonial writing at different temporal and spatial scales. There is now a robust body of work that registers the latter, which is simultaneously a remark on the historical distance of both Bhabha's trenchant interventions in the 1980s (subsequently collected in *The Location of Culture* [1994])[7] and Lazarus' appreciable riposte at the turn of the century. True, a materialist critique of postcolonial obscurantism was already in evidence and the most damning evidence of a counter-discourse was freely available from postcolonial writers themselves who, as Chinua Achebe makes clear even in the very titles of his works, did not see Modernism or literary theory as obstacles to decolonizing cultural practices. Another crucial dimension emerges in the critical work of South American anti-colonial discourse, where Aníbal Quijano's provocative "Coloniality of Power" concept (1992/2000)[8] re-focuses critique on the constitutive logic of modernity, in which colonialism as a mode of subjection is closely linked to subject reason, specific modes of rationality, bourgeois secularization, and "liberal" democracy. Modernism, while hardly an epiphenomenon of the state and colonial relations of modernity, is not an exception to coloniality's reach, especially in its European formations: the synchrony of high Modernism with the height of British imperialism is not simply a Modernist critique of the latter. As noted, it is just as clear that postcolonial engagement has been able to find contra-indications in the confluence of European Modernism and colonialism. Edward Said's readings of Yeats and

Joyce, for instance, comprise a reckoning with this troubled imbrication, not least because of the material conditions of Ireland vis-à-vis the British Empire.[9] Gayatri Spivak's work on Yeats offers a contrasting discourse of anti-colonial method. Nevertheless, whereas a materialist critique of some of the more extravagant postcolonial conceptualizations was warranted from within postcolonialism, decolonial thought has emphasized delinking from that genealogy of postcolonial theorization whenever its epistemological roots seem grounded in European thought as a posited norm. Like the Black radical tradition and critical race studies, the decolonial challenge to the institutionalization of postcolonial studies has been generative and the dynamic interaction in evidence has changed both the contours and the purview of the field as a whole. Can the interrelation of Modernist and Bakhtinian studies possibly catalyze alternative modes of postcolonial critique through such engagement?

Provocative and symptomatic interventions to date include those critics who address the imbrications between Bakhtin's aesthetic interests and his Modernist contemporaries. We know, of course, that Bakhtin did teach twentieth-century literature, and, as Stacy Burton points out, names like Brecht, Hemingway, and Neruda crop up in his writings. Of particular note is that he turns a critical eye to Thomas Mann. As Burton underlines, Bakhtin identifies *Doctor Faustus* as a text that gives support to Bakhtin's ideas of authorial complexity and polyphony, yet this only hints at the possibilities of a Modernist engagement or even the symptoms of a colonialist encounter, especially given more recent theorizations.[10] Much depends on how one construes authorship in Modernism. For Bakhtin, some Modernist writing may usefully fragment narrative modes to permit alternate voices to emerge, but often such experimentation merely confirms that the author is the organizational hub for voicing per se. This strong sense of authority in authoring is not an unproblematic relay to, say, the authoritarianism in colonial subjugation, but the author's absent presence nevertheless reveals a contradictory power over that which can exceed it. As Joyce reminds us in the *Portrait of the Artist as a Young Man*, "The artist, like the god of the creation, remains within or behind or beyond or above his handiwork, invisible, refined out of existence, indifferent, paring his fingernails."[11] The privilege of indifference in Modernism is an antinomy in the materiality of its moment from wherever it may emerge.

To some extent, this contradictory mode of authoring is another version of the impasse in the rationality of modernity, at least in its hegemonic role. Bakhtin struggled to reconcile the open-endedness of novelization in modernity with philosophical concepts that appeared to close off engagement with the Other in that process. If, for instance, coloniality actively produces encounters with Others in which some mode of Kantian reflective judgment might seem to provide solace, history shows the rational self is confounded by this event, and the agency of the Other is subsumed by versions of objectification and a process of othering that separate off people as unassimilable to reason's needs and ethical protocols. True, the eye of modernity certainly need not run through Kantian prerogatives, but Bakhtin's understanding of the Other is in part the result of interrogating the grounds of Kantian subjectivity. Whereas the logical constituents of nature and "man" might seem to preclude Othering as humanization over objectification or the projection of lack, Bakhtin argues for the promise of aesthetic reconciliation where reason itself begins in the active relation of the Other. For Bakhtinians, this is the difference between transgredience and transcendence: the former a complex linchpin of human relationality; the latter, while still relational, a condition of the unknowable as abject outsideness. Of course, Kant in the Third Critique also tries to think through the limitations of the Subject *qua* theory via aesthetic categories. Judgment itself appears predicated on the idea the Other would make the same judgment, and in aesthetics the Other may thus take up the position of the Subject in terms of experience and history. That the aesthetic here shares something of ideology's "imaginary resolution of a real contradiction" (to borrow from Althusser)[12] is to be acknowledged, if only to remind ourselves that conceptual capacities can include the refiguring of the Other as agent and othering as an alibi for continuing subjugation. If novelization can be read as a key Bakhtinian negotiation of modernity's Scylla and Charybdis ("colonization and civilization?" as Césaire put it), it is not because Bakhtin read it into his present but because the present must read it into him. For his part, Bakhtin does not reject Modernism out of hand, but any philological aspects of his approach to novelization is limited by Modernism's present and not just its methods or the specific discursive context of Soviet evaluation.

Voloshinov[13] is often invoked in this regard to allay the creeping Kantianism (and neo-Kantianism of the Marburg School) of Bakhtin's aesthetic concerns, but it is more useful for the present discussion to press the materialist symptoms of the Bakhtin Circle as a whole, for whom the prescience of aesthetic concepts was driven by a deep concern for the future of culture in the new society. Novelization, from this perspective, was not an abstract process to be read in an isolated genealogy of genre; it was an approach to narrative that permitted one to articulate the role of cultural change in social transformation itself. True, notions of the dialogic can quickly be rendered benign or anodyne, a descriptive device for cultural relations that might displace matters of conflict, contradiction, or even dialectics, but the Bakhtin Circle itself was less prone to such evasion, and, while the adjudication of its politics (which cannot simply separate itself from any gloss on its glossary) continues to generate excitable speech it is the concern for cultural futures that throws light on decolonizing modernity. Some of this is framed by a critique of modernity itself which, as Craig Brandist has pointed out, was subject to misgivings about the closed nature of Eurocentric interpretation and the kinds of philology and orientalisms, for instance, used to sustain it.[14] Cultural engagement meant more than subject/object binaries and Bakhtin's focus on utterance allowed for a provocative slide between *slovo* as word and as bodies of words and spaces of complex interactivity. Rather than typification and structuralist compartmentalization, Bakhtin and other members of the Circle looked outward and across cultural expressivity (Brandist refers to Konrad's work on Japanese and Chinese literatures, Tubianskii on Tagore, and a general Bakhtinian concern for a "world" literature beyond the idea of European foundations). This kind of openness is very much part of the concrete conditions of social change argued within Bakhtin's network in the 1920s and 1930s. Although history, including intellectual history, is quite clear on the limits and indeed failures of the period, the point is that the Bakhtin Circle did not offer a monologic or homogeneous vision of the modern or modernity and this is one reason why Bakhtin's concepts offer a symptomatic relay between Modernism and decolonization, one that speaks simultaneously to conditions of cultural engagement now (including institutional forms of knowledge) and to how the longue durée of modernity can be problematized and differentiated. While for some this means simply multiple Bakhtins, modernities, and Modernisms, the polemic implied means much more than the fact of multiplication and, significantly, is coming to terms with how decolonization takes place and the contributions of aesthetics in that process.

To think further on this re-accentuation I would suggest some critical contact zones where Bakhtinian concepts enjoin and sharpen the relations of Modernism and postcolonialism at the same time as they, in very different ways, come to inflect how Bakhtin can be thought today. If novelization describes a form of narrative becoming, it is not without constraints; indeed, one could venture that it connotes an antinomy of genre as such. The difficulty for criticism is adjudicating what is novelness in the literary from what the novel narrates as a genre. There is no doubt that the novel can ingest and perform other genres: it does, after all, participate freely as utterance and context. Yet, as the novel takes up the space of storytelling does it occlude or displace the capacity for other writing with novelness in its own way? On one level, this merely remarks on the historical links between the novel and processes of colonization; on another level, however, it highlights that the generic markers of the novel for modernity are contested by an outsideness or exotopy that the novel seeks to know but does not ineluctably contain. Novelness, like sign in Voloshinov's work, is a scene of contradiction and struggle. If the novel provides technical solutions to the limits of the epic, for instance, it is not simply a representation of the latter's knowledge despite its faith in the epistemological certitudes of written language. Modernist texts with all the novelness of Joyce's *Ulysses* certainly question novelizing and colonizing as co-constitutive, but this opening into the new worldliness of the present still only imagines aesthetic solutions to what are necessarily limits in the socio-political and economic dynamics of the modern world. The lesson of Williams is that such a shortfall is dialectically an advantage because the "subjunctive mode," as he termed it, questions the historical reality in which it is enmeshed. To that extent, novelization opens up for analysis the conceptual stress between Modernism and postcolonialism, where the "dialogical imagination" permeates a social theory of the ways utterance can be thought, expressed. If the coloniality of power, for instance, is a determinate condition of Western modernity, it is a scene of profoundly uneven coordination and impress. Modernist novels do not simply reflect such a condition (even the realist novel, as Lukács suggested, is not beyond significant aporia in that regard),[15] but neither is their technical nous an escape from it. Perhaps the logic of colonial experience is similar in this respect: the desire to decolonize does not at once escape the order that constrains it.

The value of "rethinking the colonial encounter with Bakhtin" as Brandist puts it, is not just that it suggests an alternative mode of inquiry to the Foucauldian discursive approach around postcolonialism indicated in Said's *Orientalism*, but that a dialogic dialectics (however controversial in its own right) challenges the false oppositions in the project of modernity. Again, it is important to interrogate the grounds of novelization (right down to the writing, production, translation, and distribution of novels, for instance, under actually existing colonialism), but to what extent are its assumptions and ideological affinities challenged within the novel's constitution as utterance? Bakhtin offers a metalinguistics not just of the novel's word, but of its worldliness, one where even basic ideas of the modern as a nation or national problematic, for example, find their implications rethought and re-constellated by the exigencies of anti-colonialism and decolonial critique (even when represented as a *Bildungsroman*, as in Pramoedya's *Buru Quartet*, for instance).[16] Modernism can be a source of inspiration in postcolonial writing precisely because it is already disposed to question the norming of modernity, as an aesthetic, as a way of seeing, as an expressive formation. It is a "hermeneutics of engagement" (Brandist 2018: 321) that was perhaps too present for Bakhtin to address through his historical poetics, but present enough as a longue durée now to consider its anti-colonial indications.

Holquist pointed out Bakhtin employs a distinction between novel and novelness and that clearly the latter is not confined to the novel as a characteristic.[17] To decolonize aesthetics at this level is to refuse both the elision of one in the other but also to question whether novelness serves as an alibi of modernity rather than as a potential for its critique. The newness of new genres beyond the novel (in cinema, new media, etc.) are not altogether examples of novelness, nor is a certain level of cultural embeddedness and tradition that might also partake of worldliness at different scales of perception and forms of expression. True, as my epigraph indicates, questions of non-identity and the other are also central to Bakhtin's theorization, and have a decolonial logic that may exceed Bakhtin's own. The big picture aesthetics of epicality and novelization inexorably privilege the novel as a narrative distillation of modernity, and even of its others. This may not be seen as a benevolent aesthetics the other side of its history, however magnanimous its reach. Yet the crux of decolonial aesthetics is not just to point out the questionable links between genealogies of discernment and the exclusions of modernity but also to elaborate an apprehension of artistic practices that recast the logic of intercultural relations and expression in general. This does not mean, for instance, that decolonial desire is simply more dialogical than the subject/object assumptions of Enlightenment philosophy but that it pivots on creating an interrogative space where the "eventness" of coloniality is subject to new ways of seeing and chronotopic dissent. While "novelness" does not name the material coordinates of such intervention, decolonial aesthetics share something of the spirit of Bakhtin's emphasis on "multiaccentuality," one that permits the analysis of *slovo* mediated by, for example, race and racialization, or by something akin to "Protestant ethnics" in Rey Chow's critique.[18] Similarly, the potential for chronotopic critique is open to decolonial framing because the time/space units conceived in Bakhtin's conceptualization do not privilege one dimension over another yet can be specified in their precise interaction, a materialization of time/space that may indeed question the formal and imposed hierarchization of spatio-temporal modes across colonial culture and history.

A correlative for the openness of many of Bakhtin's central ideas is that they permit an understanding of impurity and excessiveness in cultural practices which, not surprisingly, is a generic feature of the novel in its "novelness." Just as Bakhtin provides a poetics of the body in his reading of Rabelais that features the body's contradictory life-affirming leakiness and inconstancy, so the protean contours of the novel quite clearly offer carnivalizing reflection on standardization and normative will. Postcolonialism has certainly taken up these elements as a capacity for counter-critique and anti-colonialism yet these possibilities are highly mediated and overdetermined. There has been much debate about whether the writing of resistance itself is subject to the performative and where novelistic narrative can take up expected motifs as an expression of a market rather than as an exception to modernity (see, for instance, Brouillette and Walkowitz).[19] Indeed, this is a conjecture that supports aspects of Modernist experimentation, the kind that challenged analogic realism, this story is *about* rather than this story *is*, etc. Even when much discussion of Joyce elucidates his defamiliarization of the colonized space of Ireland, the principles of language in play do not find the aboutness of the real as sufficient. Concomitantly, the limits of language to express a community or a national condition knot the problem of coloniality to authoring and authority. We can say that although Bakhtin may not have extensively addressed the Modernism of his present, it was engaged symptomatically by his deep concern for the crisis of the author/authorship. The intimacy of Modernism and postcoloniality is in no small part produced by the concrete nature of this crisis: who gets to tell, and how, the story of not just the way things are ("falling apart," etc., the "about" of decolonization) but the otherwise untold stories of difference in that conjuncture? As mentioned, the assumption of authorship in tracking the colonial/postcolonial condition can produce cynicism regarding its narratological effects (exoticism, essentialism, a kind of practiced self-objectification). By decentering the author in relation to a putative "hero," Bakhtin does not erase the authority of the author but destabilizes it by changing the logic of its relation. When the author others the hero of a narrative, the latter is rendered passive in its objecthood. Bakhtin conceives of this relationship as successful aesthetically only when such othering is the active narration of at least two subjects, an authorship writing together. It would be wrong to suggest that a strong sense of authorship is denied to the postcolonial writer in the prospect of this authorial relation, just as it would be incautious to blithely state that Modernist authors eschew a god-like authority over the powers of expressivity. The point would be how to think authorship as a braided modality where the shifting bounds of authorship are "about" the meaning of authoring itself.

The above, however, is not a technical rapprochement, as if the product of a Modernist/postcolonialist dialogic is some kind of how-to blueprint. Even if one restricts an analysis of such a dialogic to a genealogy of major Anglophone postcolonial writers to the present (Ngugi, Coetzee, Rushdie, Roy, Rhys, Naipaul, Walcott, and Adichie for instance), there is little that is formulaic or generically consistent, and precedence is certainly not given over to high Modernists themselves. In addition, and as much critique indicates, the answer to the colonial discourse of absenting (in which the barbarism of its process happens elsewhere) is not simply presencing, a filling in of gaps, a making of appearance. Gayatri Spivak pointedly argued that the subaltern not speaking concerns constitutive silence and silencing, a systemic patterning of ontology and epistemology whereby the speaking subject beyond the coloniality of power is a horizon of struggle, not an arena of reparative statements sui generis, even though reparation itself is to be respected.[20] Again, Bakhtin does not directly address the politics of this as an aesthetic but his work is hardly an apology for what modernity hath wrought. When Bakhtin is invoked to aid in the reconfiguration of Modernism, a worldliness that now extends to the transnational, the global, and the planetary, one senses this is simultaneously an acknowledgment of what postcolonial writers and critics have been attempting since at least the internationalism of DuBois, Césaire, and Fanon: to read the world of modernity through a politics and aesthetics of contestation. Yet that critical inclination does not arrive value-free or beyond disputation on its own terms. Perhaps this is merely to say that, however one characterizes the dialogic of Modernism and postcolonialism, the relationship itself is subject to dialogicity, so that one might find as wildly divergent articulations of the relationship as one discerns seemingly incompatible versions of Bakhtin. The dialogic, therefore, continues to place a heavy onus on the materiality or time/space of the conjunction while assuring an openendedness or unfinishedness to the nature of the relationship at issue. Surely, a decolonial aesthetics favors a closure of sorts to the coloniality of power as a hegemonic condition of worlding? Let us say it looks to end a *dialogue* with the production and reproduction of colonial relations as such while freely engaging in the incompleteness of the *dialogic* (or of "dialogicity") to forward that process (what I have referred to elsewhere as the "dialogics of the oppressed").

We have suggested so far that postcolonial critiques in a Bakhtinian vein are longstanding, whether they begin from the broad bordering discourse of Graham Pechey[21] or specific investigations of a writer like Abdul Rahman Munif using the principle of polyphony. Similarly, we have noted that Bakhtinian investigations of Modernism are legion even if, or precisely because, Bakhtin himself addressed Modernist writers and the Modernist aesthetic relatively infrequently. Independently, there has been an ongoing engagement between postcolonialism and Modernism from artists and critics alike, not least because of the intersectional materiality of colonial history and Western modernity in particular. The third set of relations is not problematized in the same way by the provocations of the first two noted above, but would decolonial aesthetics necessarily be enhanced by Bakhtinian cultural critique or does this risk reinscribing a paradigm of worlding heavily dependent on Western intellectual traditions, neo-Kantian or otherwise? Although literary theorists are regularly subjected to their own conceptual frameworks there is a certain situatedness to such events that helps to explain the decolonial impress of Bakhtin's poetics when the project itself was not obviously legible in his worldview. One thinks of Bakhtin's discussion of canonization and canonicity in the "Discourse in the Novel" essay as a warning about single-voiced readings of Bakhtin himself, a Bakhtin perhaps safely inured from the messy politics of twentieth-century cultural critique. One could, of course, think of Bakhtin, or more precisely the meaning of Bakhtin, as part of the great heteroglossia, the subject of a matrix of conditions not fully repeatable in new contexts. This would be a Bakhtin who was less the idea of the hero he theorized, and more a symptom of the novelization he elaborated in his poetics, something paradoxically unrepeatable enough to resist unalloyed canonization. The carnivalizing of canons is a way to reveal the logic of structural hierarchy in forms and genres. Similarly, the uncrowning practices of carnivalization represent a popular riposte to hegemonic social orders that, while hardly a guarantee of overturning the systemic interconnections of colonial power, nevertheless highlight power is at stake. Even humanizing Bakhtin holds lessons for decolonizing cultural relations. Bakhtin's fascination with the grotesque offers a life-affirming appreciation of the human body's imperfections that is connected both to an aesthetic experience of his own body and a critique of the body as a basic metaphor of socialization (redolent, of course, in his study of Rabelais). The perfectability of the human is only one dimension of the discourses of Man in Western modernity but it is certainly evident in the claims to superiority by the civilizing subject of colonialism. Like the carnivalesque, the grotesque hints at a basic instability in the "natural" order of the individual, the state, and being in the world. While it would be rash to render Bakhtin a decolonial aesthetician in this light, it is not far-fetched to indicate such potential, especially where Modernism and postcolonialism are concerned.

What of decolonial delinking, however, if Bakhtin is read among the main currents of European thought? Craig Brandist takes the position that Bakhtin was European but not Eurocentric "in the sense of someone who treats European culture as a standard against which others are judged" (Brandist 2018: 312). This is a fair point but it remains complicated to adjudicate. For instance, as elaborated in a central text of decolonial theory, "Coloniality of Power, Eurocentrism, and Latin America," Aníbal Quijano proposes that within political economy colonialism entailed a "Eurocentrification" of global capitalism and that this process "concentrated all forms of the control of subjectivity, culture, and especially knowledge and the production of knowledge under its hegemony" (Quijano 2000: 540). Furthermore, the colonial project centered on distinctive forms of ethnocentrism that helped to galvanize and rationalize a hegemony of a particular kind. Again, the approach suggests that although modernity is global and diverse, a specific version claims to represent the world system as such. Enrique Dussel, who Quijano quotes in the same essay, uses a concept of "transmodernity," not to negate any benefits of modernity but to argue against Europe as the measure or distillation of what modernity can mean, which reminds us of Brandist's pertinent point.[22] Is it possible to think of Bakhtin's meta- or translinguistics as a transmodern symptom or does such a methodology participate, largely by silence, in an ethnic privileging over modernity's others? Perhaps here it is enough for the poetics to subsume the personal politics to head off the ossification of identity into some European gauge, or alternatively one could maintain the tension of delinking as an acknowledgment that such identification can re-emerge while the coloniality of power persists.

Decolonial aesthetics take the position that the work of decolonization acknowledges how authors and artists may refract rather than fully intend a break from deleterious traditions of knowledge and expression. One aspect of Modernism in this regard is that such refraction occurs across and between distinct genealogies of its practice. In her book, *Modernism after Postcolonialism*, Mara de Gennaro argues that the effect of the negotiation of Modernism and postcolonialism is a kind of aesthetic "trembling" (a term borrowed from Chamoiseau, and Glissant),[23] an answer to if not a correlative of, the "anxious worldliness" of coloniality in the modern period.[24] That prose, for Bakhtin, often refracts rather than bears the weight of authorial intention is a similar invitation to explore the vexed consciousness of comparative cosmopolitanism, where Modernist texts fracture before the prospect of an authoring that would otherwise exclude the other in its own name. True, while Gennaro's analysis offers wonderful juxtapositions of European moderns and postcolonial Modernist interlocutors (Forster/Chamoiseau, Danticat/Woolf, etc.), indeterminate poetics and what Glissant[25] calls "the opacity of the diverse," cannot in themselves complete the work of decolonization, but they do, in the spirit of Lisa Lowe's sense of "hesitant history,"[26] reflexively subvert the shibboleths of what modernity represents. To say that Modernism doubts its capacity for difficult aesthetics does not do justice to the contradictory dynamic at stake, which depends less on the luxury of indeterminacy and more on the material production of authorial outsideness, a somewhat literal marginalization of the aesthetician before the market. As Fredric Jameson[27] has noted in another context, the saturation of market logic has turned even outsideness or exotopy into a commodity niche, and *that* history finds bold Modernist experimentation now surprisingly realist within postmodern phantasmagoria.

Steeled with the experience of exile himself, we should not be surprised that Bakhtin might find aesthetic sustenance in outsideness as a form of discrepant relationality. Glissant, of course, will take this troubled marginalization even further, where the beauty of the world might be apprehended not in the wake of exile, forced or self-composed, but through an aesthetic wandering, an errancy open to worlds of "diversality" (Glissant 1993).

Is this a somewhat privileged delinking alongside the material mandates of migrancy in postcolonial conditions of severe uneven and combined development? The materialism in Bakhtinian aesthetics is to some extent overdetermined by a sensitive dependence on understanding rather than blindly performing the work of the ideological. Glissant, while very much a radical anti-colonial activist in his youth, often felt frustrated by what he saw as the torpor encouraged through Martinique's status as a Département d'outre-mer (DOM – overseas department) and, while he continued to critique French hegemony, he was not beyond a rapprochement in his aesthetics that could be read as diversionary in its own way. Glissant does not simply take up Aimé Césaire's coruscating engagement with Modernism (seen also in Suzanne Césaire's feminist decolonial deployment of surrealism) although they both share a deep distrust of representational transparency. His poetics offer a deep and trenchant reading of relation (a sort of creolization at a world scale) as a destabilization of normative subject/object priorities. My point here, however, is that Glissant's challenge to mastery and the authority in authoring can often be misread as an aesthetic solution to what is properly a social contradiction for decolonization as such. One does not have to be an avatar of structures or infrastructures of feeling to see that structure is at stake in the Modernist challenge to social hierarchization, often mediated by identitarian formulas of race, caste, gender, class, and nation. Decolonial aesthetics are at once an institutional critique, and, because of the systematicity of coloniality, must come to terms with the ideological suturing of that dynamic. This structural composite does not simply overlay the tensed conditions of Modernism and postcolonialism within modernity: some measure of the ideological implications mentioned above might complicate their pairing as aesthetic practices. Does a Bakhtinian framework participate in such critique?

I would answer this in the affirmative, but with significant caveats. However we parse the incidence and significance of dialogism in Bakhtin's theorization, "word" and words have a complex vitality that is a philosophy of relation in its own way. For the most part, his dedication to living language was not premised on either/or conditions of articulation (even when individual pronouncements like "when a human being is in art, he is not in life, and conversely"[28] offer sharp division, "answerability," or, more precisely, responsibility, undermines the binary). It is thus the case, both here and in other contributions, that the largely absent direct engagement by Bakhtin toward Modernism is an invitation to think with his historical poetics in the context of their materialization. Similarly, while an anti-colonial and Modernist aesthetics are to a notable degree co-constitutive (they both signal a crisis in modernity) their interrelationship is often symptomatic rather than asserted which intimates a space where Bakhtinian concepts appear generative. This helps explain why, for instance, the prominent anti-racist and anti-colonialist thinker, Stuart Hall, invoked Bakhtinian ideas to de-essentialize the politics of identity in contemporary cultural critique. Hall uses the term diaspora rather than exile to focus his thoughts on troubling the seeming sacred truths of center and periphery logic in modernity. In doing this he takes "multiaccentuality" from Bakhtin (or perhaps more properly Voloshinov) to problematize racial meaning and the semiosis of such meaning, not to dismiss constructions of race but rather to interrogate discursive indeterminacy as opening out racial futures. This approach is less a Foucauldian understanding of discursivity than it is a materialist approach to the dynamism of sign as a whole (one that striates the conditions of Modernism and colonialism as a decolonial problematic). Elsewhere, Hall[29] will describe his paradigm as a dialogic approach to alterity, in part to preserve the "unsettled" nature of unsettling colonial prescriptions. In his appreciation of Allon White, Hall foregrounded White's articulation of the carnivalesque as a mode of paradigm disturbance, as an "uncrowning" that proceeds from heteroglossic profusion and hybridization. Similarly, critics influenced by Hall like Kobena Mercer[30] and Paul Gilroy, have invoked Bakhtin not to preserve the immediate conditions or traditions of his scholarship but to take its implications and put theory to work. Gilroy,[31] for instance, tellingly uses the idea of the chronotope, in particular the "chronotope of the crossroads," to discuss the multi-directional influences on African and African-American/African-Caribbean cultures. While expanding an understanding of chronotope is not uncommon across critique, Gilroy shows it has particular promise in reconceiving the time/space of cultural exchange otherwise formed and striated by the longue durée of racialization and slavery. Decolonization here is not in the Bakhtinian concept but in its opening to the conflicted and material cultural logic of politics and aesthetics. Yet it is just as clear that decoloniality means creating utility on its own terms (the "human" in Sylvia Wynter's sense, "transmodernity" in Dussel's) at or through the risk of delinking from intentionalist prescriptions or originary confirmation.

Triangulating Modernism, postcolonialism, and Bakhtin is far from any theoretical correlative of Césaire's rendezvous of victory. For a discrepant decolonial aesthetics, however, the constellation continues to promise an arena of creative disjunction, especially if one begins from a Bakhtinian materialist understanding of sign, as Voloshinov does. If the coloniality of power is written into discourses of globality and globalization, the point would not be to find aesthetic matches for this fateful co-constitution but to examine further the ways in which expressivity learns and leans from paradigms forged and bequeathed by the age of empires and hierarchical conceptions of global integration. Seen in this light, when Illya Kliger[32] argues for a symptomatic approach to Bakhtin's engagement with Modernism rather than scraping his oeuvre for direct references, one can at once register the decolonial possibility of the framework explored. Is not the aesthetic arc of decolonization in Modernism punctuated, for instance, by an attention to a crisis of authorship (*krizis avtorstva*), authoring, and the author that, even in Bakhtin's neo-Kantian notions of the Subject, necessarily problematizes Kant as well as re-imagining the place of the hero? That hero is not Bakhtin himself, of course, but a concept of authoring that simultaneously decenters and de-privileges a conspicuously colonial idea of making or architectonics in modernity. Here, the material ground of the triangulation invoked is not the substance of authorial consciousness but is a realization of agency elsewhere. Thus, the decolonial agon of Modernism exists in its outsideness or exotopy, yet more provocatively still in its logic of dispute, in the word, discourse, and figuration of the Other.

Notes

1. M. M. Bakhtin, "Author and Hero," in *AA*, 4–256 (111).
2. Aimé Césaire, *Cahiers d'un retour au pays natal* [Notebook of a Return to My Native Land] (Paris: Présence africaine, 1983), 7.

3   Neil Lazarus, "The Politics of Postcolonial Modernism," *The European Legacy* 0.6 (2002): 771–82.
4   Timothy Brennan, *At Home in the World: Cosmopolitanism Now* (Cambridge, MA: Harvard University Press, 1997).
5   Raymond Williams, *The Politics of Modernism: Against the New Conformists* (London: Verso, 2007).
6   Robert Seguin, "Borders, Context, Politics: Mikhail Bakhtin," *Signature: A Journal of Theory and Canadian Literature* 2 (1989): 42–59.
7   Homi Bhabha, *The Location of Culture* (New York: Routledge, 1994).
8   Aníbal Quijano, "Coloniality of Power: Eurocentrism and Latin America," *Neplanta* 1.3 (2000): 533–80.
9   Edward Said, "Yeats and Decolonization," in *Nationalism, Colonialism, and Literature*, ed. Terry Eagleton, Fredric Jameson, and Edward Said (Minneapolis: University of Minnesota Press, 1990).
10 Stacy Burton, "Paradoxical Relations: Bakhtin and Modernism," *Modern Language Quarterly* 61.3 (2000): 519–43.
11 James Joyce, *Portrait of the Artist as a Young Man* (London: Penguin, 2003), 215.
12 Louis Althusser, *Lenin and Philosophy and Other Essays*, trans. Ben Brewster (New York: Monthly Review Press, 1972).
13 V. N. Voloshinov, *Marxism and the Philosophy of Language*, trans. Ladislaw Matejka and I. R. Titunik (Cambridge, MA: Harvard University Press, 1986).
14 Craig Brandist, "Rethinking the Colonial Encounter with Bakhtin (and Contra Foucault)," *Journal of Multicultural Discourses* 13.4 (2018): 309–25.
15 Georg Lukács, *The Theory of the Novel*, trans. Anna Bostock (Cambridge, MA: The MIT Press, 1974).
16 Pramoedya Ananta Toer, *Buru Quartet*, 4 vols., trans. Max Lane (London: Penguin, 1996–97).
17 Michael Holquist, *Dialogism* (London: Routledge, 2002).
18 Rey Chow, *The Protestant Ethnic and the Spirit of Capitalism* (New York: Columbia University Press, 2002).
19 Sarah Brouillette, "On the African Literary Hustle," *Blindfield* (2017), https://blindfieldjournal.com/2017/08/14/on-the-african-literary-hustle/; Rebecca Walkowitz, *Born Translated: The Contemporary Novel in an Age of World Literature* (New York: Columbia University Press, 2017).
20 Gayatri Chakravorty Spivak, "Finding Feminist Readings: Dante–Yeats," *Social Text* 3 (1980): 73–8.
21 Graham Pechey, "On the Borders of Bakhtin: Dialogisation, Decolonisation," in *Bakhtin and Cultural Theory*, ed. Ken Hirschkop and David Shepherd (Manchester: Manchester University Press, 1990), 39–67.
22 Enrique Dussel, "Transmodernity and Interculturality: An Interpretation from the Perspective of Philosophy of Liberation," *Transmodernity: Journal of Peripheral Cultural Production of the Luso-Hispanic World* 1.3 (2012): 28–59.

23 Patrick Chamoiseau and Edouard Glissant, *L'Intraitable beauté du monde: Adresse à Barack Obama* [The Unassailable Beauty of the World: Letter to Barack Obama] (Paris: Galaade, 2009).
24 Mara de Gennaro, *Modernism after Postcolonialism: Toward a Nonterritorial Comparative Literature* (Baltimore: Johns Hopkins University Press, 2020), 17.
25 Edouard Glissant, *Poetics of Relation*, trans. Betsy Wing (Ann Arbor: University of Michigan Press, 1993).
26 Lisa Lowe, "History Hesitant," *Social Text* 125 (December 2015): 85–107.
27 Jameson Fredric, *The Antinomies of Realism* (London: Verso, 2013).
28 "Art and Answerability," in *AA*, 1–3 (1).
29 Stuart Hall, *The Fateful Triangle: Race, Ethnicity, Nation*, ed. and intro. Kobena Mercer (Cambridge, MA: Harvard University Press, 2017).
30 Kobena Mercer, *Welcome to the Jungle: New Positions in Black Cultural Studies* (New York: Routledge, 1994).
31 Paul Gilroy, *The Black Atlantic: Modernity and Double Consciousness* (Cambridge, MA: Harvard University Press, 1993).
32 Illya Kliger, "Heroic Aesthetics and Modernist Critique: Extrapolations from Bakhtin's 'Author and Hero in Aesthetic Activity'," *Slavic Review* 67.3 (2008): 551–66.

PART TWO

Bakhtin and Modernism

9

"New Philosophical Wonder"

Bakhtin, Shklovsky, and the Re-enchantment of the World

Daphna Erdinast-Vulcan

The point of departure for this essay is an enigmatic but unmistakably wistful comment scribbled in the margins of one of Bakhtin's surviving notebooks: "New philosophical wonder at everything is needed. Everything could have been different" (*REL*: 70). As neither the meaning of this "philosophical wonder" nor the way it might have altered "everything" are made explicit in this notebook (or, indeed, anywhere else in Bakhtin's work), these sentences remain suspended as it were, an open invitation for engagement and dialogue. Taking up this invitation, this chapter suggests that this "new philosophical wonder" may be illuminated if we attend to a profound, unacknowledged temperamental affinity between the philosophical positions of Bakhtin and Viktor Shklovsky, two contemporaries often seen as ideologically and intellectually antagonistic to each other.[1] A close reading of these thinkers and an attunement to what—for reasons of political expediency and sheer survival—could be only implied or covertly suggested at the time of the writing would highlight a similar spiritual undercurrent which runs through the work of both. Some aspects of this kinship have been discussed in *Between Philosophy and Literature*,[2] and the present text would follow the discussion and take it a step further, making a detour through the concept of "re-enchantment," which may well offer some further insights as to the broader cultural significance of this implicit affinity.

I

The conception of modernity as an age of "disenchantment" has been famously copyrighted by Max Weber in "Science as a Vocation," where Weber—inspired by Schiller's vision of the departed Gods of Greece, but refusing to share what he saw as romantic nostalgia—describes the modern age as moving from the "Dark Ages" of superstition, fear, and oppression toward an age of anthropocentric enlightenment and liberation. Weber's brief comment had generated numerous discussions of the meaning and implications of disenchantment, whether related to common perceptions of magic and the supernatural, to the relations of the human to the cosmic natural order, or—most pertinently for the present discussion—to the loss of the sacred as a reference point. Nearly a century later, Charles Taylor's *A Secular Age*, a magisterial study spanning six centuries of Western history, has offered a complex account of the relations between secularization and disenchantment. Taylor subscribes to Weber's diagnosis of modernity, but the process of disenchantment, on his account, is no longer taken to be a purely emancipatory one: it has also generated a counter-narrative of "subtraction,"[3] various narratives of loss and a sense of homesickness for an "enchanted" world, where "the boundaries between the mind and the body, the self and the world, [were] blurred and permeable"; and where it was harder "to disengage from the cosmos and from society" (Taylor 2007: 42).

The historical inclusivity of Taylor's account notwithstanding, his conception of both enchantment and disenchantment is ultimately predicated on the loss of the relation to the sacred, the implications of that loss for the constitution of subjectivity, and its relation to ethics. Reiterating this sense of "subtraction" in a later essay, Taylor considers the possibility of re-enchantment, or the retrieval of the sacred, but rather than attempt an impossible return to the naïve versions of enchantment, or aim to undo the disenchantment of modernity, he proposes a version of re-enchantment which would re-establish the non-arbitrary, non-projective character of certain ethical demands on us. These demands are firmly anchored in our being-in-the-world, but they are neither mere projections of our psyche nor metaphysically or objectively derived. They arise, Taylor writes, in an "interstitial zone" between subject and world, where the sacred—no longer predicated on naïve belief—can still be recovered.[4] Concluding this essay, Taylor endorses the position of Marcel Gauchet in *The Disenchantment of the World* (published a few years earlier and introduced by Taylor), that "art, in the specific sense we moderns understand it, [is defined as] the continuation of the Sacred by other means,"[5] and similarly suggests that the best arena for the recovery of the relation to the sacred, or the re-enchantment of the world, is to be found in the "subtler languages" of poetry and art whose boundaries are, by definition, "ontologically fluid and indeterminate" (Taylor 2011: 118). In both these accounts, however, the conception of the "interstitial" zone, and the dynamics of our engagement with art and the manner in which it might continue our relation to the sacred remain undertheorized.

A more recent engagement with the concept of enchantment and its ethical implications is offered in Jane Bennett's *The Enchantment of Modern Life: Attachments, Crossings, and Ethics*, which sets out to question and resist the very premise of "disenchantment" and engagingly "tells a story of contemporary life that accentuates its moments of enchantment and explores the possibility that the affective force of those moments might be deployed to propel ethical generosity."[6] Bennett's proposed model of enchantment is, she says, "half-pagan" in that it "pushes against powerful and versatile Western traditions (in the disciplines of history, philosophy, and literature) that make enchantment depend on a divine creator, Providence, or, at the very least, a physical world with some original connection to a divine will" (Bennett 2001: 12). Against those residual, religiously oriented experiences of enchantment in "a world construed as disenchanted," Bennett proposes an alternative mode of enchantment, belonging to the "sensuous, subjective realm of taste or aesthetics" (15). Enchantment, as she conceives it, is a "mood" which involves "a surprising encounter, a meeting with something that you did not expect and are not fully prepared to engage" (5); being "struck and shaken by the extraordinary that lives amid the familiar and the everyday" (4); "a state of openness to the disturbing-captivating elements in everyday experience ... a window onto the virtual secreted within the actual ... a mood with ethical potential" (132). This, I suggest, sounds like an unintended but distinct echo of Viktor Shklovsky's concept of *ostranenie* (variously translated as "defamiliarization," "estrangement," or "enstrangement"), to which we shall now turn.

II

In December 1913, Viktor Shklovsky—a founding member of the OPOYAZ (Óbchestvo Pó izutcheniu poetítcheskovo iazyká) group—wrote a short paper, titled "Resurrecting the Word" (*Voskreshenie slova*), which laid the groundwork for a lifetime of work. It is, of course, not by accident that the title of the essay recalls Tolstoy's last novel, as the Russian author would feature more prominently than any other in Shklovsky's entire *oeuvre*.[7] What makes this essay particularly noteworthy is its uninhibited expression of religiosity which, like that of the late Tolstoy, has nothing to do with theology or doctrine. Oddly for a an ostensibly forward-looking manifesto, the note it sounds is distinctly elegiac, mourning the loss of an original living Word: "Often, when you get through to the lost, effaced image which was the original source of the word, you find yourself struck by its beauty—the beauty which existed once, and is no more."[8] Or, in a passage that recalls some of Yeats' lines:

> Nowadays, old art has already died, new art has not yet been born, and things have died—we have lost our awareness of the world; we resemble a violinist who has ceased to feel the bow and strings; we have ceased being artists in everyday life, we do not love our houses and our clothes, and we easily part with life, for we do not feel life. Only the creation of new art forms can restore to man the experience of the world, can resurrect things and kill pessimism.
> (Shklovsky 2017: 70)

Futurism, as conceived in this chapter, aims at "resurrecting things—returning the sensation of the world to the human being" (63). And here too, surprisingly for an avant-garde text, Shklovsky sounds distinctly nostalgic as he offers the example of "religious poetry" with its "semi-comprehensible language" by way of analogy with the contrived or deliberately distorted language of futurist poetry, used as a means of heightening sensation (71).[9]

A few years later, the spiritual dynamics of "Resurrection" are reworked in Shklovsky's "Art as Device" (1917/1919) through the foundational concept of *ostranenie*.[10] While this concept is familiar enough to need no introduction here, we should note that the context in which it is embedded is related by Shklovsky to Tolstoy's break with institutional religion alongside his fervent commitment to the sacred:

> This method of seeing things outside of their context led Tolstoy to the *ostranenie* of rites and dogmas in his late works, to the replacement of habitual religious terms with usual words—the result was strange, monstrous; many sincerely regarded it as sacrilegious and were deeply offended. But it was the same device that Tolstoy used elsewhere to experience and show his surroundings. Tolstoy's perception unravelled his own faith, getting to things he had been long unwilling to approach.
> (Shklovsky 2017: 87)

Sixty-five years later, in *On the Theory of Prose* (1983), Shklovsky writes of the OPOYAZ group, returning to Tolstoy, his hero, to the redeeming role of art, and to Tolstoy's unorthodox religiosity: "Art," he writes, "renews religions, testing feelings in its own court of law, art passes judgement."[11] This alignment of the dynamics of poetry in particular and art in general with a non-theological non-doctrinal conception of the sacred is, I suggest, the very version of enchantment that Taylor and Gauchet attempt to recover.

To unpack this alignment, we should look more closely at the concept of *ostranenie* inasmuch as it refers to both language and real-life ethics.

Shklovsky's initial formulation of this concept, based on Tolstoy's work, is certainly related to the latter (Shklovsky 2017: 54–5), and he fully recognizes the profound spiritual motivation underlying it in his subsequent articulations as well. "The main function of *Ostranenie* in Tolstoy," he writes, "is [the awakening] of conscience" (Shklovsky 2017 [1970]: 282). The use of the term "conscience" (rather than "consciousness"), Berlina points out, is not a translation error, but it does present a problem, as "Shklovsky uses the word *sovest'* (conscience), yet what immediately follows deals not with morals (the point stressed in his later writing) but about refreshing experience (the point of his early essays)" (282–3, n5).

This apparent translation conundrum may be easily resolved if we bear in mind that Shklovsky's reading of Tolstoy is, in fact, premised on the conflation of perception (consciousness) and ethics (conscience):

> Therefore, life is only life if it is illuminated by consciousness. So what is consciousness? What actions are illuminated by consciousness? Actions illuminated by consciousness are actions that we take deliberately, i.e. in the awareness that we could also do otherwise. Therefore, consciousness is freedom. There is no freedom without consciousness, and no consciousness is possible without freedom.
>
> ([1966/1983] 271–2)

Clearly, then, the concept of *ostranenie*, the defamiliarization of both language and reality is, for Shklovsky, a point of convergence, a nexus of aesthetics and ethics. Inasmuch as it "frees the thoughts from narrowness," it allows for freedom of will, which is a prior condition of agency and ethical choice. As Berlina notes in her introduction to the anthology, *ostranenie* "can be extraliterary, applying to the world, and also intraliterary, applying to 'poetic' language, genres, and devices" (Berlina 2017: 24).[12] The disruption of the habitual through the deployment of defamiliarization, which does not allow for smooth assimilation and reduction of otherness, revives (or "resurrects," to borrow Shklovsky's term) both our aesthetic and our ethical awareness.[13] This, I would argue, is precisely what the state of "re-enchantment" entails.

III

A complementary aspect of Bennett's theory of "material enchantment" is related to "a particular conception of how ethics work." Rather than a prescriptive code, a value system, or an ensemble of principles and rules—the "what" of ethics—which she groups under the terms "command ethics" or "code-centered ethics," Bennett insists on an engagement with the "how" of ethics, the subjective position of the agent, the "embodied sensibility," or "affective disposition," which would induce the individual to act upon the code. The formation of the self as an ethical subject and the question of ethical motivation are, she writes, closely related to the Foucauldian conception of freedom as "reflective heteronomy," and his call for "tentative explorations of the outer edges of the current regime of subjectivity" which would allow for new configurations of identity and self-direction (Bennett 2001: 132–52).

The link between ethics and the experience of enchantment, on Bennett's account, is a tentative concept of "ethical generosity":

> Enchantment is a feeling of being connected in an affirmative way to existence; it is to be under the momentary impression that the natural and cultural worlds *offer gifts* and, in so doing, remind us that it is good to be alive. This sense of fullness ... encourages the finite human animal in turn, to give away some of its own time and effort on behalf of other creatures. A sensibility attuned to moments of enchantment is no guarantee that this will happen, but it does make it more possible.
>
> (156)

Admirable as I find Bennett's work, it seems to me that this final, deliberately "weak" formulation of ethical generosity falls short of the full potential and productivity of the nexus of enchantment and ethics, and the emphasis on a sense of plenitude does not do justice to the actual circumstances in which people are called upon to make ethical choices. The crucial questions Bennett poses at the outset remain unanswered:

> What enables the jump from recognizing a moral code to living it out? How do moral injunctions become laudable acts? What are the means by which a categorical imperative, for instance, transmogrifies into the treatment of others as one wishes to be treated oneself? ... [How is it] that the moral law comes to be taken up and active upon?
>
> (133)

These questions, I would argue, are precisely the issues to which Bakhtin responds.

In his earliest surviving fragment, *Toward a Philosophy of the Act* (c. 1919–21) Bakhtin, too, challenges what he calls the "fatal theoreticism" of philosophical thinking, and his critique seems to be directed particularly at Kantian ethics, which fails to engage with the transition from a recognition of an ethical imperative or principle to the concrete ethical choices of the subject at the moment of action. He then sets out on a lifelong philosophical quest for an alternative "first philosophy" which would proceed not by "constructing universal concepts, propositions, and laws," but by offering "a description, a phenomenology of that world" (*TPA*: 31–2). Rather than a system of values or laws ("code-centered ethics," as Bennett refers to it), Bakhtin proposes to study the "ought" as "a certain attitude of consciousness, the structure of which we intend to disclose phenomenologically" (*TPA*: 6). This approach to ethics does not begin with the norms, but with the constitution and the perceptual dynamics of the "moral subiectum" (*TPA*: 6).

Having discussed this at length in my previous work, let me recapitulate briefly: Bakhtin insists on an essential asymmetry between the perceptual experience of "I-for-myself" and "I-for-the other": the human subject's perception of itself is necessarily and invariably confined to a partial "inside" perspective that can only be transcended through an external vantage point, a view through the eyes of an authorial other, positioned outside and above the subject. This "centripetal" framing of our sense of selfhood through the eyes of a "transgredient" other ("I-for-the-other") allows for social, cultural, and ideological integration, and for a sense of oneself as a fully coherent and cohesive whole. Conversely, however, there is the pull of the "centrifugal" vector ("I-for-myself") which allows the subject to break out of any and all narrative frames and resist any attempt at "finalization" from without, allowing the subject a sense of agency and self-determination. These complementary and oppositional modes of being, I have argued, feature under various labels throughout Bakhtin's work, and his conception of the dynamics, or the "architectonics" of subjectivity is often couched in terms of a tensile relation between these two vectors, or modes of self-perception.[14]

For the present discussion, the most significant aspect of this conception of subjectivity as inherently ambiguous is the relegation of ethics to the "centrifugal" vector, which clearly challenges the "centripetal," or "aesthetic" conception of the subject as a potentially coherent and cohesive entity and of ethics as a system of abstract rules, principles, and imperatives. Following from his opposition to abstract code-centered ethics, Bakhtin's approach to ethics relates to the phenomenology of choices and acts: the subject of ethics, he writes, is never adequate to itself: it is "in principle nonunitary";[15] "present to itself [only] as a task"; "incapable of being given, of being present-on-hand, of being contemplated" (*AA*: 100). If ethical practice is premised on the gap between what "is" and what "ought to be," the moment of ethical choice is a moment of internal division for the subject who must project itself forward, ahead of its "authored" self, transcending and transgressing the boundary lines of the narrative within which it is embedded. "In order to live and act," Bakhtin writes, the subject must see itself as "axiologically yet-to-be, someone who does not coincide with this already existing makeup" (*AA*: 13), inasmuch as the perspective of I-for-myself does not allow the subject to experience the whole of itself as given, completed and fully determined. This open-endedness is precisely what renders it free to transform itself, to reach out of the narrative framework in a perpetual state of becoming.[16]

The structuring metaphor for the tensile relations between the "centripetal/aesthetics" and the "centrifugal/ethical" frame of reference is that of "rhythm" vs. "loophole." Rhythm, Bakhtin writes, "presupposes an 'immanentization' of meaning to lived experience itself ... [it] presupposes a certain *predeterminedness* of striving, experiencing, action (a certain hopelessness with respect to meaning). The actual, fateful, risk-fraught absolute future is surmounted by rhythm" (*AA*: 117). The ethical moment, however, is a point of fundamental and essential dissonance, when "that which is in me must overcome itself for the sake of that which ought to be; where being and obligation meet in conflict with me; where 'is' and '"ought' mutually exclude each other" (*AA*: 118). Against the "transgredient" framing of "rhythm" that configures the subject as fully coherent and cohesive, there is always a "loophole," a counterforce (which Foucault would call a desire for "self-direction"), which enables the subject to break away from any and all external determinations. These loopholes that disrupt the rhythm of the "given" are the prerequisites of free will and agency:

> I myself as [an ethical] subiectum never coincide with me myself: I—the subiectum of the act of self-consciousness—exceed the bounds of this act's content ... [a] loophole out of time, out of everything given, everything finitely present on hand.
>
> (*AA*: 109)

Bakhtin's early essay, "Author and Hero in Aesthetic Activity," which correlates the "centripetal" mode of being with aesthetics, is clearly premised on a very conservative and distinctly nostalgic correlation of aesthetics with harmony, coherence, and cohesion. This, I would suggest, is very close to the state of naïve enchantment as described by Taylor, inasmuch as the "aesthetic" or "centripetal" framework, granted by a transgredient author (be it the author of a literary narrative, or—in real life—one's community, culture, or ideological network) generates a sense of integration, granting coherence to the subject's life. It is, therefore, not surprising that Dostoevsky is referenced in this early text as an aesthetic failure, an author who has given up the authorial "transgredient" prerogative and could not (or would not) subsume his characters' voices under his own (*AA*: 17, 20, 130, 146). A few years later, however, Dostoevsky's abdication of authority is famously celebrated, turning him into the harbinger of a "small-scale Copernican revolution" (*PDP*: 49). This revolution consists in the shift from an aesthetic to an ethical position of the author vis-à-vis his characters: rather than attempt to render them as fully known, coherent, and cohesive characters, Dostoevsky allows his characters to "act out of character," as it were, to outgrow the narrative frames and challenge the voice of their author.

What makes this authorial abdication truly "Copernican" in its magnitude becomes evident when it is related to life rather than literature: the polyphonic quality of Dostoevsky's novels, the "plurality of independent and unmerged voices and consciousnesses" (*PDP*: 6), and the capacity of his characters to "outgrow, as it were, from within and to render untrue any externalizing and finalizing definition" of themselves (*PDP*: 59) is not only a literary strategy; it is an offer of a new paradigm of ethical subjectivity, a "new artistic model of the world" (ibid., 3). The foundational principle of his new model of the world is the "non-coincidence" of the subject— fictional/literary or historical/real— with itself, or rather, with any "secondhand," "finalizing" definition of itself: "As long as a person is alive he lives by the fact that he is not yet finalized, that he has not yet uttered his ultimate word" (*PDP*: 59). The ethical implications of this paradigmatic shift are clearly related to the move from "code-centered" abstract systems to a phenomenology of the ethical subject who lives on its own borderlines and is always "axiologically yet-to-be" (*PDP*: 13, 16). What Bakhtin cherishes and values so highly in Dostoevsky's work is, arguably, the leap from the safety of ideological and aesthetic containment to the risk-fraught and heavy responsibility of ethics and freedom.

What Tolstoy does for Shklovsky, Dostoevsky does for Bakhtin.[17] The dichotomy of "rhythm" and "loophole" as the respective metaphoric vehicles for the "centripetal," and the "centrifugal" modes of being is, I suggest, very close to Shklovsky's juxtaposition of "habituation" and "defamiliarization." Indeed, as observed by Holquist and Kliger, if Shklovsky is the first and obvious figure in the historical poetics of estrangement, Bakhtin also features in this history by virtue of his recognition that language itself is "interwoven with an irreducible otherness" and his reading of the Dostoevskian heroes "who persist in their refusal to be finalized."[18]

But the affinity between Shklovsky and Bakhtin does not end there. Much like Shklovsky, whose profound temperamental need for re-enchantment is articulated through the concept of *ostranenie*, Bakhtin, too, seems to retain a profound sense of the sacred, which has nothing to do with religious orthodoxy or dogma. If "Author and Hero" reflects a sense of nostalgia for "enchantment," a state of religious and aesthetic naïveté, conflating the author with a benign, all-knowing Auctor Mundi, *Problems in Dostoevsky's Poetics* not only recognizes the impossibility of returning to this kind of enchantment but is also keenly aware of its attendant dangers. Given the historical and biographical circumstances of Bakhtin's work, it would be pointless to expect a full and explicit articulation of a Bakhtinian version of re-enchantment in his extant work. But there is, I believe, sufficient textual evidence which would enable some tentative conclusions on this matter. In his notes toward a revision of the Dostoevsky book, written at a time of relative relaxation of state censorship, Bakhtin obliquely relates to the question of faith: Dostoevsky's religiosity, he writes,

> [was] not faith (in the sense of a specific faith in orthodoxy, in progress, in man, in revolution, etc.) but a *sense of faith*, that is, an integral attitude

> (by means of the whole person) toward a higher and ultimate value. Atheism is often understood by Dostoevsky as a lack of faith in this sense, as indifference toward an ultimate value which makes demands on the whole man, as a rejection of an ultimate position in the ultimate whole of the world.
>
> *(PDP:* 294)

The juxtaposition of the "centripetal" and the "centrifugal," "I-for-the other" and "I-for-myself," "rhythm" and "loophole" is echoed once again in Bakhtin's wartime fragments. In "Rhetoric, to the Extent that It Lies" (dated "12 Oct. 1943"), he goes back to the premise of "Author and Hero," reiterating the claim that "the point of view from without, its surplus and boundaries" and "the point of view on one's own self from within" (respectively designated as "I-for-the-other" and "I-for myself" in the early essay) "cannot, in principle, overlap with one another, cannot fuse," and claiming that there is an "eternal tense struggle in the process of self-consciousness between 'I' and 'other'" (*REL:* 205). Both these positions are available to the subject, and we are all constituted in and through the tug-of-war between the desire for integration, containment, and narrative framing on the one hand, and the need for self-direction and free will on the other. Significantly, however, Bakhtin's view of the "centripetal" mode of subjectivity is now decidedly bleaker than it was in "Author and Hero." After decades of personal and historical calamities and the experience of ideological state terrorism, Bakhtin seems to mistrust the coherence of selfhood afforded by total immersion in the narrative of the other, no longer seen as benign. He is fully aware that a narrative that defines and enframes the subject monolithically is an act of violence, subjugation, and ethical "deadening" that deprives the self of its "future open-endedness," its freedom and its "inner infinity" (*REL:* 205, 209).[19]

This fragment, I have suggested, is actually an oblique reference to Bakhtin's earliest surviving fragment, *Toward a Philosophy of the Act*, and his conception of ethics as premised not on a code or an abstract set of imperatives and principles but on the absolute singularity of the subject, who has "no alibi in being." Bakhtin seems to go back to this premise, but now concedes that "the majority of people live not by their exceptionality, but by their otherness" (*REL:* 221). To translate this into the terms of the present discussion, Bakhtin seems to concede that most people are closer to the "centripetal" limit, living according to the rhythm of the framing narratives, authored through the eyes of others (society, ideology, or institutional religion) in "a world of other people's words," as he would later call it.[20] This, however, does not do away with the force of the "centrifugal" movement, as the boundary lines between "our own" and "others" words are never fixed, and invariably serve as the arena for "a tense dialogic struggle" (143). It is not difficult to guess which side of this dialogic struggle

Bakhtin would have picked at that point in his life. Against this closed, authoritative framing of subjectivity, he would insist on his own version of "re-enchantment"—the loophole which allows a mode of resistance to the grammar of ideology, with "neither a first nor a last word."[21]

Both Shklovsky and Bakhtin are metaphysical exiles, living in a disenchanted world, where the "vertical" metaphysical superstructures have lost their validity and force; both are primarily concerned with the nexus of ethics and subjectivity at a cultural junction where morality is no longer anchored in metaphysics, and "code-centered" ethical systems no longer suffice to account for ethical agency and choice. And both, I suggest, set out to recover a measure of "horizontal" transcendence and a re-enchantment of the world through the engagement with radical alterity, beginning with the literary works of Tolstoy and Dostoevsky, extrapolating their readings of fictional texts to the arena of lived experience, and working their way, against all odds, toward a renewed sense of philosophical wonder.

Notes

1. Berlina's Slavonic spelling of the first name (Viktor) has been followed throughout this essay.
2. Daphna Erdinast-Vulcan, *Between Philosophy and Literature: Bakhtin and the Question of the Subject* (Stanford: Stanford University Press, 2013), 57–65.
3. Charles Taylor, *A Secular Age*. The Gifford Lectures Series (Cambridge, MA: Belknap Press of Harvard University Press, 2007), 28–9.
4. Charles Taylor, "Recovering the Sacred," *Inquiry* 54.2 (2011): 113–25 (117–18).
5. Marcel Gauchet, *The Disenchantment of the World*, trans. O. Burge (Princeton: Princeton University Press, 1997 [1985]), 203.
6. Jane Bennett, *The Enchantment of Modern Life: Attachments, Crossings, and Ethics* (Princeton: Princeton University Press, 2001), 3.
7. Indeed, toward the end of his career, Shklovsky wrote: "All my life I have been studying Tolstoy, and Tolstoy keeps changing for me; it's as if he was growing young. He is always ahead of me." *On the Theory of Prose* (1983), quoted in *Viktor Shklovsky: A Reader*, ed. and trans. Alexandra Berlina (New York and London: Bloomsbury Academic, 2017), 306.
8. Viktor Shklovsky, "Resurrecting the Word," in *Shklovsky: A Reader*, 63–72 (63–4).
9. Galin Tihanov's astute discussion of Shklovsky's early writings observes a fundamental ambivalence or coexistence of radicalism and a deep-seated "conservatism," which he defines as a propensity to "look to the past for values," a belief in "the permanent and unalterable substance of things, and

nostalgia for the temporarily lost, but no doubt still recoverable, intimate proximity of word and object, which is posited as an ideal and set as a pressing task for the artist." Galin Tihanov, "The Politics of Estrangement: The Case of the Early Shklovsky," *Poetics Today* 26.4 (2005): 665–96 (673). I would whole-heartedly subscribe to this diagnosis, which relates to Shklovsky as yet another thinker in what I have elsewhere called "the exilic constellation" (see Erdinast-Vulcan, *Between Philosophy and Literature*).

10 *Shklovsky: A Reader*, 73–96.

11 *Shklovsky: A Reader*, 293–343 (307).

12 Indeed, Svetlana Boym writes of "emigration" of *ostranenie* "from text to life," and of its "historical metamorphosis ... from a technique [or a device] of art to an existential art of survival and a practice of freedom and dissent," which she traces through Shklovsky's experimental autobiographical texts of the 1920s, read in dialogue with Hannah Arendt's reflections on distance, freedom, and political dissent. Svetlana Boym, "Poetics and Politics of Estrangement: Victor Shklovsky and Hannah Arendt," *Poetics Today* 26.4 (2005): 581–611 (581).

13 For an extended discussion of this issue see Erdinast-Vulcan, *Between Philosophy and Literature*, 57–65.

14 In their foundational study of Bakhtin's work, Morson and Emerson relate to a "shifting ratio of finalizability to unfinalizability" through various phases along his philosophical itinerary and to the concomitant dichotomy of "rhythm" and "loophole." Caryl Emerson and Gary Saul Morson, *Mikhail Bakhtin: Creation of a Prosaics* (Stanford: Stanford University Press, 1990), 193, 217. In a later study, however, Emerson movingly relates to Shklovsky's conception of *ostranenie* (enstrangement) and to Bakhtin's *vnenakhodimost'* (variously translated as "transgredience," or "outsideness") in terms of "distancing," focusing on both the convergences and the divergences of their respective responses and aesthetic economies to the experience of physical pain, which was all too familiar to both of them. Caryl Emerson, "Shklovsky's *ostranenie*, Bakhtin's vnenakhodimost'" (How Distance Serves an Aesthetics of Arousal Differently from an Aesthetics Based on Pain), *Poetics Today* 26.4 (2005): 637–64. The thesis offered in the present discussion relates the concept of *ostranenie* to the opposite, "unfinalizable" end of the spectrum in Bakhtin's work.

15 M. M. Bakhtin, "Author and Hero in Aesthetic Activity," in *AA*, 4–256 (83).

16 Another perspective on the issue of freedom and narrative ethics is offered by Gary Saul Morson whose approach focuses on narrative structure (rather than characterization). Morson reads Dostoevsky's work as a project of resistance to the novelistic predisposition toward a "closed view of time," inasmuch as the structural indeterminacy of Dostoevsky's work allows for a "throb of presentness," retaining an openness to alternative ethical choices and endings. Gary Saul Morson, "Strange Synchronies and Surplus Possibilities: Bakhtin and Time," *Slavic Review* 52.3 (1993): 477–93 (478). For a more extensive engagement with Morson's thought-provoking conceptualization, see Erdinast-Vulcan, *Between Philosophy and Literature*, 123–4.

17 In *Energy of Delusion: A Book on Plot* (1981), Shklovsky writes: "This might sound strange, but rereading Tolstoy surprises me more often that reading Dostoevsky [for the first time]. In Dostoevsky's books, all characters think alike, as if they had only ever read a single author—Dostoevsky" (*Shklovsky: A Reader*, 291)—clearly, an echo of his implicit polemic with Bakhtin. The point of the present discussion, however, is not to pick sides, but to suggest that whatever the merits of their respective literary preferences, Bakhtin and Shklovsky are, in fact, closer than they know or acknowledge, inasmuch as both engage with the dynamics of literature as a mode of re-enchantment which may lead back to lived experience.

18 Michael Holquist and Ilya Kliger, "Minding the Gap: Toward a Historical Poetics of Estrangement," *Poetics Today* 26.4 (2005): 613–46 (634); for a more extensive discussion of this essay, see Erdinast-Vulcan, *Between Philosophy and Literature*, 62.

19 For a discussion of the wartime fragments and of Bakhtin's philosophical anthropology and the dynamics of autobiography as both an inscription and a performance of subjectivity see Erdinast-Vulcan, "Heterobiography: A Bakhtinian Perspective on Autobiographical Writing," *Life Writing* 15.3 (2018): 413–30.

20 M. M. Bakhtin, "From Notes Made in 1970–1971," in *SG*, 132–58 (143).

21 M. M. Bakhtin, "Toward a Methodology for the Human Sciences," in *SG*, 159–71 (170).

I am grateful to the Israel Science Foundation (ISF) for the generous support of my work.

10

Gide, Bakhtin, and the Threshold of Modernism

Tara Collington

> As *"longue durée"* work on modernity continues, the absence of modernist texts from Bakhtin's essays appears less a judgment than an invitation.
>
> (STACY BURTON)

In the introduction to the *Cambridge History of Modernism*, Vincent Sherry notes that "modernism" comes from the Latin root *modo*, a word denoting "not simply 'today' or even 'now', but '*just now*' … a temporality pressured by an immense sense of eventful change: a special present, a brink of time, a precipitous instant, all in all, a crisis time."[1] This impression of an accelerated pace of change in turn gives rise to the sensation of "time itself in crisis" (ibid., 2–3). Sherry describes this doubly charged sense of temporality as "the idea of a perpetual threshold moment in history" (ibid., 15) and he finds "advance signals" of this new Modernist sensibility at "specific points of mid-late nineteenth-century European culture, especially in France" (ibid., 20). In the same volume, Jean-Michel Rabaté reminds us that "'Modernism' happens to be a loaded word when understood in a French context" and that French critics adopted this term "only recently and reluctantly" in place of the more typical "modernité" (modernity).[2] The use of "modernité" in a critical context can be traced back to an article published by Balzac in 1822[3] and, more famously, an 1863 essay by Baudelaire.[4] As such, the beginnings of a "modernist" current in France may be seen earlier than in the Anglo-Saxon sphere, where it is generally more narrowly considered to apply to the early twentieth century. Rabaté traces the emergence of French Modernism from the early 1870s through the Symbolist movement and into the 1920s, noting a remarkable evolution of the French novel during this period, as "French modernism crossed genre boundaries and transformed the psychological novel of the last decades of the nineteenth century ... into a polyphony of voices even when they inhabit one single consciousness" (ibid., 578). Without naming Bakhtin, Rabaté nonetheless frames French Modernism in Bakhtinian terms by underlining its essential polyphony. In his analysis of Gide's contribution to this Modernist current in French literature, Rabaté notes that the author's later works shifted from "post-Symbolist experimental writing to an ethical Modernism in which daring experimentation with values dominated" (ibid., 584). This ethical Modernism is grounded in Gide's acceptance of his homosexuality, resulting in the "new frankness" and "direct mode of writing" that typifies the autobiographical *If It Die* (ibid., 585). Finally, Rabaté asserts that "the lever that helped André Gide put a distance between the Parisian aesthetes and his own vitalism was a combined influence, the discovery of Nietzsche's philosophy and the reading of Dostoevsky's novels" (ibid., 583).

Not surprisingly, Dostoevsky's impact on both Gide and Modernism has been much studied. In an analysis of Gide's reception of Dostoevsky, Donald Rayfield explains that very often, "Dostoevsky was read as an act of defiance against the conventions of the realist or naturalist novel," and that the "complex process of influence" that the Russian writer had on other European authors is best appreciated in the works of Gide.[5] Rayfield declares that "Dostoevsky's death and spectacular funeral procession in 1881, rather than his work, awoke the attention of France's literary circles to his crucial modernity" (ibid., 340) and he affirms that "it is easy, with hindsight, to see that Dostoevsky had been following a path that ran parallel to those pursued by Baudelaire, Verlaine and Huysmans" (ibid., 341). Prior criticism has thus established a direct line between early expressions of French Modernism, the works of Dostoevsky, and the novels of Gide. Peter Kaye similarly explores what he terms "the disruptive presence of Dostoevsky in the English house of fiction"[6] and provides a useful summary of the primary attributes of the Modernist movement:

> skepticism about the creeds, ideals, and artistic traditions of the past; disdain for the middle class and its conventions; a preoccupation with change; an interest in the workings of perception, consciousness, and what Virginia Woolf called "the dark places of psychology"; a profound sense of alienation, often separating the artist from family, community, or the general audience; an obsession with technique and an attendant delight in formal experimentation; and a conviction that the present time differed radically from all previous eras.
>
> (Kaye 1999: 3)

For many Modernist authors, Dostoevsky's novels proved to be an early expression of certain of these ideas and literary techniques, and his works influenced the development of Modernism in a variety of contexts.

Taking these observations as a starting point, this paper will explore links between Bakhtin, Gide, and Modernism, as construed through the intermediary figure of Dostoevsky. I will first briefly consider Bakhtin's engagement with French literature, then explore Bakhtin and Gide's profound and shared interest in the novels of Dostoevsky. I will then turn my attention to the link between Modernism and the threshold chronotope, examining its embodiment in the work of André Gide.

At first glance, any connection between the Russian philosopher and the French author seems tenuous. While it is true that Bakhtin was intimately familiar with French literature, his evocation of French authors rarely ventures into the twentieth century. In addition to devoting an entire book to Rabelais, Bakhtin's writings are peppered with references to canonical French authors from the Renaissance to the nineteenth century. Moreover, the essay "Forms of Time and of the Chronotope in the Novel" seems particularly influenced by French literary works, as two entire sections are devoted to the "Rabelaisian chronotope," while the section on the idyllic chronotope evokes the novels of Rousseau. Bakhtin posits the overturning of this chronotope in the subsequent works of Stendhal, Balzac, and Flaubert, and he traces its fragmentary form in the presence of characters of "idyllic descent," such as "Françoise in Proust" (*DI*: 235)— one of the rare references to contemporary French literature to be found in Bakhtin's writings. Furthermore, the chronotope of the salon is derived from the novels of Stendhal and Balzac, and that of the provincial town from Flaubert. The chronotope essay also contains a short discussion of the representation of death in Baudelaire as "a phenomenon on the border between my life here and now and a potential other kind of life" (*DI*: 200), with a footnote mentioning the Symbolist poets Rimbaud and Laforgue. Caryl Emerson notes that Bakhtin "had a thorough scholarly knowledge of Symbolist poetry and its successor movements in Russia"—and, we can add, at least a passing familiarity with French Symbolist poetry as well—but she concludes that "as far as we can tell, he was profoundly unresponsive to the major works of twentieth-century modernism."[7]

Bakhtin's indifference to contemporary literature is particularly noticeable in the chronotope essay, which only briefly evokes Proust. Evidently unmoved by Proust's madeleine, involuntary memory or experiments with narrative temporality, Bakhtin instead finds in Proust the last vestiges of the idyll. Interestingly, Gide was similarly initially unimpressed by Proust and, as a reviewer for the *Nouvelle Revue française*, rejected *In Search of Lost Time*, which was then published elsewhere (Rabaté 2017: 579). In "Discourse and the Novel," Bakhtin makes another passing reference to contemporary French literature when he declares that "when an aesthete undertakes to write a novel, his aestheticism is not revealed in the novel's formal construction, but exclusively in the fact that in the novel there is represented a speaking person who happens to be an ideologue for aestheticism," citing as one example "the early André Gide" (*DI*: 333). This is the only reference to Gide that I have been able to find in Bakhtin's writings and the Russian philosopher seems to narrowly categorize (and dismiss?) the French novelist as an "aesthete."

Bakhtin, Gide, and Dostoevsky

In the early 1920s, Bakhtin was working on the monograph that would become *Problems of Dostoevsky's Poetics* (first published in 1929 then revised in 1965). For his part, as early as 1908, Gide published an article on Dostoevsky and was working on a biography which he abandoned at the start of the First World War.[8] In 1921, Gide gave a series of invited lectures to mark the centenary of Dostoevsky's birth which were subsequently published in 1923—six years before the publication of the first edition of Bakhtin's book. Both Gide and Bakhtin assert that prior critics have fundamentally misunderstood the importance of the Russian author's contributions to literature. Gide is bemused that "certain minds are still obdurately prejudiced against his [Dostoevsky's] work" (1961: 13–14), while Bakhtin laments that "the fundamental innovation" of Dostoevsky's writing "has received far too little elucidation in the scholarship" (*PDP*: 3). For both critics, the works of Dostoevsky–who had already been dead for forty years—represent a radical shift in novelistic discourse. Gide finds Dostoevsky's novels to be "of all the books I know ... the most palpating with life" (1961: 16) and the author himself "the greatest of all novelists" (1961: 17), while for Bakhtin Dostoevsky is "one of the greatest innovators in the realm of artistic form" (*PDP*: 3).

Olga Tabachnikova observes that, "anticipating Bakhtin's revolutionary study of Dostoevsky's poetics," Gide "recognized the deep personalization of Dostoevsky's world and emphasized the role of ideas presented through particular personalities."[9] Like Bakhtin, Gide deems dialogue to be the central characteristic of Dostoevsky's works, stressing that in Dostoevsky's novels "ideas are never presented in their crude state, but always through the medium of the character expressing them" (1961: 48–9) and must be "sought in the speeches of his characters" (92). Bakhtin, of course, develops a more complete theory of the "polyphonic novel" in which a "character's word about himself and his world is just as fully weighted as the author's word usually is" (*PDP*: 7) and the hero is "not an objectified image but an autonomous discourse, *pure voice*; we do not see him, we hear him" (*PDP*: 53). For both Gide and Bakhtin, the innovative nature of Dostoevsky's writing thus resides in the apparent autonomy and dialogue of his characters. Stacy Burton notes that this decentering of authorial privilege to the benefit of the character prefigures the narrative experimentation of later Modernist writers: "As Bakhtin reads Dostoevsky, the nineteenth-century writer's greatness lies in his exceptional modernity."[10]

Gide also underscores both the relativity and temporal specificity of ideas in Dostoevsky's novels:

> His ideas are practically never absolute, remaining relative always to the characters expressing them. I shall press the point even further and assert their relativity not merely to these characters but to a specific moment in the lives of these characters. The ideas are, as it were, the product of a special and transitory state of his *dramatis personae*, and relative they remain, subservient to and conditioned by the particular fact or action which determines them or by which they are determined.
>
> (1961: 92–93)

This passage highlights those same temporal markers of modernity defined by Sherry—the "special present" and "perpetual threshold moment" that characterize the "*just now*"—and situates Dostoevsky as a proto-Modernist. For Gide, another signal feature of Dostoevsky's characters is their inconsistency or "disquieting duality" (1961: 106) as demonstrated by the coexistence of contradictory feelings and impulses. This combination of dialogue and duality results in characters who, according to Gide, are "never finished, ever changing," being "always in course of formation" (17). Finally, Gide examines characters' struggles with their own conscience, remarking on the "demonic" nature of their dualism (90). These observations are strangely prescient of Bakhtin and his assertion that a

> stubborn urge to see everything as coexisting, to perceive and show all things side by side and simultaneous, as if they existed in space and not in time, leads Dostoevsky to dramatize, in space, even internal contradictions and internal stages in the development of a single person—forcing a character to converse with his own double, with the devil, with his alter ego.
>
> (*PDP*: 28)

Similarly, Bakhtin also stresses the "unfinalized" (*PDP*: 73) nature of Dostoevsky's characters, stating that the author "always represents a person *on the threshold* of a final decision, at a moment of *crisis*" or a "turning point for his soul" (*PDP*: 61). This idea of crisis time on the threshold will prove for Bakhtin to be a defining characteristic of Dostoevsky's writing, one that we can also find in the works of Gide.

Crisis Time and Threshold Space

In *Problems of Dostoevsky's Poetics*, Bakhtin stresses the compositional originality of Dostoevsky's novels which signals a break with literary conventions as his works do not conform to the "generic and plot-compositional forms of a biographical novel, a socio-psychological novel, a novel of everyday life or a family novel" (*PDP*: 101). In combining into one work a multiplicity of generic forms, Dostoevsky's experimentation was perceived as "a crude and absolutely unjustified violation of the 'aesthetics of genre'" (*PDP*: 105). In addition to the polyphonic principle, Bakhtin identifies the representation of time as another important compositional feature of Dostoevsky's work:

> Those events that Dostoevsky portrayed on the *threshold* or on the *public square,* with their profound inner meaning ... could not have been explored in ordinary biographical and historical time. And in fact polyphony itself, as the event of interaction between autonomous and internally unfinalized consciousnesses, demands a different artistic conception of time and space.
>
> (*PDP*: 176)

If we return to Sherry's assertion that Modernism is principally concerned with the representation of time as both a "crisis time" and a "time in crisis," then we can see in Dostoevsky's novels the same generic experimentation and precursors of Modernism's temporality that both Sherry and Rabaté identify in the French Symbolist movement. Moreover, Sherry's description of the Modernist preoccupation with time as embodied by a "threshold moment" corresponds to Bakhtin's identification of the threshold as a defining feature of Dostoevsky's novels.

Throughout *Problems of Dostoevsky's Poetics*, Bakhtin returns time and again to the image of the threshold, locating the origins of the "threshold scene" in Menippean satire and tracing its evolution from medieval mystery plays through to the seventeenth and eighteen centuries (*PDP*: 116). Whereas, in earlier genres, these scenes take the form of veritable dialogues at the gates of heaven, in Dostoevsky's novels the scope of the scene has expanded; his characters stand more metaphorically on the threshold of "life and death, falsehood and truth, sanity and insanity" (*PDP*: 147). In terms of time, Dostoevsky thus concentrates action "at *points of crisis, at turning points and catastrophes*" and, in terms of space, on an actual threshold: "in doorways, entrance ways, on staircases, in corridors," or "on the *public square,* whose substitute is usually the drawing room (the hall, the dining room)" (*PDP*: 149). As such, the *metaphoric* threshold moment in a character's life unfolds in the *literal* threshold space represented in the novel. After listing numerous scenes in which important plot points concerning life-changing events occur in physical threshold spaces in *Crime and Punishment*, Bakhtin concludes:

> There is certainly no need to enumerate further all the "acts" that take place on the threshold, near the threshold, or that are permeated with the living sensation of threshold in this novel. The threshold, the foyer, the corridor, the landing, the stairway, its steps, doors opening onto the stairway, gates to front and back yards, and beyond these, the city: squares, streets, facades, taverns, dens, bridges, gutters. This is the space of the novel.
> (*PDP*: 170)

This interlinking of the crisis time of a life and the physical space of the threshold is more fully developed in the Concluding Remarks to the chronotope essay, where Bakhtin proposes a series of new chronotopes which have a "different degree and scope" than the "major" chronotopes outlined in the body of the essay (*DI*: 243). Among these minor chronotopes we find: the road, the castle, the salon, and the threshold. A single paragraph is devoted to this most intriguing of chronotopes, deemed by Bakhtin to be "highly charged with emotion and value" (*DI*: 248). The threshold represents a "chronotope of *crisis* and *break* in a life" and is associated with "the decision that changes a life (or the indecisiveness that fails to change a life, the fear to step over the threshold)" (*DI*: 248). Once again, Bakhtin links the representation of crisis time in Dostoevsky to a particular spatial setting, observing that in his works the main events of the plot typically occur in the physical space of a threshold or in the spaces of "the staircase, the front hall and corridor" as well as in "the street and square that extend those spaces into the open air" (1981: 248). In the threshold chronotope, time seems "essentially instantaneous" as if it "has no duration and falls out of the normal course of biographical time" (248). I will use the term "threshold chronotope" to encompass the broad range of spatial manifestations (doorways, stairs, halls, streets, public gardens, and waiting rooms) linked to this arrested time in which a character faces a moment of decision or crisis, "the falls, the resurrections, renewals, epiphanies, decisions that determine the whole life of a man" (*DI*: 248). I will now turn to selected works of André Gide, examining their expression of a new, ethical Modernism and the manifestations of the threshold chronotope in his writings, most particularly in his novel *The Counterfeiters*.

The Threshold Chronotope in Gide

Several of Gide's works contain what may be described as threshold scenes. For Rayfield, *The Vatican Caves* is the "most Dostoevskian work" in the Gidean canon (2000: 341) and Lafcadio's murder of Fleurissoire explicitly echoes Raskolnikov's murder of the old woman "not for profit, not out of illness, despair or protest, but 'to see if I could'" (2000: 348). As Lafcadio commits this "*acte gratuit*" (crime without motive) by throwing his victim out the door of a moving train, time seems to grind to an interminable halt as he considers the possibilities then decides to act, thinking to himself: "It's not so much about events that I'm curious, as about myself."[11] Rayfield observes that Gide is fascinated by "the life-and-death, surrender-or-rebellion predicament of Dostoevsky's heroes" (2000: 342), and this scene perfectly illustrates Gide's imitation of Dostoevskian crisis time and what Bakhtin terms "testing the 'man in man'" (*PDP*: 105), as Lafcadio puts his disregard for moral conventions to the test. Rabaté notes that Gide himself asserted that this "was to be a 'demoralizing book', an undoing of any bourgeois morality testifying to a deep sense of crisis, more than just a literary parody of the picaresque novel."[12] Gide had, of course, already long been exploring what Rabaté terms "ethical modernism" (2017: 584), more particularly the break with the traditional values most often represented by the family unit. And this break is often embodied by the spatial image of crossing a threshold. As early as 1897, with the publication of *Fruits of the Earth*, Gide has Menalcas express his disdain for the traditional family with the famous line "Families, I hate you!", which continues with a spatial image: "Closed circles round the hearth; fast shut doors; jealous possession of happiness."[13] Menalcas, looking through a window and seeing a boy doing his homework under his father's watchful eye immediately longs to lure the boy away, across the threshold of a conventional, domesticated life to "live a wandering life on the roads" (Gide 1949: 67).

This same image of crossing a threshold into a more authentic life occurs repeatedly in the autobiographical *If It Die*. The first evocation of a threshold marks an epiphany concerning the cousin Gide would eventually marry. Arriving unexpectedly at her house, Gide discovers his aunt's infidelity and cousin's sorrow, declaring that "On the very threshold I scented something unusual."[14] He makes his way up a darkened staircase to his cousin's bedchamber, where he knocks on the door to comfort her. Her grief and shame bring about a revelation for Gide: the discovery that she is the "mystic lodestar" (1977: 106) of his life, the focus of a love so pure that their subsequent marriage would never be consummated. This relationship is fictionalized in *Strait Is the Gate*, whose very title evokes the image of a difficult, if not impossible, threshold to cross.

A second threshold epiphany in *If It Die* relates to Gide's acceptance of his homosexuality. While traveling in North Africa, Gide hesitates before accepting the sexual invitation of a male guide, and in recounting the scene wonders, "Was I still hesitating on the threshold of what is called sin?" (1977: 248). After succumbing to temptation, Gide attempts to normalize his sexuality through encounters with a female prostitute, this time framing his failure in terms of an impassable threshold: "The door which hope had pushed ajar for a moment was too heavy; it had slammed back again; it always would: I was shut out for ever" (254). Unable to enter into the realm of conventional sexuality, on an evening out with Oscar Wilde, Gide is captivated by the sight of a young musician as he hesitates on the threshold of a café. Later, in an alleyway, a space which, according to Bakhtin, extends the threshold into the public square, Wilde asks, "would you like the little musician?" and Gide finally sums up the courage to openly declare his sexual preference by saying "Yes" (281). In the subsequent passages, Gide crosses a threshold both in terms of his sexuality and his narrative. Hitherto extremely circumspect in describing his sexual adventures, he now feels free to reveal them in astonishing detail, relating that he "reached the summit of pleasure five times" (285) on that remarkable night. Throughout various texts published between the late 1890s and 1926, Gide thus explores threshold moments associated with a crisis or a break in a life, as characters—or the author himself—seek to free themselves from the constraints of social convention and create a new, modern sense of self.

Gide did not consider any of the texts mentioned above to be novels, preferring the terms "récit" for the first-person confessional narrative and "sotie" (originally a medieval satirical farce) for *The Vatican Caves*. The dedication of *The Counterfeiters* (*TC*) indicates that Gide considered this work his first and only novel, and it is here that the threshold chronotope is most fully deployed as the location where "the knots of narrative are tied and untied" (*DI*: 250) in a text with a notoriously complex structure involving multiple intersecting plotlines. The very first line of the novel—"'The time has now come for me to hear a step in the passage,' said Bernard to himself"[15]–references a threshold space, which reflects Bernard's liminal state, poised on the point of abandoning his family. Having just discovered that he is the product of his mother's extramarital liaison, Bernard acts out the scenario envisaged by Menalcas, quitting the family home with nothing but the clothes on his back. He first articulates his plans to Olivier in the Luxembourg gardens, a public space that becomes the extension of the threshold. After spending one night at Olivier's, Bernard sleeps on a public bench on the quays and seems stuck in a threshold space as he tries to determine what to do next. Having freed himself from the conventional family where he never felt at ease, he hopes to live by a new credo: "If I don't do it, who will? If I don't do it at once, when shall I" (1973: 57) but the narrator quickly points out the emptiness of his enterprise: "He thinks: 'Great things to do!' [...] If only he knew what they were!" (57). Bernard's next life-altering decision takes place in another threshold space, the waiting room of the St. Lazare train station, where he picks up the cloakroom ticket inadvertently discarded by Edouard and proceeds to steal his suitcase, an immoral act which only gives him slight pause before he overcomes his scruples. The theft of the suitcase allows him to read the journal he finds therein and to present himself to Edouard as a possible secretary. Toward the end of the novel, while in the Luxembourg gardens meditating on his future, Bernard encounters an angel who takes him through the streets of Paris, first showing him the wealthy boulevards and then opening his eyes to the harsh realities of the city's squalid quarters. Bernard's subsequent wrestling match with the angel remains unresolved, as he continues to seek his future path in life.

As for Bernard's family, M. Profitendieu learns of Bernard's decision to leave in a way which prolongs the opening threshold scene, as Antoine, their servant, makes sure to catch him "in the passage" (1973: 13) to inform him of his son's departure. While contemplating the caustic letter Bernard has left for him, Profitendieu is constantly interrupted by noise, knocking on the study door, irruptions into the room, and, finally, a ring of the doorbell as his wife arrives home. The steps in the passage proliferate as if to underscore the missed opportunity: they come too late to stop Bernard.

Edouard's first meeting with Georges Molinier takes place in a liminal space, the quays along the Seine, where (without knowing it is his nephew) he spies a boy trying to shoplift a travel book on Algeria from a bouquiniste. Georges cites his interest in geography as the reason for wanting the book, but Edouard rather suspects that "an instinct for vagabonding was concealed behind this liking" (1973: 88), recalling Menalcas' image of a "wandering life." Georges will make a life-altering decision in a similarly public threshold space, as he accepts a counterfeit coin from Ghéridanisol while walking on the Boulevard Saint-Michel and passes it off in a tobacco shop.

Other characters are similarly poised on the threshold of life-changing moral decisions. The entire plotline concerning Vincent and Laura plays out within a threshold chronotope. They meet on the garden terrace of a sanatorium in Pau and, convinced that they only have a short while to live, embark upon an adulterous affair. This idyll, which seems to be a suspended moment outside of biographical time, results in a pregnancy which will become a turning point in each of their lives, as Vincent abandons her and gambles away (then wins back) the money he had intended to give her. Once again, their storyline unfolds in a threshold space as Laura waits until 3 o'clock in the morning "on the steps which led to the Moliniers' flat," to entreat with Vincent; but he repudiates her, telling her to return to her husband and "shut[s] the door against her," leaving her sobbing in the hallway (1973: 39). Later, when his conscience gets the better of him and he seeks her out, Vincent is left "wait[ing] in the hall" as she rejects his belated offer of financial assistance (146). The narrator maps out the evolution of Vincent's character as he invents for himself a "new ethic" to "legitimize his conduct" toward Laura (143). In fact, Vincent is acting under the influence of Lady Griffith, whose own conduct has been determined by a prior threshold moment. During a shipwreck which she survived, she witnessed sailors chopping off the hands of passengers desperate to climb into already-full lifeboats, and this sight has influenced her subsequent conduct: "I realized that I was no longer the same ... that henceforth there would be a whole heap of delicate feelings whose fingers and hands I should hack away to prevent them from climbing into my heart and wrecking it" (1973: 64). At the end of the novel, we learn that Vincent either "thinks himself possessed by the devil," or "thinks he *is* the devil" (376), probably having murdered Lady Griffith by drowning her.

The reader first learns of Vincent and Laura's affair when Olivier explains that from his bedroom he can hear the comings and goings of his older brother whose door also opens out onto the common landing. In a novel in which very few physical spaces are described in any detail, the narrator frequently insists upon the unusual nature of various bed chambers and the possibilities for transgression that these spatial arrangements afford. Olivier's bedroom "opens straight on to the staircase, half a floor below [the] flat" (1973: 7), allowing him to secretly harbor Bernard for a night. From Saas-Fée, Bernard writes to Olivier explaining that he and Edouard are traveling with Laura, who is pretending to be Edouard's wife. They have taken adjoining rooms and every night Laura crosses the threshold into the single room to sleep alone while Edouard and Bernard share the other room. Filled with "impure visions" (173) and "tortured" by the thought of them sharing a room, Olivier decides to join the Comte de Passavant on his travels. Later in the novel, Edouard rescues him from Passavant and takes him to his own apartment, where Olivier attempts suicide. He tries to convince Edouard that he is not certain of his own motives but clarifies that the act was not related to feeling "ashamed" (322). In fact, Olivier's attempted suicide is rather an explicit reference to Dostoevsky, as Bernard had asked him if he understood the idea of killing oneself "out of a mere excess of life, 'out of enthusiasm' as Dimitri Karamazov says" and Olivier had responded in the affirmative, saying that "he understood killing oneself, but only after having reached such heights of joy, that anything afterwards must be a descent" (310). The source of this transcendent joy, Olivier's new intimate relationship with Edouard, is confirmed by the description of Olivier's room as adjoining that of his uncle, with the door between being "left open" (313).

Similarly, Sarah Vedel's room can only be reached by passing through her parents' room or through that of Armand, and she is thus caught between the strict puritanism of her parents and the decadence of her brother. Sarah sneaks out through Armand's room which conveniently opens "on to the backstairs," where she will first meet Bernard in the dark "passage" (1973: 290) before going with him to the banquet for Passavant's new literary review. When they return, Armand ushers them through his room and into Sarah's, only to abruptly lock them in together, bolting the door behind him. Armand has effectively pushed his sister over a moral threshold, playing Pandarus to this modern Troilus and Cressida.

Landings, passageways, doorways, staircases, and windows are privileged spaces in *The Counterfeiters*, locations where characters experience moral crises related to their sexuality and/or their sense of self-identity. It is not a coincidence that Edouard speaks with Laura on her wedding day "in the embrasure of a window" where a decade before they had written their names on the frame (1973: 101). Laura has made her choice: she weds Douviers rather than continue pining for Edouard whose love for her is as chaste as the author's own love for his cousin. At this same reception, Sarah embraces Olivier on the bed in Laura's old room, then leads Edouard "out on the landing" to show him her father's old diary, the one in which he recounts his struggles to give up "smoking," with both of them thinking "that 'smoking' stood for something else" (112). The sexual hypocrisy of Pastor Vedel is thus revealed on the threshold of his daughter's old bedroom.

Perhaps the most crucial threshold scene in the novel involves the suicide of Boris, who is goaded by the young counterfeiters into the gesture to demonstrate his bravery. They set up an elaborate scenario "fixing the hour, and the place, which they marked on the floor with a bit of chalk," selecting as the ideal location "a recess, formed by a disused door, which had formerly opened on to the entrance hall" in the school (1973: 387). As the fatal moment approaches, time seems to slow down. Ghéridanisol places his watch on the table next to Boris and cruelly announces the countdown: "you've only got a quarter of an hour more," then: "only ten minutes more" (389). As if to underscore the threshold nature of the scene, the narrator equates Boris with "a foreigner who, on arriving at the frontier of the country he is leaving, prepares his papers" (389). Boris walks to the appointed place "slowly, like an automaton," and as the fatal shot is fired the scene retains a slow-motion quality, with La Pérouse "rooted to the spot" and the boy's body "stay[ing] upright for a moment" before collapsing (391). Only afterwards does time resume a normal rhythm, with George leaping over the desks to grab the pistol and Ghéridanisol running unnoticed in the confusion to return it to La Pérouse's room, as the boys attempt to conceal their cruel game.

From its opening pages to this climactic scene, every plotline of the novel shows characters in threshold spaces such as doorways, stairs, halls, landings, public terraces, streets, and gardens where decisions are made which change the course of a life, contributing to what Bakhtin terms a "chronotope of *crisis* and *break* in a life" (*DI*: 248). Time in these scenes often appears to have slowed and fallen out of the course of normal biographical time. Armand Vedel aptly summarizes the overall feeling of threshold chronotope which dominates the novel as he explains to Olivier:

> I am calculating the extremest point. It is possible. It is still possible … It is no longer possible! My mind walks along that narrow ridge. That dividing line between existence and nonexistence is the one I keep trying to trace everywhere. The limit of resistance to—well, for instance, to what my father would call temptation. One holds out; the cord on which the

devil pulls is stretched to breaking ... A tiny bit more, the cord snaps—one is damned.

(1973: 287)

He then asks Olivier: "Do you understand now what it is to feel that one is always 'on the border line'?" (1973: 288). Here then is the dilemma of the characters in *The Counterfeiters*: how to inhabit this border line of their moral choices in the perpetual threshold moment presented by this Modernist novel.

The *Journal of "The Counterfeiters"*

Gide began work on *The Counterfeiters* in 1919 but the novel itself was not published until 1925. He also maintained a diary of his writing process, published two years later as the *Journal of the Counterfeiters*, which traces important aspects of the evolution of the novel, such as the initial intent to have the text narrated by Lafcadio from *The Vatican Cellars*, the development of certain plot lines, and Gide's own reflections on the construction of the novel as a genre, many of which find their way into *The Counterfeiters* in Edouard's journal. Both Gide and his fictional author are seeking a new novelistic form, one freed from the conventions of the excessive descriptions of the realist novel. "Purge the novel of all elements that do not belong specifically to the novel" (1973: 432) admonishes Gide, in his *Journal*, while Edouard writes: "I should like to strip the novel of every element that does not specifically belong to the novel" (1973: 73). Similarly, both accord far greater autonomy to the reader in the co-creation of the story, for, according to Edouard, "The novelist does not as a rule rely sufficiently on the reader's imagination" (74), while Gide concludes that "The story requires his collaboration in order to take shape properly" (416). *The Counterfeiters* satirizes the reader's expectation that every aspect of a novel is fully mapped out by the author, as a character bemoans of a book he is reading, "'I've got as far as page thirty without coming across a single colour or a single word that makes a picture. He speaks of a woman and I don't know whether her dress was red or blue. As far as I'm concerned, if there are no colours, it's useless, I can see nothing" (5). *The Counterfeiters* itself contains very little intervention on the part of the narrator to provide concrete descriptions of its characters. These details are rather gleaned from the characters' speeches, such as when Edouard wonders if he could have guessed from one of her letters that Laura's hair was black, then reflects on the disservice that authors do to their readers by providing too much descriptive detail.

For Rayfield, the very structure of *The Counterfeiters*, "a novel about a novelist writing a novel about a novelist writing a novel, could not be less Dostoevskian" (2000: 353), and yet both Gide's *Journal* and Edouard's fictional journal testify to a preoccupation profoundly influenced by Gide's reading of Dostoevsky: the desire to allow characters to speak for themselves. In the *Journal*, Gide declares: "I should like events never to be related directly by the author, but instead exposed (and several times from different vantages) by those actors who will be influenced by those events" (1973: 416). In a passage reminiscent of Bakhtin's distinction between the monologic and the polyphonic novel, Gide also observes that "The poor novelist constructs his characters; he controls them and makes them speak. The true novelist listens to them and watches them function; he eavesdrops on them even before he knows them. It is only according to what he hears them say that he begins to understand who they are" (1973: 444).

In *The Counterfeiters*, Edouard expresses a similar desire to allow his characters to speak for themselves, thinking, "[I]t would be a better plan to make the boy tell the story himself; his point of view is of more signification than mine" (87), as he debates whether to narrate a scene himself or allow the character to relate it from his own perspective.

Another Dostoevskian feature of *The Counterfeiters* lies in its unfinalizability, as the fate of many characters remains undetermined. Bernard and George have each returned to their families, but how long this reconciliation will last and where it will lead remain unknown. What will befall Vincent, the reconciliation of Laura and her husband, and the future of Edouard and Olivier's relationship–not to mention the fate of the Edouard's novel–all remain uncertain. For Daphna Erdinast-Vulcan, the unfinalizability of Dostoevsky's novels is a form of "resistance to narrative closure" and may also be considered a "distinct feature of modernist fiction."[16] Gide notes in his journal "I am fond of sudden endings" (1973: 450) and *The Counterfeiters* ends with an excerpt of Edouard's journal, the last sentence being "I feel very curious to know Caloub" (Bernard's younger brother, who appears only tangentially in the novel) (397). Earlier, Edouard had written in his journal "'Might be continued'–these are the words with which I should like to finish my *Counterfeiters*" (335), a sentence which prefigures the novel's absence of a true ending.

Perhaps the most interesting aspect of the *Journal of the Counterfeiters* is Gide's acknowledgment of his difficulties in writing the novel. Very little of the initial idea centering around Lafcadio is preserved. It is unclear exactly when the action of the novel is set, and in the *Journal* we also find clues regarding this temporal ambiguity, as Gide reflects: "Probably it is not very clever to place the action of this book *before* the war, or to include *historical* considerations; I cannot be retrospective and immediate at the same time" then goes on to add: "The future interests me more than the past, but even more what belongs neither to tomorrow nor to yesterday but which in all times can be said to belong to today" (1973: 407). Here we find that quintessentially Modernist idea of the "*just now.*" In the second-to-last journal entry, dated March 1925, Gide offers some final observations on his writing process and notes: "one of the peculiarities of this book ... is the excessive difficulty I find in beginning each new chapter—a difficulty almost equal to the one that held me marking time on the threshold of the book for so long" (1973: 449). Like his characters, Gide views himself as being caught in a life-changing moment, marking time on the threshold of producing his first (and only) Modernist novel.

Notes

1. V. Sherry, ed., *The Cambridge History of Modernism* (Cambridge: Cambridge University Press, 2017), 2.
2. J. M., Rabaté "French Modernism: Gide, Proust, and Larbaud," in *The Cambridge History of Modernism*, ed. V. Sherry (Cambridge: Cambridge University Press, 2017), 575–95 (575).
3. This article, "Considérations sur la littérature romantique" is presented and edited by Rolland Chollet in "Balzac critique littéraire en 1822. Une importante découverte balzacienne" [Balzac as a Literary Critic in 1822. An Important Balzacian Discovery], *L'Année balzacienne*, 13 (2012): 231–42.
4. C. Baudelaire, "Le Peintre de la vie moderne" [The Painter of Modern Life], in *Œuvres complètes, tome 3* (Paris: Calmann Lévy, 1885), 51–6.
5. D. Rayfield, "A Virgil to His Dante: Gide's Reception of Dostoevsky," *Forum for Modern Language Studies* 36.4 (2000): 340–56 (340).
6. P. Kaye, *Dostoevsky and English Modernism, 1900–1930* (Cambridge: Cambridge University Press, 1999), 6.
7. C. Emerson, "Introduction: Dialogue on Every Corner, Bakhtin in Every Class," in *Bakhtin in Contexts: Across the Disciplines*, ed. A. Mandler (Evanston: Northwestern University Press, 1995), 1–30 (17).
8. A. Gide, *Dostoevsky*, trans. A. Bennett (New York: New Directions, 1961), 48.
9. O. Tabachnikova, "'Dialogues with Dostoevsky' from Two Corners: Lev Shestov versus André Gide," *New Zealand Slavonic Journal* 42 (2008): 55–76 (65).
10. S. Burton, "Paradoxical Relations: Bakhtin and Modernism," *Modern Language Quarterly* 61.3 (2000): 519–43 (532).
11. A. Gide, *The Vatican Cellars*, trans. D. Bussy (London: Penguin, 1959), 185.
12. J.-M. Rabaté, *1913: The Cradle of Modernism* (Malden: Blackwell Publishing, 2007), 53.
13. A. Gide, *Fruits of the Earth*, trans. D. Bussy (London: Secker & Warburg, 1949), 67.
14. A. Gide, *If It Die*, trans. D. Bussy (Harmondsworth: Penguin, 1977), 104.

15 A. Gide, *The Counterfeiters and Journal of the Counterfeiters*, trans. D. Bussy (New York: Vintage Books, 1973), 3. For an extended analysis of the importance of the novel's opening line and the privileging of the "instant," see S. Gallon, "La Fissure étroite: De la première phrase des *Faux-Monnayeurs* de Gide," *Questions de style* [The Narrow Crack: On the First Sentence of Gide's *Counterfeiters*], 10 (2013): 49–82.

16 D. Erdinast-Vulcan, "Narrative, Modernism, and the Crisis of Authority: A Bakhtinian Perspective," *Science in Context* 7.1 (1994): 143–58 (153).

11

Sensation and Abstraction

The Station as a Modernist Chronotope

Anker Gemzøe

Introduction

Focusing on the station as an iconic image of a modern conception of time and space, a primary aim of the present chapter is to examine the scope of the concept of the chronotope as presented by Mikhail M. Bakhtin and further developed by a number of Bakhtin scholars. With its "four dimensions" fusing time and space, the concept of the chronotope corresponds better to the task of reading modern poetry than the "two-dimensional" concept of place often one-sidedly preferred in recent years. In this article, I suggest a philosophical contextualization for Bakhtin's concept in the Modernist discussion of sensation and abstraction, referring to Theodor W. Adorno, Frederick Jameson, Sanford Schwartz, and Patricia Waugh. Methodologically, I explore the analytical power of the concept of the chronotope in a philosophically informed close reading of two important Modernist poems: the Danish Nobel Prize-winner Johannes V. Jensen's "Paa Memphis Station" (At Memphis Station, 1906)[1] and Ezra Pound's "In a Station of the Metro" (1913).[2] The aforementioned literary scholars contribute to demonstrate how some of the aspirations of Modernist poetry progressed in interaction with fundamental endeavors in contemporary science and philosophy. This interaction was not a one-way influence of theory on art. As emphasized by Jacques Rancière, among others, literature and other art forms have often anticipated developments in theory[3]—or accomplished parallel developments through their special "mimetic" devices.

Another aim of this paper is to demonstrate the relevance of a "Bakhtinian" approach to (modern) poetry. Although Bakhtin himself focused mainly on prose fiction, his first analysis of a literary work was indeed of a poem: an analysis of "Parting" by Alexander Pushkin was included in the posthumously published work of youth *Toward a Philosophy of the Act* (*PTA*). In the subsequent, likewise posthumously published essay, *Author and Hero in Aesthetic Activity*, he considerably expands his reading (*AA*: 211–27). In an anticipation of his theories of dialogue and polyphony, he concludes that the poem holds three evaluative centers: that of the heroine, of the hero, and of the author. The word of the heroine is encompassed by that of the hero, and both are encompassed by the form-giving activity of the author—"and, consequently the intonation of almost every word in the poem must be performed likewise in three directions: the real-life intonation of the heroine, the equally real-life intonation of the hero, and the formal intonation of the author/reader" (*AA*: 212f.).

In "The Problem of Content, Material, and Form in Verbal Art" he claims that the word is maximally charged in poetry, especially "in lyric, where the body, generating the sound from within itself and feeling the unity of its own productive exertion, is drawn into form" (*AA*: 314). Finally, in "Epic and Novel. Toward a Methodology for the Study of the Novel" (1941), Bakhtin calls attention to the "novelization" of all the remaining genres in modern literature, "even lyric poetry (as an extreme example Heine's lyrical verse)."[4] This offers a good argument for the overall applicability of Bakhtin's theories about the "prosaic" word to modern poetry.[5] Moreover, Bakhtin's relation to poetry was much more enthusiastic than is implied in a polemical statement like the simplified comparison between the poetic and the prosaic word in *Discourse in the Novel*.[6]

The Modern Sublime

In Theodor W. Adorno's aesthetics,[7] beauty, in the modern art and literature the philosopher seeks to characterize, appears as a form-creating reaction to experiences of the ugly, the repulsive, the shocking: "What codifies the category of beauty is the transition to the primacy of form. Beauty at once shows and reduces the terrible, from which it elevates itself in a process of formalisation" (Adorno 1997: 97, my translation).[8] "The terrible stares at us from beauty, even in the coercion that radiates from form," he adds (99): in its wish to impose pure form on living diversity, art itself has an affinity to death. Beauty increasingly shifts into the dynamic totality in the new art, rather than being found in beautiful words and passages. For the sake of beauty, modern art avoids the beautiful, since beauty no longer exists in modernity. For the sake of art itself, it may be necessary to renounce art (cf. 101).

For Adorno, the *sublime* constitutes a central conceptual approach to the transformations of beauty in modernity. The sublime, he argues, is art that becomes shocking as it suspends its artistic character in favor of truth, and yet retains it (cf. 340). "The sublime that Kant reserved for nature became, after Kant, what constitutes art itself historically" (341). Through a more rigorous demand for truth, including the terrifying and the ugly, art separated itself from a traditional concept of beauty that was increasingly regarded as kitsch. At the same time, the sublime itself—in the sense of unmediated, anointing pathos—became problematic. "The legacy of the sublime is relentless negativity, naked and unadulterated" (344), Adorno concludes, adding that it can also lend the sublime a shade of the comical.

Adorno focuses solely on the reassignment of the sublime from nature to art. In his aesthetics he disregards another historical development: the shift of the sublime from nature to society. Such a displacement—located in a later historical phase—is one of the key points in Fredric Jameson's groundbreaking essay "Post-Modernism, or, The Cultural Logic of Late Capitalism." Here he points to the technology of the latest stage of capitalism, the stage of "multinational capital,"[9] as an expression of a "radical eclipse of Nature itself" (77), as a

> shorthand to designate that enormous properly human and anti-natural power of dead human labor stored up in our machinery, an alienated power, what Sartre calls the counterfinality of the practico-inert, which turns back on and against us n unrecognizable forms and seems to constitute the massive dystopian horizon of our collective as well as our individual praxis.
>
> (Ibid.)

This is represented by, for example, "the computer whose outer shell has no emblematic or visual power" (79). Yet both technology and "the most energetic postmodernist texts" seem to offer

> some privileged representational shorthand for grasping a network of power and control even more difficult for our minds and imaginations to grasp—namely, the whole new, decentralized network in the third stage of capital itself [...] It is therefore in terms of that enormous and threatening, yet only dimly perceivable, other reality of economic and social institutions that in my opinion the postmodern sublime can alone be adequately theorized.
>
> (79f)

It seems to me entirely possible to step historically backward to a concept of "the modern sublime." The defining metaphors of industrialization and urbanization—the huge factory, the giant machine, the railway station, the metro, the ocean liner, and the locomotive—have a marked visibility, which, counterintuitively, only enhances their aura of myth and mystery. As expressions of technological and organizational complexes that, though human-made, express a natural-like autonomy and uncontrollability, they can inspire in the viewer a numinous awe—a mixture of fascination, fear, and an awkwardly comical sense of powerlessness. I would argue a complex mimetic relationship between "the modern sublime" in this social sense and in the aesthetic sense envisaged by Adorno.

Sensation and Abstraction: Structural Mimesis and Chronotope

Modernism and the avant-garde express aesthetically mediated reactions to modernity, an experience of it. Modernism and the avant-garde, however, distinguish themselves from realism "by not only, not primarily or not at all seeking to reproduce modernity as a 'content', but rather performing some kind of *structural mimesis*."[10] The transgression of tradition inherent in Modernism, its effort to mirror modernity with modern aesthetic devices, its acute form consciousness and self-reflexivity—everything converges in a structural mimesis that combines sensation and abstraction.

In *The Matrix of Modernism: Pound, Eliot, and Early Twentieth-Century Thought*, Sanford Schwartz offers a broad presentation of the motif of sensation and abstraction in contemporary philosophy and in Modernism. With a point of departure in very different but nonetheless related philosophers like Nietzsche, William James, Bergson, and (the lesser known) F. H. Bradley, he explains the importance of the relationship between sensed experience and abstraction—and thus also reflects on the role of art in philosophy around the year 1900. He also convincingly demonstrates in detail how a similar preoccupation with sensation and abstraction was central to the Modernist poetics developed by T. E. Hulme, Ezra Pound, and T. S. Eliot, among others. Without adhering to one philosophical position, they moved within a spectrum, often taking the middle ground, seeing "art as a form of mediation between the abstract and the concrete, between the unifying power of the concept and the diversity of sensory particulars it relates."[11] Schwartz's ideological-historical contextualization of this branch of Modernism is compelling, his review of Pound and Eliot's poetics competent and detailed. It contains, however, certain limitations. To some extent, he disregards Pound's explicit contempt for philosophy. Pound did not care for the philosopher T. E. Hulme, his "rival" as a theorist of imagism, and could reject modern philosophy entirely with one of his typical nonchalant maxims: "Philosophy since Leibniz (at least since Leibniz) has been a weak trailer after material science, engaging men of tertiary importance."[12] Pound aligned literature not with philosophy, but with science, mathematics, and possibly psychology. A more serious limitation—which to some extent reproduces blind spots in Pound and Eliot's poetics—is the lack of any clear notion of modernity in Schwartz's account. In Pound's case, as referred without comment by Schwartz, it reveals itself in his very treatment of "In a Station of the Metro," when he writes about the poem's second verse as an "interpretive metaphor": "The image functions as a kind of lens through which to 'interpret' the natural object" (Schwartz 1985: 93). That is, to put it mildly, a generalization, an abstraction of "the natural object," which thus could just as well be a mountain landscape as a metro station. The latter, however, is not a "natural" but a highly social and urban phenomenon.

In her essay "Beyond Mind and Matter: Scientific Epistemologies and Modernist Aesthetics," Patricia Waugh has shown that the issue was equally relevant to Modernist prose fiction. On the mutually inspiring relationship between British scientific philosophers and Modernist theorists between 1910 and 1930, she concludes:

> What unites [Roger] Fry in painting, [Bertrand] Russell and [Alfred North] Whitehead in philosophy of science, and [Virginia] Woolf in fiction, is the desire to explore modes of knowing and representing which might discover a bridge between the sensory world of experience and the formal world of structural relations.[13]

The Modernist reaction to a conventional realism-as-style includes a search for a sub-empirical structure, a matrix or abstraction.

Originating in the same period, Mikhail Bakhtin's concept of the chronotope expresses a similar effort to connect sensation and abstraction. The word chronotope is a combination of *chronos* (time) and *topos* (place, space), meaning time-space. Space, however, is the phenomenological starting point. In the outer forms of space, the inner experience of time can be traced and interpreted. The chronotope is thus also a concept for Goethe's "ability to *see time*, to *read time* in the spatial whole of the world, and, on the other hand, to perceive the filling of space [...] as an emerging whole" ("The *Bildungsroman* and Its Significance in the History of Realism: Toward a Historical Typology of the Novel" (*SG*: 25)).

The concept of chronotope is inspired by new scientific theories. It is a term borrowed from Einstein's Theory of Relativity that connects time and space more closely than envisaged before. Bakhtin became acquainted with the term in 1925 during a lecture by the famous Russian brain researcher A. A. Uxtomskij. He writes about the concept:

> This term [space-time] is employed in mathematics, and was introduced as part of Einstein's Theory of Relativity [...] What counts for us is the fact that it expresses the inseparability of space and time (time as the fourth dimension of space). We understand the chronotope as a formally constitutive category of literature; we will not deal with the chronotope in other areas of culture. ** [Note]: In the summer of 1925, the author of these lines attended a lecture by A.A. Uxtomskij on the chronotope in biology; in the lecture questions of aesthetics were also touched upon.
>
> (*DI*: 84)

Bakhtin developed the concept in a series of essays written around 1937–38, but upon publication much later, he added some important "Concluding Remarks." They are from 1973 and are thus some of Bakhtin's last reflections. Corresponding to the introductory characterization of the chronotope as "a formally constitutive category" fusing form and content, in "Concluding Remarks," he also speaks of the "general (formal and material) chronotopicity of the poetic images conceived as an image of temporal art, one that represents spatially perceptible phenomena in their movement and development" in a commentary on Lessing's *Laokoon* (1766) (ibid., 251).

In his essay "The Fugue of Chronotope," Michael Holquist has strongly emphasized the function of chronotopes as mediations between concrete sensation and abstract form. Holquist gives a thorough account of Bakhtin's critical inspiration drawn from Immanuel Kant: "the *fons et origo* of Kant's system is to be found in the act of joining a priori, transcendental categories in the mind with sensed intuitions coming from the external environment."[14] I have also commented on this relation:

> Time and space, according to Kant, are inescapable for the good reason that they are "transcendental forms of perception", properties of all human perception, the very forms that enable us to perceive the world at all [...] For Bakhtin, however, time and space were not (merely) transcendental forms of perception, but concrete properties of reality itself, including thought and language. Thus time and space became in no way less omnipresent.[15]

Holquist's detailed account of the relationship between Kant and Bakhtin goes a step further in determining the peculiarity of the concept of the chronotope. Two conclusions deserve particular emphasis. First, Bakhtin's dialogical understanding of existence—a dialectic between the self and the other in time and space perceived as a chronotope—entails "a new degree of specification into the general understanding of time-space [...] Time and space in the chronotope are never divorced from a particular time or a specific space [...] Bakhtin introduces chronotope to name the existential immediacy of fleeting moments and places" (Holquist 2010: 31). Second, in relation to Kant, Holquist reminds us, Bakhtin has a completely different focus on language, which will always anchor one's dialogue with the world historically as an event:

> the coupling of the first person pronoun with indicatives such as "then," "now" and "here," "there" serves to calibrate positions in abstract space and time that are always conditioned ("thickened") in the event by the specific values that society attaches to them in any particular time and space.
>
> (Ibid., 32)

The station as a Modernist chronotope is a particularly lucid example of the artistic exploration of the encounter between experience and modernity as an unescapable condition through sensory as well as structural mimesis.

The Tone of Modernity and the Stations

In the autofictional travel journal *Intermezzo* (1899) and the documentary report *Den gotiske Renaissance* (The Gothic Renaissance, 1901),[16] Johannes V. Jensen had already listened to the tone of modernity. That tone is solely available to the fresh senses; the *sum* of modernity is a buzzing hum of discordant voices representing mobility and provisionality, presupposing a cynical acceptance of a life in pieces and polarities, resonating with interference and ambivalence. *Places* are for permanent residents; the infinite and all-connecting *space* is the non-place of modernity. Its time—time-space—is that of technology, which also dictates a new rhythm to poetry, demanding a new poetics.

Jensen's overall acceptance of modernity as an inevitable condition does not prevent him from being challenged by its inherent contradictions, its painful contingency. In his *Digte* (Poems, 1906)[17]—inspiration and stumbling block for Danish poetry for the remainder of the twentieth century—the most startling and famous section is a collection of poems in free verse. In the first of them, "Interferens" (Interference),[18] the ego lies awake at night while contemplating the agonizing inner tensions that characterize his sense of life. He experiences them as an inner encounter of wave trains and as noisy frictions between ill-fitting machine parts:

> This groan of the axles, this devilish clash of psychic sound
> releases the transcendental pain vibrations
> which are the form of my innermost self.
> My consciousness expresses itself as psychic interference.

> The very screaming relationship between all otherwise harmonious
>   realities
> is the penetrating key of my mind.
>
> (Jensen 2006: 1, 44)

"It is the monologues of space, whose rings meet/with the toneless circles of time"—these lines begin and end the poem. It is an astonishingly epistemological poem. On the one hand, it presents the problem of the ego's relationship to the outside world in abstract-philosophical—Kantian—terms: I–space–time. On the other hand, it concretely pictorially urges three aspects of a modern sense of life to interfere poetically. First, the *cosmic*—as perceived in a scientific worldview: "It is the sound of a thousand miles of emptiness/between the grinding stone globes" (ibid.). Next, the inner *psychic*—as a conflict between impulses and instances, the self as a "clash of psychic sound," "transcendental pain vibrations." And third, the confrontation with a *vital-banal everyday life*: "Tomorrow I will get up/ charged with curses and zest for life/like all mornings before./Tomorrow I will be confronted with washbasin, shoehorn, toothbrush and the whole history,/tobacco and sunshine and draught Tuborg" (43).

In later editions, the section with the six free verse poems carries the title "The Journey around the Globe." Jensen had in fact made just such a journey in the years 1903–04. During the journey—on which he visited the Malacca Peninsula, China, Japan, and the USA—he spent many months among Danish immigrants in Chicago, with an excursion to the South, where he passed through Memphis, Tennessee. "Paa Memphis Station" (At Memphis Station) is the penultimate of the six free verse poems and a fairly direct result of the journey around the globe.

This poem can be seen as a radical alternative to a well-known poem by Jensen's predecessor and rival, the late Romantic and early Modernist poet Sophus Claussen: "Rejseminder" (Travel Memories 1899), with its chorus-like repetition of the words "Paa Skanderborg Station" (At Skanderborg Station). Although traditional in its form, smaller in scope, and located in the petty-bourgeois Danish province, it is nevertheless related in both scene and motif. In an international context, the poem is evidently inspired by travel poems in free verses such as Goethe's "Harzreise im Winter" (1789) and Heine's poems in *Die Nordsee* (1826). In both cases, the natural sublime is the scenery, and, especially in Goethe's poem, a main motif is the complexity, the contingency of emotions, corresponding to the natural sublime.

"At Memphis Station" is a travel poem, a troubled soliloquy during a forced halt on a railway journey, triggered by a flood disaster. The stage is the Memphis train station. Memphis was/is an industrial center and important junction between the rail network and shipping traffic on the Mississippi River; yet in the mind of the lyrical ego, the city's name evokes the classical Memphis of ancient Egypt, the capital of many Pharaohs, home to pyramids, and an avenue of sphinxes. With the sphinx on his mind, he immediately recalls its function in Greek mythology and tragedy. When a traveler (e.g., the king's son Oedipus) met the sphinx, it presented him with a riddle on life and death; he had to solve the riddle or else meet his death.

The first stanza presents the self between two worlds:

Half-awake and half-dozing,
rammed by a clammy reality but still off
in an inner sea-fog of Danaid dreams,
I stand here my teeth chattering
at Memphis Station, Tennessee.
It's raining.
(Jensen 1977: 23, translation by Alexander Taylor)

The state of mind is the dangerous *hypnagogic* state between dreamy sleep and wakefulness, known from Edgar Allan Poe's poems and tales, from the beginning of Franz Kafka's fantastic tale "Die Verwandlung," and his novel *Der Prozess*, and from many of Jensen's experimental prose texts, his *myths*. The outer time, as mentioned, is a forced stop on a train journey, an empty waiting time, a kind of hole in his life, a pocket of time. The inner time is a time of crisis, the full time of a struggle of the soul (*psychomachia*) over the last crucial questions, an inner struggle between impatience and patience, between the pull of nomadic life and the urge for a settled home life.

The outer space, Memphis Station, is perceived with concise realism:

The day ruthlessly exposes
the cold rails and the masses of black mud,
the waiting room with its candy machines,
the orange peels, the stumps of cigars and matches.
The day grins with spewing gutters
and an eternal grille of rain.
Rain, I say, from heaven and to earth.
(Ibid.)

The inner space includes at least three spheres: myth, psyche, and everyday life. First, there is the (Greek) mythological space, filled with eerie "Danaid dreams." King Danaus' fifty daughters all killed their husbands on their wedding night. In the underworld, they were condemned to fill a bottomless vessel with water for eternity as punishment for their deeds. The endlessly flowing rain is associated with eternal punishment in an underground realm of the dead. The nightmare of the murderous women expresses the protagonist's fear of perishing should he let himself be caught by a woman and settle down with her. This mythical level reveals the basic tonality of the internal debate between the two alternatives: to continue a life on the go, or to settle down, have a family and a home. Both poles appear as antinomies; they are equally right and wrong—that is the riddle of the sphinx. The value struggle manifests itself in the competing images in which he imagines the place where he is to settle down: prison and home. Both in nature and in human-made modernity, he can find arguments for either alternative.

In the course of the first five stanzas, the focus shifts from the inner misery—the frightening Danaid dreams—to the outer one—the dreary waiting room and the pouring rain that, like a vertical wall, blocks the horizontal movement of the journey. He sees the rain as iron bars in a prison, but grinning gargoyles from Gothic cathedrals are also implied: "The day grins with spewing gutters/and an eternal grille of rain./Rain, I say, from heaven and to earth." His vision activates a widespread image of the railway station as a cathedral of modernity[19] but in grotesquely grinning negativity. Like his ancestor Hamlet, he is seriously in doubt as to whether life is worth living or not.

In the sixth stanza, his mood improves, and an extensive attempt at inner persuasion commences. It manifests itself in a shower of verbs in the imperative, especially as an appeal to the sense of sight: look, look, look—and pull yourself together; that is the counter-voice in his dialogical soliloquy. It appeals to the Stoic ideal of patience, represented by the *machine*, the locomotive: "Quiet! Look, how the engine,/that mighty machine, stands there calmly seething/wrapping itself in smoke—it is patient" (24). He tries to reject his idealistic, eternal yearning and fantasizes about settling in Memphis. Here, like everywhere else, a pretty young woman is just waiting to meet him. He no longer sees the rain as prison bars but tries to hear it as "an amorous murmur,/a long, hushed love-chat/mouth against mouth/between the rain and the earth?" (ibid.). He hears a similar appeal from the "natural sublime," from the very power of another, majestic appearance of the catastrophic water: the mighty Mississippi which has just shown its power by going far beyond its banks: "Look how it sweeps a gigantic paddle-wheeler/in its deluge embrace/like a dancer who is lord of the floor!" (25).

But in stanza 13, the inner discussion derails and he can no longer take his reassuring claims seriously. His continued attempts at self-persuasion are increasingly permeated with irony and exhibit the "sleaziness," the predictability and conformity that would characterize such a life without riddles as he imagines remaining "in sphinx-forsaken Memphis ... " (ibid).

At this point in his unfinished inner discussion, he is saved by external events. The reason for the journey stoppage is revealed to be a train accident, caused by the flood disaster. A "wretched freight train" enters "with broken sides," "the cars staggering on three wheels," and "on the tender among the coal/four still forms are lying/covered with bloodwet coats." "The track is clear" (26).

The forces of nature, while awe-inspiring and sometimes deadly, do not have the power to stop the expansive force concentrated in the human-made machine, only to temporarily hold it back. The riddle of the Sphinx has not really been solved—the antinomies continue in the lyrical ego's relationship to woman as a threat or promise, and to life as a traveler or as a resident. But they are temporarily relegated to a sidetrack by the basic opposition between life and death.

"At Memphis Station" explores the chronotopic dimensions of the station by combining the chronotope of the road with that of the threshold. In the chronotope of the road, "Time, as it were, fuses together with space and flows in it (forming the road); this is the source of the rich metaphorical expansion on the image of the road as a course: 'the course of a life', 'to set out on a new course'" (*DI*: 244). The threshold symbolizes "crisis and break in life … In this chronotope, time is essentially instantaneous; it is as if it has no duration and falls out of the normal course of biographical time" (248). The poem is Modernist in its untraditional form and mixed tonality, with a decisive element of "prose": "the orange peels, the stumps of cigars and matches," "poster-howling buildings," "bloodwet coats." Throughout the twentieth century, this poem became a uniquely important source of inspiration in Danish/Nordic poetry due to this diction and a subtle interweaving of three worlds: a mythical sphere, an emotional and intellectual chaos in the form of a silent but wordy psychomachia, and a sensitive sensory perception of modern reality.

Apparitions of the Station

IN A STATION OF THE METRO
The apparition of these faces in the crowd;
Petals on a wet, black bough.

(Pound 1967: 113)

The modern work of art also requires, according to Adorno, interpretation. It is an illusion that its self-reflexivity has made interpretation superfluous, and that obscurity and absurdity have made it impossible (Adorno 1997: 56f.). Yet, the ambiguous and polysemic should not be eradicated, but respected in the reading: "The character of riddle survives the interpretation that requires answer" (222). The literary world has seen a large number of published readings and characterizations of Ezra Pound's short poem "In a Station of the Metro," and it is a hopeless endeavor to list and take a position on all of them. Many of the readings I know of, however, are limited by a biographical-poetological approach. Ezra Pound's (early) poetry, his poetics and literary criticism have fascinated me since my youth, and I present here a close reading of a poetic "equation" in the wider, motivic, and chronotopic perspective of the station.

The poem, first published in the journal *Poetry* (1913) and then included in the collection *Lustra* (1915), is generally regarded as a model example of the poetics of imagism. It consists of a title indicating the scene and two verses. The two verses represent a juxtaposition of two separate, fragmentary images. The sound dimension includes the use of alliteration ("black bough"), assonance, and even half-rhyme ("crowd"—"bough"). In addition, there is the sound symbolism, inherent in the dominance of dark vowels—interrupted by the i-sound and the hissing consonant sound in "apparition."

Metrically, the poem is practically a classic distichon: a hexameter followed by a pentameter. The use of *catalex* in the final verse, consisting of one two-syllable word followed by five monosyllabic words in a row, is a distinctive rhythmic device. After the first verse with twelve syllables, the last one has only seven. Through the rhythm and the pause effect (from the pattern laid out in the first verse), the words "wet, black bough" gain great weight in a kind of spondaic ending. The rhythm pattern of the verse can be notated as follows: - x - x - [x] - [x] - [x]. The form of enunciation is the programmatic, Imagist "direct presentation" of images, without a lyrical ego. Deprived of verbs, the images immediately appear quite static, while their dynamization is apparently left to the readers, to their abilities of association and combination.

There is, however, an imperceptible but important movement contained within the substantiated verb "apparition." That word leaps to the eye and the ear both for its sound qualities and for syntactic reasons. The dynamic of "apparition" encompasses both verses and is crucial to establishing the poem's character of *event* in the addressee's senses and mind.

Moreover, this word possesses an unusual semantic richness. "Appear" (to come in sight; to show up; to become manifest; to look like; to reveal itself ...) is a key word in one of the most important currents of contemporary philosophy, namely phenomenology, whose main goal is to dissolve the dualism between subject and object by describing the world as it appears to the human consciousness. Closely related to this philosophical dimension is the metapoetic significance of the word, which condenses a basic idea from the poetics developed in T. E. Hulme's early essays: "Style short, being forced by the coming together of many different thoughts, and generated by their contact. Fire struck between stones";[20] likewise in Pound's own famous definition of the image: "An image is that which presents an intellectual and emotional complex in an instant of time" (Pound 1963: 4); and in James Joyce's idea of "epiphany," as presented in *Stephen Hero*:

First we recognise that the object is one integral thing, then we recognise that it is an organised composite structure, a thing in fact: finally, when the relation of the parts is exquisite, when the parts are adjusted to the special point, we recognise that it is *that* thing which it is. Its soul, its whatness, leaps to us from the vestment of its appearance. The soul of the commonest object, the structure of which is so adjusted, seems to us radiant. The object achieves its epiphany.[21]

But "appearing like," "looking like" can also—e.g., in rationalism—mean to "be an illusion," to exhibit a false, seductive surface. Apparition can further denote the central mystery of numerous religions—the revelation itself: the incarnation of the avatar, the descent of the deity to earth. Finally, "apparition" can have the eerie, "gothic" meaning of a revenant, a ghost, a phantom.

The second part of the first verse deictically emphasizes the synecdochical expression "these faces in the crowd," a typical variant of the figure *pars pro toto*. Significant is the fragmentary character of the sensation and the pointillistic tendency of the image. "A face in the crowd" is a fixed term in English—with a wide range of literary implications, later expanded by famous movies (e.g., Elia Kazan, *A Face in the Crowd*, 1957) and songs. In my reading of the poem, the term contains at least two important intertextual references. First, to Edgar Allan Poe's short story "The Man of the Crowd" (1840). The scene is set in London, and the story is a confusing and eerie parable about life in the modern metropolis, marked by the presence of ubiquitous masses, and imbued with crime. The short story begins with a French quote by Jean de La Bruyère: "Ce grand malheur, de ne pouvoir être seul." Second, to Baudelaire's famous poem "À une passante," from the section "Tableaux Parisiens" in *Les Fleurs du Mal* (1857). With the deafening street noise howling around him, the lyrical ego sees a beautiful woman passing by:

> Dans son oeil, ciel livide où germe l'ouragan,
> La douceur qui fascine et le plaisir qui tue.
> Un éclair ... puis la nuit! Fugitive beauté
> Dont le regard m'a fait soudainement renaître,
> Ne te verrai-je plus que dans l'éternité?[22]

The poem is an exquisite example of the metropolitan *flaneur*'s sensuous, emotional, and aesthetic shock experience, so thoroughly analyzed by Walter Benjamin.[23] Notice the sharp color contrast and sudden movement in "Un éclair ... puis la nuit!"; furthermore, the metaphorical identification between the expression in the woman's eye and a lead-gray sky in which a hurricane lurks; and, finally, the ambivalent emotions ("tue"–"renaître"). A number of more individualized "passante" poems in Pound's *Lustra* form a leitmotif in the collection: "Gentildonna," "Passing" (in the poetry cycle "Ladies"), "The Encounter," and "Shop Girl."

The second verse points toward Japanese and Chinese poetry. In his passages about the poem in *Gaudier-Brzeska. A Memoir*, Pound has described the catalytic experience and the lengthy process of finding a form for it. First, an "equation" of color spots: "I do not mean that I found words, but there came an equation ... not in speech, but in little splotches of colour" (Pound 1916: 100). Passing through longer poems that were discarded, it ended up as a kind of haiku: "a form of super-position, that is to say, it is one idea set on top of the other [...] A year later I made the following hokku-like sentence" (103). In later commentaries, he highlighted the ideogram idea from a small pamphlet by Ernest Fenollosa: *The Chinese Written Character as a Medium for Poetry*, which he edited and published in 1920. The poem, together with several others from *Lustra* and the re-creation of Chinese poems in the subsequent collection *Cathay* (likewise in 1915), is a marked expression of the oriental influence on European literature and art around and after the year 1900.

This verse too contains an implied action. Petals do not typically grow on thick, black branches, but a spring storm can leave wet branches with scattered petals glued to them. In the immediately preceding poem in *Lustra*, "Ts'ai Chi'h," we also encounter detached petals falling into the well; "their ochre clings to the stone." Storms occur more often in the spring than in the summer. Indicating a season is a traditional element in haiku poetry and is very important in *Lustra* as well.

The title sets the scene of the poem, which is very literally metropolitan: the infrastructure of Paris in the form of its *Métropolitain*. It implies the chronotope of the road. An underground station—a place for arrivals and departures, for random encounters—further implies the chronotope of encounter. In a cultural sphere, characterized by the mechanical, the first verse unfolds an outer, sensory image, a fragmentary appearance of human faces against an anonymous background. In an underground, the spatial dimension is of course subterranean, a "cave" in a system of tunnels.

The second verse, an "interpretive metaphor" according to Pound's definition, unfolds an inner, psychic image in a natural, organic sphere. Its spatial position is literally above the ground; metaphorically, branches are seen from below and thus face the sky. These contrasts are superimposed by the sharp (implicit but obvious) color contrasts between the illuminated station and the dark tunnel, the luminous faces and the blurry crowd, the bright petals and the wet, black branch.

The short poem thus contains a maximally condensed encounter between contrasting spheres and dimensions. One aspect is the perfect combination of a classic European epigram (elegiac distich and couplet) with a Japanese haiku poem. In the criticism, interest has mostly been concentrated on the oriental background of the short form. Eliot, however, offers a good balance in his "Introduction" of 1928 to Pound's *Selected Poems*. On the one hand, he names Pound "the inventor of Chinese poetry for our time" (Pound 1967: 14). On the other, he points to "a class of Pound's poems which may be called the Epigrams" and notes Pound's "acquaintance with Martial" (16). Moody presents the same duality: "Pound, in 1913, was only doing for contemporary London what Martial had done for Rome, and he knew well enough that it was a low sort of job for a poet."[24] Yet, especially about "In a Station of the Metro," he claims that it rises above narrow satire to a vision of "deeper, more ultimate things—on those things the smuggled self-satisfied will not see. It had taken the poet over a year to refine an experience in the Paris Metro into that nineteen-syllable *haiku*" (209).

Another aspect is the poetic "mimesis" of a general phenomenological perception process, noted by Pound himself in his reflections on the poem: "In a poem of this sort one is trying to record the precise instant when a thing outward and objective transforms itself, or darts into a thing inward and subjective."[25] In reproducing this process of appropriation, he clearly emphasizes the precise moment and its striking, "outgoing" character. But he rejects the passive, impressionistic reflection in favor of the actively shaping, conceiving reception:

> There are two opposed ways of thinking of a man: firstly, you may think of him as that towards which perception moves, as the toy of circumstance, as the plastic substance of receiving impressions; secondly, you may think of him as directing a certain fluid force against circumstance, as conceiving instead of merely reflecting and observing.
>
> (Ibid.)

The ability of the actively shaped image to recreate an existential, crisis-like experience of an instant that transcends the continuous biographical time and outer space boundaries, is described more precisely in the second part of Pound's definition of the image in the manifesto "A Few Don'ts": "It is the presentation of such a 'complex' instantaneously which gives that sense of sudden liberation; that sense of freedom from time limits and space limits; that sense of growth, which we experience in the presence of the greatest works of art" (Pound 1963: 4). This Modernist version of the chronotope of threshold is the secular, aesthetic equivalent to mystical or religious phenomena such as the vision, the epiphany, the revelation.

What then does the vision reveal? The answers of the antique oracles and the Christian revelations were obscure words and visions. Phenomenology maintained focus on the composite experience in an attempt to dissolve the dualism between subject and object. In the same way, the project of the new philosophers of science, as previously mentioned, "was to develop a theory of knowledge which could reconcile the world of sensation and the experience of objects, the basis of empiricism, with the world of pure formal relation, of abstraction" (Waugh 2001: 9). It also preceded Niels Bohr's and Werner Heisenberg's subsequent attempts "to formulate a new epistemology in the terms of indeterminacy or uncertainty" (ibid.).

The early Pound constantly draws parallels between science and literature (Gemzøe 2003a: 65f). In "The Serious Artist," which was published in the same year and in the same magazine (*Poetry* 1913) as "In a Station of the Metro," we find the following comparison: "The arts, literature, poetry, are a science, just as chemistry is science. Their subject is man, mankind and the individual" (Pound 1963: 42). "Bad art is inaccurate art. It is art that makes false reports" (43). In science as in poetry, incorrect reports can lead to disasters, he points out. Criticism must also avoid false reports. I think we mistake the nature of the true reality report in "a poem of this sort" if we do not reckon with its "indeterminacy," its multiple virtuality, i.e., if we do not attempt a juxtaposition of potentially conflicting interpretations that take into account the contingent manifestations of modernity.

One line of interpretation would be a positive version of the *flaneur*'s experience of the large city. Pound himself highlights this approach in his explanation of the inspiration for the poem: "Three years ago in Paris I got out of a 'metro' train at La Concorde, and saw suddenly a beautiful face, and then another and another, and then a beautiful child's face, and then another beautiful woman" (Pound 1916: 100). The unforgettable faces are pointed out deictically in their abrupt appearance. In this direction of understanding, the faces may appear as positive exceptions that stand out from the anonymous, negatively assessed metropolitan masses. The crowd, however, in the image of "a wet, black branch," could also be conceived as something fertile, a force of nature that breeds attractive faces and fascinating personalities. In this positive line of interpretation, a mythical overtone would be the sudden, divine descent of heavenly beauty in the midst of the trivial weekday.

Readings that emphasize the negative, critical possibilities of signification should include the mythical suggestions of all these ghostly *apparitions* of pale faces: a horrific sight of doomed souls in a Dantean Inferno—or of shadowy corpses in Avernus or Hades, antique realms of death, both of which appear elsewhere in *Lustra*. Pound was later influential in the final version of Eliot's Inferno poem "The Waste Land" (1922), which is also dedicated to him. Here the word "crowd" forms, so to speak, the gateway to the realm of the dead: "A crowd flowed over London Bridge, so many,/I had not thought death had undone so many."[26]

In his poem "Les sept vieillards" (The Seven Old Men), also from "Tableaux Parisiens," Baudelaire had, through a morning scene in a Paris street, created "a mysterious, ghostly, spectre-haunted submarine world,"[27] an alienated caricature of civilization as a wasteland, a dreary non-place. An underground or submarine specter-world as a "reverse" image of the normal world was familiar from a long tradition of ballads and folktales, and was renewed by the Romantics and highlighted in Edgar Allan Poe's gloomy poetic death fantasy "The City in the Sea." As I point out, however, Baudelaire's Modernist specificity is the "metaphorical multi-dimensionality that fuses merciless city realism with images from nature, from fantasy and from myth" (165). This fusion of dimensions was re-created and renewed by Modernist urban poets such as Jensen, Pound, Eliot, and many others.

The critical image in that kind of "merciless city realism" that I see as an indispensable dimension in a reading of "In a Station of the Metro" could be formulated as follows: In the dark, underground tunnel of city life (transport to and from work) the stations with their luminous faces are merely short intermezzi. Nature is present only in its absence: as the inner, psychic creation of a compensatory counter-image. Personality is nothing but a ghostly glimpse against the background of a black, slimy anonymity; individuality is scattered to the winds, swirling away like petals in a spring storm.

If we take all the above dimensions equally into consideration, the apparitions of the station for Pound appear as a report on the human situation in modern metropolitan life that does not falsify its complexity and contingency.

The Station as a Chronotopic and Motivic Junction

The station is a junction where many of the social and psychological lines of modernity have been crossed and captured in aesthetic glimpses. It represents urbanization, industrialization, science, and technology; the overcoming of distances linked to capitalist globalization; separation and thus transport between home and work. It is inextricably linked to a vectorized, mechanical—and stressful—temporality.

At the station, an encounter between the most heterogeneous phenomena takes place: between man and technology, between all kinds of people, from all social classes and from every corner of the world. It connects places for living with places for working, but as an anonymous transit space it is itself a modern *non-place*. Train stations and metro stations are spaces where spatial horizontality—rails, tracks, roads—collides with spatial verticality (floors, tunnels, bridges, stairs, and elevators), and a diverse *temporality* (the fourth dimension of space) inherent in timetables and travel—and the countless points on the life trajectories of travelers.

In modern art from Impressionism onwards, the station is an iconic premiere motif. Realistic prose writers have portrayed the station as a topos in modernity. Modernist literature, often poetry, presents the station through structural mimesis. In "At Memphis Station" and "In a Station of the Metro," the encounter with the station triggers a violent clash between sharp realist sensations, fragments of Greek mythology, and strong images of nature. The combined chronotopes of the encounter, of the road and of the threshold merge with the cosmic vision, with myth, and with the ecstatic lyrical instant. "At Memphis Station" and "In a Station of the Metro" are epochal poems, both as an expression of an acute sense of epoch and as epoch-making literature. As epiphanies of "the modern sublime," the poems are mimetic in Joyce and Adorno's sense: they show in their poetic form more of the whatness of modernity than concepts can convey. In poems like these, the rings of the monologues of space have a resounding interference with the toneless circles of time.

Notes

1. Johannes V. Jensen, "At Memphis Station," trans. A. D. Taylor, in *Contemporary Danish Poetry: An Anthology*, ed. Line Jensen et al. (Copenhagen and Boston: Gyldendal / Twaine, 1977).
2. Ezra Pound, *Selected Poems* (London: Faber & Faber, 1967).
3. Cf. Jacques Rancière, "The Politics of Literature," *SubStance* 33.1 (2004): 10–24 (20f.).
4. "Epic and Novel: Toward a Methodology for the Study of the Novel," in *DI*, 3–40 (6).
5. An important example of such an application is Peter Stein Larsen's Danish doctoral thesis *Drømme og dialoger. To poetiske traditioner omkring, 2000* [Dreams and Dialogues. Two Poetical Traditions around the year 2000] (Odense: Syddansk Universitetsforlag, 2009).
6. Cf. my published opposition to Larsen's thesis that has a main paragraph about "Bakhtin and Lyrical Poetry." Anker Gemzøe, "Andreopponent Anker Gemzøe," *Edda* 4 (2010b): 407–16.
7. Theodor W. Adorno, *Ästhetische Theorie. Gesammelte Schriften* [Aesthetic Theory. Collected Writings], vol. 7 (Frankfurt: Suhrkamp, 1997).
8. Unless otherwise indicated, all quotations in English from sources in languages other than English are in my translation.
9. Fredric Jameson, "Post-Modernism, or, The Cultural Logic of Late Capitalism," *New Left Review* 146 (1984): 59–92 (78).
10. Anker Gemzøe, "Modernisme og mimesis" [Modernism and Mimesis], in *Modernismens historie*, Modernismestudier 2, ed. Anker Gemzøe and Peter Stein Larsen (København: Akademisk Forlag, 2003a), 49–75 (50).
11. Sanford Schwartz, *The Matrix of Modernism: Pound, Eliot, and Early Twentieth-Century Thought* (Princeton: Princeton University Press, 1985), 48.

12 Ezra Pound, *Literary Essays* (London: Faber & Faber, 1963), 76.
13 Patricia Waugh, *Beyond Mind and Matter: Scientific Epistemologies and Modernist Aesthetics*, Working Paper 14 (Aalborg: Significant Forms: The Rhetoric of Modernism, 2001), 17.
14 Michael Holquist, "The Fugue of Chronotope," in *Bakhtin's Theory of the Literary Chronotope: Reflections, Applications, Perspectives*, ed. Nele Bemong et al. (Gent: Academia Press, 2010), 19–33 (22).
15 Anker Gemzøe, "Tid og rum i Bachtins værker"[Time and Space in Bakhtin's Works], in *Smuthuller: Perspektiver i dansk Bachtin-forskning* [Loopholes: Perspectives in Danish Bakhtinian Studies], ed. Nina M. Andersen and Jan Lundquist (København: Politisk Revy, 2003), 63–88 (64).
16 Johannes V. Jensen, *Intermezzo* (København: Det nordiske Forlag, 1899); Johannes V. Jensen, *Den gotiske Renaissance* [Gothic Renaissance] (København: Samlerens Bogklub, 2000).
17 Johannes V. Jensen, *Samlede Digte* [Collected Poems] (København: Gyldendal, 2006), 1–2.
18 In the scientific sense: "Physics. The mutual action of two waves or systems of waves, in reinforcing or neutralising each other, when their paths meet or cross" (*Oxford English Dictionary*).
19 Cf. Louise Mønster, *Mødesteder: Om Tomas Tranströmers og Henrik Nordbrandts poesi* [Meeting Places: On the Poetry of Tomas Tranströmer and Henrik Nordbrandt] (Aalborg: Aalborg Universitetsforlag, 2013), 103.
20 T. E. Hulme, *Further Speculations* (Minneapolis: University of Minnesota Press, 1955), 80.
21 James Joyce, *Stephen* Hero (London: The New English Library, 1966), 217f.
22 Charles Baudelaire, *Les Fleurs du mal* [The Flowers of Evil] (Paris: Garnier, 1961), 103f.
23 Walter Benjamin, *Gesammelte Schriften* [Collected Writings], 5.1–5.2, *Das Passagen-Werk* [Arcades Project] (Frankfurt am Main: Suhrkamp, 1982).
24 Anthony David Moody, *Ezra Pound: Poet. A Portrait of the Man and His Work*, vol. 1: *The Young Genius 1885–1920* (Oxford: Oxford University Press, 2009), 208.
25 Ezra Pound, *Gaudier-Brzeska: A Memoir* (London: Laidlaw and Laidlaw, 1916), 103.
26 T. S. Eliot, *Collected Poems 1909–1962* (London: Faber & Faber, 1968), 65.
27 Anker Gemzøe, "Morning at the Window. The City as a Sea in T. S. Eliot, Charles Baudelaire and Otto Gelsted," in *English and Nordic Modernisms*, ed. Bjørn Tysdahl et al. (Norwich: Norvik Press, 2002), 159–74 (164).

12

Bakhtin and the Protomodernist Dickens From an Anthropological Perspective

Michael Hollington

As Antonia Byatt writes, discussing Frazer and Freud in relation to postmodernist fiction, it was none other than the erstwhile New York literary guru Lionel Trilling who pronounced in 1961 that "perhaps no book has had so decisive an effect upon modern literature as Frazer's"—by which of course he meant *The Golden Bough*.[1] The essay in which this quotation is to be found is contained in a volume entitled *Sir James Frazer and the Literary Imagination: Essays in Affinity and Influence* edited by Robert Fraser, which offers substantiation and celebration of this view.[2] Here writers as significant as Yeats and T. S. Eliot, Lawrence and Conrad, along with many others, are each given individual chapters that probe their debt to *The Golden Bough*. Were it not for the fact that the book is confined to the English language sphere, it would be entirely appropriate, I believe, to add the name of Mikhail Bakhtin to its roster.

He signals as much in *Rabelais and His World* in two telling references to Frazer. The first is a magisterial parenthetical sentence during discussion of the humorous tradition to which, he claims, Rabelais and his work belong, which pays homage to the "folklorists [who] performed a considerable task in the study of the origins and character of various themes and symbols pertaining to the culture of folk humor," and then waives detailed consideration of any particular individual with "it is sufficient to recall Frazer's monumental *The Golden Bough*" (*RHW*: 54). The second, at the very outset, is perhaps yet more significant, consisting as it does of a quotation from Michelet which ends by asserting that Rabelais' "entire book is a golden bough" (2). Writing before Frazer, Michelet was equally enthralled by the passage in Vergil's *Aeneid* which concerns Aeneas' encounter with the Cumaean Sybil and her command that he should pluck the *rameau d'or* in order to descend into the underworld, which he saw as an allegory for the task of the historian wishing to enter the world of the past. It is surely permissible to speculate that Bakhtin too, placing this quotation at the head of his book, saw a connection with the comparable anabasis into the lower regions of the grotesque body of the carnival tradition offered in his last and perhaps most influential book, thanks to the golden bough of his own powerful method.

Yet nowadays, among professional anthropologists at least, Frazer's stock stands virtually at zero. Of all the grand theorists of the nineteenth and early twentieth centuries, he has suffered the most complete eclipse— greater perhaps even than that of the matriarchalist Bachofen. "Frazer is an embarrassment," runs the first sentence of Robert Ackerman's authoritative *J. G. Frazer: His Life and Work*,[3] a book in which "work"—in library or study, and, damnably in the eyes of professionals, never in the field— occupies significantly more attention than "life." And so, not surprisingly, discussions of Bakhtin in relation to Frazerian anthropology are hard to come by. A valuable exception, though, is provided by Hilary Bagshaw in her book *Religion in the Thought of Mikhail Bakhtin*,[4] which also provides useful material on the general reception of Frazer in Russia upon which Bakhtin was able to draw.

She quotes Rachel Polonsky's view that "unlike Nietzsche's, Frazer's influence in Russia was submerged."[5] The proof of that pudding can perhaps be found in the vagueness and inaccuracy of the enthusiastic celebration of his work in Sokolov's *Russian Folklore* of 1938, assigning to Frazer in anticipation of Bakhtin "one of the most prominent positions in contemporary world folkloristics." He is seemingly unaware of the history of the publication of *The Golden Bough* as he asserts that "in 1890 Frazer published his famous book ... in twelve huge volumes," when it was only a one-volume work that was published in that year, the twelve-volume third edition first appearing twenty-five years later. Bagshaw is therefore careful not to overdo the relationship: she admits that there are other, diverse anthropological influences, some of them specifically Russian, and she also sees that in many ways Bakhtin, in putting forward his theory of the carnivalesque, transcends his source. At the same time she offers pointers for an enterprise that might be thought worth undertaking, but which does not, to my knowledge, as yet exist: a careful critical study of Bakhtin in relation to Frazer and to the anthropological tradition as a whole that was available to him in his time.

What follows here is certainly not that. It merely uses Frazer and some other later nineteenth-century anthropologists as one means among others of bringing together a range of writers and texts linked by their relationship, in the first instance, to what might seem to be the most important section of *The Golden Bough*, both for Bakhtin and for a number of high Modernist writers, that concerning the connection between the Roman Saturnalia and the Christian Carnival. This segment, published originally as a two-part essay in the *Fortnightly Review* of October and November 1900, seems to have generated considerable interest among a number of writers when it first appeared—H. G. Wells, for instance, excitedly telling George Gissing in a letter how his own copy passes around among friends first to his next door neighbor Popham and then to Joseph Conrad.[6] Along with some other European festivals, such as Christmas, the Feast of Fools, and May Day, it will be given prominent attention here.

It is commonplace to observe that Modernists were drawn to Frazer by the powerful "primitivist" strand in the intellectual and cultural fabric of late nineteenth-century and early twentieth-century Europe—although writers like D. H. Lawrence, for instance, liked to promote the paradox that it was their contemporaries, at the time of the First World War, who were the real "savages," and the so-called "savage mind" of past and present "primitives" more deeply civilized. There is not much more than a trace in Bakhtin of that nostalgia for past cultures to be found, particularly in conservative Modernists like Eliot and Pound, and yet, like them, his version of cultural tradition places a fall from grace in the sixteenth or seventeenth century that bears a degree of relation to such concepts as Eliot's "dissociation of sensibility." Along with Wyndham Lewis, for example, Eliot can be seen as favoring an earlier, more "savage" style of comedy against a more modern "sentimental" version thereof, finding varying traces of each in the novels of a writer who was one of his heroes: Charles Dickens.

He will appear at centre stage in what follows. I approach him through the lens of Ludwig Borinski's 1957 essay, "Dickens's Late Style,"[7] which sees him as a "proto-modernist" able to "bring together non-logical incongruities, as in the art of T. S. Eliot or James Joyce," or to offer "foreshadowings of the full-blown Surrealism of our century" (428, 429). His remarks link up with such earlier comments as that in 1929, made by Hugh Walpole, the friend of Virginia Woolf with whom she liked to discuss Dickens in her last years, expressing the view that Dickens' late novels have "not been sufficiently studied in their strange and almost uncanny relationship to certain aspects of the modern novel," or such later opinions as that of the American critic Steven Marcus, declaring in 1961 that "true respect for Dickens as an artist had to wait until the work of Joyce, Proust, and Faulkner had made his techniques more familiar." I shall present a Dickens with a foot in both camps, that of folk tradition and that of urban modernity and literary Modernism, appealing very strongly at one point in the history of the reception of his work to anthropologically oriented critics who themselves reflect the Modernist yearning "after strange gods."

To such a view of the novelist as protomodernist, Bakhtin, inheriting the universal nineteenth-century Russian reverence for Dickens, from Tolstoy and Dostoevsky and Turgenev alike, and referring to him on a number of occasions, can perhaps be brought into alignment. Employing a variant of the triangular method employed in Keith Booker's useful book *Bakhtin, Joyce and the Literature Tradition*,[8] remarkable for its ability to shed light on both writers despite the slender direct connections between the pair of them, I shall attempt to do this here, considering Bakhtin in relation to Frazer and other anthropological or anthropologically inspired voices of the late nineteenth century, and tangentially to James Joyce, himself indebted to Frazer, according to T. S. Eliot's influential review of *Ulysses*, and to other, later commentators. These two writers can be regarded as the authors of the finest comic masterpieces of the modern era, and to consider Dickens, and in the background, Joyce, in the light of their respective relation to the anthropology of the Frazerian era may help to place Bakhtin's theory of comedy in relation to grotesque and carnivalesque "folk humor," with its own relationship to *The Golden Bough*, within a Modernist context.

It is noteworthy that Frazer, in his discussion of Carnival in that *magnum opus*, considers himself the inheritor of a robust previous tradition by declaring at the outset that "the resemblance between the Saturnalia of ancient and the Carnival of modern Italy has often been remarked" (634). Thus, for our purposes, the most obvious place from which to start this undertaking, because Bakhtin himself makes so much of it in *Rabelais and His World*, is the account of the Roman Carnival of 1786 in Goethe's *Italienische Reise*. In his preamble to this, he remarks with a degree of humorous amusement how delighted the inhabitants of Rome have been ever since, that the introduction of Christmas in celebration of Christ's birth between pagan Saturnalia in December and Christian Carnival in February/March merely succeeded in delaying the former for a few weeks.[9] And as his careful, detailed account proceeds, he enumerates a number of features of the carnivalesque prominent in Bakhtin's work—the complete absence of rules in a festival that belongs to the people, not to the authorities, the election of a mock king among the clowns, or Pulcinellas, of the occasion, and the festive parricide deposition of such kings expressed in the concluding and climactic symbolic battle of the *moccoli*—candles born by the participants—in which boys yell out to their fathers, as they extinguish their "weapons": *Sia ammazzato il padre!* (Die, father, die!). The accent of Goethe on the Roman Carnival of 1786 is thus very much on its reenactment of *"vive le roi, le roi est mort"*—even down to the detail of his noticing the presence in Rome of Bonny Prince Charlie, the Young Pretender, as an expression of "the Carnival comedy of his kingly pretensions" (*PDP*: 458). These are the words with which the entire twelve-volume *Golden Bough* draws to a close, and which Bakhtin develops into that organicist Viconian celebration of the unbroken continuity of birth and death, destruction and creation in the vegetal and animal kingdom which he sees as fundamental to the Carnivalesque view of life.

After Goethe, as part of the essential background in the British tradition to Bakhtin's anthropology, we might briefly take notice of a passage in one of Sir Walter Scott's novels, *The Abbot* of 1820. Himself a keen student of Scottish folklore, Scott punctuates this and other novels with footnotes that curiously anticipate T. S. Eliot's thoroughly Frazerian *The Waste Land* in their attention to a background of symbolic ritual. These must have been of particular interest to the Scot Frazer, steeped in childhood in the reading of the novels of his "anthropological" predecessor. In this one Scott refers to a "species of general license, like that which inspired the ancient Saturnalia, or the modern Carnival, [that] has been commonly indulged to the people at all times and in almost all countries," and goes on to describe, from his own conservative point of view, a turning upside down of the normal hierarchy of social order, in which the "rude vulgar" elect "some Lord of the revels, who, under the name of the Abbot of Unreason, the Boy Bishop, or the President of Fools, occupied the churches, profaned the holy places by a mock imitation of the sacred rites, and sung indecent parodies on hymns of the church."[10]

From Scott it is only a short step to Dickens' account of the Roman carnival in *Pictures from Italy*. The writer whom he sought to emulate in popularity, and did, very early in his career, may well be in his mind when he writes his own account of the *Moccoletti* ritual, fully comparable with Goethe's; had he known of it, Bakhtin must surely have given it his full attention. Here, Dickens refers to some (like Scott) who have taken it to be "a remnant of the ancient Saturnalia,"[11] and revels like Goethe in the remarkable sublimation of violence and disorder in the rituals of Carnival (Dickens 1866: 123) For Goethe, "everyone accosts everyone else, all good-naturedly accept whatever happens to them, and the insolence and license of the feast is balanced only by the universal good humour;" for Dickens, "I shall always remember it, and the frolic, as a brilliant and most captivating sight, no less remarkable for the unbroken good-humour of all concerned, down to the very lowest" (123). Both of them see it as an occasion where clear traces of original sexual abandon are on display in the "license" with which men and women interact in the course of Carnival, which, however, never spills over into "licentiousness." For Goethe "I can remember seeing only one obscene mask," for Dickens it as "free from any taint of immodesty as any general mingling of the two sexes can possibly be" (123). In terms that are current in anthropological criticism of Dickens in the Frazer era, it is a great folk celebration that is "popular" but not "vulgar."

With Dickens we of course reach an author whom Bakhtin explicitly acknowledges as belonging in some degree to the carnivalesque tradition, especially as seen by Dostoevsky, when he declares that "a combination of carnivalization with a sentimental perception of this was found by Dostoevsky in Sterne and Dickens." Bakhtin would seem to be aware of Dostoevsky's debt to Dickens here and elsewhere in his work—greater than that to Sterne, in fact; we know, for instance, of only two books that he read in prison in Siberia, and these are *Pickwick Papers* and *The Old Curiosity Shop*—described by Henry Gifford as an "underground passage" comparable perhaps to the "submerged" influence of Frazer on Bakhtin suggested by Bagshaw and Podolsky. But not so "underground," in fact, as to pass unnoticed by a number of English language writers in the early twentieth century, who strengthen the idea of Dickens as protomodernist by linking him to Dostoevsky as forerunner. There is Ottoline Morrell, who wrote that "Dickens gave birth to Dostoevsky," or T. S. Eliot, who described Dostoevsky as "Dickens's Russian disciple," or indeed Virginia Woolf herself, who emerged from a family background in which her father and uncle tended to dismiss Dickens—violently, in the case of the uncle— to celebrate him alongside Dostoevsky in her later life.

Here I shall give more emphasis to the carnivalization than to the sentimentality that Bakhtin finds in Dickens, and in any case Bakhtin may be applying the word "sentimental" in a relatively neutral manner, as a term in literary and cultural history (cf. "Empfindsamkeit" in the era of C. P. E. Bach) —as Joyce does when he asserts that "Dickens is a great caricaturist and a great sentimentalist (using those terms in their strict sense and without any malice)," and compares him to Hogarth in the former and Goldsmith in the latter respect.[12] In considering Dickens from a Bakhtinian perspective we might use the word "sentimental," for instance, in connection with a pervasive sense of the gradual loss in the nineteenth century, in the face of the massive ongoing encroachment of urban industrialized society, of a tradition of folk culture—festivals, customs, literature, humor—that is to be found scattered throughout his prodigious output. Even in Dickens' earliest work, *Sketches by Boz*, he notes, in "The First of May," that popular customs and rituals celebrating growth and fertility in spring are very much on the decline, and are chiefly kept alive by an urban under-class:

> in former times, spring brought with it … merry dances round rustic pillars, adorned with emblems of the season, and reared in honour of its coming. Where are they now? … Well, many years ago we began to be a steady and matter-of-fact sort of people, and dancing in spring being beneath our dignity, we gave it up, and in course of time it descended to the sweeps.[13]

But if only vestiges of the past remain, the prominence in these festivities of chimney-sweeps, who are, or should be, children, ensures that some semblance of the turning upside down of the class structure characteristic of Saturnalia and Carnival is still apparent. The narrative voice pours scorn on those who welcome the triumph of propriety in modern times: "What would your sabbath enthusiasts say, to an aristocratic ring encircling the Duke of York's column in Carlton-terrace—a grand *poussette* of the middle classes round Alderman Waithman's monument in Fleet Street?"[14]

This, and many another passage in Dickens concerning popular tradition that we might cite, pale in significance, however, in comparison to the statement that deserves prominence as the central justification for the approach adopted here. A famous passage in Forster's biography of Dickens, quoting from a letter of 1858, notably underlines the importance of the word "popular" in his artistic practise and signifies a consciousness of a tradition under threat in the age of realism. It is clear that the novelist regards it as a major part of his mission as a writer to uphold this:

> in these times, when the tendency is to be frightfully literal and catalogue-like—to make the thing, in short, a sort of sum in reduction that any miserable creature can do in that way—I have an idea (really founded on the love of what I profess) that the very holding of popular literature through a kind of popular dark age may depend on … fanciful treatment.[15]

That concern, evinced quite literally by the unprecedented popularity it enjoyed after the introduction of Sam Weller, can clearly be seen in Dickens' first novel *Pickwick Papers*. Here the carnivalesque world of exuberant laughter is more pronounced, perhaps, than anywhere else in Dickens' work. As he falls asleep in a wheelbarrow that has carted him to a shooting session, Pickwick himself murmurs "cold punch," which sparks comic interpretation by bystanders as evidence of his name and identity—that he is a Mr. Punch. As such, he can be seen to operate as a kind of "Lord of misrule," a fool elected king of the fools, in a novel where slapstick comic violence is everywhere, as in a Punch and Judy show. Pickwick himself fully enters into the carnivalesque spirit of things, seemingly at one moment about to engage in a game of leapfrog with his equally mature friend Tracy Tupman, as we shall soon see.

It is not my intention here, however, to develop or demonstrate to any great extent the possibilities of a direct Bakhtinian account of the grotesque and carnivalesque in Dickens. But it is difficult to avoid the temptation of at least naming a few of the "gargoyles," in Orwell's phrase, that might yield dividends to such an approach. There are for instance, the references to Holbein's *Dance of Death* in many of the novels, reflecting the fact that Dickens consulted that work as a young man in the British Museum in the 1830s and remained fascinated by it ever thereafter. Bakhtin himself refers to it, when he writes that "the image of death in medieval and Renaissance grotesque (and in painting also, as in Holbein's and Dürer's 'dance of death') is a more or less funny monstrosity" (*RHW*: 50–1). And surely this is the spirit in which death is presented in *Pickwick Papers*, a novel that contains literally hundreds of jokes about death, from Mr. Jingle's opening funny story of the lady on top of a stagecoach eating a sandwich who has her head knocked off by an archway to Sam Weller's memorializing of Richard III's murders in the Tower of London[16] but very few actual deaths.

There are likewise humorous demons galore in Dickens' work, including Alain-René Lesage's *Le diable boiteux* [The Lame Devil], the comically deformed and grotesque lame devil who offers Don Leandro a ride on his back in the sky above Madrid if he is liberated from the bottle in which he is imprisoned, known to Dickens from an early stage in Smollett's translation, and figuring as a significant gargoyle in *Oliver Twist* and *Dombey and Son*, for instance. There is the figure of "Nobody," with the potential for numerous jokes and paradoxes, traced by Gerta Calmann in popular culture, as reflected in Renaissance art, in her article "The Picture of Nobody," who turns up in the original title of *Little Dorrit* or as "Captain Nemo" in *Bleak House*.[17] And, finally, to conclude this brief parade of some of the riches on offer for any discussion of Dickens in relation to the tradition of grotesque humor with a trivial but revealing anecdote, there is, near his home in Kent, the church in the village of Chalk, which Dickens used to pass regularly on his walks. Here there are carvings above the porch of literal gargoyles, rather squeamishly described by John Newman in the "West Kent and the Weald" volume of Pevsner's *Buildings of England* as "loathsomely contorted grotesques" who "disport" themselves, by which he means in particular a *sheela na gig* female figure obscenely displaying her genitals to ward off devils, to be found in many such places in England and Ireland.[18] Dickens is known regularly to have uttered words of greeting to this figure as he went by, as if in homage to his debt to anonymous popular folk culture.

But my primary intention is to link Bakhtin's thinking, not only with Frazer, but with other anthropologically oriented critics and theorists, particularly as they write about Dickens, and it is time to introduce some other relevant contemporaries of Frazer in the field. He himself makes no reference to Dickens, or indeed to any other contemporary English writer, but other anthropologists of his generation certainly do. Chief of these is the folklorist Andrew Lang—an opponent of Frazer, in fact, who wrote four hostile reviews of *The Golden Bough*—whose introductions to the 1898–99 Gadshill edition of the *The Works of Charles Dickens* in 34 volumes were influential in disseminating a view of the novelist at the turn of the century as a writer in touch with centuries of expressions of "the primitive mind" in popular culture, humor, and folklore. In a significant recent article, "Devulgarizing Dickens: Andrew Lang, Homer, and the Rise of Psycho-Folklore,"[19] Caroline

Sumpter describes these introductions as "championing a mythic Dickens whose fictions tapped into humans' earliest feelings and mental impulses." For Lang and others of his generation including Arthur Machen, *Pickwick Papers* was a modern, humorous *Odyssey*—and thus in essence prefigured Joyce's *Ulysses*.

In a number of essays, including "Realism and Romance" and "King Romance," Lang develops arguments that can be seen to be "imagining popular culture as the product of a primitive past," in the words of Caroline Sumpter. They link Dickens more closely to the tradition of "romance" than to that of realism, at least as this is defined by the American novelist William Dean Howells, who was Lang's contemporary and opponent in dismissing Dickens as an inadequate realist. Lang argues that writing would soon turn its back on realism of the nineteenth-century variety, and return to closer relationship with the older tradition—a prediction that is arguably borne out in Modernist practice, and partly in its debt to Frazer. His work may also be said to look forward to the major, influential recategorizing of Dickens as a "romantic realist," along with Dostoevsky, Balzac, and Gogol, in Donald Fanger's *Dostoevsky and Romantic Realism* of 1965.[20]

The reminder of this essay will be devoted to an examination of what may at first sight seem an unlikely comparison between Bakhtin and the major early twentieth-century Dickens critic G. K. Chesterton, who can be seen in relation to Andrew Lang. Chesterton was a conservative who converted to Catholicism, but in this he is obviously not alone in the company of conservative enthusiasts for folk tradition assembled here, with Scott before him and T. S. Eliot after. His work is imbued with Frazerian and other anthropological writings of the period, and he admired in particular the work of his fellow Dickensian Andrew Lang. Like Dibelius in Germany in 1915, to whom Bakhtin refers, he is among the earliest critics to write and publish in 1906 a full-length study of Dickens, followed up by a volume in 1911 that collects his many introductions to the novels and short stories.[21] The first of these would have been available in Russia, at least in a German translation, read for instance by Walter Benjamin for his own valuable notes on Dickens in the *Passagenwerk*. Absorbing Frazerian anthropology in connection with carnival and Saturnalia, Chesterton finds aspects of both in Dickens. Though he lacks anything like the same philosophical rigor—his "method" consists largely of a predilection for paradoxicality that amounts almost to an addiction—it is worth surveying here, I believe, some of the features of his work that link him to Bakhtin. I shall consider three.

The first thing to say, simply, is that Chesterton is a lover of Rabelais, who praises him in terms that prefigure Bakhtin's in their responsiveness to many similar aspects of his work, including what Joyce might have called the "jocoseriousness" of *Gargantua and Pantagruel*. In a review of Rostand's *Cyrano de Bergerac*, for instance, he finds that in the play "the gigantesque levity, the flamboyant eloquence, the Rabelaisian puns and digressions were seen to be once more what they had been in Rabelais, the mere outbursts of a human sympathy and bravado as old and solid as the stars," asserting in the same piece that "great comedy, the comedy of Shakespeare or Sterne, not only can be, but must be, taken seriously."[22]

Elsewhere, he links Rabelaisian comedy specifically to that of Dickens, and in this can be directly compared to Bakhtin. He claims of Dickens that "his books were in some ways the wildest on the face of the world. Rabelais did not introduce into Paphlagonia or the Kingdom of the Coqcigrues satiric figures more frantic and misshapen than Dickens made to walk about the Strand and Lincoln's Inn," again pausing to insist again that "you come in the core of him, on a sudden quietude and good sense. Such, I think, was the core of Rabelais, such were all the far stretching and violent satirists." In drawing this comparison Chesterton makes stronger claims than does Bakhtin himself, meditating on food and eating in Rabelais and Dickens respectively, and seeing a carnivalesque relationship between them. Bakhtin writes of Gros Guillaume's belly and Mr. Pickwick's paunch as follows— "There is much of Gros Guillaume in this character, or rather, there is much of his English equivalent, the popular clown. The English applaud Pickwick and will always applaud, but his paunch is far more ambiguous than Gros Guillaume's barrel of wine" (*PDP*: 292)—correctly seeing Pickwick as a clown king in a feast of fools, but stopping short, unlike Chesterton, in giving him the same status as Rabelais in relation to the tradition of the grotesque.

Second, Chesterton celebrates throughout his work the festivals of Carnival and Saturnalia, and like others before him, albeit in his case from a Christian and specifically catholic enthusiasm for the Middle Ages, sees the two as essentially one. His view of Dickens' "philosophy of Christmas," for instance, is that he treats the contemporary festival as a modern version of the Feast of Fools: "it is exactly because Christmas is not only a feast of children but in some sense a feast of fools that Dickens is in touch with its mystery."[23] In a piece entitled "The Winter Feast," moreover, he explores a conception of Saturnalia that he finds reflected in Dickens. He takes as a paradigm what is now only practiced as a sport for children—the very Bakhtinian carnivalesque game of leapfrog. But as Aries shows in *Centuries of Childhood* many games for children were previously shared with adults, and late in *Pickwick Papers* when Pickwick meets with Tupman it looks as if the two are about to indulge in it. Of Bartholomew Smallweed in *Bleak House* Dickens writes satirically that "he could as soon play at leap-frog or at cricket as change into a cricket or a frog himself." Chesterton enters into the spirit of this kind of joke when he remarks, of Jerry Cruncher's spiky hair in *A Tale of Two Cities* that "you wouldn't like to leapfrog him."

Third, he takes up a view of grotesque humor that bears important relation to Bakhtin's own, in its emphasis on the playfulness and abandon of its emphasis on hybridity, rather than on its combination with Gothic elements of the sinister and terrifying, as in the influential work of Wolfgang Kaiser. For Chesterton, Dickens is the master of a "genial grotesque" who "devoted his genius in a somewhat special sense to the description of happiness" (Chesterton 1920: 105) for which grotesque humor is indispensable, which he defines as "the natural expression of joy," for, paradoxically again, "happiness is best expressed by ugly figures" (111): "We have a feeling that Scrooge looked even uglier when he was kind than he looked when he was cruel," he writes (112).

> Upon him descended the real tradition of Merrie England [...] Dickens had in his buffoonery and bravery the spirit of the Middle Ages [...] in fighting for Christmas he was fighting for the old European festival [...] he defended the medieval feast which was going out against the Utilitarian spirit which was coming in [...] he looked on the living Middle Ages, on a piece of the old uproarious superstition still unbroken.
> (Chesterton 1906: 164)

Which brings us naturally enough, by way of conclusion, to Dickens and Christmas. In its intimate connection with Dickens in Chesterton's work, Christmas can be seen as the counterpart of Carnival for Rabelais in Bakhtin's book. For Chesterton, it is "a half pagan and half Catholic festival" (Chesterton 1920: 103) which in theory Dickens, as a progressive Radical, ought to have despised, but which, in a manner anticipating that of Jung, and the notion of the "collective unconscious," as in the work of Andrew Lang, "it was by a great ancestral instinct that he defended Christmas, by that sacred sub-consciousness ... which is much too deep to be called heredity" (105). There are three elements that typify Christmas in Chesterton's work, all of them to be found abundantly, he claims, in Dickens—the first, its "dramatic quality" (and there is no need to reiterate here the essentially theatrical aspects of Dickens' writing), the second, what Chesterton calls "the quality of divine obstruction," of oppositional anti-Christmas feeling, as in *A Christmas Carol*. Finally, for him, "the third great Christmas element is the element of the grotesque" (110). He continues by declaring that "the grotesque is the natural expression of joy," abundantly present in the utopian writing of *Pickwick Papers* for instance, and contrasts Utopias that celebrate it with those that do not—William Morris' for instance: "A man in most modern Utopias cannot really be happy." We are reminded here of the distinctive stress of Bakhtin's version of Carnival and Saturnalia as grotesque utopian celebrations of the return to Rome of the reign of King Saturn.[24] Ultimately, though, the conservative Chesterton looks back for his notion of Utopia, while Bakhtin looks forward.

Notes

1 Sir James George Frazer, *The Golden Bough: A New Abridgement*, ed. Robert Fraser (Oxford: Oxford World's Classics, 1994), 270.
2 Robert Fraser, ed., *Sir James Frazer and the Literary Imagination* (London: Macmillan, 1990).
3 Robert Ackerman, *J. G. Frazer: His Life and Work* (Cambridge: Cambridge University Press, 1987).
4 Hilary B. P. Bagshaw, *Religion in the Thought of Mikhail Bakhtin: Reason and Faith* (London: Routledge, 2016).
5 Rachel Polonsky, *English Literature and the Russian Aesthetic Renaissance* (Cambridge: Cambridge University Press, 1998).
6 Robert Hampson, *Sir James Frazer and the Literary Imagination* (London: Macmillan, 1990), 172.
7 Ludwig Borinski, "Dickens's Late Style," in *Charles Dickens: Critical Assessments*, ed. Michael Hollington (Robertsbridge: Helm Information, 1995), vol. 3: 617–39.
8 M. Keith Booker, *Joyce, Bakhtin and the Literary Tradition* (Ann Arbor: The University of Michigan Press, 1997).
9 "In diesen Tagen freuet sich der Römer noch zu unsern Zeiten, daß die Geburt Christi das Fest der Saturnalien und seiner Privilegien wohl um einige Wochen verschieben, aber nicht aufheben konnte" [During this time, even to this day, the Roman rejoices because, though it postponed the festival of the Saturnalia with its liberties for a few weeks, the birth of Christ did not succeed in abolishing it] https://www.projekt-gutenber.g.org/goethe/italien/ital2a11.html "The Roman Carnival," in *Italian Journey*, trans. W. H. Auden and E. Mayer (New York: Pantheon, 1962), 446.
10 Sir Walter Scott, *The Abbot* (Boston: Dana Estes, 1893), 314.
11 *Pictures from Italy and American Notes* (London: Chapman and Hall, 1866), 123.
12 Unlike the hostile American protagonist for classic realism William Dean Howells, castigating Dickens' *Christmas Books* and *Christmas Stories* as "child's-play, in which the wholesome allegiance to life was lost. Artistically, therefore, the scheme was false, and artistically, therefore, it must perish. It did not perish, however, before it had propagated itself in a whole school of unrealities so ghastly that one can hardly recall without a shudder those sentimentalities at secondhand to which holiday literature was abandoned long after the original conjuror had wearied of his performance."
13 Charles Dickens, *Sketches by Boz*, ed. Denis Walder (London: Penguin Books, 1995), 202.
14 Another sketch in the same work, "Greenwich Fair," in which such grotesque and carnivalesque creatures as "a dwarf, a giantess, a living skeleton, a wild Indian, a young lady of singular beauty, with perfectly white hair and pink

eyes," and two or three other natural curiosities are on display, is similar. It describes a turning upside down of normality, in which for a period, disorder reigns: "if the parks be the 'lungs of London' we wonder what Greenwich Fair is—a periodical breaking-out, we suppose, a sort of spring rash; a three days fever, which cools the blood for six months afterwards, and at the expiration of which, London is restored to its old habits of plodding industry" (Dickens, *Sketches by Boz*, 143, 135).

15 Cited in John Forster, *Life of Charles Dickens*, ed. J. W. T. Ley (London: Cecil Palmer, 1928) 727–8.
16 "[B]usiness first, pleasure arterwards as King Richard the Third said ven he stabbed the t'other king in the Tower, afore he smothered the babbies." Charles Dickens, *Pickwick Papers* (Oxford: Oxford University Press, October 1987), xxv, 329.
17 Gerta Calmann, "The Picture of Nobody," *The Journal of the Warburg and Courtauld Institutes*, 23.1–2 (1960): 64–104.
18 John Newman, *West Kent and the Weald* (London: Penguin Books, 1969).
19 Caroline Sumpter, "Devulgarizing Dickens: Andrew Lang, Homer and the Rise of Psycho-Folklore," *ELH* 87.3 (2020): 733–59.
20 Donald Fanger, *Dostoevsky and Romantic Realism* (Chicago: Phoenix Books, 1967).
21 G. K. Chesterton, *Charles Dickens: A Critical Study* (New York: Dodd, Mead and Co., 1906); *Appreciations and Criticisms of the Works of Charles Dickens* (London: J. M. Dent & Sons, 1911).
22 G. K. Chesterton, "Rostand," *Varied Types* (New York: Dodd, Mead and Company, 1905), 73–84.
23 G. K. Chesterton, *The Uses of Diversity* (London: Methuen, 1920), 153.
24 Christian Roy, *Traditional Festivals: A Multicultural Encyclopedia* (Santa Barbara: ABC/Clio, 2005), II, 424.

13

"An Irish Clown, a Great Joker at the Universe"

Joyce and the Modern Carnival

Yann Tholoniat

James Joyce claimed "the modern writer must be an adventurer above all,"[1] but when a young man asked to kiss the hand that wrote *Ulysses*, he quipped: "No, that hand has done a lot of other things as well."[2] From his young age onward—let us say, from his verse satire "Holy Office"— Joyce does not only pose as a rebel, but he also actively disrupts many of the Victorian and Edwardian values and practices, both in real life and in his fictional narratives. Another early example is the libel "The Day of the Rabblement," which attacked the evolving artistic standards of the Irish Literary Theatre. According to Kevin Barry, even in his journalistic articles, Joyce offers a "collapsing inward of previously sustained stereotypes" about Ireland:

> Italy is in Galway; Ireland, both medieval and modern, is in Europe; Dante's *Divine Comedy* is a belated version of St Fursa's *Vision*; Christopher Columbus is a belated discoverer of America; [...] before Defoe there was no English literature; Cromwell was a Celt; the triumph of William of Orange 'signifies a crisis of race, an ethnic revenge' by the Germanic upon the English: the English, 'that hybrid race which lives a tough life on a small island in the northern sea'.[3]

Of course, Joyce's way of action is not sabotage or bomb-attack. His is a meticulous and subtle performance of debunking social and literary conventions through elaborate writing. This aspiration toward subversion is embedded in his work, and this is why it has been read through the Bakhtinian lens a number of times in books[4] and articles. By comparison, the necessary limited scope of this chapter will be to provide an overview of, and to sketch and point at a number of elements that fall under the label "Bakhtinian" phenomena in James Joyce's four main narratives, *Dubliners* (1914), *A Portrait of the Artist as a Young Man* (1916), *Ulysses* (1922), and *Finnegans Wake* (1939). I shall develop three aspects of Bakhtinian theory: the polyphonic quality of Joyce's novels, the carnivalesque, and his sweeping debunking of literary practices, the radical quality of which can still be felt in the twenty-first century.

Polyphonies

Dubliners (1914) is a collection of short stories.[5] From the variety of milieus which are evoked, a number of voices can be heard, and "so many utterances of so many imaginary persons," not Joyce's, to paraphrase the poet Robert Browning in his advertisement to his *Dramatic Lyrics* (1842). Moreover, there are stories within stories, as exemplified by the story of Michael Fury in "The Dead." As opposed to words uttered in direct speech, there are several occasions in which other expressions are mentioned as if they belonged to no one, as if they occurred per se, as in the first short story, "The Sisters": "It was an unassuming shop, registered under the vague name of *Drapery*. The drapery consisted mainly of children's bootees and umbrellas; and on ordinary days a notice used to hang in the window, saying: *Umbrellas Recovered*." Shop-signs can also be found in "Araby" and in "Two Gallants." Other anonymous materials without any specific origin are the songs, such as "I Dreamt that I Dwelt" ("Clay"), and extracts from newspapers, for instance in "A Painful Case." Linguistic areas and idiolects clash: the English spoken by most Dubliners is unobtrusively called into question by Celtic references and phrases. The juxtaposition of short stories reinforces the de-centerment of any single narrative voice, which keeps changing from one story to the next, and sometimes even from within the same story. The narrative instances range from the omniscient narrator, the intradiegetic narrator (as in "Araby"), to the "subjective" narrator espousing the point of view of one character (as in "Evelyn" and "The Dead").

Changes of point of view and in narrative voice in *A Portrait of the Artist as a Young Man* come from the evolution of the same narrator, Stephen Dedalus. As a consequence, each chapter of the *Bildungsroman* is characterized by an evolution in style, each style being suggestive of the

Bildung of the narrator at this point. In the incipit, the syntax, observations, and concerns of the child-narrator are rather simple, fragmentary, and down to earth ("When you wet the bed, first it is warm then it gets cold"), whereas, with the help of ambition and education, the grown-up narrator of the last chapter wishes "to forge in the smithy of [his] soul the uncreated conscience of [his] race." Chapter 3 of *A Portrait* includes Father Arnall's vehement sermon about hell and damnation, as perceived by the narrator. This *outré* purple patch runs over several pages and contributes to the polyphony of voices on the topic of religion.

Joyce also makes abundant use of school slang, Irish jargon, and foreign words. The challenge of being confronted with another language than English occurs right from the beginning of *Ulysses* ("*Introibo ad altare Dei*"). *Ulysses* is famously built—as the Gilbert and Linati Schemata indicate[6]—on a great variety of literary, rhetorical, and symbolic devices which evolve all along the eighteen episodes. The novel—which has also been compared to a prose poem and which contains an episode, "Circe," built like a play—is arguably a medley of (sometimes anonymous) oral manifestations including "jokes, speeches, slogans, letters, street-signs, and printed ephemera"[7] as well as soundbites and songs. The border between the written word and the spoken word is a very narrow one, if not sometimes thoroughly inexistent, as the pun on "fowl [foul] crime" in the "Cyclops" episode suggests. What might appear as a cacophony is precisely what T. S. Eliot praised in *Ulysses*, as he famously described Joyce's "mythical method" as "a way of controlling, of ordering, of giving a shape and a significance to the immense panorama of futility and anarchy which is contemporary history."[8] The various narrators are embodied in various styles which imply different worldviews. If, for instance, "Eumaeus" foregrounds Bloom's voice (Parrinder 1984: 180) and a Bloomian point of view, Molly Bloom finally tells her own version of the day's events in the last episode ("Penelope"). The interior monologues of Stephen Dedalus (see the incipit of the "Proteus" episode) blend the voices of the philosophical, theological, and literary traditions, which are colored by his own opinions and responses. "Oxen of the Sun" covers a wide spectrum of parodied texts, ranging from anonymous documents to the idiosyncrasies of particular authors (Sterne, De Quincey, Dickens, among many others). "Circe" contains ghosts and even inanimate objects which are endowed with human speech.

The incipit of "Calypso" provides an example of the polyphony of voices which always surfaces in *Ulysses*. Leopold Bloom's cat "speaks" in direct speech as in "—Mkgnao!" (53). The onomatopoeia is followed by: "Prr. Scratch my head. Prr." The cat probably does not speak English, but these reported words are ascribed to her. Is it the narrator ventriloquizing it or, more probably, Bloom? And what about the onomatopoeia "Prr"? Is it the cat, the narrator transcribing the sound into letters, Bloom's rendering of his cat's purring—or, in the end, the narrator rendering Bloom's rendering of the cat's sound? The overlapping of instances is intentional and is part of the game played by Joyce with his readers. The "Aeolus" episode contains regular intrusions of an objective narrator in the form of capitalized headlines taken from newspapers which indirectly and ironically comment on the narration.

"For the reader," the interplay of voices and allusions sounds like "scanning a linguistic collage" (Parrinder 1984: 132), or "like a tape-recording of innumerable conversational fragments overheard in the street and in the pub" (176). This holds true for the whole novel, which contains an encyclopedic farrago of trivia, historical events, and scientific facts of all kind. Indeed, *Ulysses* has been described as an "encyclopaedia of styles" by Arnold Goldman (Parrinder 1984: 163): rhetorical figures ("Aeolus"), musical forms ("Sirens"), the Bible, and child's reading-books ("Cyclops"), to quote but a few examples of some of the texts that are included in Joyce's literary melting pot. All these elements resurface in the form of parodies and rhetorical matrixes which in turn re-inform the events and blur the narrative voices and other narrative instances (such as circulating rumors and gossip).

Let us now consider the "Cyclops" episode. The name of the Cyclops in the *Odyssey* is Polyphemus, which means literally "of the numerous voices." The polyphony stems from a double technique of writing called the "alternated asymmetry" in the Gilbert and Linati Schemata and pitting against one another "the Nameless One" and the parodies. But in a figurative acceptation, *poluphemos* means "much spoken about." Now, this too reveals a dimension of the episode which highlights the role of rumors. It seems that each detail is, has been, or will be repeated in an infinite succession of echoes in analeptic or proleptic digressions. In *Ulysses*, all that is said is repeated, and transformed, and reinserted, and reappears at a later stage. Thus, this passage from "Cyclops" reappears in "Circe" (545). A similar process of rewriting is also going on in the parodies. Their status is beyond the traditional dichotomy between diegesis and mimesis inherited from Aristotle's *Poetics*. The parodies serve neither one nor the other. Parodies are to be distinguished from the pastiches which aim at a specific person, whereas parodies aim at styles. Here, the parodies are not a mere amplification of the action they follow, but they are the reproduction of specific writings. By their form—a description of common events in a bombastic style—they belong to the genre of the *parodia sacra* (*RHW*: 14) or, in other words, to what Gérard Genette calls the "desecrating burlesque" ("burlesque degradant," as opposed to mock-heroic or "burlesque dignifiant"):[9] they are parodic doubles of elements from the religious dogma, entailing a mutual transvestism of the popular and the noble. As a consequence, the text seems to be spoken from within by heterogeneous voices. This is all the more striking as they parallel the slangish glibness of the narrator. Furthermore, the rendering of the rambling conversation by "the Nameless One" implies a frequent shift from the direct style to the indirect speech and free indirect speech. The "pure" orality of the direct style infects the indirect styles, and it entails a new, composite style, as in this sentence: "and he asks Terry was Martin Cunningham there" (290). The sentence begins in the indirect style but the correct syntactic form ("if he was there") does not follow; on the other hand, "was Martin Cunningham there" is like a question in the direct style, but it is not introduced by a colon or quotation marks, neither does it end with an interrogation mark. Moreover, the verb is not in the present tense but in the preterit as in the observance of the sequence of tenses implied by the reported speech.[10]

If on the one hand the parodies appear as a cubist collage of miscellaneous elements, on the other hand they contribute to the elaborate and far-reaching network of resonances inside *Ulysses*, and beyond. Indeed, the styles parodied in various episodes crop up again in "Oxen of the Sun," and the characters from various episodes reappear in "Circe" again. But there are also links beyond *Ulysses* with other parts of Joyce's work. For example, the shotgun wedding story of Bob Doran and Polly Mooney is told in *Dubliners* ("The Boarding House"), and the "old one there" described in "Cyclops" appears under the name of Dante in chapter 1 of *A Portrait of the Artist as a Young Man*.

In the "night-language" of *Finnegans Wake* (Parrinder 1984: 207), the body of stories jumbled together takes the form of dreamwork. The stream of consciousness morphs into a "stream of unconsciousness," as Harry Levin puts it.[11] Meaningful and playful phonic and visual displacements in the morphology and etymology of words, in the syntax and in paragraphs are involved in this funeral which is also a "funferal."[12] The *Wake* equally includes a wide gamut of oral performances such as quizzes, riddles, seances, courtroom scenes, intermingled with catchphrases, book and song titles alluded to and parodied. Narrators vary and fuse in an extraordinary display of polyglottism—65 languages have been identified (Parrinder 1984: 229)—including hundreds of river-names, uttered by a great number of "english spooker[s], multaphoniaksically spuking" (178: 6–7). In the incipit of the novel, the onomatopoeia imitative of the sound of a fall—"bababadalgharaghtakamminarronnkonnbronntonnerronntuonnthunntrovarrhounawnskawntoohoohoordenenthurnuk!"—is in itself polyphonic and polyglot as it contains the word "thunder" dramatized under various linguistic guises. Indeed, written in "babelic" language (suggested by "babadal"), this nonce-word is made up of a number of words meaning "thunder" ("thun" stands in the middle) in languages other than English, such as Hindi "gargarahat" ("gharaghta"), Japanese "kaminari" ("kamminarronnkonn"), Greek "brontê" ("bronn"), French "tonnerre" ("tonnerronn"), and so on. If it is possible to disentangle and isolate some phenomena (such as male soliloquy, and female soliloquy), one of the joys and surprises of *Finnegans Wake* is that it is very much "pure untamed verbal wilderness" (Parrinder 1984: 236), which contains the "defence and indictment of the book itself," as Joyce wrote in a letter

(237). The available reading aids are necessary to explore and perceive various levels of meanings.

In this novel, as in *Ulysses*, you "never know whose thoughts you're chewing" (162): "Often the reader is expected to decode material without necessarily enjoying full knowledge of who is speaking" (Kiberd 2009: 169). "The word in language is half someone else's. It becomes 'one's own' only when the speaker populates it with his own intention, his own accent, when he appropriates the word, accepting it to his own semantic and expressive intention" (*DI*: 293). *Finnegans Wake* is a celebration of the variety of languages and of linguistic performances the world over. In both novels, "All sides of life should be represented" (190).

A Carnivalesque Kaleidoscope

From *Dubliners* onwards, the reception of Joyce's narratives was always accompanied either by silent refusals or loud uproar at their socially subversive content. Delays for publication, trials for obscenity, and censorship weigh on the publishing history of *Dubliners*, *The Portrait of the Artist as a Young Man*, and *Ulysses*, in various English-speaking countries: *Ulysses* was finally published in France in 1922.

Dubliners debunks many father figures in the fields of family, nationalism, and religion. Most families in *Dubliners* are dysfunctional: a parent is missing, fathers tend to be drunk or violent, mothers tend to be manipulative. Priests are suspected pedophiles; heroes from Irish nationalism are mocked. In the wake of *Dubliners*, *A Portrait of the Artist as a Young Man* identifies three nets—nationality, language, religion—which are the butt of the narrator's perspective. In chapter 1, family members and friends quarrel over the roles of nineteenth-century nationalist characters. Later on in the same chapter, the young Stephen Dedalus is punished by a priest who uses a pandybat to whip his hands. In this scene, symbolical positions are inverted: Dedalus is turned into a martyr, whereas the priest behaves like an executioner. Chapter 3 consists mainly of a speech on hell given by a priest in Stephen's school. It is not morality which is encouraged, but intimidation which is used in order to foster good behaviors in teenagers. Through the priest's speech, hell appears more bureaucratic than demonic. As far as language is concerned, the dialogue taking place in chapter 5 between Stephen and an English priest over the designation of the same utensil (funnel/tundish) ends up with Stephen's victory over the colonizer and his language.

Ulysses and *Finnegans Wake* are, to borrow Bakhtin's words about the work of Rabelais, an encyclopaedia of folk culture. *Ulysses* occurs on the day when Bloom is cuckolded, a situation often celebrated on carnival days.

Finnegans Wake draws on funeral merrymaking in the Irish fashion. Leopold Bloom in *Ulysses* is a deracinated hero: Western, British, and Irish cultures are filtered through the de-centered eyes of the Jewish character. The events in "Cyclops" have much to do with the revelries of a carnival. First, the central scene takes place in a pub, a place of sociability and of informality; the tipsy customers are not out of place. Following Mikhail Bakhtin's analysis of the carnival in *Rabelais and his World*, Patrick Parrinder defines carnival as "a forum in which a behaviour that is normally frowned upon—such as ogling another person's physical attributes, or flaunting one's own—becomes sanctioned and overt .... The world, as ordinarily experienced, is turned bottom upwards" (7). Bakhtin underlines the predominance of "the material bodily principle, that is, images of the human body with its food, drink, defecation, and sexual life" (*RHW*: 18). This is indeed a description of the world of *Ulysses*, in which the characters are not only shown drinking, eating but also defecating ("Calypso"), urinating ("Cyclops," "Penelope"), vomiting ("Eumaeus"), farting ("Sirens"), and masturbating ("Nausicaa").[13] All the physical orifices are wide open and great stress is laid on the exchanges between the inside and the outside of the body. This is a distinguishing feature of what Bakhtin calls the "grotesque body," which "transgresses its own limits" (*RHW*: 28), as with the tears falling from the eyes of Bob Doran or the hanged man's erection, which is "philoprogenitive" (it ends with an ejaculation), and is "standing up in their faces like a poker," in "Cyclops."

Let us take "Cyclops" as an example again. When Bloom comes in, the drinking session is like a symposium (as analyzed in *RHW*, ch. 4) in full swing. Throughout the conversation, toasts are made in the name of various persons and institutions. This is done after the Irish custom, which implies that everybody takes their turn to pay a round. Eating, too, is present. The dog Garryowen does not swallow the content of the tin of biscuits: "Gob, he golloped it down like old boots and his tongue hanging out of him a yard long for more." Excess occurs in the process: "Near ate the tin and all." During carnival time, as Bakhtin notes, things are turned upside down, there is "a continual shifting from top to bottom, from front to rear" (*RHW*: 11), and a great emphasis is laid on the nether parts of the body. In this respect, allusions to Molly Bloom's bottom (293) and to Polly Mooney (called the "bumbailiff's daughter") are made. "Bumbailiff" is a derogatory word which designates a policeman who catches thieves from behind ("bum"). Slang words and swearwords making reference to bodily aspects, such as "bloody" and "bugger," occur all along the text. The erection of the hanged man goes indeed to show that the boundaries between life and death are no longer clear. Life laughs at death—something which is also to be found in *Finnegans Wake*, a "funferal" based on the custom of the Irish wake. The grotesque is characterized by ambivalence and by a state in which the mineral, vegetal, animal, and human reigns are intermingled ("plant, animal, and human forms [...] seemed to be interwoven," *RHW*: 3). Thus, Bob Doran's sobbing is at the same time moving and ridiculous (284). Moreover, the expression "the tear is pretty near your eye" alludes to a poem by Thomas Moore, "Erin, the Tear and the Smile in Thine Eyes," which develops the ambivalence between laughter and tears. The narrator is disgusted ("give you the bloody pip") by the sight of Bob Doran using baby-talk for the dog: "Give us the paw, Doggy" (293). The dog Garryowen is "humanized" by the pronoun "he." On the contrary, Polly Mooney is called "a bitch," and her lovers are implicitly compared to horses. The phrase "fair field and no favour" designates a horse race where all the contestants have equal chances (290). This may be seen as a prologue to the metamorphoses of "Circe."

In his fellows' eyes, Bloom is a know-all and a killjoy; he does not abide by the rules of pub hospitality, by refusing not only to join in the drinking session but also to pay his round (it is true, unwittingly): "As a liminal person, Leopold Bloom disrupts the complacencies of all the settled codes with which he comes into contact" (Kiberd 2009: 189). Bloom is at the same time "the passive centre of the action in "Cyclops" and its active focus."[14] This is considered all the more severely as they believe him to have won in horse-racing bets. Bloom introduces a dissonant voice and he embodies seriousness and science; on his first appearance, he is compared to a policeman: "He's on point duty up and down there." He becomes the Lord of Misrule of the feast: in a carnival, the king (or the highest authority) "is mocked by all the people. He is abused and beaten" (*RHW*: 197).[15] This is to be linked with the end of the episode and the pogrom attempted by the citizen on the person of Bloom. "Cyclops" ends in a traditional "transformation scene," with Bloom's apotheosis.

Bakhtin remarks that a carnival manifests "the familiar speech in the marketplace" (*RHW*: 15). The feast of the body parallels a feast of words. The narrator's Irish pub banter in "Cyclops" is but one example of the verbal grotesque in this episode, as in the whole novel. Here, to take a few instances, a chiasmus is combined with an antanaclasis ("Good Christ! [...] —Who said Christ is good?," 290), and other examples of wordplays include fancy etymology (barber/barbarous/barbarian, 291); unintentional puns (foul/fowl, 291), and intentional ones such as the one on "cod";[16] neologism ("codology," 292); nonsensical logic: "Talking about new Ireland he ought to go and get a new dog so he ought" (292). One would like to add "etc." to imitate the lists in *Ulysses* which give way to almost infinite potentialities.[17] Thus, the narrator of "Cyclops" concludes his speeches with: "and so forth and so on," "phenomenon and science and this phenomenon and the other phenomenon," "and new Ireland and new this, that and the other" (292). Amid "all [the] kinds of drivel" (291) proffered in Kiernan's pub, and in order to understand the polymorphous language of Joyce, one has to be a polyglot. In addition to the alternated styles of "Cyclops," one meets with

Saxon English and Latin English words, English and Irish slang ("I beg your parsnip," "a kip," "stravaging," "the wampum," 290, 293), familiar Celtic phrases ("loodheramaun," "Sinn Fein!," 293), German and Latin words ("Blumenduft," "corpora cavernosa," 292). The great variety of curses[18] ("Christ M'Keown," "by herrings," 290, 293), and oaths ("God's truth," "True as you're there," "Faith he was," "I could have sworn it was him," 290, 292), and other significant misspellings,[19] contribute to the great kaleidoscope of linguistic forms, in which even God undergoes metamorphoses: Jesus, begob, Good Christ, Christ M'Keown, The Lord, God, dog?, Gob, the holy farmer, herrings ... in a scatological debunking of Irish pieties. Forgetting that a carnival, as in Brueghel's *The Fight between Carnival and Lent* (1559), is a time when religion is defied and parodied, H. G. Wells deplored what he called Joyce's "cloacal obsession."[20] However, the spectator/reader is implicitly invited to join in the performance through the personal pronoun which works as a shifter: "True as you're there." *Finnegans Wake* dramatizes bodily fluids in other scenes, and adds the evocation of incest as another assault against the so-called institution of the family. As such, Joyce's work is a "humanisation of epic" (Kiberd 2009: 328).

A Radical Debunking of Literary Codes

In Joyce's work, the opening up of the body is paralleled with the opening up of the word and even with the opening up of the book. If *Dubliners*, by and large, pays homage to the nineteenth-century novels of Flaubert and Dickens, *A Portrait of the Artist as a Young Man* starts to declare war against the novel, a war which is going to be waged in its last extremities in the final novels. The story of Stephen Dedalus' formation begins and ends with fragments. In chapter 3, it contains a catalog of horrors, which heralds the lists in *Ulysses* and *Finnegans Wake*. The growing use of the stream of consciousness in Joyce's novel implies that events are viewed not in terms of chronology but according to the importance of the emotions as they are felt within the speaker. Stephen's development in *A Portrait* evolves from a fascination for words in themselves, to words in relation with other words, the relation between words and reality, words and semantics, and words with wordplays. In a postcolonial turn, English language is subverted.

The notion of character is also undermined. Dedalus' father in *A Portrait* has many facets, being: "a medical student, an oarsman, a tenor, an amateur actor, a shouting politician, a small landlord, a small investor, a drinker, a good fellow, a storyteller, somebody's secretary, something in a distillery, a taxgatherer, a bankrupt and at present a praiser of his own past."[21] Stephen's identity evolves by leaps from chapter to chapter and within each chapter, from section to section. In the network of references of *Ulysses*, Stephen Dedalus is not only Telemachus but also Hamlet, the Prodigal Son, Wagner's Siegfried, and many other lesser-developed intertextual figures. Jennifer Levine warns: "To read *Ulysses* as a novel is to ask, at every turn, 'who speaks?' and, beyond that, 'what do these words say about the own who "owns" them?'"[22] In her *Census of Finnegans Wake*, Adaline Glasheen gives a telling title to the section dedicated to the characters in the novel: "Who is Who when Everybody is Somebody Else."[23] Indeed, the characters reappear under various names (or variations on their former name), and under various aspects, as for instance in a seance at the beginning of section III.3.

In the spirit of Laurence Sterne's *The Life and Opinions of Tristram Shandy*, *Ulysses* and *Finnegans Wake* play with the potentials of the printed layout and develop Joyce's own innovative use of punctuation. The reading of the letter[24] in "Cyclops" is problematic: only the reader of *Ulysses* and the "actual" reader, Joe Hynes, can perceive the errors of punctuation, the misspellings (and especially the homophonic pun foul/fowl), and the presentation of the text (the position of the heading and of the signature). The "graphical dimension" (Derrida 1987: 46) of the pun on "foul/fowl" is but one instance of many "gramophone words"[25] in *Ulysses*. In *Finnegans Wake*, for example in section II.2, the marginal notes by the two brothers Shem and Shaun form a counterpoint with the text in the central column. Shem's notes are at first on the left and Shaun's notes are on the right, but they swap after page 292, while another character, Issy, provides footnotes. Section III.4 revolves around four points of view or camera positions.[26] Novels include musical scores, drawings, lists, tables, and symbols of all kinds, which invite and/or channel reading into creative directions.

Joyce's work challenges and straddles literary genres. If *Dubliners* is at first glance a succession of short stories, it is also a novel about Dublin—as all the other novels are. Is *Ulysses* a play, a poem, a succession of short stories, a novel? Common literary categories collapse and evaporate. Take the stream of consciousness in *Ulysses*, for instance. The parodic styles of the later sections of the novel reveal the deceptiveness of the stream of consciousness realism of the earlier episodes (Parrinder 1984: 121).

Joyce also subverts classical literature through modernization—not only through the modernization of myths and mythical figures (the *Odyssey* in *Ulysses* for instance), but also through the introduction of modern practices with the handling words. For instance, *Ulysses* draws not only on the surfacing art of advertising which already contaminated headline journalism (see the textual breaks in "Aeolus"), it probably also takes into account some of the recent development of editing in the cinema (as shown in the scene-switching in "Wandering Rocks"). In *Finnegans Wake*, the telephone, radio, and television programs come into play as well, showing the attention paid by Joyce throughout his life to new, emerging media he would blend in his omnivorous novels.

Joyce's final work, *Finnegans Wake*, proliferates and expands in fancy morphology, broken up syntax, coinages (which include several one-hundred letter words), puns,[27] and portmanteau-words, to such an extent that "a paragraph, a sentence, a phrase, or even a word can offer a mini-narrative to the reader."[28] Consequently, the final revelation of meaning is always for "later" as Stephen Heath suggested.[29] "I have discovered I can do anything with language I want," Joyce exulted (Parrinder 1984: 200). One of the paradoxes of the novel is that, although considered virtually untranslatable, it has been fully translated into eight languages.[30]

Indeed, his work evolves toward a literary kaleidoscope in which the exiled Irish writer celebrates a great number of elements of modern popular culture including the "modern art of advertisement" whose "infinite possibilities (have been) hitherto unexploited" (636). Another paradox of Joyce's last novels—*Ulysses*, and, more so, *Finnegans Wake*—is that, although they celebrate the epic of the common man and woman, they discourage many readers belonging to this category. Instead of exploring the new ways of reading invented by Joyce, many are daunted by the myriad possibilities of interpretations. Reading aids are therefore of great help to make better sense of the proliferation of literary devices and echoes and intertextual and retroactive effects of the novels, so that Gertrude Stein's prediction proves true: "*Ulysses* is incomprehensible but anybody can understand it" (Kiberd 2009: 312). Joyce, like Rabelais, encourages readers to enjoy the precarious stability of meaning: "I am nothing but an Irish clown, a great joker at the universe."[31]

Notes

1. Finn Fordham, *Lots of Fun at Finnegans Wake: Unravelling Universals* (Oxford: Oxford University Press, 2007), 6.
2. Declan Kiberd, *Ulysses and Us* (Faber & Faber: London, 2009), 25.
3. James Joyce, *Occasional, Critical, and Political Writing* (Oxford: Oxford University Press, 2008), xxi–xxii; see also xxix.
4. Keith M. Booker, *Joyce, Bakhtin, and the Literary Tradition: Toward a Comparative Cultural Poetics* (Ann Arbor: University of Michigan Press, 1996); R. B. Kershner, *Joyce, Bakhtin, and Popular Literature, Chronicles of Disorder* (Chapel Hill: University of North Carolina Press, 1989).
5. James Joyce, *Dubliners* (London: Penguin, 1992 [1914]).
6. James Joyce, *Ulysses* (Oxford: Oxford University Press, 1993 [1922]), 734–9.
7. Patrick Parrinder, *James Joyce* (Cambridge: Cambridge University Press, 1984), 119–20.

8. T. S. Eliot, "*Ulysses*, Order, and Myth," *Selected Prose of T. S. Eliot* (London: Faber & Faber, 1975 [1923]), 177.
9. Gérard Genette, *Figures III* (Paris: Seuil, 1972), 186.
10. These examples are close to what Hugh Kenner called the "Uncle Charles Principle." Hugh Kenner, *Joyce's Voices* (Berkeley: University of California Press, 1978), 15–38.
11. Harry Levin, *James Joyce: A Critical Introduction* (New York: New Directions, 1960 [1941]), 140.
12. James Joyce, *Finnegans Wake* (Oxford: Oxford University Press, 2012 [1939]), 120: 10.
13. Molly Bloom, in addition to the above mentioned activities, also copulates and menstruates. Leopold Bloom appears neither masculine nor feminine but "pansexual" (Kiberd 2009: 189) in various episodes: "How a man eats an egg, said Joyce, could reveal more about him than how he goes to war" (77).
14. Clive Hart and David Hayman, eds., *James Joyce's Ulysses: Critical Essays* (Berkeley: University of California Press, 1974), 249.
15. In *A Portrait of the Artist as a Young Man*, Stephen's father embodies a similar Lord of Misrule.
16. A cod is a fish, but as a verb it means "to talk nonsense" (hence, the paradoxical probable meaning of the coinage "codology"), and as a noun, in slang, it designates a testis.
17. "[Joyce's] work functions as a library and archive" (Parrinder 1984: 4), an idea taken up and developed by Derrida (1987).
18. They belong to the grotesque realism: "Profanities and oaths (jurons) are in many ways similar to abusive language. They too invaded billingsgate speech" (*RHW*, 17).
19. These frequently occur in *Ulysses*, especially in letters, as in Martha Clifford's letter to Bloom, in which she writes "world" instead of "word" (*Ulysses*, 74).
20. H. G. Wells, "*A Portrait of the Artist as a Young Man* by James Joyce," *The New Republic*, 10 (March 1917).
21. James Joyce, *A Portrait of the Artist as a Young Man* (Oxford: Oxford University Press, 2008 [1916]), 203.
22. Jennifer Levine, "Ulysses," in *The Cambridge Companion to James Joyce*, ed. Derek Attridge (Cambridge: Cambridge University Press, 1990), 122–48 (157).
23. Adaline Glasheen, *A Second Census of Finnegans Wake* (Evanston: Northwestern University Press, 1963).
24. The letter is part of the "telegramophone" network of postal services in *Ulysses*. Jacques Derrida, *Ulysse gramophone. Deux mots pour Joyce* (Paris: Galilée, 1987), 33.
25. A gramophone word is "a mark which is at the same time spoken and written, vocalized as a grapheme and written like a phoneme" (Derrida, *Ulysse gramophone*, 76).

26 One of the symbolic keys of *Ulysses* is parallax—an apparent change in the position of an object resulting from the change in position of the observer. The term appears in "Lestrygonians" and "could have served as a title for this novel," according to Marilyn French (in Parrinder 1984: 153).

27 Vladimir Nabokov, who dedicated a number of lectures to Joyce, particularly *Ulysses*, called the novel *Punnigans Wake*. Vladimir Nabokov, *Lectures on Literature* (London and New York: Harvest Book, 1980); Vladimir Nabokov, *The Annotated Lolita* (Penguin: London, 1991 [1955]), 413.

28 Derek Attridge, *Joyce Effects* (Cambridge: Cambridge University Press, 2000), 129.

29 Stephen Heath, "Ambiviolences: Notes for Reading Joyce," in *Post-Structuralist Joyce: Essays from the French*, ed. Derek Attridge and Daniel Ferrer (Cambridge: Cambridge University Press, 1984): 31–68 (31).

30 See Topia for some of the difficulties and options faced by translators of *Finnegans Wake* into French. André Topia, "*Finnegans Wake*, la traduction parasitée," in Palimpsestes 4 (1990), accessed March 5th, 2021, http://journals.openedition.org/palimpsestes/602.

31 Willard Potts, ed., *Portraits of the Artist in Exile: Recollections of James Joyce by Europeans* (Seattle: University of Washington Press, 1979; New York: Harcourt, Brace & Jovanovitch, 1986), 229.

14

Mikhail Bakhtin, Modern Dance, and the Body's Unmediated Presence in the World

Marsha D. Barsky and Robert F. Barsky

> *Dance is the unification of expression and function, Illumined physicality and inspired form. Without ecstasy no dance! Without form no dance! (Ohne Ekstase kein Tanz! Ohne Form kein Tanz!)*[1]

> *Instinctively [the dancer] accepts this medium of self-expression, an art form achieved through and dependent on the body.*[2]

> DANCE. Soft and gentle, vehement and wild. (Wigman 1975: 122)

Scholars have mostly agreed that Mikhail Bakhtin, to quote Caryl Emerson, "was profoundly unresponsive to the major works of twentieth-century modernism."[3] This is a strong claim, which reverberates menacingly in a volume devoted to the overlap between Bakhtin's work and Modernism as a movement. Ilya Kliger has measured the implications of Emerson's words, and agrees that in spite of his "brief lectures, flickering with enthusiasm, on more than a dozen contemporary poets and prose writers," "nowhere in his work does Bakhtin's treatment of Modernist authors approach the intensity of his engagement with the Hellenistic novel, with Rabelais, Fyodor Dostoevskii, Johann Wolfgang von Goethe or, for that matter, with Aleksandr Pushkin, Charles Dickens, or Nikolai Gogol" (551). He then provocatively notes that "one might be tempted to conclude from this relative lack of attention to Modernist works that Bakhtin was essentially opposed to the fundamental presuppositions underlying literary modernism as such"; or else, he suggests that one could also assert "that it is precisely the modernist novel that is most consistently guided by the narratological principles elaborated by Bakhtin" (551).[4] Kliger doesn't land up pursuing either tack, however, but instead works to explore "a more general Bakhtinian conception of the modernist condition as characterized by what [Bakhtin] calls 'a crisis of authorship' (*krizis avtorstva*)" (552).

In this chapter, we will suggest that the Bakhtinian conception of the Modernist condition is indeed discernable, but it's situated in his approach to dialogism, which offers a distinctly modern approach to the relationship between bodies in space and in time. Part of this approach involves a careful examination of the self in relation to the body, the other, and the surrounding environment. Kliger envisions this process in a literary realm, in which "even the most abstract and lifeless of objects" are animated and endowed "with a temporal trajectory of a hero," allowing for an engagement with abstract or "objectless" art (553). This is interesting as regards literary texts, but it's even more applicable to bodies moving in space, and with time, for which modern dance provides a particularly salient microcosm.

Kliger looks back to knowledge debates originating at the end of the eighteenth century, but for our approach to dialogism and the dancing body we go further back in time, and recall characteristics that Bakhtin assigns to the carnivalesque, including masks; betwixt-and-between spaces; carnival time; double-voicedness; the grotesque body; the language of symbolic concretely sensuous forms; the suspension of normal social and behavioral codes; the "atmosphere of joyful relativity," and, to cite Bakhtin, "free and familiar contact among people" who in the normal course of things are divided by "impenetrable hierarchical barriers" (PDP: 122–3). These carnivalesque forms, present in many manifestations of modern dance, enable, to cite Bakhtin, a "new mode of interrelationship between individuals, counterpoised to the all-powerful socio-hierarchical relationships of noncarnival life" (123). One way to enter that space is through the mask, a central tool for the seminal modern dancer and choreographer Mary Wigman, who used it to transport herself toward the carnivalesque space:

> Why should a dancer use a mask? Always when his creative urge causes a split process in him, when his imagination reveals the image of an apparently alien figure which ... compels the dancer to a certain kind of metamorphosis. The mask never can and never ought to be an interesting addition or decoration. It must be an essential part of the dance figure, born in a world of visions and transported as if by magic into reality. The mask extinguishes the human being as a person and makes him submit to the fictive figure of the dance.
>
> (Wigman 1973: 124)

This fictive figure of the dance is, from Wigman's perspective, indistinguishable from the dance itself. For Wigman, the dancer was freed from Enlightenment codes of reason, order and rationality, and thereby able to create a distinctly modern woman. In the words of Mary Anne Santos Newhall, "along with a radical reordering of what was acceptable for the body, roles for women and men became fluid, leading to a dynamic shift in how the body was trained, presented and performed on the concert stage. Deep links to ritual and occult practices served as justification and aesthetic foundation for these experiments."[5] These practices create links to Bakhtin's carnivalesque, in a space of dialogic encounters between and within moving, dancing bodies.

Modern Dance

Modern dance is in many ways a quintessential modern artform, since from its earliest manifestations in America, Europe, and Russia dancers stripped away the rigid constraints of codification, and the frivolous subject matter associated with classical ballet, in favor of pure movement and emotion. The American dance critic John Martin wrote in 1933[6] that modern dance "is not interested in spectacle, but in the communication of emotional experiences—intuitive perceptions, elusive truths—which cannot be communicated in reasoned terms or reduced to mere statement of fact" (22–3). These embodied states are, and have been, central to the practice and performance of modern dance. They can also be perceived in the body by "kinesthesia," a term coined by H. C. Bastian in 1887[7] to describe the ability to sense the position and movement of our limbs and trunk. For him, it's "a mysterious sense since, by comparison with our other senses such as vision and hearing, we are largely unaware of it in our daily activities":[8]

> Through kinesthesis, any bodily movement arouses a sympathetic reaction in the mind of the spectator. If it is a representational movement, the spectator recognises it at once because in performing the same action he has utilised the same movement. If it is non-representational movement, the same process holds true. The maker of the movement has a purpose, an intention, in making the movement; the movement is transferred in effect by kinesthetic sympathy to the muscles of the spectator, and because he is used to associating movement with intention, he arrives by induction at the intention of the particular movement under consideration; it is inconceivable that any bodily movement should be made without intention, even if that intention is nothing more than to make a movement without intention.
>
> (Bastian 1878: 85)

This approach offers a helpful connection between kinesthesia and modern dance, and, as we'll see, many of the points of overlap between the two are aptly described by Bakhtin's approach to dialogism, particularly as developed in the work of Michael Holquist. Irina Sirotkina and Roger Smith[9] expand upon the kinesthesia–modern dance relationship by suggesting that "when properly cultivated by the choreographies, dance movement can unite both dancer and viewer in the experience of fundamental human emotion" (3). They thereby lay the claim that kinesthesis was a source for innovation and personal knowledge for (Russian) dancers during the early twentieth century.

> Put in its simplest form, the claims for kinaesthesis hinge on the argument that this sense gives unmediated contact with the world, while the other senses offer a mediated relationship. The very word "contact" communicates the point: in movement and touch there is contact, a direct relationship with; in the other senses there is not. With touch and movement, a person is at one with the world; with the other senses, so it may be felt, there is subject and object, self and other. In this way of thought, dance becomes the most powerful metaphor, and it also becomes the reality, of unmediated being alive as part of a world.
>
> (4)

There is no objective in this description of dance, no narrative, no teleology, but rather a celebration of movement as the "reality" of being alive, which in turn provides knowledge about the world itself. The movement "gives both unmediated expressions to being-in-the- world and unmediated knowledge of the world," which helps the modern subject "to realize the ancient hope 'to know' by rendering the knower part of the larger whole, not an outside observer of it." This distinctly modern approach to the subject relies on a recreation of intuition, insight, and belief in a higher or more profound knowledge of which "the modern dancer is its personification, its celebrant." From this standpoint, "knowledge is in the body, and the body the vessel of truth," connecting "our historical story with present debate about the nature and understanding of dance and embodied performance" (10). This echoes the work of Martin, for whom modern dance communicated emotional experiences through movement: "The modern dancer, instead of employing the cumulative sources of academic tradition, cuts through directly to the source of all dancing."[10]

The link between emotion and movement here is based precisely on the kind of feedback loop that we would consider dialogic, in that it implies a move from self to other and self to environment whereby, according to Martin, "the sense organs which report movement and postural change are closely connected with that part of the nervous system which belongs primarily to the inner man where emotions are generated."[11] Interestingly, from the perspective of dance and Bakhtin, this process is also akin to a kind of language, since it "opened the body from a new direction, a direction that speaks'" (Sirotkina 2017: 65).

Citing S. M. Volkonsky, and Friederich Nietzsche, Sirotkina, and Smith also suggest that time and space meet in "plyaska" (inspired dance, or dance with spirit), quieting that "dissension" that exists between "our 'I wish' and 'I may'." Dance in this view resounds with carnivalesque characteristics that generate a meeting of imagination with reason, illuminate the play of the imagination, and blend it all into one "beautiful person" (65):

> Nietzsche's metaphors of dance, the extensive, if not systematic, reference to the importance of rhythm, movement and dance in the writings of innovative artists like Rimbaud (who recognized that rhythmic poetic forms were spatial, like dance) and Cézanne (who, it has been said, choreographed his thought in painting), along with innovations in dance performance itself, suggest that dance may be a key, perhaps even the key, to a more satisfactory comprehension of modernism as a conceptual category.
>
> (66)

This "blending" that occurs in modern dance is the key to our situating this conception of Modernism in the body itself, which from this standpoint isn't differentiable from the movement that it performs. All of this resonates with Bakhtin's conception of the dialogized body which, as we'll see, is not a sign of something else, or the medium that gestures toward meaning: the body itself *is* the meaning.

The Ideality of Modern Dance

A fascinating source for a Modernist approach to movement and the dancing body, one which resonates with what we are describing here, is the modern writer Stéphane Mallarmé, whose small corpus of observations about dance has become remarkably influential. For him, "the dancer—whom he perceives as inseparable from the dance—constitutes an ideal sign. His belief in the ideality of dance … is, however, also determined by his perception of the dance sign as being not only a representation but also a symbolic embodiment of whatever ideal form of beauty the spectator interprets it to represent." Furthermore, "dance signs seem to constitute their own referents; they do not merely name, copy, or suggest but actually materially incorporate what they signify." Recalling Théophile Gautier's suggestion that the primary subject of dance is dancing, "Mallarmé deemed 'the mobile synthesis' of the dancers' attitudes to be the ultimate signified of every dance and of the art of dance on the whole." For this reason, Mallarmé "dismisses the plots of both Viviane (an allegorical battle between light and darkness) and Les Deux Pigeons (a fable about love, separation and reconciliation) as pretexts (albeit charming) for the exposition of the signifying process of dance itself."[12]

Bakhtin seldom focused on twentieth-century materials, in part because he spent most of his life in provincial towns, and he never elaborated a full-blown "theory of modernism." Nevertheless, that Mallarmé's depiction of the modern dancer corresponds with Bakhtin's approach to plyaska is not surprising, because he was a member of the circle of Zelinsky's students in St. Petersburg, who discussed it.

> According to Bakhtin, a person achieves 'presence' only in special circumstances, of which one, a principal one, is plyaska …. In dance, my exteriority, only visible by others and for others who exist, flows together with my inner, self-aware, organic activity; in plyaska, everything inner in me strives to come out, to combine with exteriority, and in plyaska I must strengthen being and join the being of others. My presence (confirmed as a value from without), my Sophia [*sofiinost'*, divine wisdom], dances in me, another dances in me.
>
> (Sirotkina 2017: 42)

Bakhtinian Bodies in Theater

Dick McCaw, a British actor-trainer and mind-body specialist, has explored Bakhtin's writings from a similar perspective, but much as we find value in his approach, he concludes that Bakhtin, who himself was immobilized by osteoporosis, gets things wrong in regards to the body because he uses visual scenarios which, like his own immobilized body, don't move. By way of example, McCaw refers to this oft-cited passage:

> When I contemplate a whole human being who is situated outside and over against me, our concrete, actually experienced horizons do not coincide. For at each given moment, regardless of the position and the proximity to me of this other human being whom I am contemplating, I shall always see and know something that he, from his place outside and over against me, cannot see himself: parts of his body that are inaccessible to his own gaze (his head, his face and its expression), the world behind his back and a whole series of objects and relations, which in any of our mutual relations are accessible to me but not to him.
>
> (*AA*: 22–3)

McCaw comments on this passage that

> The first thing to note is that this is a static act of contemplation, and, as such, extremely limited as a foundation for a theory of action, drama or dialogue. To extend the visual metaphor further Bakhtin's body is about sight and site: neither parties change position in order to offer themselves multiple points of view and neither actually speaks to each other. There is no to and fro of exchanges and no challenging of views. They sit, mute and immobile, and think to themselves about what they see. It is all about visually apprehended images of 'whole humans'. The senses of movement, smell, touch, taste and hearing play very little active role in this primordial situation.[13]

For McCaw, this represents Bakhtin's propensity to figure the moving body as a series of fixed images, rather than in continual movement. His conclusion is that

> Bakhtin's categorical distinction between sense and meaning, between the inner and the outer body, is driven by his reliance on the single sense of sight, as is the distinction between the roles of observer and actor; there is no question of the other assisting in any practical way to change the situation. Bakhtin's notion of how we understand the body revolves around it being able to be grasped immediately as a static image rather than a mobile organism. At every step of his argument he is dealing with fixity rather than movement. (105)

For McCaw's criticism to stand up to scrutiny, Bakhtin's approach must be devoid of active engaging, unfolding movement in time and space. But this seems hardly to be the case. For example, throughout his work, McCaw distinguishes between the idea of the self as image with the self as agent, leading him to propose that "Bakhtin's notion of body, time and space are grasped as static, frontal images" (122). But what is it in the Bakhtinian situated self in a particular chronotope that suggests a complete immobility on the part of the body that he describes?

> Bakhtin argues that even when I look in the mirror it is only a partial reflection of myself and not an image, because I cannot grasp myself as another would see me; I am still, as it were, attached to the reflected image. Furthermore he argues that all self-portraits lack ontological weight because they lack an 'optical purity of being' and have an 'emptiness' and 'ghostliness' because of the 'fact that we lack any emotional and volitional approach to this outward image that could vivify it and include or incorporate it axiologically within the outward unit of the plastic-pictorial world'. Would Bakhtin's approach provide a very fruitful reading

of the self-portraits that Rembrandt made during his life? Bakhtin doesn't actually argue the connection between seeing, knowing and valuing, it is just taken as a given of his categorical distinction between I and other and then repeated over and over again.

(108)

There are several presuppositions here that don't stand up to scrutiny. His claim is that one's self-image is necessarily partial, but this doesn't mean that the inner experience of the self is empty or ghost-like, but that it's just that: partial. McCaw himself makes this clear when he writes that "For Bakhtin the only way to understand your body as a whole is through the intercession of a loving other; in his philosophy the gaze of the Other (capital 'O' indicating the more negative conception of Other) is not intrusive but a welcome means of offering the incomplete (incompletable) 'I'"[14] (244). For us the operative term here is "whole," and none of the theorists he cites to correct Bakhtin can make this any more clear than Bakhtin himself: "In this sense, one can speak of a human being's absolute need for the other, for the other's seeing, remembering, gathering, and personality could not exist if the other did not create it: aesthetic memory is *productive*—it gives birth, for the first time, to the *outward* human being on a new plane of being" (*AA*: 35–6). Notice Bakhtin's use of gerunds: "seeing," "remembering," and "gathering," which all suggest a self in movement, in time, and in space.

From Egocentric and Allocentric Orientations to Dialogism

McCaw's contributions are nevertheless interesting for our broader project relating Bakhtin's work to dance, and a Modernist conception of body. Indeed, McCaw himself suggests that "Bakhtin does acknowledge this flow in time and argues that it characterises the experience of selfhood." For Bakhtin, people are always in the process of becoming, the future yet-to-be, which is "an intuitively experienced loophole out of time, out of everything given" (*AA*: 109). For McCaw, "[t]he body should not be thought as the generator of once-and-for-all acts whose meaning lies in the actualisation of a potential philosophical meaning, but as the source of meanings that come through the sensory awareness of the (often unseen) possibilities inherent in these actions as they unfold in time" (McCaw 2018: 246).

McCaw's fixation on reading Bakhtin's work as static forestalls his ability to recognize the dynamism of the dialogic approach that he himself has just described. For example, he writes that "for Bakhtin the skin is simply a boundary, one that neither provides a sensory interface with the world nor a sense of the embodied self as a whole" (248). Therefore, in his view Bakhtin is arguing "against the possibility of a direct experience of our bodies, arguing instead for a philosophical theory which involves the body" (248). But Bakhtin's work is often specifically about interstitial and liminal spaces, such as skin, as is clear when he suggests that "aesthetic self-activity always operates on the boundaries (form is a boundary)" (*AA*: 85). The problem here is semantic, though, so for McCaw the fact that Bakhtin uses "boundary" rather than "skin" is evidence that he "thereby privileges the sense of sight over touch." This, we think, is a trivial distinction. One final example comes from the realm of theory of mind, for which McCaw cites McConachie: "Because we are often in social situations when attuning ourselves to [the] emotions of others and reading their minds is important for achieving our goals, empathy is ubiquitous and commonplace; we deploy it (mostly unconsciously) all the time." Indeed! We need this constant empathetic feedback because, as McCaw says "Our body is a theatre of sympathetic sensation whose function is shaped and educated by our every experience" (McCaw 2018: 250).

In her article called "Bakhtin and the Actor,"[15] Caryl Emerson provides crucial insight that helps clarify how a Bakhtinian reading connects to what McCaw wants to ascribe to other theorists. In her description of stage directors' interactions with actors, she suggests that the actor "is obliged, not only as a mind but as a body, to sustain both perspectives at once. The actor is simultaneously the author of the hero (that is, the creator of the role, with all its unseen inner complexity) and its first spectator, who must constantly keep the outer body of this emerging 'creature' before his eyes" (193). This movement from inside of the body, to a place from which the body can be observed, demands constant awareness, and thus undermines any kind of habitual response. Once again, the dancer or actor thereby becomes what Bakhtin calls an "author/contemplator." Emerson acknowledges that "at times, this authoring task is considered the work of the actor alone, shuttling between self and other, between 'seeing' the role and being seen in it" (193). Her approach here, helpfully connected to theater, is very specifically dynamic; she is talking about a process that unfolds in time, with constant feedback, and recognition of the give-and-take that is the very hallmark of dialogism.

Bakhtin and the Dialogic Body

We have taken a rather deep dive into McCaw's work to challenge the reading of Bakhtin that he offers when he describes it. We agree with him that there is in the very act of being alive an ongoing dialogue that exists within the self, an inner dialogue that helps us to think about our actions in ways connected to such categories as sensation, perception, auto-regulation, feedback, and listening. This inner dialogue is connected to, rather than distinct from, the context or environment in which the self is situated. Dance pioneer Doris Humphrey describes this process with elegant simplicity in her seminal work *The Art of Making Dances*,[16] not in regards the audience member, but rather the dance maker when she sits in the audience: "The dance maker must stand away from his work spatially ... first in a literal sense, of space between himself and the dance, but also psychologically, so that he is sitting in an imaginary tenth row, looking at his dance for the first time, listening to the music, and receiving these impressions as an audience would, all just once through" (149). This is a tall task, since it demands that the dance maker be situated in several places at once, watching the movement unfold in time.

This, we would suggest, is where Michael Holquist's description of dialogism can help advance our consideration of dance as a dialogic process. For Holquist's conception of dialogism, "motion ... has only a relative meaning. Stated differently, one body's motion has meaning only in relation to another body; or—since it is a relation that is mutual—has meaning only in dialogue with another body."[17] This other body, in dance, can be that of the spectator, who witnesses the movement unfold, quite literally, in time and in space, from a particular situated vantage point: "If motion is to have meaning, not only must there be two different bodies in a relation with each other, but there must as well be someone to grasp the nature of such a relation: the non-centeredness of the bodies themselves requires the center constituted by an observer" (21).

For Holquist, even the dancers themselves don't move completely independently, statically, out of place, or out of time. On the contrary, their movement is affected by, inspired by, or in response to, the movement anticipated by the choreography, the other dancers in the work, and even the audience that is anticipated to view, and then actually does view, the performance. This is at the very heart of the dialogic relationship Holquist describes: "Bakhtin's observer is also, simultaneously, an active participant in the relation of simultaneity. Conceiving being dialogically means that reality is always experienced, not just perceived, and further that it is experienced from a particular position. Bakhtin conceives that position in kinetic terms as a situation, an event, the event of being a self" (21). This is very powerful, because while we are used to thinking about what the audience feels or observes, we are less likely to consider how movement is crafted in an ongoing fashion by the very presence and reactions of other dancers, or observers. Bakhtin provides us with a way of thinking about the dancer in relation to these observers according to what he refers to as the "law of placement" in dialogism, which, according to Holquist, "says everything is perceived from a unique position in existence; its corollary is that the meaning of whatever is observed is shaped by the place from which it is perceived" (Holquist 2003: 21). To return to our critique of McCaw, this "position" is not static, it's living, shifting, changing, and unfolding in time. One could argue that something similar happens during performances because the dancer sees, or knows of, the audience's existence.

All of this flows from another important discussion in Bakhtin's work, relating to what he described as the "self–other relationship," which McCaw insisted upon as being visual. But in Holquist's description, participants to the dialogic relationship have constant and ongoing agency, they are never just fixed points in space: "We are both doing essentially the same thing, but from different places: although we are in the same event, that event is different for each of us. Our places are different not only because our bodies occupy different positions in exterior, physical space, but also because we regard the world and each other from different centers in cognitive time/space" (Holquist 2003: 22). This "thing" that (for our example) the dancers are "doing" is a process of "filling-in" for the perspective of the other, and responding to it with movement in time. "For the perceivers, their own time is forever open and unfinished; their own space is always the center of perception, the point around which things arrange themselves as a horizon whose meaning is determined by wherever they have their place in it" (22). The consequence of this is that the dancer, like the dance, or like the dialogic conversation in language, is constantly in the process of being created, neither as a "cognitive necessity" nor a "mystified privilege." We will see this—and the intimate relation dialogism bears to language—if we understand that cognitive time/space is "ordered very much as time and space categories are deployed in speech" (22).

Holquist's insistence here upon "dialogism" as a "relation" in time and space is also made to contrast with the Formalist approach, articulated during Bakhtin's lifetime. Formalism[18] sets the basis for modern theories of art that focus upon form, which often led Formalist-style critics to extract the work from the context in which it was created. Bakhtin likened the identification of formal elements to an autopsy, which allows the pathologist to identify and isolate parts of the being, but sheds very little light on the way that those parts interacted with the whole body when the being was still alive. If we were to imagine a corollary in dance, it would be as though the dance maker took static pictures of her dancers, and then pointed out what they were doing with reference to the body divorced from motion in time and space. Bakhtin's dialogism challenges an approach to, say, dance, that insists upon the objects, forms, and symbols that are fixed in time and space. On the contrary, the dancer always experiences the work from both inside and the outside simultaneously, and to communicate this experience to the dancers. In her article on collaboration and responsible citizenship, Julie Mulvihill[19] states that "dance makers improvise, reflect, edit, adjust, evaluate, and critique the work and the process along the way. The soil of rehearsal is fertile for nurturing listening and being present and voice and bodying and exploring principles of responsible citizenship" (118). The product in a choreographic sense is of course important, but the "soil of rehearsal" provides the necessary space for transmission of somatic education and experiencing. So, for Bakhtin, all movements, just like all utterances, are saturated in their surroundings, bathing in polyphony (multiple sounds) and heteroglossia (multiple texts), which are combined artistically in the body moving in space.

What's fascinating about this approach to the body is that in its purest form, it presupposes a liberation from standard or formal categories. This is undoubtedly the reason that so many scholars find in Bakhtin an approach that is valuable for the study of the modern or postmodern novel. But in the context of dance, as we've seen, the overlap is even more powerful, because it corresponds directly to the kind of thinking we associate with Modernism, but also the actual events that were occurring which promoted such thoughts. Once again, Mary Wigman is fascinating from this perspective, because she developed her sense of modern dance on Monte Verità, in Ticino, Switzerland. She was there during the amazing period, from 1900–20, when a group of extraordinary writers, philosophers, psychoanalysts, dancers, and artists came to search for new forms of expression beyond the crushing demands of consumer capitalism in Europe. The likes of Otto Gross, Hermann Hesse, D. H. Lawrence, Mikhail Bakunin, and Rudolf von Laban were forerunners to the counterculture that emerged in the 1960s, as they foraged, sun-bathed, and moved in harmony with nature on this amazing "Mountain of Truth":[20]

> When Mary Wigman arrived at Monte Verità, she was directed to follow the sound of drums. By doing so she would find Rudolph von Laban and his students. Wigman recalled walking down a path on a hot summer day. Dressed from head to toe in her summer whites, she came upon a clearing where Laban was leading a group improvisation. Shedding hat, stockings, shoes and clothing, she joined the group.

Wigman's description of this encounter with Laban is extraordinary:

> Aha-a drum! I followed the sound, reached a meadow, and on the other side of the meadow a man stood in a white shirt and shorts, a drum in his hands and a few girls and a midget jumping around. I was fascinated, staring motionless. Laban turned around and said to me: —What do you want?—I would like to join you.—Fine, get undressed behind that bush and come over here. I did it. It was like coming home. This wonderful feeling I will never forget. I stood there and suddenly, under the guiding rhythm of his drum, I felt marvelous.[21]

This commune at Monte Verità was ideally suited to create a free an unfettered space of carnivalesque exploration, a kind of utopian world that was

> dedicated to radical ideas about lifestyle, art making, ritual, nature worship, feminism, birth control and free love. Along with a radical reordering of what was acceptable for the body, roles for women and men became fluid, leading to a dynamic shift in how the body was trained, presented and performed on the concert stage. Deep links to ritual and occult practices served as justification and aesthetic foundation for these experiments. Martin Green focuses on the cultural function of alternative belief systems in efforts to resist social norms.
>
> (Newhall 2010: 78)

Bakhtin's ideal spaces are always rich in possibility, like the carnival, the public space, the unfettered dialogue, or, as we've seen, the space of dance as conceived of by Laban and Wigman. Michael Holquist writes:

> It was his sense of the world's overwhelming multiplicity that impelled Bakhtin to rethink strategies by which heterogeneity had traditionally been disguised as a unity. In his several attempts to find a single name for the teeming forces which jostled each other within the combat zone of the word–whether the term was 'polyphony,' 'heteroglossia,' or 'speech communion'—Bakhtin was at great pains never to sacrifice the tension between identity and difference that fueled his enterprise.[22]

Communication of any sort, and movement of any sort, when viewed from the perspective of Bakhtin's work, exists in constant dialogue, on a range of levels: the self is in dialogue with the environment, and in dialogue with other selves. Beyond that, there is in the realm of creation (dance making) what Bakhtin calls the author–hero relationship, or the dialogism that's implicit in self–other relations. Then there is the dialogue between self and environment: we move through space, but we also move in relationship to space, and we are always situated in a given place, and not in another. Each movement, and even each non-movement, unfolds in time, and in space. From this perspective, stasis can't exist, except as a postulate, because human bodies don't exist in a move/not-move compendium, but rather in a situated space, and a chronotope that ties our "selves" to these relationships. The modern world gave new voice to bodies, suddenly unfettered from traditional ties. And modern dance, as we've seen, was its expression.

Notes

1. Mary Wigman in Rudolf Bach, *Das Mary Wigman Werk* (Dresden: Carl Reissner Verlag, 1933), 19.
2. Mary Wigman, *The Mary Wigman Book: Her Writings*, trans. Walter Sorrell (Middletown, CT: Wesleyan University Press, 1975), 105.
3. Caryl Emerson, "Introduction: Dialogue on Every Corner, Bakhtin in Every Class," in *Bakhtin in Contexts: Across the Disciplines*, ed. Amy Mandelker (Evanston: Northwestern University Press, 1995), 17.
4. Ilya Kliger, "Heroic Aesthetics and Modernist Critique: Extrapolations from Bakhtin's 'Author and Hero in Aesthetic Activity,'" *Slavic Review* 67.3 (2008): 551–66.
5. Mary Anne Santos Newhall, "Like a Moth to the Flame: Modernity and Mary Wigman 1886–1973," (2010) https://digitalrepository.unm.edu/hist_etds/68, 78. See also Mary Anne Santos Newhall, *Mary Wigman* (Abingdon: Routledge, 2009).
6. John Martin, *The Modern Dance* (New York: A. S. Barnes & Co., 1933).
7. H. C. Bastian, "The 'Muscular Sense'; Its Nature and Cortical Localisation," *Brain* 10 (1887): 1–137.
8. Uwe Proske and Simon C. Gandevia, "The Kinaesthetic Senses," *The Journal of Physiology* 587.17 (2009): 4139–46.
9. Irina Sirotkina and Roger Smith, *The Sixth Sense of the Avant-Garde: Dance, Kinaesthesia and the Arts in Revolutionary Russia* (London: Methuen, 2017).
10. John Martin, *Book of the Dance* (New York: Tudor, 1963), 138.
11. John Martin, *Introduction to the Dance* (New York: Dance Horizons, 1939), 47.
12. Mary Lewis Shaw, "Ephemeral Signs: Apprehending the Idea through Poetry and Dance," *Dance Research Journal* 20.1 (1988), 3–9 (4).
13. Dick McCaw, *Bakhtin and Theatre: Dialogues with Stanislavski, Meyerhold and Grotowski* (London: Taylor & Francis Group, 2015), 104.
14. Dick McCaw, "Toward a Philosophy of the Moving Body," in *Mikhail Bakhtin's Heritage in Literature, Arts, and Psychology: Art and Answerability*, ed. Slav N. Gratchev and Howard Mancing (Lanham: Lexington Books, 2018).
15. Caryl Emerson, "Bakhtin and the Actor (with Constant Reference to Shakespeare)," *Studies in East European Thought* 67.3/4 (2015): 183–207.
16. Doris Humphrey, *The Art of Making Dances* (New York: Grove, 1987 [1957]).
17. Michael Holquist, *Dialogism: Bakhtin and His World* (London: Routledge, 2003).
18. See Peter Steiner's *Russian Formalism: A Metapoetics* (Ithaca: Cornell University Press, 2016).

19 Julie A. Mulvihill, "COLLABORATION," *Journal of Dance Education* 18.3 (2018): 112–19.
20 See the magnificent work of Martin Green, most notably *The Mountain of Truth: The Counterculture Begins, Ascona, 1900–1920* (Boston: Tufts, 1986).
21 Mary Wigman cited in Walter Sorell, *Mary Wigman: Ein Vermächtnis* [Mary Wigman: A Legacy] (Wilhelmshaven: Forian Noetzel Verlag, 1986), 34.
22 Michael Holquist, "Answering as Authoring: Mikhail Bakhtin's Trans-Linguistics," *Critical Inquiry* 10.2 (1983): 307–19 (307).

PART THREE

Glossary

15

Introduction to the Glossary

Sergeiy Sandler

Any glossary of Bakhtinian terms should be read with caution because these are not quite terms in the usual sense. On the most fundamental level, Bakhtin is trying to paint a picture, to communicate a complex philosophical image, rather than to construct a logical argument or build a system, and his use of terms serves this overarching purpose.

Critics (most notably Gasparov)[1] noted that Bakhtin's terms are very evocative, but daringly imprecise, while Bakhtin himself noted his "love for variations and for a diversity of terms for a single phenomenon."[2] But this is so by design: when trying to describe an image, evocativeness is a virtue, while rigorous precision is often a vice.

Moreover, Bakhtin habitually used other people's terms—terms he found to be useful, or ones that were in vogue, or sanctioned by the powers that be in the U.S.S.R.—but not in their original sense. Instead, he twisted and bent them to fit into the image he was trying to evoke.

Add to this the fact that the vast majority of Bakhtin's writings were published late in life or posthumously. This means Bakhtin never published any definitive statement of his philosophical vision that he had to remain committed to as an author. And that meant he was free to (indeed, even compelled to) play around and experiment with different ways of presenting his image. Some terms were adapted in different ways in different places, even resulting in what superficially looks like a contradiction.[3] Some features in the underlying image received different names in different periods, resulting in several terms effectively conveying the same idea (though often from different aspects). And, above all, Bakhtin's terms are enmeshed with one another, overlapping and interconnected. They should rather be understood in terms of the image they paint jointly, than in terms of the designation each has separately.

With that in mind, this glossary should be seen not only as an attempt to explain the outline of Bakhtin's key terms, but also, equally importantly, as an attempt to forestall misunderstandings that might arise from treating Bakhtin's terms as if they were terms of the more usual kind, not less an explanation of how these terms should be read than an explanation of how they should not.

Notes

1   Mikhail Leonovich Gasparov, "M. M. Bakhtin v Russkoj Kul'ture XX Veka" [Bakhtin in Twentieth-Century Russian Culture], in *Mikhail Bakhtin: Pro et Contra*, ed. Konstantin Glebovich Isupov (St. Petersburg: Russkij khristianskij gumanitarnyj institut, 2002), vol. 2, 507–10.

2   M. M. Bakhtin, "From Notes Made in 1970–71," in *SG*, 132–58 (155); M. M. Bakhtin, "Rabochie zapisi 60-kh—nachala 70-kh godow" [Working Notes from the 1960s to Early 1970s], in *SW6*, 371–439 (431).

3   Sergeiy Sandler, "Whose Words Are These Anyway?" in *Dialogues with Bakhtinian Theory*, ed. Mykola Polyuha, Clive Thomson, and Anthony Wall (London, Ontario: Mestengo Press, 2012), 227–42.

16

Architectonics (*arkhitektonika*)

Sergeiy Sandler

This entry is also related to the notions of event (*sobytie*), eventness (*sobytijnost'*), event of being (*sobytie bytiia*) and being-event (*bytie-sobytie*).

The notion of the event was primarily developed by Bakhtin in his early philosophical works, *Toward a Philosophy of the Act*, and "Author and Hero in Aesthetic Activity," but the term remained important to Bakhtin throughout his life.

An event, in Bakhtin's sense, always involves the meeting and interaction of at least two consciousnesses. This is also suggested by the Russian word *sobytie* itself, which can be read as *so-bytie*, literally, "co-being." Bakhtin, without explicitly suggesting this reading of the word in any extant text, implicitly encourages it by frequently placing the words "event" (*sobytie*) and "being" (*bytie*) next to each other.

The resulting "being-event" is Bakhtin's main early metaphysical term, a means to designate being in its entirety. It refers not only to the objective reality all conscious subjects share (which was the main point of interest for Kant), nor only to the world constituted by a single consciousness, individual or collective (as, e.g., in Hegel's philosophical system), but also to the irreducible multiplicity of all conscious perspectives. This multiplicity forms the true totality of being for Bakhtin, and is thus what a "first philosophy" would need to account for.

For Bakhtin's purposes, it would not be useful to describe the event, as an interaction between consciousnesses, from a neutral, outside perspective. Instead, the event has to be understood and philosophically described from within, from the point of view of its participants. From this first-person perspective, the world of my experience (and, more generally, of my *deed*) is organized by an *architectonics* with three pivotal points: I-for-myself, the-other-for-me, and I-for-the-other.

I-for-myself is the center from which I perceive, evaluate, and act in the world, the center from which I come forth (*iskhozhu*). In the world, I come upon (*nakhozhu*) others.[1] I do not, however, come upon myself in the world (see also: *Outsidedness*). In forming any notion of my self, I am totally dependent on others—on the language they taught me, on their forms and values, for seeing, evaluating, and expressing myself. Even my outward appearance, whenever I manage to get a glimpse of it, refuses to coalesce into a coherent image with my sense of myself from within (most compactly illustrated in Bakhtin's analysis of a person looking into a mirror.[2] A Cartesian subject that naively combines consciousness with introspection is impossible without the crucial contribution of the other, who can grant me an image of myself (I-for-the-other) as a gift.

Notes

1 "K Filosofii Postupka" [On the Philosophy of the Deed], in *CW1*, 7–68 (67). Translation in *TPA*, 74.

2 See M. M. Bakhtin, "Mikhail Bakhtin. Selections from the Wartime Notebooks," ed. and trans. Irina Denischenko and Alexander Spektor, *The Slavic and East European Journal* 61.2 (2017): 201–32 (216–17).

17

Author and Hero (*avtor i geroj*)

Sergeiy Sandler

This entry is also related Bakhtin's notions of to authorship (*avtorstvo*) and hero (*geroj*)

The relations between author and hero (understood in the sense of a character in a literary work; no heroism is implied) is a central concern for Bakhtin in all periods, and in several different contexts. Foremost, it offers Bakhtin a way to explore, in detail, the relations between I and the other (including the divine "absolute otherness"), where I may be considered in both roles. And note that this is not merely a metaphor for Bakhtin.[1] In all his discussions of author–hero relations, an ethical dimension is always involved. Conversely, literature is of interest for Bakhtin above all because it offers ways to create, or at least approximate, an image of a person, as a conscious being with an inner world, not merely an object—an image that would be a true gift of self, given to the hero by the author (a gift the hero would need truly so as to become a subject).

This set of themes is explored by Bakhtin in the greatest detail in his early incomplete treatise "Author and Hero in Aesthetic Activity." (The title was given to the work by its publishers. Bakhtin's original title for the work is lost.)[2]

Beyond this core engagement with these concepts, both "author" and "hero" are used in several additional, and related, senses, especially in later works. Thus, at one point, Bakhtin even uses his notion of "hero" in the context of linguistic analysis, on the school-grammar level: The phrase: "The news, which I heard today" has two "heroes," while: "The news heard by me today" has only one.[3]

Authorship in particular is of interest to late Bakhtin in the context of the author's relation to previous authors. Bakhtin essentially asks how a hero becomes an author, how, despite my dependence on words and forms

I inherited from others for the very possibility of my self-expression, I can still develop a voice of my own. Bakhtin's solution to this conundrum is summarized succinctly in a metaphor he uses at one point: an author is "A conductor, but not a composer";[4] that is, the author can create, but can do so only by arranging, interpreting, and adding overtones to others' voices.

Notes

1. Daphna Erdinast-Vulcan, *Between Philosophy and Literature: Bakhtin and the Question of the Subject* (Stanford: Stanford University Press, 2013.
2. M. M. Bakhtin, "Author and Hero in Aesthetic Activity," in *AA*, 4–256; M. M. Bakhtin, "Avtor i geroj v esteticheskoj deiatel'nost" [Author and Hero in Aesthetic Activity], in *CW1*, 69–263.
3. M. M. Bakhtin, "Voprosy stilistiki na urokakh russkogo iazyka v srednej shkole" [Questions of Stylistics in Russian Language Lessons in Secondary School], in *CW5*, 141–56 (142–3); M. M. Bakhtin, "Dialogic Origin and Dialogic Pedagogy of Grammar in Secondary School," *Journal of Russian and East European Psychology* 42.6 (2004): 12–49 (13–14).
4. M. M. Bakhtin, "Rabochie zapisi 60-kh—nachala 70-kh godow" [Working Notes from the 1960s to Early 1970s], in *CW6*, 371–439 (420).

18

Becoming

Jonathan Hall

When Bakhtin made his "linguistic turn" toward theorizing the relationship of consciousness to language, he retained his ethics of individual "answerability" (*otvetstvennost'*) to others, but he reformulated it in terms of the dialogical nature of language. This led him to criticize Saussure's influential concept of a linguistic science which abstracts the system of language (*langue*) from actual linguistic performances, which Saussure designated as a distinct and purely secondary *linguistique de la parole*. In contrast with this now familiar categorical distinction between *langue* and *parole*, which separates the structural "synchronic" study of language from its unsystematizable "diachronic" histories, Bakhtin and Voloshinov insisted on the primacy of the "utterance" (*vyskazyvanie*). They rejected the systemic definition of language propounded by Saussure and his successors, not only because they refused the determinist view which Fredric Jameson has called the "prison house of language," but also because they insisted that the study of language should focus on the inherent creativity of the dialogical "utterance" and the consequent human capacity for historical change or "becoming" (*stanovlenie*).

In developing their views on linguistic "becoming," Bakhtin and Voloshinov drew extensively on Ernst Cassirer's *Philosophy of Symbolic Forms*. Voloshinov may have initiated this because he had translated three sections of the first volume of Cassirer's work into Russian. Cassirer's overall argument is that all human experience is mediated through the "symbolic forms" (including language) which human beings have created for themselves in the course of their socio-historical development. This means that a history of knowledge, up to and including modern science, must be more than a positivist record of the accumulated knowledge of its objects. It must also be a historical anthropology of the changing "symbolic forms" through which those objects have become conceptualized by human understanding.

Cassirer's *longue durée* historical anthropology is concerned with the development of the different modes of symbolic abstraction which are the prerequisite for all human thinking about the world, from the minimal level of abstraction brought into being by the "totemic" forms of mythical consciousness, followed by the higher levels of abstraction enabled by religious consciousness, which then lay the basis for modern scientific forms of enquiry with their reliance on mathematical abstraction. Cassirer's concern with this overall process of "becoming" led him to affirm that every developmental phase involves a higher degree of abstraction made possible by the different "symbolic forms" through which knowledge is pursued. This unidirectional and universal track can certainly be criticized, and should perhaps be pluralized to investigate cultural histories quite different from Cassirer's European model, but the crucial point for both Bakhtin and Voloshinov is that the dialogical nature of language means that as human beings we are not predetermined by nature or by our cultural forms; we always have the potential for reflection upon our own socially inherited symbolic modes of understanding, and for changing them. Bakhtin and Voloshinov argue that it is the dialogical nature of language which gives any individual, or any social collective, the potential for "becoming" by enabling them to assume a position of "outsideness" (*vnenakhodimost'*) in relation to the discourses which have shaped their consciousness. A detectable Hegelian influence is, therefore, evident in this indebtedness to Cassirer's philosophy, but, unlike the Hegelian teleology, which Bakhtin considered to be yet another "monological" system, the dialogical version of "becoming" means that it is always an unfinalizable process open to further unanticipated development. The dialogical nature of language itself means that while structures have come into existence historically and can certainly be investigated (under Foucault's influence they are usually labeled "discourses"), they are nonetheless always subject to the dialogical processes of "becoming." These are not necessarily unidirectional or uniformly "progressive." Bakhtin and Voloshinov did not give sufficient attention to the ways in which contestation, or even reactive resistance to "becoming," are also dialogical. But their adoption of Cassirer's developmental schema afforded them the possibility of historical insights freed from the predestined track prescribed by the official (neo-Hegelian) *diamat* of Stalin's Russia. Moreover, its anti-systemic potential persists beyond Bakhtin's covert resistance to that particular form of would-be "monological" control over the supposedly predictable future. The "last word" (Bakhtin's *poslednee slovo*) is never spoken.

19

Carnival

Yann Tholoniat

Perhaps Goethe has defined in a nutshell the main characteristics of carnival after attending one in Rome in 1788:

> the Roman Carnival is not really a festival given for the people but one the people give themselves ... All that happens is that, at a given signal, everyone has leave to be as mad and foolish as he likes, and almost everything, except fisticuffs and stabbing, is permissible. The difference between the social orders seems to be abolished for the time being; everyone accosts everyone else, all good-naturedly accept whatever happens to them, and the insolence and licence of the feast is balanced only by the universal good humour.[1]

Indeed, carnivals have a long history stemming from a Babylonian feast in the third century BC, where a mock king was celebrated before being whipped and put to death. Later on, in the Roman Saturnalia, the stress was laid on the turning of the social tables, in a reversal of traditional hierarchy. In modern times, carnival celebrations occur at specific moments of the year, and their pagan origins have gradually been concealed, or replaced, by Christian ones: "carnival" comes from "carne vale," "farewell to meat," and it designates the period before Shrove Tuesday, a period of feasting before Lent, which is a period of fasting. An allegorical depiction of this opposition can be seen in Peter Bruegel the Elder's painting *The Battle between Carnival and Lent* (1559). At carnival time, people often wear masks, parade through the city, and accompany wooden floats showing grotesque puppets which are the caricatures of contemporary political and moral leaders. Carnival time stages a topsy-turvy world, and its depiction of "the culture of the market place" (Bakhtin) often takes the form of grotesque realism. The body, its functions and fluids, are put to the fore, even glorified. As carnival constantly plays with values, and undermines civil and social ceremonies and rituals, it dramatizes the relativity of all values. To some extent, it can be related to the expression of humanism against rigid dogmas. As such, carnival is often feared by the powers that be: they try to channel popular energy in choreographed events so as to subdue the subversive power of the people.

Note

1   Finn Fordham, *Lots of Fun at Finnegans Wake: Unravelling Universals* (Oxford: Oxford University Press, 2007), 6.

20

Chronotope (*khronotop*)

Sergeiy Sandler

The word "chronotope" is composed of the Greek words for "time" and "place." Bakhtin adapted it, as he himself explains,[1] from a lecture delivered by Russian physiologist Aleksej Alekseevich Ukhtomskij. From Ukhtomskij's notes for that talk,[2] it is clear that the term is derived from the Einsteinian notion of space-time, but with the focus turned to the concrete experience of a living organism: stable objects in Euclidian space are a construct, while immediate experience is dynamic, situated in a space-time continuum. The term appears very frequently in Bakhtin's working notes from the latter half of the 1930s, occasionally in works from the 1940s and from the early 1960s, and more frequently in the late 1960s and 1970s. A substantial body of notes from 1937–38 was centered around this term, and was reworked by Bakhtin in 1973 into the essay "Forms of Time and of the Chronotope in the Novel" (*CW3*; *DI* 341–511).

Bakhtin's use of the term has links both to his early philosophical writings and to his writings on carnival. First of all, as for Ukhtomskij, the chronotope for Bakhtin involves the perception of time and space from a subjective point of view. For Bakhtin, this directly implies that chronotopes have an inherent evaluative aspect to them: subjective values and preferences are built into how time and space are felt and conceptualized (see: "Deed"). These values can be relatively pragmatic (e.g., a *road*, for the traveler, has a point of origin and a destination, and one's spatial location along the road is evaluated in relation to these two points). It can also be more global and cosmic, as in the case of values linked to the top and the bottom, both of the entire cosmos and of the human body—a theme explored in depth in Bakhtin's book on Rabelais.[3]

Chronotopes also provide Bakhtin with yet another way to explore intersubjectivity, the interaction between individuals, between literary characters, and between authors, their readers, and their characters (see: "Architectonics," "Author and Hero"). This includes occasional remarks that directly reference the relationship between the chronotopes of the author, the narrator, the characters, and the readers. (e.g., CW3: 504).[4] But even where Bakhtin is speaking about concrete chronotopes in literature (e.g., the chronotope of the road, the meeting, the threshold, etc.), he considers them as configurations for the interaction of multiple subjective perspectives (see: "Architectonics"). To clear a common misunderstanding, these specific chronotopes are *not* treated by Bakhtin as simple literary motifs. Thus, the road is of interest to Bakhtin not for any symbolic value it may have in a particular novel, but as a concrete setting for the meeting of two or more characters, which becomes meaningful to them and to us, readers, in the context of the structure of space, time, and value, that traveling on a road implies.

Notes

1   M. M. Bakhtin, "Forms of Time and of the Chronotope in the Novel: Notes toward a Historical Poetics," in *DI*, 84–258 (84); M. M. Bakhtin, "Formy Vremeni i Khronotopa v Romane" [Forms of Time and of the Chronotope in the Novel], in *CW3*, 340–511 (341).

2   Aleksej Alekseevich Ukhtomskij, *Dominanta Dushi: Iz Gumanitarnogo Naslediia* [The Dominant of the Soul: From the Human-Sciences Heritage], ed. Liudmila Vladimirovna Sokolova, Galina Mikhailovna Tsurikova, Igor' Sergeevich Kuz'michev, and Ol'ga Vasil'evna Ivanova (Rybinsk: Rybinskoe podvor'e, 2000), 77–80.

3   While in the book on Rabelais, Bakhtin mostly uses the term "topography" to refer to this evaluative perception of space and time, he viewed the terms "topography" and "chronotope" as closely linked. At one point, he writes about "The study of the spatio-temporal topography (chronotope) of the world in literature," 1996. M. M. Bakhtin, "Dopolneniia I Izmeneniia k 'Rable" [Additions and Changes to *Rabelais*], in *CW5*, 80–129 (110).

4   See also M. M. Bakhtin, "From Notes Made in 1970–71," in *SG*, 132–58 (134); M. M. Bakhtin, "Rabochie zapisi 60-kh—nachala 70-kh godow" [Working Notes from the 1960s to Early 1970s], in *CW6*, 371–439 (387, 392).

21

Completion (*zavershenie*)

Sergeiy Sandler

This entry is also related to the notions of finalization, consummation and unfinalizable/Unfinalizability. Other related terms: *nezavershimyj* (that which cannot be brought to completion, unfinalizable) and *nezavershimost'* (impossibility of bringing to completion, unfinalizability).

Writing for a lay audience, Bakhtin opens his earliest surviving text by introducing a distinction central to a lot of nineteenth-century philosophy, especially in Germany—that between a mechanical and an organic whole.[1] This distinction is indeed a crucial starting point for interpreting Bakhtin's thought, and the notion of completion is directly linked with it. In Bakhtin's early aesthetics, to bring an image to completion simply means to shape it into an organic, not just a mechanical, unity. Attaining completion is, in this context, the greatest virtue for a work of art, and a complete, that is, organically whole, image of me is the greatest gift I can receive from others (see: "Outsidedness," "Architectonics").

However, bringing the image of a person, a conscious human being, to completion is no mean feat. Much of the discussion in Bakhtin's "Author and Hero in Aesthetic Activity"[2] can be read as a catalog of ways in which literature fails in this task, without any examples of clear success. A holistic image of myself is, according to Bakhtin, strictly impossible to form from my own perspective (see: "Outsidedness"). Literary images that are fundamentally autobiographical, based on the author's first-person perspective, are thus doomed to fall apart, to never reach completion. Yet, images of a person from an outside perspective risk entirely missing their object by ignoring their object's subjectivity and freedom, not directly accessible from the outside.

Ignoring the subjectivity and freedom of the image's object is not only a matter of the image's form or content but also a matter of its function.

There is, for Bakhtin, a fundamental difference between the organic unity of an image that is submitted to its object as a gift (in an act of love, in true dialogue) and the organic unity of an image that is imposed on its object as a would-be definitive statement (in an act of cognition, which can also be an act of violence). This distinction becomes a central concern for Bakhtin in the first edition of his book on Dostoevsky (1929) and remains a recurring theme in his writings from that point on. This shift in focus is also linked to a shift in Bakhtin's understanding of what creating an organically holistic image of a person implies. His early understanding of completion involves, for example, reflecting features in the person's body and surroundings not accessible to that person, while, in the later period, the very fact that these features are not accessible to the person becomes problematic, and the capturing of subjectivity and freedom themselves in the image becomes Bakhtin's paramount interest and concern.[3]

Related to this variation is also a subtle shift in the way the term "completion" itself is used by Bakhtin. "Completion" implies closure. An image that has been completed is not meant to undergo further change. As a result, from 1929 onward, Bakhtin rarely speaks about literary images as complete. He often stresses that an image of a person remains ever *incomplete*, that it *cannot* be completed. He avoids using the term "completion" in reference to examples of an image that is properly given to its object as a gift; for instance, in the book on Dostoevsky, he uses such terms as "dialogic penetration" and "penetrated discourse" instead.[4]

And yet, "completion" never turns into a negative term in Bakhtin's vocabulary. Dostoevsky, in Bakhtin's reading, goes beyond completion, but does not invalidate completion in an image as such. And "completion" is still the term Bakhtin uses to denote the highest level of aesthetic achievement in contexts where reflecting human freedom and subjectivity is not relevant.[5]

Notes

1. "Iskusstvo i Otvetstvennost' [Art and Responsibility]," in *CW1* [2003b], 5–6 (5). Translated as "Art and Answerability," in *AA* [1990a], 1–3 (1).
2. "Avtor i geroj v esteticheskoj deiatel'nosti" [Author and Hero in Aesthetic Activity], in *CW1* [2003a], 69–263. Translation in "Author and Hero in Aesthetic Activity," in *AA* [1990b], 4–256.
3. Sergeiy Sandler (2016), "Tema karnavala v kontekste filosofii M. M. Bakhtina" [The Place of Carnival in the Context of Mikhail Bakhtin's Philosophy], *Studia Litterarum* 1. 3–4: 10–28.
4. "Problemy poetiki Dostoevskogo," in *CW6* [2002], 6–630 (73, 80–1, 97–8. 277ff.). Translation in *PDP*, 59, 61–2, 86, 249ff.
5. For example with reference to the Homeric epic in "Roman Kak Literaturnyj Zhanr" [The Novel as a Literary Genre], in *CW3*, 608–54 (647).

22

Contemporaneity (*sovremennost'*)

Ken Hirschkop

The novel, Bakhtin said in 1941, is the genre of contemporaneity [*sovremennost'*]. He didn't mean that novels began to appear in the seventeenth and eighteenth centuries. In fact, Bakhtin believed that the first examples of novelistic writing appeared in Greek and then Roman Antiquity, and that these works were also full of contemporaneity. Contemporaneity stood not for a distinct period in human history, but for a distinct conception of it. The novels of ancient Greek and Rome were contemporaneous because they narrated events of their time, without the reverential distance of the epic, the tragic, or the mythical, and they narrated them as if their significance was not yet fixed.

But these were just the roots or germs or of contemporaneity, which only comes into its own with the Renaissance, the epoch when modern science is established, and national vernaculars displace the hegemony of Latin and Greek. At that point novels acquire historical ambitions and develop narrative structures equal to those ambitions. As a consequence, Bakhtin believes, novels create different kinds of heroes, represent temporality differently, and evolve a distinctive dialogizing style, which reflects and refracts the heterogeneous speech forms of their time.

Bakhtin describes this change in several works: two long series of notes, called "On the *Bildungsroman*" (1937–39) and "On Issues in the Theory and History of the Novel" (1940–41); in two lectures, "From the Prehistory of Novelistic Discourse" (1940), and "The Novel as a Literary Genre" (1941, later retitled "Epic and Novel"); and in his numerous writings on Rabelais. In these works contemporaneity stands for a distinct conception of historical time, summarized in the following passage:

The *present* as a, so to speak, 'whole' (although it is precisely not a whole) is essentially and in principle unfinished: according to its very essence it demands continuation, it moves into the future, and the more actively and consciously it moves forward into this future, the more tangible and essential is its unfinishedness [...] For artistic-ideological consciousness time and the world become, for the first time, historical: they unfold, although in the beginning unclearly and uncertainly, as becoming, as uninterrupted movement into a real future, as a single, all-encompassing and unfinishable process.[1]

In many respects this is a more comprehensive and detailed account of the "historical becoming" Bakhtin claimed, in "Discourse in the Novel," was the motive force behind the novel's dialogization of language. What is critical to it, as to the earlier conception of becoming, is the claim that the future pulls the present along, that what motivates historical change and movement is a future that always stands in front of it.

That future is messianic in form and substance. In the part of "On the *Bildungsroman*" that became "Forms of Time and of the Chronotope in the Novel," Bakhtin speaks of the future as consisting of ideals of justice, harmony between people, and human perfectedness. History, in this conception, moves toward the future in an effort to realize these goals, however imperfectly, in human society. The upshot is that, contrary to the way it's sometimes presented, Bakhtin does not draw ethical conclusions from the fact that time moves on, things change, life is unpredictable and so on—life moves on and things change because of the ethical force of the future.

One more crucial consequence: the change may be sudden and unexpected, a transformation and not an incremental improvement. The future is radically different from the present and it may affect it in dramatic fashion. Novels are founded, he wrote in 1943, not on "the ordinary course of life, but faith in miracles, in the possibility of its radical violation" (*REL*: 202–3). Contemporaneity is about a present that isn't closed in on itself.

Note

1   M. M. Bakhtin, "The Novel as a Literary Genre," in *CW3*, 608–43 (633). English translation as "Epic and Novel," in *DI*, 4–40 (30).

23

Deed (*postupok*)

Sergeiy Sandler

A central notion in Bakhtin's early philosophical works. While some connection with Franz Brentano's term "intentional act" cannot be excluded (probably motivating the use of "act" in translating this term), Bakhtin's term is significantly different in content. It is much closer, instead, to Kierkegaard's notion of "existence," in that both are based on the distinction between the actual and the potential. Thus, when faced with a moral dilemma, various ethical principles may be considered for and against each of its horns, but, in the end, I do the *deed*—I actually *potentially* follow through on one course of action, for which I now bear responsibility and which I cannot take back.

A deed does not have to be an action. Thoughts, feelings, utterances, can all be considered deeds so long as I indeed think, feel, utter them, but they would not be deeds when considered merely hypothetically, in theory. Deeds also do not have to be discrete actions. On the contrary, "my entire life as a whole can be considered as a certain composite deed."[1] My deed comprises the entire subjective world of my experience, evaluation, and action. Everything in this world is evaluated by me in relation to my purposes and actions. Space and time are perceived from my position and orientation, and are conceptualized in categories relative to this position (up, down, left, right, in front, behind, past, future, etc.).

My deeds are also fundamentally unique: "That which can be accomplished by me, can never be accomplished by anyone" (*CW1*: 39; *TPA*: 40). Note that Bakhtin (in the Russian original) does not write "by anyone else," but just "by anyone," thus implying that this is not a matter of my unique circumstances, or even unique properties. My deeds have to be done, and lived through, by me, not by anyone like me, nor by anyone in my position, nor even by me, considered as a mere "anyone," who just happens to be me. My deeds can only be done by "the only I in the world."[2]

For Bakhtin, deeds are, philosophically speaking, more fundamental than objective facts or theoretical generalizations. This is not to deny the objectivity of objective facts nor the validity and importance of theoretical generalizations, but a first philosophy has to be grounded in the deed as its starting point. Thus, in a poem by Pushkin that Bakhtin analyzes in his early writings (e.g., *CW1*: 60ff, *TPA*: 66ff), Pushkin depicts the departure of a lover for a long journey to her family, never to return. Objectively speaking, this is one journey, but we have here (at least) two deeds: for the poet, she is sailing away, to a foreign land, seen from the port of departure; as for her, she is on the ship, sailing back to her homeland. The objective journey is one, while the deeds are many, but the objective journey is not actually experienced by anybody. The information about it can be abstracted from the deeds and experiences of the two protagonists, and of others (this is, of course, only possible assuming individuals do interact with one another, as Bakhtin indeed argues they must—see: "Architectonics"). However, the deeds cannot possibly be deduced from objective information or theoretical knowledge alone. Thus, Bakhtin concludes, the deeds, despite their greater number, are philosophically more fundamental.

Notes

1   "K Filosofii Postupka" [On the Philosophy of the Deed], in *CW1* [2003], 7–68 (8). Translation in *TPA* (3).
2   "Rabochie zapisi 60-kh—nachala 70-kh godow" [Working Notes from the 1960s to Early 1970s], in *CW6*, 371–439 (380). Translation in "From Notes Made in 1970–71," in *SG*, 132–58 (147).

24

Dialogue/Dialogical/ Dialogization

Ken Hirschkop

The slashes for this entry aren't just a way of covering all the bases: they point to an ambiguity, an ambiguity that was a direct consequence of Bakhtin's philosophical style. When Bakhtin claimed that Dostoevsky and, later, the novel itself, were distinguished by a dialogical style, he wasn't saying that Dostoevsky's works and the novel as a genre contained a lot of dialogue. Bakhtin was taking an ordinary concept, that of "dialog," and applying it in a way that required a dramatic extension and transformation of the original sense. Most of the confusion that attends the idea of a "dialogical" style of discourse stems from the uncertainty about just how far the transformation should go. The answer is that it should go very far and is often not taken far enough.

When Bakhtin first uses the term, in his 1929 book on Dostoevsky, it describes the relation between the "author's discourse" and that of the characters: the former "is oriented toward the hero as toward a discourse and is therefore dialogically addressed to it. The author speaks, by means of the entire construction of its novel, not about the hero, but with the hero."[1] The confusion is evident: on the one hand, Bakhtin's account implies that the author is a speaking voice, carrying on a conversation with the characters; on the other hand, it is clear there is no such authorial voice and that the speaking takes place metaphorically, by virtue of the "entire construction of the novel." In this scheme, the author's voice is the form of the novel.

When Bakhtin makes dialogical style the defining feature of novels as such (and not just a Dostoevskian specialty), the ambiguity remains. Discourse in the novel is typically, Bakhtin argues, double-voiced. But the doubling is an effect of a distinct style or socio-ideological dialect, drawn from heteroglossia, being incorporated into the architecture of a novel, with other languages, characters, a narrative structure, and so on. Thus "[e]ach separate element of the language of a novel is in the first instance defined by the subordinated stylistic unit that it is immediately part of: the stylistically individualized speech of a hero, the everyday *skaz* of a narrator, a letter, etc.," but this immediate significance is then refracted by its subordination, the role it plays in the "higher stylistic unity of the whole," that is, by the form of the novel.[2] Double-voicing isn't only asymmetrical—the unity of the whole determining the role played by its stylistic parts—it is ontologically inconsistent, the author/novel being present in the structure of the novel (rather than, say, a narratorial voice).

As Bakhtin's favorite novels will feature many quite distinct "subordinate stylistic units" (language varieties), it's tempting to think dialogical style is a matter of how voices within a novel intersect and play off one another. But dialogical writing is first a matter of how the narrative form of a novel affects the force and significance of its constituent styles, of how, to use the sociolinguistic term, it indexicalizes them (attributes contextual significance to them). You can have a dialogical novel that is stylistically homogeneous. (Bakhtin himself points to Dostoevsky as an example.) When novels are stylistically heterogeneous, the crucial dialogue is still between the incorporated style and the novel as a whole, through which it will be ironized, stylized, parodied, endorsed, or whatever.

Now why does Bakhtin use this ambivalent terminology? Because he hoped to ground this aesthetic phenomenon in our everyday experience of others, when we give to their experience, their words, their lives, a meaning they cannot give it themselves. On this account, no one can blame him for being unambitious.

Notes

1   *PDA*, 70. English translation in *PDP*, 63.
2   M. M. Bakhtin, "Discourse in the Novel," in *CW3*, 9–179 (15). English translation in *DI*, 259–422 (262).

25

Genre (*zhanr*)

Sergeiy Sandler

The term "genre" appears in Bakhtin Circle works from the mid-1920s and becomes increasingly significant in Bakhtin's (undisputed) own writings from about the mid-1930s. The term has two main, mutually complementary contexts of use: first, the context of discussing literary traditions (especially the novel and Menippean satire) and second a linguistic context ("speech genres").

In Pavel Medvedev's book *The Formal Method in Literary Scholarship*, genres are understood primarily as encapsulating *ways of seeing and interpreting the world*.[1] In terms of Bakhtin's early philosophy, this would place genres among the forms of evaluation and of self-expression that one receives from others (see: "I and Other," "Architectonics"). Bakhtin's treatment of literary genre from the 1940s on puts greater emphasis on the historical continuity and evolution of genres, possibly inspired by Bakhtin's reading of Olga Freidenberg, who views genres as traditions, held together not by any formal features but by historical continuity in interpreting images.[2]

In a linguistic context, genres ("speech genres") become a central concern for Bakhtin in the 1950s and early 1960s. Speech genres are "relatively stable typical *forms of constructing the whole*"[3] of an utterance (see: "Utterance"). Thus, again, genres are forms of self-expression the speaker inherits from others.

While etymologically, as well as in its most common use, "genre" refers to a category within a taxonomy of artistic or literary works; this is emphatically *not* how Bakhtin understands genre. For Bakhtin, literary works and other utterances do not simply "belong to" a genre. Instead, they *use* it and *respond* to it.

It is impossible—Bakhtin claims (*CW5*: 198–99; *SG*: 93–94)—to create an utterance that would be entirely novel, totally unrelated to past utterances. It would be at once impossibly onerous to create and meaningless to its audience. One cannot directly, naively, state one's meaning on virgin linguistic ground. Instead, one expresses one's own meaning by adding overtones to others' voices (see also: "Author and Hero").

By making use of a genre, one also responds to its past users and contributes to the genre's future evolution. While Bakhtin does not express it directly, he clearly considers genres to be enabling, not restricting authorship, and deviations from genre conventions are ways of responding to the genre tradition, on a par with upholding them.

Moreover, one work or utterance could easily interact simultaneously with multiple genres. Bakhtin's own examples of such a multiplicity of genres concern a distinction he makes at one point (*CW5*: 161–2: *SG*: 61–2) between "primary" and "secondary" genres, where primary genres can be embedded within utterances belonging to secondary genres (for instance, letters included in an epistolary novel). Note that this distinction is (probably deliberately) oversimplified. Thus, ample evidence[4] exists of such embedding taking place in ordinary conversational turns and other utterances Bakhtin would label as "primary." Bakhtin, however, would surely welcome such "counterexamples" to the distinction he introduced, as they strengthen rather than weaken the evidence for the inherently dialogic nature of language.

Genres, then, are linked to events (see: "Architectonics") and thus to situations. A trivial example would be that of a greeting, linked to a situation in which two people meet. Over time, genres can accumulate rich information about human attitudes and values linked to these situations. Bakhtin at one point[5] speaks about a genre as having a memory of its own. An author, by working with and responding to a genre can revive important features of the genre even without being directly exposed to past works exemplifying these particular features.

Notes

1   Pavel Nikolaevich Medvedev, *Formal'nyj Metod v Literaturovedenii: Kriticheskoe Vvedenie v Sotsiologicheskuyu Poetiku* [The Formal Method in Literary Scholarship: A Critical Introduction to Sociological Poetics] (Leningrad: Priboi, 1928), 180; translated as *The Formal Method in Literary Scholarship: A Critical Introduction to Sociological Poetics*, trans. Albert J. Wehrle (Baltimore: Johns Hopkins University Press, 1991), 133.

2   Ol'ga Mikhailovna Freidenberg, *Poetika Siuzheta i Zhanra* [The Poetics of Plot and Genre], ed. Nina Vladimirovna Braginskaia (Moscow: Labirint, 1997).

3   "Problema Rechevykh Zhanrov" [The Problem of Speech Genres], in *CW5*, 159–206 (180). Translated in "The Problem of Speech Genres," in *SG*, 60–102 (78).

4   See Esther Pascual, *Fictive Interaction*, vol. 47, *Human Cognitive Processing* (Amsterdam: John Benjamins Publishing Company, 2014).

5   "Problemy Poetiki Dostoevskogo" [Problems of Dostoevsky's Poetics], *CW6*, 6–300 (137). Translation in *PDP*, 121.

26

Heteroglossia (*raznorechie*)

Ken Hirschkop

Heteroglossia led a strange life in Bakhtin's texts, appearing suddenly and dramatically in "Discourse in the Novel," retaining a crucial position in the theory of the novel from the 1930s and 1940s, and leaving the stage, quietly, and without fuss, immediately afterwards. It has led an equally strange life in translation. The Russian word *raznorechie* consists of the prefix *razno-*, which means different, disparate, discrepant, and of the root *rechie*, an abstraction of the noun *rech'*, almost invariably translated as "speech." It could therefore be translated as something like "differences in speech" or "speech variety." In "Discourse in the Novel," however, Bakhtin—as so often is the case—wants linguistic variation to be the index of something larger and a signal to us that we must think about language in a philosophically new manner, so translators have aimed for something more colorful and distinctive. Tzvetan Todorov translated it into French by calquing it with Greek loans, arriving at *heterologie* (with *hetero-* standing in for *razno-* and *logie/logos* standing in for *rechie/rech'*), and when his book was translated into English *raznorechie* was rendered as "heterology," which sounds more like a new academic discipline than a linguistic situation. When Michael Holquist and Caryl Emerson came upon it, they took more or less the same road, christening the new phenomenon *heteroglossia*, although they also translated the term as "social diversity of speech types."

Its classic definition is offered in the opening pages of "Discourse in the Novel," when Bakhtin says that a prerequisite of the novel is "[t]he internal stratification of a unified national language into social dialects, group manners, professional jargons, generic languages, languages of generations and age groups, languages of movements and parties, languages of authorities, languages of movements and passing fads, languages of socio-political days and even hours (each day has its own slogan, its own lexicon, its own accents)."[1] Each of these so-called styles or socio-ideological languages consists of linguistic features (at all levels: phonological, morphological or lexical, syntactic) linked by a context of usage or a type of speaker: in sociolinguistic terms, they are registers, combinations of features that specify a context or speaker indexically. That much Bakhtin had drawn from the work of Soviet dialecticians at the time, who had worked extensively on social dialects in urban environments.

But heteroglossia means more than just the pervasiveness and inevitability of linguistic variation. At the basis of each of the languages of heteroglossia, Bakhtin notes, "lies a completely different principle of differentiation and formation" (*CW3*: 44; *DI*, 291): in some cases it's lexicological, in others stylistic, and it may be rhetorical or thematic as well. But "all these languages, whatever the principle of specification, are specific points of view on the world, forms of its verbal interpretation, particular referential-semantic and value horizons" (*CW3*: 44; *DI*, 291–2). "Therefore," Bakhtin insists, "we always foreground the referential-semantic and expressive, that is, intentional moment, as the force that stratifies and differentiates a common literary language, and not the linguistic features" of heteroglot languages (*CW3*: 45; *DI*: 292).

Bakhtin did not mean to say only that these languages encoded or constrained ways of thinking, in the manner of Sapir–Whorf: he wanted to identify intentionality with "the forces of historical becoming that stratify a language" (*CW3*: 79; *DI*: 325). Indeed, most of the essay is devoted to showing how the dialogism of novels harnesses and exploits "the socially contradictory historical becoming of language" (*CW3*: 84; *DI*: 330). Novels don't just reproduce the styles of heteroglossia; they artistically organize it, or turn "heteroglossia-in-itself" into "heteroglossia-for-itself" (*CW3*: 155; *DI*: 400). Novels, we might say, are meant to display where these languages of heteroglossia are going, what their implications are, how they might develop, seeing each as something aimed at the future (hence, "becoming"). That's why the characters who speak these languages are ideologues—committed to a project—and why "[t]he idea of the testing of the hero and their discourse may be the fundamental organizing idea of the novel" (*CW3*: 144; *DI*: 388). The ideologies bound to the socio-ideological languages of heteroglossia are meant to be concrete, socially embodied, and so forth, which means they are projects whereby their speakers aim to achieve something in the future. When novels represent these languages, when they create images of them, they don't limit them so much as reveal their potential.

Note

1   M. M. Bakhtin, "Discourse in the Novel," in *CW3*, 9–179 (15). English translation in *DI*, 259–422 (262–3).

27

I and other

Philippe Birgy

One's unique position as a conscious being is related to one's responsibility (see: "Responsibility") which Bakhtin delineates in his philosophy of the act and of existence—both falling under the scope of phenomenological enquiry. Even putting one's own interest and perspective in abeyance would not mean the erasure of one's consciousness, for in the renunciation of my claims I fully realize the uniqueness of my position in being. I am for myself, and nothing can be an I in being except myself. The unique place that I occupy as an I is the guarantor of my singular act in relation to everything that is not I, and only from this place can I act. All the evaluative moments of being that are individually valid are revealed to me because I occupy that unique place: such is the foundation of my lack of "alibi" for existence.

As for Bakhtin's understanding of the other, it can be approached through the perspective of his observations on parody. The parody of the other's language, and the worldview that underlies it, are linked to that of knowing at least two languages, Bakhtin insists. The other's language forces me to change position so as to perceive the limits and arbitrariness of my own language. When I mock the weaknesses and inadequacies of a language, I implicitly pose an alternative to it; thus parody is not conceivable outside a system of at least two languages. Parody is only possible if "this (my) language is structured and perceived in the light of another language."[1] Such a confrontation between two languages, one of which is perceived externally as the other's, forces us out of the presumed universality and overall unity of a single language system that would supposedly be sufficient to express the experience of the self and the perception of the world in which we are embedded.

In parody, the other's language is kept at a distance, put in inverted commas better to expose its limits and inadequacies. From this confrontation results a relationship of co-presence and unceasing attempts at mutual apprehension or seizure. Now, in that scheme, the respective positions of the self and the other are obviously a matter of point of view, for on both sides an I relates to another. Otherness, and particularly the relation of the perception of an acting subject to the perception of another subject which is foreign to it, is the formula of dialogism, of the displacement of points of view and of their opposition as well as their combination. The I is characterized by its intentionality, while the other is always considered as coextensive with its environment, which means its consummation as a defined entity, and the perception that results from it.

On the process of authoring, Bakhtin suggests that the relationship of the author to the character he shapes is similar to that by which, as a subject, I shape myself and others. In order to access perception, there must be a completion; there must be an attempt at circumscribing the other. And in the process of reading, where the reader co-authors the text, the relationship is that between me, the reader, and another. This is the architectonics of answerability. In this relationship I construct the hero/author relationship on the model of the I/other relationship, but I myself am an I that is foreign to them.

Thus, levels of otherness exist in language: the more it is stretched toward others and articulated for others, the more efforts it requires from me to produce it, and through this work I constitute myself as a subject. One cannot transmit the words of the other without working on them, without striving to perceive oneself according to the perception of the other. This should not suggest that my language natively belongs with my constitution. On the contrary, Bakhtin holds that my own language is not really my own, and that my own intentions can only be made intelligible in the form of overtones riding on top of others' words, tones, forms of expression, etc. In the field of writing and literary composition, there is likewise an effort on the part of the author to make himself a stranger to himself.

Note

1   "From the prehistory of novelistic discourse" (*DI*, 41–83 (75). Again, this should not imply that any priority is given to the "I" while the other would somehow be dependent on it. It is the other who gifts me with my own image. To clarify this point, one should keep in mind that: 1) The other is someone I can see (or come upon) in the world; 2) The other is someone that can see me as a coherent image—something I am unable to do; 3) The other is the only possible source I have for a coherent image of myself, and so is the only medium in whom introspection is possible.

28

Menippean Satire

Yann Tholoniat

Menippean satire gets its name from the Cynic philosopher Menippus, whose work has been lost. To define the specific generic features of Menippean satire is a challenge. Northrop Frye, in *Anatomy of Criticism* (1957), preferred the term "anatomy." Broadly speaking, it shares with traditional satire a mixture of verse with prose, it tackles a variety of topics, and its aim is to lambaste or make fun of its satiric target. More specifically, Menippean satire takes its root in the Cynics' outspokenness and often makes use of marginal narrators (as in Petronius' *The Satyricon*) to offer a philosophical point of view on a particular topic, which is discussed in dialogues among fools or knaves (as in Lucian of Samosata's work, such as *Dialogues of the Courtesans* and *Dialogues of the Dead*—in which Menippus himself speaks from the underworld). Bakhtin, in *Problems of Dostoevsky's Poetics* (ch. 4), adds that Menippean satire provocatively uses such devices as the fantastic or scandal scenes in order to test philosophical truths or explore contemporary social issues. Moral and psychological experimentation is the rule; it "reaches directly back into carnivalized folklore" (*PDP*: 112). The protagonists are free from common social norms and behaviors, and the dialogic form includes parodies, inserted genres, and abrupt changes in tone. Julia Kristeva, in Σημειωτική (*Semeiotike*) (1969), insists on the ambivalence of Menippean satire. According to her, it dramatizes two poles of Western literature: the staging of language, and the exploration of language as a correlative system of signs.

29

Outsidedness (*vnenakhodimost'*)

Sergeiy Sandler

Alternate translation: "Exotopy." Also related to Bakhtin's notions of "surplus of seeing" and "other."

Outsidedness is a central term in all periods of Bakhtin's thought, but especially in his early and late work. Outsidedness is the position of the other in relation to me, and, conversely, my position in relation to the other. The other has a surplus of seeing, i.e., can see more of me and of my context or surroundings than I can see myself. It is therefore only from the other's point of view, from a position of outsidedness, that a coherent image of me can be formed.

On the other hand, my inner first-person sense of the world (my horizon or purview) and my ability to act in the world and to change myself, are only accessible to me from within, and not to the other. This is why the other's surplus of seeing can also be abused, can become an act of violence, if the image of me is not given to me freely as a gift, but is imposed on me in an attempt to define me, or to make me an object of external knowledge.

Bakhtin also extends the notion of outsidedness beyond the strictly intersubjective sphere, to the relations between cultures, languages, and historical periods.

30

Present/Past/Future

Philippe Birgy

See "Author and Hero," and "Contemporaneity," where these topics are also discussed.

Bakhtin is careful to point out that the present can only be conceived in tension and continuity with the past and the future. In his considerations of the ancient novel, he remarks that "If taken outside its relationship to past and future, the present loses its integrity, breaks down into isolated phenomena and objects, making of them a mere abstract conglomeration. Even the ancient novel had a certain minimum fullness of time peculiar to it alone."[1] The openness of the present, its lack of closure, result in its exposure to the future: "The present, in its so-called 'wholeness' (although it is, of course, never whole) is in essence and in principle inconclusive; by its very nature it demands continuation, it moves into the future, and the more actively and consciously it moves into the future the more tangible and indispensable its inconclusiveness becomes."[2]

At the same time as the division between past and present is accomplished as the relation of eternally established facts, essences and remarkable models, to the uncertainty and indecision of current acts in the process of being accomplished, the past also takes upon itself all the qualities of ideality, of perfection, and of these glorious projections which should normally belong to the future, since that future alone offers unlimited perspectives. The future is thus divested of its project, and the contents that should legitimately constitute it are deported to the past, emptying it of its substance (all the possible outcomes that it spells). Thus, it loses "[t]he force and persuasiveness of reality."[3]

The novel inaugurates a literary space of "maximal contact with the present"[4] characterized by its openness and inconclusiveness. This is in contrast to earlier genres which celebrate and memorialize a heroic and historically defining past. Such an absolute past requires a break and a distance from the authorial position. This absoluteness also means that past is closed and univocal, cut off from the present, from change and becoming, which are the proper attributes of the present. "The epic, as the specific genre known to us today, has been from the beginning a poem about the past, and the and the authorial position immanent in the epic and constitutive for it (that is, the position of the one who utters the epic word) is the environment of a man speaking about a past that is to him inaccessible, the reverent point of view of a descendent" (*DI*: 13). Sandler signals a major caveat in this pattern of opposition; it might be that it is overdone for rhetorical purpose since not all novelistic works are expressions of the present while older forms are not systematically past-oriented. Moreover, Bakhtin repeatedly indicates in the examples he takes their frequent failure to conform entirely to that dichotomy.

The present as an evocation of the prosaic conditions of the moment, of everyday life, as I perceive it, was nonetheless for Bakhtin associated with the popular comic forms from which the novel emerged.

> The present, contemporary life as such, "I myself" and "my contemporaries," "my time"—all these concepts were originally the objects of ambivalent laughter, at the same time cheerful and annihilating. It is precisely here that a fundamentally new attitude toward language and toward the word is generated. Alongside direct representation—laughing at living reality there flourish parody and travesty of all high genres and of all lofty models embodied in national myth.
> (*D*: 21)

By default, such a form presents everything that does not deserve to appear in the chronicles of the remarkable deeds performed by the distinguished beings who make history. Conversely, the novel creates a language that allows us to speak of the present experience. This sense of the present, in Bakhtin's view—and this has frequently caused a rapprochement with Bergson—[5] implies that being must be conceived and felt as existence in progress, as an ongoing process. A living consciousness moves and evolves in the flux of existence as the latter unfolds.

Bakhtin draws a distinction between the content and the meaning of an act on the one hand, and the real immediate historical conditions of its being on the other—that is: the unique and irreproducible experience of this moment of existence.

The latter constitutes a vital or living relationship not only because it is felt in the present but also because this present is caught up in a historicity, and that coextensivity with a past precisely allows the flow or circulation which animates the subject's here-and-now.

Notes

1. M. M. Bakhtin, "Forms of Time and Chronotope in the Novel," in *DI*, 84–258 (146).
2. M. M. Bakhtin, "Epic and the Novel," in *DI*, 3–40 (30).
3. M. M. Bakhtin, "Forms of Time and Chronotope in the Novel," 147.
4. M. M. Bakhtin, "Epic and the Novel," in *DI*, 3–40 (11).
5. Gary S. Morson and Caryl Emerson, *Mikhail Bakhtin: Creation of a Prosaics* (Stanford: Stanford University Press, 1990), 177–9.

31

Responsibility

Philippe Birgy

This entry is also related to "Answerability" *otvetstvennost'* is the ordinary word for "responsibility" in Russian. Published English translations use the English word "answerability" instead, probably to highlight the etymological connection to the word "answer" (Russian *otvet*), but, to be sure, "responsibility" is similarly derived from the more or less synonymous "response."

The term is central to Bakhtin's early works. It appears in the title of his earliest known publication, the brief essay "Art and Answerability," published in 1919, and features prominently in *Toward a Philosophy of the Act*. And it is still in use in "Author and Hero in Aesthetic Activity," yet it falls mostly out of use in his later works (which is not to say Bakhtin abandons the underlying notion, but he opts for different terms, with a somewhat different focus in his mature works, possibly also because the early works are the only explicitly philosophical works Bakhtin wrote).[1]

In his preface to *Toward a Philosophy of the Act*, Holquist (1993) describes responsibility as "the ground for moral action." Since I must take responsibility for my actions, situate and locate them intimately with reference to my personal coordinates in this situation, registering how they impact me, they are necessarily infused with a sense of immediacy and intimate proximity, being specifically lived by me as a subject. Responsibility thus consists in the taking upon me of an action that could not be actuated otherwise.

This responsibility is antithetical with the formula of the "alibi in being" whereby my acts and thoughts would be justified by external determinations, exempting me from all responsibility, but by the same token alienating me from my own existence. Conversely, the absence of any external cause or explanation leaves me perfectly responsible for my actions (though it may be that I am not entirely the master of these actions).

The dissociation of culture and life, Bakhtin argues, is due to the fact that the reality experienced by the subject immersed in a unique situation and the fact of his being in action are set aside in the judgment made in the field of culture. What is at stake in the notion of responsibility, conversely, is that the contents and the meaning of a particular experience that I undergo and that I experience are joined to my acts, the latter involving my moral responsibility. Content and meaning are thus bound together with the acts in responsibility or answerability: "This answerability of the actually performed act is the taking-into-account in it of all the factors–a taking-into-account of its sense-validity as well as of its factual accomplishment in all its concrete historicity and individuality" (*TPA*: 18, translation slightly modified).

Even if I perform an act as the representative of a group, mandated to do so on behalf of others, it remains nonetheless my individual responsibility, for I participate in social rituals as a person.

Even self-denial, which intuitively would spell the extinction of my agency as a subject, belongs to the responsible act of the subject, owing to the form of local and personal existence that it requires.

Paradoxically, "the performed act concentrates, correlates and resolves within a unitary and unique and, this time, final context both the sense and the fact, the universal and the individual, the real and the ideal, for everything enters into the composition of its answerable motivation" (*TPA*: 29). It is therefore more than instrumental, it is the very activity whereby finalization (see "Completion") can be achieved.

Eventually, it is a unique consciousness that gathers up all the moments and circumstances making up the event in its totality and unifies them in a responsible act: "Responsibility is possible not as answerability for meaning in itself, but as responsibility for the once-occurrent affirmation or non-affirmation of it. It is possible, after all, to pass by meaning and it is also possible to lead meaning irresponsibly past Being" (*TPA*: 14, translation slightly modified)

Note

1 For this entry as well as the one concerning I and other, I am greatly indebted to Sergeiy Sandler who carefully read and annotated the manuscripts.

32

Style

Ken Hirschkop

Isn't style, and the idea of style, the very essence of Modernism? Its study, the discipline of stylistics, was formally inaugurated by Saussure's student (and editor) Charles Bally, who published his *Traité de stylistique française* in 1908. Its founding father in literary circles was Leo Spitzer. In Russia, it was represented by the idea of "poetic language," a distinctive, stylistically experimental form of writing, the technical minutiae of which were carefully dissected by Viktor Shklovsky, Lev Iakubinskii, and Roman Jakobson. It's what Flaubert singles out as the overriding goal of the modern writer.

When Bakhtin takes aim at the concept of style in the opening pages of "Discourse in the Novel," he is therefore playing on Modernism's home turf. His argument will be that Modernist theoreticians have formulated a poetic concept of style that's cramped in its range and based on a mistaken philosophy of language (the belief that a language is a code, which speakers might employ in personally idiosyncratic—i.e., stylish—ways). Understanding the style of the novel depends on a new philosophy of language, one alive to "the social life of discourse outside the artist's study, in the open spaces of squares, streets, cities and villages."[1] Fine, Bakhtin seems to be saying, style is the essence of literary art. But if you don't understand the stylistic uniqueness of novels, that only goes to show you don't understand what literary art is and what it's capable of.

That uniqueness can be summed up in a sentence and a phrase. The sentence is "*the style of a novel lies in its combination of styles; the language of a novel is a system of 'languages'*" (CW3: 15; DI: 262); the phrase is "double-voiced discourse." The former tells us that novels aren't distinguished by consistent linguistic patterns, but by the way they display and coordinate heterogeneous forms of speech. Novels take different kinds of language—character speech, generic forms, different kinds of public written and oral speech, social dialects, and so on—and orchestrate them. Each of these constituent styles derives its sense and feel from the significance it has outside the novel (as a recognizable pattern of speech, indexing a particular context) and its place "within the higher stylistic unity of the work as a whole" (*CW3*: 15; *DI*: 262). When a particular kind of speech, drawn from heteroglossia, appears in the context of a novel's plot, character set, and world, it acquires a meaning and force it may not have had originally. The sentimental young man appears naïve and foolish; the narrator sounds like a chatterbox; the solemn judge sounds pompous.

In that sense every constituent "language" that appears in a novel is double-voiced, made significant by the meaning it has outside the novel and the refraction it receives within the novel. But double-voicing is not an entirely suitable metaphor for novelistic style, insofar as the second, framing voice is not a voice at all, but the form of the novel as a whole. A close look at the actual examples Bakhtin provides of double-voicing only reinforces this suspicion, for most of them involve parody, stylization, and irony, in which the direct claims of a borrowed style are undercut. A better starting place is probably Bakhtin's claim that "the central problem for a stylistics of the novel may be formulated as *the problem of artistically representing a language, the problem of the image of a language*" (*CW3*: 90: *DI*: 336). Novels make images of languages: they draw together co-occurring features, associate them with a context and perhaps a category of speaker, and display the project behind such a way of speaking. That's their style.

Note

1   M. M. Bakhtin, "Discourse in the Novel," in *CW3*, 9–179 (10–11). English translation in *DI*, 259–422 (259).

33

Utterance (*vyskazyvanie*)

Sergeiy Sandler

The word *vyskazyvanie* literally means "saying-out," or "what is said-out." In Russian scholarly discourse, it was used in several different senses, including as the Russian equivalent of the English terms "proposition" (in logic), "statement," and "enunciation." The term was first extensively used in Bakhtin Circle writings in Valentin Voloshinov's 1926 article "The Word in Life and the Word in Poetry."[1] A close equivalent of "utterance" in Bakhtin's early philosophical vocabulary would be the "deed-in-word," mentioned a few times as one kind of deed in "Author and Hero in Aesthetic Activity" (see also "Deed," "Word/Discourse").[2] Voloshinov also used this term as the Russian equivalent of Ferdinand de Saussure's term "la parole"[3]—a usage we find occasionally in Bakhtin's writings as well.[4]

The term received its most significant development, however, in Bakhtin's draft linguistic article from the early 1950s, "The Problem of Speech Genres" (*CW5*; *SG*). Here, Bakhtin for the first time considers the utterance as an operational unit of linguistic analysis. The extent of an utterance in this sense is delimited by the succession of speaking subjects (*CW5*: 172ff.: *SG*: 71ff.). In the context of a face-to-face conversation one utterance is thus the same as one turn of talk. In other contexts, a single utterance would be a single piece or work—a single story, poem, article, lecture, speech, novel, etc. In all contexts, a person (an author; see also "Author and Hero") holds the floor within the utterance, while others hold the floor before it and after it.

From within, the utterance reflects at least some level of design (Bakhtin uses the Russian word *zamysel*, literally "thought behind") on its author's behalf and is intended to end on a point of closure indicated by the author. Looking outward, the utterance is engaged in dialogic relations (see also "Dialogue/Dialogical/Dialogization") with other utterances: it responds to past utterances, and is addressed to, and anticipates a response from, future utterances. Moreover, upon closer examination, a single utterance can be viewed as dialogic from within, analyzed internally as consisting of utterances in an internal dialogue embedded within it (furthermore, in principle, these "internal" utterances can in turn also be analyzed dialogically in the same way). In Bakhtin's words, the utterance is "all furrowed, as it were, by the distant and barely audible resonances of speaking subject successions and dialogic overtones, boundaries between utterances that have been weakened to their limit" (*CW5*: 198; *SG*: 93)

Notes

1   Valentin Nikolaevich Voloshinov, "Slovo v Zhizni i Slovo v Poezii" [The Word in Life and the Word in Poetry], in *Filosofiia i Sotsiologiia Gumanitarnykh Nauk*, ed. Dmitrij Aleksandrovich Iunov (St. Petersburg: Asta-press, 1995b), 59–86. Translation in "Discourse in Life and Discourse in Poetry," in *Bakhtin School Papers*, ed. Ann Shukman, trans. John Richmond (Oxford: RPT Publications, 1983), 5–30.

2   "Avtor i geroj v esteticheskoj deiatel'nosti" [Author and Hero in Aesthetic Activity], in *CW1*, 69–263 (173). Translation in *AA*, 4–256 (98).

3   Valentin Nikolaevich Voloshinov, "Marksizm i Filosofiia Iazyka" [Marxism and the Philosophy of Language], in *Filosofiia i Sotsiologiia Gumanitarnykh Nauk*, ed. Dmitrij Aleksandrovich Iunov (St. Petersburg: Asta-press, 1995a), 216–380 (273). Translation in *Marxism and the Philosophy of Language*, trans. Ladislav Matejka, and Irwin R. Titunik (Cambridge, MA: Harvard University Press, 1986), 59.

4   "Problema Rechevykh Zhanrov" [The Problem of Speech Genres], in *CW5*, 159–206 (183–4). Translation in "The Problem of Speech Genres," in *SG*, 60–102 (81).

34

Word/Discourse (*slovo*)

Sergeiy Sandler

The Russian word *slovo* usually means "(a) *word*," but, like its English counterpart, it has an older and broader meaning (which, in English, can still be observed in such expressions as "mark my *word*," "upon my *word*," or "the written *word*"). It is in this older original sense that this word is used by Bakhtin.

For Bakhtin (as well as for his friend Valentin Voloshinov), *slovo* offers a way to speak about language without conjuring up grammatical relations, formal systems, or the lexicon in the technical sense ("*a* word"), that have become so closely associated with the very concept of language throughout much of the twentieth century. In this, it is close in meaning to how, in more recent times, the term *discourse* has been used in some branches of linguistics and discourse analysis (the use of *discourse* in the work of Foucault or Lyotard, on the other hand, is quite irrelevant and misleading if read into Bakhtin's texts).

The word, alongside the image, is a central concern for Bakhtin's aesthetics. Early on,[1] we find references in Bakhtin's writings to a "deed-in-word" (*postupok-slovo*), which is one kind of *deed*, alongside the deed-in-thought, the deed-in-feeling, and the deed-in-action. In later texts, we can observe two main overlapping, and not fully differentiated, uses of the term.

First, word/discourse is used to refer to language in general, understood as a fundamentally social or intersubjective phenomenon. In this sense, the term often appears in the titles of texts and chapters: "*Discourse* in the Novel," "From the Prehistory of Novelistic *Discourse*," "Image and *Word* in Rabelais' Novel" (the original title of the final chapter in Bakhtin's book on Rabelais).

The second sense has more to do with how language concretely functions in a text or in other forms of human interaction. In this second sense, we find the term used in such expressions as "double-voiced *discourse*," "the *word* with a loophole," or "another's *word*" (*chuzhoe slovo*). In this sense, the term can apply to any stretch of discourse, short or long, examined in terms of how it responds and relates to what others said in the past, and in terms of what it concretely means to an addressee in a given situation.

Note

1. "Avtor i geroj v esteticheskoj deiatel'nosti" [Author and Hero in Aesthetic Activity], in *CW1*, 69–263 (173). Translation in "Author and Hero in Aesthetic Activity," in *AA*, 4–256 (98).

INDEX

Adorno, Theodor W. 180–2, 189
Anderson, Perry 81–2, 95
Anthropocene 122
architectonics 247–8
author 138, 158, 249

Balzac 19, 76, 101, 163
Bakhtin's works
    "Author and Hero in Aesthetic Activity" 85, 88, 156
    "Discourse in the Novel" 20, 22–3, 87, 103, 140, 165, 260, 269–70, 283
    "Forms of Time and of the Chronotope in the Novel" 24, 66, 68, 110, 165
    "From the Prehistory of Novelistic Discourse" 28, 43, 259–60
    "Notes towards a Reworking of the Dostoevsky Book" 105
    "On the Bildungsroman" 19, 24, 46
    Problems of Dostoevsky's Art 19, 83, 89, 94
    Problems of Dostoevsky's Poetics 157, 166, 168
    "Rabelais and Gogol: The Art of Discourse and the Popular Culture of Laughter" 46
    Rabelais and His World 199
    "Response to a Question from the Novyj Mir Editorial Staff" 33, 69
    Speech Genres and Other Late Essays 69
    "The Bildungsroman and Its Significance in the History of Realism: Toward a Historical Typology of the Novel" 183
    "The Novel as a Literary Genre" 259–60
    "The Two Stylistic Lines of Development in the European Novel" 43
    Towards a Philosophy of the Act 56–7, 127, 154, 158, 281
Baudelaire, Charles 67, 111, 165, 191, 194
Benjamin, Walter 20–1, 71, 72, 73–5, 112
Bildungsroman 24
body 13, 229, 232, 235

carnival 22, 124, 201–2, 207, 208, 218–20, 228, 253–4
carnivalization 140, 209
Casirer, Ernst 25, 251–2
Chesterton, Gilbert Keith 207–9
chronotope 5, 9–10, 24, 43–4, 45, 66–7, 68, 69–70, 75, 77, 144, 179, 183–4, 189, 192, 239, 255–6
chronotope of the threshold 65, 75, 110, 165, 168–9, 171–2, 193
citability 74
completion 257–8
contemporaneity 21, 26, 27, 28–9, 259
contextualization 2
crisis time 78, 110, 163, 168, 169, 187, 193
culture 34–5

dance 13, 227–39
dialogism 93, 100–3, 140, 236, 285–6
Dickens, Charles 19, 201, 203–6, 209
Discourse 94, 252, 263, 287–8

Dostoevsky, Fyodor Mikhailovich 19, 28, 65, 67, 86, 101, 105, 110–11, 164, 167, 204
double-voicing 94, 264, 283–4, 288

Eliot, Thomas Stearns 201
ethics 10–11, 154–7, 170, 260
ethical turn 10, 170

Felski, Rita 9, 33, 37–9
Fraser, Nancy 118
Frazer, Sir James 199–201, 202
futurism 6, 152

genre 35, 39, 175, 265–6
Gide, André 164, 166–7, 169–74, 177
Glissant, Edouard 142–4
Goethe, Johann Wolfgang von 46, 93, 183, 202–3
great time 11, 35, 40, 69–71, 76, 78–9, 126

Habermas, Jürgen 12, 115–17, 119, 123
Hall, Stuart 143
hero 28, 138, 158, 249
heteroglossia 87
history 111
    historical becoming 23–4
    historical criticism 38
    historical time 20, 22, 24–5, 116
    historicism 68, 71
    literary history 36
Höderlin, Friedrich 76–7, 78, 79
humanism 82
hyperobject 119–23

I and other 52, 248
    I 103–4, 186
    I for myself 84–5, 158, 248, 271
    I for the other 155, 158, 248
    other 84–5, 103, 124, 134, 155, 275
individuality 90, 121
irony 23

Jakobson, Roman 40
Jensen, Johannes Vilhelm 179, 185–8
Joyce, James 19, 134, 138, 190–1, 213–23

Koselleck, Reinhart 20
Kraus, Karl 71
Kristeva, Julia 36

Lacan, Jacques 71
Lukacs, Georg 27

Mallarmé, Stéphane 231–2
Mayakovsky, Vladimir 91–3
McCaw, Dick 232–3, 234, 35
Medvedev, Pavel 36, 41
Menippean satire 273
modernity 3, 5–6, 8, 20, 70, 81, 83, 116, 119, 122, 131, 133–4, 138, 141, 150, 163, 182, 185, 195

Nietzsche, Friedrich Wilhelm 73, 88
non alibi in being 84
novelness 136–7

orientalism 136
outsidedness 275

parody 29, 271
postcolonial 131–3, 137–9
postmodern 2, 117
Pound, Ezra 179, 183, 189–94
Proust, Marcel 165

Rabaté, Jean-Michel 163–4, 168, 170
Rabelais, François 45, 208, 218–19
realism 24, 207
responsibility 103, 143, 281–2
Rimbaud, Arthur 111
Russian Formalism 41

Shakespeare, William 57, 68
Shklovsky, Viktor 42, 149–53, 157
Simondon, Gilbert 93
situatedness 13, 52, 117, 126, 236, 239
Sloterdijk, Peter 124
style 283–4
subject 82–3, 90, 157
    self 84–5, 90–1, 154, 233–5, 271–2
    subjectivity 5, 52, 90, 92, 104, 155
succession 54–5, 57

Taylor, Charles 150
threshold 109, 168, 171, 174
time 68, 72, 93, 193
    conception/perception of time 10, 93
    future 21, 23, 260
    future and present 26, 277
    now time 72–3
    present 11, 47, 277–8
    past and present 11, 47, 277

time/space 5, 43–4, 68, 75, 117, 126, 138, 140, 144, 179, 183–4, 185–6, 189, 228, 231–3, 237, 255–6

unfinalizability 176, 252, 257–8

Voloshinov, Nikolaevich 99, 106–8, 135, 143, 251–2

Wagner, Richard 68
Williams, Raymond 132
Woolf, Virginia 111

www.ingramcontent.com/pod-product-compliance
Lightning Source LLC
Chambersburg PA
CBHW050323020526
44117CB00031B/1616